Entrepôt of Revolutions

Entrepôt of Revolutions

*Saint-Domingue, Commercial Sovereignty, and the
French-American Alliance*

MANUEL COVO

OXFORD
UNIVERSITY PRESS

OXFORD
UNIVERSITY PRESS

Oxford University Press is a department of the University of Oxford. It furthers
the University's objective of excellence in research, scholarship, and education
by publishing worldwide. Oxford is a registered trade mark of Oxford University
Press in the UK and certain other countries.

Published in the United States of America by Oxford University Press
198 Madison Avenue, New York, NY 10016, United States of America.

Library of Congress Control Number: 2022943896
ISBN 978–0–19–762639–9 (pbk.)
ISBN 978–0–19–762638–2 (hbk.)

DOI: 10.1093/oso/9780197626382.001.0001

me substantially reframe the manuscript. Fellows in my cohort, in particular Randy Browne, Aston Gonzalez, Brian Luskey, and Rachel Walker, contributed to make my Philadelphia stay very productive. I discovered new archival sources thanks to the John Carter Brown Library fellowship and benefited from the insights of Kathryn Burns, Bérénice Gaillemin, Sarah Newman, Justin Pope, Lorenzo Ravano, and Nancy E. Van Deusen. I want to give special mention to Neil Safier whose indescribable help was decisive in the course of my research career. Last but not least, I was highly privileged to write most of the chapters of this book as a postdoctoral fellow at the Huntington Library. That was an extraordinary experience: there I benefited from exchanges with director Steve Hindle, librarian Sara Austin, and fellows Daniela Bleichmar, Kristen Block, Katherine Cox, Marjoleine Kars, Gregory Nobles, Jessica Rosenberg, Martha Sandweiss, Alexander Statman, and Danielle Terrazas Williams.

As I was revising final drafts of the book, Paul Cheney, Ashli White, and François Furstenberg gave me incredibly helpful feedback. I was able to reorient and sharpen the ideas of *Entrepôt of Revolutions* thanks to their generous and close reading. I could not be more grateful for Emily Clark's brilliant mentoring and Michael Kwass's insightful guidance at decisive stages of the writing process. Marcus Rediker invited me to deliver a lecture at the University of Pittsburgh and to meet the fantastic faculty and graduate students. I will always remember how welcoming, supporting, and inspiring he was. Trevor Burnard taught me so much when he shepherded the publication of my very first article in *French History*. Catherine Desbarats asked all the tough questions and helped me formulate the best possible responses with care and brilliance. Rebecca Scott dedicated immeasurable time to my project and made enlightening suggestions: I could not be more thankful. I could always count on the excellent advice, sharp criticism, and warm support of Marc Belissa, Elizabeth Cross, Quentin Deluermoz, Alyssa Goldstein-Sepinwall, Christopher Hodson, Eddie Kolla, Bertie Mandelblatt, Megan Maruschke, Gregory O'Malley, Nathan Perl-Rosenthal, and Pernille Røge. All have played a decisive role in the making of this book and created a cherished environment of scholarly camaraderie. I want to express my debt to Tyler Stovall, a remarkably inspiring and supportive scholar, whose passing has been deeply felt by the community.

Along the way, I presented portions of my work at various conferences, workshops, and gatherings and enormously profited from exchanges with many scholars. I want to thank David Andress, Anja Bandau, David Bell, Rafe Blaufarb, Claire Cage, Hannah Callaway, Audrey Célestine, Jean-Jacques Clère, Paul Cohen, Myriam Cottias, Christian Crouch, Marlene Daut, Lauren Derby, Nicholas Dew, Nathan Dize, Alexandre Dubé, Alec Dun, Robert Duplessis, Sarah Easterby-Smith, Nathan Elliot Marvin, Mathieu Ferradou, Carolyn Fick, Albane Forestier, Allan Forrest, Niklas Frykman, Julia Gaffield, Guillaume Garner, John

Garrigus, Malick Ghachem, Arad Gigi, Alejandro Gómez-Pernía, Allan Greer, Jean-Sébastien Guibert, Mark Hanna, Jennifer Heuer, Tamar Herzog, Katie Jarvis, Martha Jones, Delide Joseph, Asheesh Kapur Siddique, Wim Klooster, Joseph La Hausse de la Louvière, David Lambert, Silyane Larcher, Jean-Pierre Le Glaunec, Boris Lesueur, Mary Lewis, James Livesey, Noam Maggor, Rahul Markovits, Marguerite Martin, Silvia Marzagalli, Sermin Meskill, Matthias Middel, Philip Morgan, Carla Pestana, Steve Pincus, Laure Pineau, Janet Polasky, Jeremy Popkin, Lara Putnam, Karine Rance, Marie-Jeanne Rossignol, Brett Rushforth, Eric Saunier, Eric Schnakenbourg, Elena Schneider, Will Slauter, Miranda Spieler, Bertrand Van Ruymbeke, Giovanni Venegoni, Charles Walton, Rachel Waxman, Carl Wennerlind, Thomas Wien, Wendy Wong, Laurie Wood, and Anya Zilberstein.

Transforming a manuscript into a book is no easy process. I had been told that Susan Ferber was the ideal editor, but I quickly realized this designation is an understatement. Her prompt, meticulous reading and her care carried me through difficult stages, especially when time was running out. I was very fortunate that Joanna Baines reviewed and copyedited drafts of the manuscript–every phrase that sounds *un petit peu trop française* is solely my doing. I want to extend my thanks to Jungki Min, who helped me format the footnotes, and Elizabeth Schmidt, whose brilliant paleographical skills helped me overcome Nathaniel Cutting's terrible handwriting. Jeremy Toynbee at Oxford University Press and Jefferson Lamb have also been extraordinarily helpful.

My colleagues in the history department at the University of California, Santa Barbara, have created a remarkably supportive and intellectually animating environment. I am especially grateful to Hilary Bernstein, Verónica Castillo-Muñoz, Utathya Chattopadhyaya, Juan Cobo-Betancourt, Adrienne Edgar, Lisa Jacobson, Kate McDonald, Katie Moore, Harold Marcuse, Cecilia Méndez Gastelumendi, Stephan F. Miescher, Alice O'Connor, Ann Plane, Erika Rappaport, Sherene Seikaly, and Xiaowei Zheng. I learned also so much from our research group on "slavery, captivity and the meaning of freedom" and want to thank Jeannine DeLombard, Rose MacLean, Giuliana Perrone, and Evelyne Laurent-Perrault.

My friends and family have aided me in innumerable ways. Morwenna Coquelin who provided feedback on multiple drafts deserves special mention. Thanks to my friends and siblings who have helped me make important decisions at crucial stages and supported me in many different fashions: Alison Annunziata, Farid Azfar, Rémi Blanc, Emilio Capettini, Clémence Cattaneo, Rodrigo Cattaneo, Lisa Covo, Samy Covo, Edward Crouse, Hélène Demeestere, Rosie Doyle, Omar El, Fanny Fihman, James Geist, Nathalie Gendrot, Cyrielle Hébert, Anne Jégou, Augustin Jomier, Emmanuelle Josse, Rebekah Maggor,

David Marcilhacy, Olivia Nicol, Thomas Rigaud, Solange Rameix, Itay Sapir, and Malika Temmar.

I dedicate this book to my parents: my father, Léo, was always enthusiastic about my research and would probably have placed *Entrepôt of Revolutions* on the coffee table in the living room. My mother, Chantal, eagerly listened to the litany of new archival finds I made and encouraged the earliest rumination that made this book possible. Thank you.

Entrepôt of Revolutions

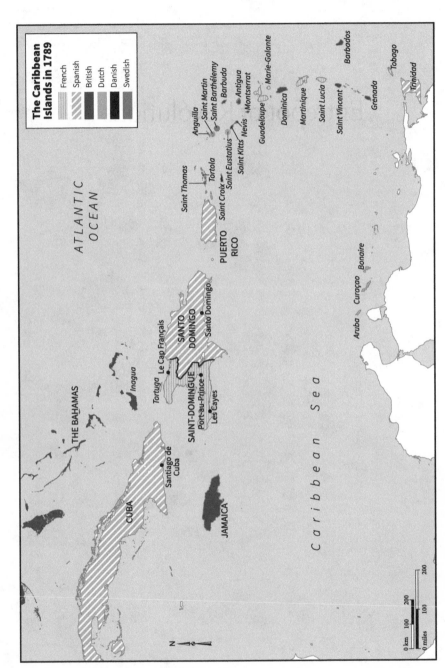

Figure 0.1 The Caribbean Islands in 1789

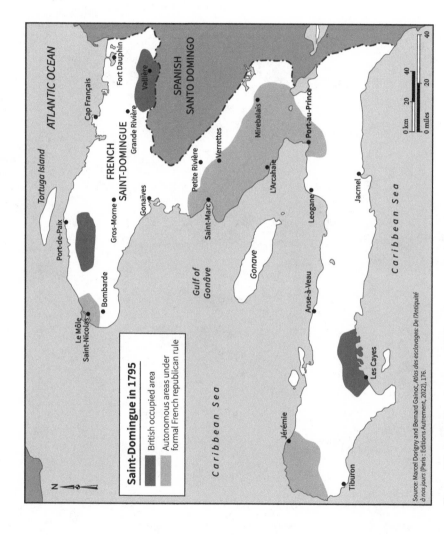

Figure 0.2 Saint-Domingue in 1795

Source: Marcel Dorigny and Bernard Gainot, *Atlas des esclavages: De l'Antiquité à nos jours* (Paris : Editions Autrement, 2022), 176.

Introduction

On September 11, 1794, Captain Joshua Barney received France's highest honor. The National Convention, legislative body of the first French Republic, invited him to accompany the new US ambassador, James Monroe, to ceremonially present the union of the French and American flags to the Assembly. The Baltimorean had made a name for himself during the American Revolutionary War, becoming a naval lieutenant at the age of sixteen and, in the seven years he served, capturing British frigates much larger than his own ship. Proud of his achievements for the cause of "liberty," Barney delivered a much-applauded speech at the Convention advocating a permanent politico-commercial union between France and the United States. The deputies, who viewed Barney as a living symbol of the republican and revolutionary ties binding the two countries, awarded him an *accolade fraternelle*, and offered him French citizenship to herald the Revolution's universalism. Finally, the deputies invited the young American to join the French navy as a ranking officer. A few weeks later, on October 11, Barney had a front-row seat when the remains of Jean-Jacques Rousseau were transferred to the Pantheon, the national mausoleum dedicated to distinguished French citizens. Being granted such high honors was no doubt thanks to Barney's embodiment of the core qualities associated with revolutionary republicanism. He incarnated the intrepid youth of the United States whose very founding aided the regeneration of France. His invitation to revolutionary France expressed a cosmopolitan ambition for universal liberation. The call to join the French navy also reflected ferocious hatred of the common English enemy still closely associated in the United States and France with royalist tyranny.[1]

These official ceremonies, however, did not refer to Barney's true purpose for visiting Paris: to maximize the profits from his business in the French colony of Saint-Domingue (now Haiti). Barney was, first and foremost, an entrepreneur. As a shrewd merchant, he paid little attention to French pomp, being preoccupied with selling a substantial cargo of wheat imported from the United States. In return, Barney received payment promised by the Saint-Domingue authorities for

Entrepôt of Revolutions. Manuel Covo, Oxford University Press. © Oxford University Press 2022.
DOI: 10.1093/oso/9780197626382.003.0001

provisioning the island. Saint-Domingue, whose sugar and coffee production had made it one of the most profitable colonies in the world, was in revolution. A mass uprising led by revolutionaries of African descent had brought about the abolition of slavery on the island on August 29, 1793, a decision validated by the National Convention on February 4, 1794. A friend of the republican commissioner, Léger-Félicité Sonthonax, who had announced the proclamation of "universal liberty" in Saint-Domingue, Barney did not hesitate to conduct business with newly freed Blacks. Yet, earlier in his life, Barney had been a smuggler and slave trader in the Spanish Caribbean, and his support of the French Republic had not deterred him from acquiring the enslaved people he would later take back to his plantation in Kentucky. Barney thus spent the four decades between the American Revolutionary War and the War of 1812 navigating between the United States, the Antilles, and France, alternating between slave trading and supporting the Haitian Revolution, all the while making and losing money. The one constant was his willingness to fight the British at every opportunity. His chaotic journey was not an anomaly; it perfectly embodied the Franco-American relationship in this era of imperial rivalry and revolution, the heart of which was Saint-Domingue, the *entrepôt* uniting France and the United States.[2]

Entrepôt of Revolutions: Saint-Domingue, Commercial Sovereignty, and the French-American Alliance situates the French Revolution in both the context of the American and the Haitian revolutions and the longer history of colonial capitalism. Rather than examining notions of personal freedom and citizenship as the sole sources of revolutionary upheaval, this book emphasizes the significance of commercial sovereignty as a key concept that both connected revolutions and brought them into conflict. Its focus on the interactions between merchant circulation and the transformation of political entities decenters the core of the French-American relationship from the revolutionary capitals, Paris and Philadelphia, and underscores the centrality of Saint-Domingue as the hub of global capitalism in an age of revolutions.

By placing Saint-Domingue at the core of this history, the book identifies imperial trade as a driving force in the age of revolutions. In the aftermath of the Seven Years' War, the French government envisioned a new organization for its empire, redesigning the connections between North America and the French Caribbean. This experiment in political economy was supposed to strengthen France's imperial position in the Atlantic world. However, the creation of the United States, which had vast economic interests in the "Pearl of the Caribbean" through the smuggling of sugar, coffee, flour, and captives, sparked new anxieties and generated intense debate in France about the "liberty of commerce" and the nature of its own imperial sovereignty. Commercial reforms, with their broader moral and political ramifications, were hotly contested by lobbies, deputies, merchants, white planters, free people of color, and administrators. The debate transformed over the course of the French Revolution with multiple attempts to republicanize sovereignty through commerce and purge colonial trade of its Old Regime, monarchical features. Commercial republicanism was the effort to put trade at the service of a political agenda that aimed to expand citizens' rights internally and generate more equal relationships with foreign nations externally. Although most of the French revolutionary leaders understood that political sovereignty derived from economic independence, they relentlessly claimed that political goals should prevail. . Yet the adaptation of merchant networks and the outbreak of the slave revolution in Saint-Domingue in 1791 transformed the parameters of debate. Within a wider context of rivalry with Britain and Spain, the French colonial system was compelled to remake its commercial infrastructure and invent new forms of political association that called into question the categories "colonial," "imperial," and "national." *Entrepôt of Revolutions* reveals the multiplicity of imperial and colonial experiments that contemporaries such as Barney envisioned, traversed, influenced, and profited from to various degrees, within and beyond national boundaries in a rapidly globalizing economy.

French Trade in the Imperial Crisis of the Late Eighteenth Century

The French Revolution did not unfold within the framework of a ready-made nation-state but in a colonial empire with origins dating to the beginning of the seventeenth century. Since the French monarchy had claimed sovereignty over Acadia and the St. Lawrence Valley in Canada and the West Indian island of Saint-Kitts, the role of the colonies in the kingdom's economy had steadily increased. French colonial expansion followed a nonlinear route and generated an uncertain empire that escaped positive definitions of an imperium (supreme power or sphere of control and monopoly). The French Empire emerged from a laborious process involving private entrepreneurs and semi-governmental organizations in the form of charter companies. Louis XIII's and Louis XIV's prime ministers Armand Jean Du Plessis de Richelieu and Jean-Baptiste Colbert had made colonies a central element of their geopolitical strategies. Adept at the nascent science of "political economy," they were convinced that colonies were essential to commerce, and that commerce was the foundation of a formidable navy. If the king of France wanted to challenge the maritime supremacy of the United Provinces (the Netherlands) and, later, Great Britain, he needed to support and facilitate the expansion of French trade across the world. Conquests accompanied or followed the extension of trading networks with Native Americans in North America and Indian merchants in South Asia where France secured a multitude of commercial outposts. Although fishermen, settlers, missionaries, filibusters, and pirates spearheaded this expansion, the monarchy supported many of these enterprises, contracting charter companies and in some cases affirming its jurisdiction over newly claimed territories. From the focus on mineral resources that characterized much of the early Iberian colonization in the Americas, the French government collaborated with private stakeholders and "rogue colonists" or interlopers to sustain a capitalist agriculture destined to export such products as tobacco and indigo, then sugar, coffee, cocoa, and cotton from the Caribbean and Mascarene islands.[3]

During the eighteenth century, France emerged as one of the leading slave trading countries in Europe, second only to Britain and Portugal. Merchants in Nantes, Bordeaux, Le Havre, Marseille, La Rochelle, Dunkerque, and a few other smaller ports deported more than 1.1 million captives from Africa to the Greater Caribbean in that century alone. The extreme violence of the slave trade sustained the development of French slave societies in Martinique, Guadeloupe, Tobago, other smaller islands in the Lesser Antilles, Louisiana, Guyane, Ile-de-France (now Mauritius), Bourbon (now Réunion), and, above all, Saint-Domingue. Saint-Domingue's economy rapidly thrived through extreme forms of brutality against the Black workforce, whose forced sacrifices, often their lives, in turn enriched metropolitan port-cities. Its production levels dwarfed those of any other Atlantic colony, fostering jealousy with the British and Spanish empires. The technical sophistication of the irrigation system and labor organization provided a striking picture of capitalist modernity, described by historian Michael Kwass as the "dark side of globalization."[4]

Colonies, however, remained vulnerable to imperial warfare, natural disasters, epidemics, and revolts, exposing the volatility and fragility of capitalism. Distance created vast problems in communication and control: crossing the ocean from Europe could take between thirty and seventy days, depending on the prevalence of hurricanes and other unforeseen incidents. In the face of such challenges and despite uncertainties about colonial profitability, the monarchy's ongoing concern was to sustain an enduring source of income through a favorable "balance of commerce," feeding off and channeling the greed of colonists. The Code Noir of 1685 was an unsuccessful judicial project to assert metropolitan sovereignty while legalizing and encouraging slavery. To counter a potential invasion by European rivals, the monarchy financed the building of shipyards and arsenals, extended premiums to merchants, and encouraged an increase in trained sailors to be drafted in future wars. The resources of the French fiscal-military state partly depended on colonial income but also involved costly expanses in naval protection. The wealth extracted from the colonies and their financial burden were critical factors in an ever-shifting set of international alliances and enmities. For France, the many wars of the eighteenth century took place largely in the colonies and at sea, and the treaties ending each of these conflicts dealt prominently with commercial matters, from Utrecht in 1713 to Versailles in 1783. To a certain extent, France was enmeshed in a second "Hundred Years' War" with Britain for global hegemony, yet wartime was interspersed with inter-imperial cooperation "from above" and "from below." The French Empire was entangled in other European imperial formations and indigenous polities, generating gaps and loopholes.[5]

Control over trade was central to the French king's claim of imperial sovereignty and would remain crucial for revolutionary republics. Mimicking the policy of Oliver Cromwell in the Act of Navigation (1651) and responding to Dutch commercial power, the French government established the principle of colonial monopoly: the *exclusif*. Under pressure from metropolitan merchants, the monarchical government under Colbert produced a set of regulations later formalized in the laws of 1717 and 1727 (*lettres patentes*), through which French merchants not only monopolized colonial produce on the kingdom's markets but also reexported these commodities to other European countries (the "carrying trade") and provisioned the colonies with foodstuffs and goods from the metropole. In the *Encyclopedia*, economist François Véron Duverger de Forbonnais clarified the purpose of such legislation. "These colonies being established only for the utility of the metropolis, it follows: 1 °. That they must be under its immediate dependence, and therefore under its protection. 2 °. That the trade must be exclusive to the founders." In many ways, the colonial *exclusif* was just one item on an endless list of privileges that made up the Old Regime legal system, based on exceptions, tariffs, franchises, and a set of *libertés*. The exclusif coexisted with charter companies claiming to monopolize markets in Senegal and the "East Indies."[6]

Just as metropolitan regulations were contested, the exclusif did not go unchallenged. From the outset, colonial societies flouted, ignored, and resisted regulations crafted by European powers. In the Americas, rampant smuggling was almost universal, and colonial officials were often complicit in a trade regarded as both essential and "natural." The extreme agricultural specialization of several Caribbean colonies, which often developed economies of scale based on single commercial crops, was sustained by imports of foodstuffs from far-flung territories. The results led to precarious economic arrangements on the ground. In the seventeenth century, French colonies in the Antilles were only able to grow, expand, and thrive due to a flourishing Dutch trade, officially prohibited by the Crown but actually tolerated and even covertly encouraged. Over time, the French colonies became increasingly reliant on imports of cod and timber from New England, while the rum distilleries of Massachusetts depended on molasses from Martinique, Saint-Domingue, and Guadeloupe. Mules from Tierra Firme, essential for functioning plantations, were imported into many islands via Curaçao. The Spanish piaster of Mexican silver was the common currency in non-Spanish colonies. Connections fostered by dense networks of traders and sailors produced what historian Ernesto Bassi has termed an "aqueous territory" spanning the greater Caribbean, incorporating the Antilles, the shores of New Granada (Colombia and Venezuela), and the spaces bordering the Gulf of Mexico and the Atlantic seaboard of North America. The entrenchment of intercolonial and inter-imperial connections engendered an interdependent economy that refuted the monopolistic rhetoric of European monarchies and exposed the gap between rhetoric and reality.[7]

European political economists were divided on the relevance and usefulness of colonial monopolies for a variety of reasons. Thinkers on both sides of the Channel and the Atlantic engaged with political, diplomatic, fiscal, and legal issues, beyond what today would narrowly be defined as economics. Arguments deployed a variety of understandings associated with the "liberty of commerce," which cannot be reduced to a contest between mercantilism and free trade. One of the most contentious topics concerned the dialectical tensions posed by commerce between "cosmopolitanism" and "patriotism." In the books of *philosophes* such as Gabriel Bonnot de Mably, Denis Diderot, Voltaire, and Rousseau, a merchant's "cosmopolitanism" was at times regarded as a vector of peace and intercultural encounter, at others as a symptom of harmful, greedy, and selfish passions. Commerce facilitated connections between diverse peoples of the world and offered an alternative to conquest, laying the groundwork for what economist Victor Riquetti Marquis de Mirabeau labeled the "universal confraternity of commerce." But many commentators also pointed out that desire for profit could become the basis of exploitation, corruption, predation, and domination, the most pernicious manifestation of which was colonialism. The profitability of enslaved labor versus free labor was debated, as was how to regulate trade so that private interests could contribute to public interest, both on a national and global level. Whether an absolute monarchy could successfully rule a commercial society was another crucial source of political tension in eighteenth-century France.[8]

The Seven Years' War (1756–1763) sparked a reorientation of French colonial policy using a new language of patriotism that mirrored global transformations and was entangled with British, Spanish, Portuguese, and Danish reforms. This new direction in political economy was integral to what historian Christopher Bayly termed the "imperial crisis." In the context of British expansion in India, the increasing inter-imperial trade in the Americas clashed with a growing metropolitan centralization and concrete assertions of state power beyond the empty rhetoric of sovereignty and the practice of colonial neglect. The French defeat in 1763, prompting the loss of Canada to Britain and the cession of Western Louisiana to Spain, was a catalyst. On the one hand, Britain tightened restrictions on North American trade and reformed the Navigation Act, increasing taxation on the thirteen colonies and contributing to political unrest. On the other, it implemented a system of "free ports" in the Caribbean, which circumscribed and taxed the flows of "foreign" goods and vessels into Jamaica, Barbados, and other British West Indies. While such commercial hubs were far from new, in the Americas these had previously been confined to tiny islands claimed by less powerful empires, such as Dutch Saint-Eustatius and Curaçao, and Danish Saint-Thomas. Opting to recover Guadeloupe and Martinique by abandoning Canada in 1763, the French monarchy embraced a broader program of experimentation toward non-territorial forms of empire based on maritime expansion. In 1767, after much controversy, the French designed an *exclusif mitigé* that legalized the import of specific goods into controlled entrepôts while reasserting a French monopoly over shipping and trade of the most lucrative goods. Under this new policy, the French colony of Saint-Domingue, which had become the uncontested engine of French colonialism, was granted one such entrepôt at Môle Saint-Nicolas, a remote outpost of the colony.[9]

Because of the immense territorial amputation of 1763, many scholars have narrated the history of the early modern French colonial empire up to Haitian independence in 1804 as one of decline. French imperial crumbling was compounded by the country's geopolitical fragility on the European continent. The expansion of Russia and Prussia in Eastern Europe, the worrying vulnerability of France's Austrian and Spanish allies, and the enduring strength of the British navy positioned France as a beleaguered player in Europe's political system. The period between the Seven Years' War and the French Revolution is therefore generally viewed by historians as a time of "collapse." Within this narrative, France's participation in the American Revolution is often presented as a peripheral event, a phony victory driven by a fruitless appetite for revenge ending in the financial disarray that engulfed a monarchy in chaos. The ever-shrinking territory of the French colonial "assemblage" has led historians to doubt the very idea that France was an empire at all. This perspective often aligns with an assumption that the French Revolution was an economic disaster happening in a backward agricultural country, another capitalist failure accelerating the British rise to global hegemony via the industrial revolution. This historiographical legacy partially explains why the French Revolution is rarely discussed as an important factor by proponents of the "new history of capitalism."[10]

Although this book positions French-British colonial rivalry as an important feature of the revolutionary Atlantic and explores the entanglement of imperial formations, it also challenges this British-centric teleology. Rather than making the case for a successful French Empire or presenting a new genealogy of French industrialization, it aims to reconnect Saint-Domingue's plantation complex with an imperial history of France and a broader debate over free trade that a fascination with the "rise of Britain" has concealed. Historian Guillaume Daudin has shown that "the largest trading power in Europe at the end of the 1780s was France," not Britain, and its main support was "the plantation system." As will be demonstrated, the devaluation of the power and scope of the French commercial empire leads to biased interpretations: first, it minimizes the significance of the Haitian Revolution and the wealth that France derived from Saint-Domingue; second, it overlooks the fact that the political economy of the French Empire interacted with the nonlinear construction of the French nation-state. Not unlike the Spanish "polycentric polity," France underwent a phase of imperial revolution characterized by many short-lived experiments and unacknowledged continuities. The features of the French-American alliance set the stage for a French free-trade imperialism in the nineteenth century with old regime roots, as well as the "new colonization" centered on Africa and based on wage labor. Regarding Saint-Domingue as an entrepôt makes the connections between trade, revolutions, imperial formation, and nation building visible.[11]

A Triangular Relationship

Focusing on the implications of US-Saint-Domingue trade, *Entrepôt of Revolutions* places political economy at the center of the revolutionary narrative yet rejects a Eurocentric retelling of the Age of Revolution. This book engages with the notion of Atlantic revolution that historians Robert Palmer and Jacques Godechot conceptualized as a transatlantic democratic wave. It also draws from the more recent scholarship that has exposed the mutual influences of the French and Haitian revolutions and illuminated the multiple and contrary ramifications of events in the Caribbean and the United States. The book expands on this rich, layered work by showing that US trade with Saint-Domingue shaped the French-American relationship, contributed to state and imperial building in these three polities, and defined overlapping but distinct forms of republicanism.[12]

It argues that commercial tensions around colonialism were integral to revolutionary sovereignty. The liberty of commerce did not necessarily align with personal freedom, and commercial sovereignty could negate human rights. The meaning of commercial sovereignty remained contested throughout the revolutionary era; it was defined not only by ideas deployed by white thinkers in Europe or the desires of metropolitan consumers, but it was also shaped in the United States by a variety of elite and non-elite players. The new country and its 4 million inhabitants, partially isolated by European powers, coexisting with powerful Indian polities, and deprived of a standing navy, was a weak player compared to France, a global superpower. In fact, the French government ordinarily viewed the United States as peripheral to its colonial interests. Yet the founders challenged this subordination from the outset, envisioning the United States as a universal *entrepôt* and breaking down the boundaries drawn by European colonial empires. A market revolution preceded, accompanied, and promoted a broader geopolitical revolution. Moreover, the existence of the new country disrupted the metropole-colony binary, as John Adams, the first representative of the US confederation at Versailles, explained:

> The Commerce of the West India Islands is a Part of the American System of Commerce. They can do Neither without Us nor We without them. The Creator has placed us upon the Globe in Such a situation, that We have Occasion for each other, We have the means of assisting each other, and Politicians and Artificial Contrivances cannot separate Us.

Adams was not only making a lofty statement about natural law and the commercial ambitions of the nascent power he represented but was also accurately calculating that the West Indies, and Saint-Domingue above all, were the nation's principal non-British market. France needed the United States to supply its colonies, but the US government and many ship owners also believed they needed Saint-Domingue to sever their commercial subservience to the former metropole.[13]

While many white American elites, farmers, and migrants on the borderlands from the Great Lakes to the Floridas looked toward western expansion, powerful groups of traders in Atlantic port-cities advocated for and implemented an aggressive commercial policy, notably, albeit not exclusively, toward the French West Indies and the French Mascarene Islands. Under the US flag, ships from New York, Philadelphia, Boston, Salem, Charleston, and Baltimore flocked to harbors in Martinique, Ile-de-France, and Saint-Louis in Senegal. Saint-Domingue was by far the most significant French colonial market for the new country, and access to the Pearl of the Caribbean became integral to establishing the United States on the global stage. The enforcement of customs regulations, in parallel and in conjunction with settler colonialism and Native dispossession, was a major building block on the transition from a confederal state into a more centralized federal polity. Saint-Domingue was one of the sites where the co-construction of French and US republican empires intersected for revolutionary state formation and nation building.[14]

While the colony's production enriched French and American capitalists and catered to consumer needs on both sides of the Atlantic, Saint-Domingue's society did not remain a passive object of imperial scheming and commercial profiteering, and an array of actors from the colony shaped the French-American relationship. Although this was most visible during the tenure of general

Toussaint Louverture between 1797 and 1801, the colony's commanding influence had been unfolding since the birth of the United States. Caribbean players
were active participants within a multi-centered, Atlantic framework. Le Cap-
Français, Port-au-Prince, and, to a lesser extent, Les Cayes Saint-Louis, were
cosmopolitan hubs importing foodstuff and timber from distant lands and exporting colonial commodities. They were connected with West Africa through
the slave trade. These port cities were also part of a Caribbean network of trade,
having long-standing connections with Jamaica, Cuba, Curaçao, the Danish
West Indies, Martinique, Guadeloupe, North American ports, and, at its border,
the Spanish part of the island. This commercial landscape contextualizes Saint-
Domingue's "layered sovereignty" within French imperial formation and the
emergence of the Haitian state.[15]

This book follows the story of US-Saint-Domingue traffics and flows from
a variety of angles. It examines the competing ideas that defined the legal
framework of this trade, their intellectual sources, and their strategic use by
individuals, rival factions, and pressure groups. The debate intersected with but
was distinct from the history of abolitionism. Beyond concerns regarding taxation and monopolies, the nature of the relationship among Saint-Domingue and
France and the United States was at stake and, in turn, raised broader questions
about the national and imperial nature of the new composite polities emerging
from revolutionary situations. Being a crossroad and a patchwork of overlapping
sovereignties until the Haitian war of independence began in 1802, the status of
the colony remained unclear: was it a *département*, a French-US entrepôt, or a
new, unacknowledged polity? Examining the entangled commercial regulations
illuminates the rise of a Haitian state connected with but autonomous from metropolitan, US, British, and Spanish designs. This ambiguity was foundational to
a new French imperial republic.[16]

Entrepôt of Revolutions provides the first detailed study of the Saint-Domingue
merchants whose networks traversed national and imperial boundaries and
argues that they were major stakeholders in the debate over revolutionary
commercial sovereignty. Although businessmen have always been prominent
characters in narratives of the American Revolution, traders and sea captains
have never been acknowledged as significant players in the Haitian Revolution.
There are many reasons for this lack of recognition. The first relates to sources.
While plantation records have made it possible to recount the fate of *habitations*
(plantations in French colonies), and while ample business correspondence
from French merchants has shed light on commercial matters in metropolitan ports, comparable sources for traders based in the colony are sparse and
scattered in depositories outside Haiti. Much of this archival material has also
been lost through fire and warfare. Most traders were continually moving from
one port-city to another, and as transnational agents, they did not easily fit

within traditional historical narratives. For example, Guadeloupe's privateers, immortalized by Cuban novelist Alejo Carpentier, have obscured similar characters in Saint-Domingue, whose role was deemed peripheral to the Haitian Revolution. Put bluntly, these merchants were for the most part unsavory characters. Unlike Black sailors, they were not radical forces spreading revolt, and, far from challenging the plantation system, they generally contributed to keeping it afloat. The vast majority of traders who had access to and specialized in the US market were young white men like Barney. Unlike the more diverse world of planters and the urban middle classes, traders formed a racially exclusive milieu and social class clearly separated from that of modest retailers. Beyond this specific group, informal traffics took place between Black insurrectionists and American sea captains. However, the lack of archival material on informal trading makes it impossible to measure its volume.[17]

A current of Atlantic history has tended to depict transnational commercial networks as self-organized and self-regulated, existing beyond state oversight. Yet merchants did take state-sponsored regulations into account and jostled to infiltrate state institutions to strengthen their credit and reputation. The meaning of this activity amid revolutions, when the nature, function, boundaries, and definition of the state were in turmoil, remains unclear. Merchants strived to profit from ever-changing environments and negotiated with local public officials to facilitate trade. These individuals with fluid identities were able to manipulate how they were categorized, transforming themselves from French to American, from privateer captain to diplomat or smuggler. In so doing they also contributed to the transformation of polities. Maintaining cross-border solidarity, trans-imperial actors created links that alternately strengthened and contradicted the projects defined in the metropole. These informal links on the fringes of empire caused friction, distorted colonial dreams, and reinvented metropolitan rules. Merchants also attempted to occupy leading roles within political entities where influence was there for the taking. They organized rings and cartels, did battle in the name of merchants' interests, and fought each other for the control of specific trades. In a context of entangled crises, the divide between the market and the state was constantly under negotiation.[18]

The *Jeux d'échelle* of Entangled Revolutionary Crises

Entrepôt of Revolutions contributes to efforts to globalize the French Revolution with the tools of "connected history." Rather than settling on one scale of analysis, I practice what historian Jacques Revel calls a *jeu d'échelles* (game of scales): it examines the triangular relationship between Saint-Domingue, France, and the

United States, on an Atlantic, imperial, regional, local, and even individual level. The use of various scales is not only a descriptive and rhetorical device; it also sheds light on the collision of forces, parameters, and circumstances that have produced historical consequences. Although people, money, ideas, and goods circulated, commercial sovereignty provoked countless clashes on multiple scales of analysis. The French–US–Saint-Domingue relationship was part of a greater global framework of trade and empires, but it also materialized in the smallest of settings. It was fashioned by and intersected with the British and Spanish Atlantic worlds and was embedded in its Caribbean environment. Imperial centers such as Versailles, Paris, and London were also sites that defined the meaning of this trade. At times a central concern, at others a vague unarticulated afterthought, commercial sovereignty had very different meanings when viewed from a small port in Saint-Domingue, the National Assembly in Paris, a political club in New York, or a merchant house in Curaçao.[19]

This study crosses traditional boundaries between political, social, and economic history by employing an abundance of widely dispersed primary sources from France, the United States, and Britain. Published reports, memos, and newspapers open a window on debates in the public sphere; handwritten notes, letters, and drafts reveal behind-the-scene discussions in Versailles, London, Philadelphia, and Le Cap-Français. Administrative correspondence between metropolitan authorities and colonial officials in Saint-Domingue show that implementation of commercial regulations remained a central concern in the last decades of the eighteenth century. Boxes from the DXXV series at the Archives nationales in Paris, a major source for writing the history of the Haitian Revolution, also offered a wealth of information on trade and financial transactions. Customs documents from US National Archives provided data on the flow of ships and goods between Saint-Domingue and New York, Baltimore, and Philadelphia.

Relying solely on public archives creates biases and risks overstating the power of governmental authorities as well as the consistency of their policies. Centering attention on traders provides a different picture. In addition to consular correspondence, repatriated archives from French consulates in US port-cities provide information on the commercial and political world underpinning this trade. Furthermore, Saint-Domingue's notarial records detail the trajectories of commercial firms. Records from the High Court of Admiralty at the British National Archives contained papers providing new insights on US trade. Business letters, diaries and autobiographies, scattered in a great number of depositories, described the intricate commercial worlds from a personal perspective.

Although the layout of this book is largely chronological, the constant shifting of scales and a multi-centered framework produce a narrative that resists linearity.

The first chapter places diplomatic discussions at Versailles in their Atlantic context, examines the French-American alliance of 1778, and suggests that Louis XVI entered the war for colonial and economic reasons that entailed a global reappraisal of the French Empire. The creation of the United States sparked heated transatlantic debate on free trade, colonial relations, and diplomacy. The immediate consequences of the French-American alliance are explored in chapter 2, which also reveals the multi-faceted world of smuggling that linked US ports to Saint Domingue in the aftermath of the American Revolutionary War. Benefiting from cheap resources imported from North America, the Pearl of the Caribbean's economy developed at an unprecedented rate. Although Saint-Domingue's expanding plantation complex relied on US complicity, this development did not unfold seamlessly in the metropole, prompting concerns about "looting" of the nation.

Chapters 3 and 4 examine the contrast between conflicting perceptions of trade and merchants' actual commercial practices, which created a politically explosive climate and set the stage for the imperial crisis triggered by the French Revolution. Far more than a dispute over doctrine, the struggle over the "liberty of commerce" revealed competition between colonial pressure groups at a time of democratic creativity entangled with slavery and race politics. With the creation of the French Republic in 1792, new concerns about colonial loyalty, national allegiances, and commercial connections surfaced and combined to create a shaky French-American "empire of liberty." Decisions in Paris had consequences on the other side of the Atlantic—but not those expected by legislators, as white colonists weaponized commercial rules to attack free people of color and attempted to create new diplomatic connections with the United States. Chapter 5 exposes the contradictions between supposed high politics and merchants' attitudes to events in Saint-Domingue and on the imperial level. Many traders in the Americas understood the slave insurrection as a potential boon and a way to eliminate French metropolitan competition. While some seized the opportunity to start intercolonial slave trading, others pulled strings to secure monopolistic contracts in the guise of "free trade." At the same time, Black revolutionaries took advantage of the French-American crisis to abolish slavery on the island. These critical events exploded the fantasies associated with commercial republicanism.

The sixth chapter situates the emergence of the French commercial republic in the context of a new global war with Britain and US neutrality. While debate on the "liberty of commerce" mostly preoccupied a small minority of experts in Paris and London, it provoked a major democratic crisis in the United States and contributed to the embryonic bipolarization of party politics. French commercial republicanism failed in Philadelphia. Chapter 7 discusses how the breakdown of the colonial system almost entirely isolated Saint-Domingue from the

French metropole. Increasingly dependent on the United States for provisions, the colony suffered fragmentation and foreign occupations. The "newly free" practiced an informal free trade, which the government claimed to favor but hastened to regulate. Chapter 8 describes how new patterns of commercial circulation in a Caribbean at war challenged and generated political identities in the new revolutionary polities. Merchants played scales, shifting positions and crossing imperial/national boundaries in their own self-redefinitions, prompting state efforts to strengthen regulations and refine national definitions. Chapter 9 follows the formation of Toussaint-Louverture's quasi-state as the subverted hub of commercial republicanism. This apotheosis was also the final episode in a series of economic and political experiments that concluded in French counter-revolution, the end of the special relationship between France and the United States, and the War of Haitian Independence.

The Greatest Revolution
in Commerce and Politics,
1776–1784

"Who could say that the happiness of the human kind is no motive for the alliance between the French and the Americans?" It was with great optimism that Thomas Paine contemplated the likely consequences of the French-American treaty of amity and commerce of 1778. Paine, who in 1776 had heralded the beginning of the American Revolution with his best-selling pamphlet *Common Sense*, thought that this new connection would spark a cosmopolitan realignment and a diplomatic revolution. He had no doubt that the liberty of commerce between the early American republic and the French kingdom would shatter the grounds of national jealousies. The world would only become increasingly open thanks to the shared *entrepôt* of America and the civilizing virtues of trade. Therefore, the new economic union would inevitably destroy the basis of the European colonial system. Paine's prophetic vision was all the more powerful as this pamphlet specifically targeted the *abbé* Raynal, whose controversial *Histoire des deux Indes* had been one of the bestselling and most translated books of the time. Yet Raynal, distancing himself from his radical reputation, had not shown any enthusiasm for the 1778 treaty. In the *abbé's* opinion, the alliance was just another by-product of an old-style diplomacy that inexorably weakened the British "natural enemy" by taking revenge after the 1762–1763 agreement that stripped France of Canada and Louisiana. Raynal was quite certain that the young nation's aspirations would rapidly collide with the colonial interests of European powers—including France—putting an end to the commercial and political revolution that Paine had imagined.[1]

This exchange between two of the most read authors of the late eighteenth century revealed the uncertainties that surrounded the emergence of the United States. The disagreement between Paine and Raynal should not,

Entrepôt of Revolutions. Manuel Covo, Oxford University Press. © Oxford University Press 2022.
DOI: 10.1093/oso/9780197626382.003.0002

however, detract from the common premises on which they based their views—particularly the colonial lens through which they understood the events. Both of them knew that the birth of a new state in the Americas occurred in a world where political communities were organized as colonial empires, not as nation-states. The United States was tentatively emerging out of a diverse coalition of British colonies whereas France was centering its empire on the slave colony of Saint-Domingue. What was really at stake in the alliance was not the question of whether the United States would be allowed to trade with European metropoles but the question of whether it would have access to colonial markets, and the political consequences of this access for European politics more broadly. What would the alliance mean for the French Empire, its relationships with other empires, and its internal links between the metropole and the colonies?[2]

These questions unleashed a series of anxieties about the national boundaries of France and America. The possible institutionalization of commercial ties threatened to sever the international and colonial borders that had been established in the previous decades. The thriving "science of commerce" and discourse of political economy had already been shaping a number of reforms in the French Empire since the Seven Years' War. In the 1770s and the 1780s, the colonial stakes of the French-American alliance galvanized the public sphere. It was not just ministers, diplomats, and economists but also merchants, planters, and public officials whose ideas circulated across the English Channel and the Atlantic Ocean in brochures, pamphlets, and encyclopedia articles. If most of the themes had been elaborated before, US independence would make those new ideas concrete and their actualization more likely. French officials extended a rethinking of empire already under way, taking the concrete existence of a new political entity into account. The controversy produced the conceptual categories with which the French-American connection would be examined during the revolutionary era. By looking at what happened as Franco-American diplomacy met the colonial history of the French Caribbean, this chapter reframes the origins, evolution, outcomes, and significance of the 1778 treaty.

A War in the Name of Colonies?
Vergennes Against Turgot

The terms of the debate over the fate of the French West Indies during the British imperial crisis emerged from the crucible of a conflict between members of the French state council. On one side of the debate was Charles Gravier, Count of Vergennes and secretary of state for foreign affairs, who fully backed an overt war with Britain. On the other side was Anne Robert Jacques Turgot, who as general controller—the French equivalent of finance minister—warned the king of the great risks that the French involvement entailed. Both parties grounded their views on the theories of political economy that had, ever since the 1750s, increasingly replaced and complicated politics that had once been based on honor and conquest.[3]

Analyzing the debate between these two figures demonstrates how far economic ideas had penetrated beyond the public sphere and into the domains of Old Regime diplomacy. If Vergennes was not a *philosophe* or expert in the science of political economy, he was hardly impervious to the *science du commerce*. In the *Reflections* that he submitted to the king in April 1776, he underlined the importance of colonies in international relations after the Seven Years' War. England, he insisted, was the "natural enemy of France," a "greedy, ambitious, unfair and hypocritical enemy." British hegemonic ambitions were destabilizing the balance of Europe, and he deemed it a matter of the utmost urgency to reestablish France as the sole arbitrator of Europe. This, he argued, would maintain the status quo and, by extension, peace in the continental and maritime realms. This economic language of balance, in fact, was the leitmotif of his writings. Secondary powers needed to be able to counteract the powers of the first rank; mutual jealousies were necessary to keep each country in its rightful position. It was based on an entirely defensive presupposition that he argued for the importance of supporting the American colonies. By weakening England, France would be able to protect its colonies from covetous Britons. The French intervention would not be a war of revenge but a preventive act destined to protect French commerce and reduce England to its "natural," secondary rank among nations.[4]

Vergennes insisted on the centrality of commerce in the power of states. The strength of England was backed by its navy, whose superiority derived from the possession of colonies and exclusive trade agreements. As such, Vergennes was the heir of his predecessor Etienne-François de Choiseul who had been in charge of foreign affairs, the navy, and war when France was fighting its first truly global war. Choiseul had concluded from the outcome of the Seven Years' War that navigation and commerce constituted the power of empires, not territorial expansion. For that reason, Vergennes carried on Choiseul's policy of rebuilding the French Navy so as to reestablish international balance. Both Choiseul and Vergennes implemented some of the theories of Vincent de Gournay's "liberal circle," which had translated a number of British economic treaties into French and popularized the idea that France should adopt British conceptions of commerce and the navy. Vergennes drew one major conclusion from this set of ideas: France had to diminish the extent of the British Empire if it was going to protect the French colonies from British envy, and the creation of a new state in America would fulfill this goal.[5]

While the need to contain British colonial inroads into French colonial territories had brought Vergennes to this pro-American position, his vision had a much broader scope. He predicted that France, by gaining access to the North American market, could secure new markets for its own output. The alliance would engender a special relationship, a "connection" shaped by the "necessary ties of commerce." A long-term "chain" would stimulate the French manufactures and attract low-cost commodities, "increasing national labor while diminishing the rival's power." Yet, in Vergennes's view, this commercial prospect was only a secondary object that lost much appeal through the discussions with American commissioners. Benjamin Franklin, although a Francophile, made clear that the United States would not grant France any commercial privilege. Franklin, who held many of the same views as the French physiocrats, refused to create "artificial" rules that thwarted the "natural order" of free trade. Congress, like its representatives abroad, consistently maintained that it would not substitute one metropole for another. However, Vergennes thought that a Franco-American alliance would indirectly benefit French commercial strength. The French Antilles would, in particular, gain from trade with the United States. This was an idea that had been hovering since Choiseul's ministry, according to which smuggling was supposed to root a French-American relationship and progressively detach the North American continent from the British metropole. Whereas a French conquest would incur new demographic and financial burdens, an independent and allied North America could become extremely useful to provision islands "in times when it was impossible to feed them from Europe." This new spatio-economic arrangement would turn out to be much more advantageous to the French Atlantic trade than the opening of an unpredictable US market.[6]

The proposal was not without its dangers. Couldn't the creation of the United States threaten the political security of the Antilles? What if the new independent power contemplated conquering the French colonies for itself and by itself? Vergennes presented these anxieties only to discount them. A United States drained by the war could not sustain such expansionist ambitions. British Canada would manufacture an insecurity that would dissuade the United States from a southward repositioning of its military forces. In any case, the United States did not need more land to develop, as the agricultural possibilities of the North American continent seemed thoroughly unlimited. And most important, it was going to form a republic, not just any republic but one that was defined by the looseness of its ties. Reprising Montesquieu's argument, Vergennes recalled that republics seldom had a "spirit of conquest" and insightfully predicted that the confederation would be composed of different states with different interests, making the United States a weak player among nations. The allied state in North America was expected to provide military security to French colonial commerce and save money for the state. A few years earlier, Canada had been imagined as playing that role in a reformed French Empire, but the United States could be a cheaper and more effective option. Congress deftly foregrounded this strategic interest in making a deal with France. An allied country hostile to England would be able to check British expansion in the Caribbean without incurring the expense of territorial occupation.[7]

These, then, were the currents of strategy and political calculation that would grow in the following years. Commerce, not new colonial conquests, became increasingly central to the operation of geopolitical thinking. The new country would come to be imagined as the "satellite-state" of the French Antilles, providing them with protection and feeding their demand for resources. The United States was to be the fort and the granary of Saint-Domingue.

In response to Vergennes's memorandum, Turgot submitted his observations to the king, in which he clarified his own views on political economy. Far more than Vergennes's proposal, Turgot's was saturated in the physiocratic debates about the value of colonies. Since the 1750s, Turgot had been close to a group of economists, including Doctor François Quesnay, Victor Riquetti de Mirabeau, Nicolas Baudeau, and Pierre Paul Lemercier de La Rivière, who assailed the colonial monopoly. More recently, Pierre-Samuel Dupont de Nemours and Guillaume-François Letrosne, with whom Turgot was in constant dialogue, had again supported the liberalizing of colonial trade. Most thought that the colonies should be regarded as provinces of the kingdom, emancipated from the prohibitive regime that plagued their development. Mirabeau had already predicted that the European metropoles would provoke the independence of American colonies if they clung to this protectionist catechism. Following the Boston Tea Party, it was the time to prevent a similar conclusion by applying what Turgot had consistently called for.[8]

This memorandum allayed Vergennes's anxieties and revoked the supposed benefits of a French involvement at a time when the kingdom was in dire financial straits. Full military support of the patriots, Turgot firmly believed, would not improve the security of the Antilles. If the insurgents were to be defeated, there would be no momentum for another ruinous war in the Caribbean. But in the long run, the independence of the North American colonies would be unavoidable, with or without French support. Yet this text went well beyond such circumstantial considerations. Turgot took the opportunity to ask three fundamental questions: what would be the consequences of an independent state in North America? Was the colonial system advantageous to European countries? How could it be reformed in a way that could countervail an emerging power on the North American continent? Turgot could not emphasize more the revolutionary significance of the events that were currently under way. Far from being a banal episode in another colonial standoff, the American independence would mark "the age of the greatest revolution in commerce and politics, not only in

England, but in all Europe." The relationship of power between both continents would be rebalanced in radical ways. Quoting Franklin, very popular in France, Turgot prophesied the emergence of a new polity obsessed with buying and selling. Serving its "true interest," the commercial state would reach an unprecedented level of power.[9]

The United States, despite its cosmopolitan inclinations, would not carry out a *doux commerce* (a gentle, civilizing commerce) with European colonies when monopoly ruled the whole colonial system. In his denunciation of commercial monopolies, Turgot took as an example the Spanish Empire, instead of the French one: he certainly hoped to be provoking less controversy by deflecting the blame to Madrid, the strongest ally of France since the end of the Seven Years' War. It was indeed commonplace to denounce the Spaniards for their jealousy concerning precious metals. The United States would pose a direct threat to its Spanish neighbors, as American patriots were described by Turgot as quintessential smugglers. If Madrid persisted in its selfish system, the Americans would encourage the Spanish colonists to follow their example and "shake off the yoke of the metropole." Otherwise, the North Americans would engage in a "lucrative war, without danger for themselves." Turgot was a pioneer in articulating the theory of dominos. Contraband would be all the more revolutionary as a new state would fully support this trade. It was not unlikely that the Americans would go from "armed contraband" to open war and help other colonies to "liberate themselves," only to eventually "integrate" them into a broader "union of interests." As the United States pushed its agenda forward, European powers would no longer be able to escape the necessity of reforming their colonial empires.[10]

Turgot seized the opportunity to synthesize the long-standing physiocratic take on colonial empires. Instead of monopolies, which harmed the true interests of the nation, international competition should stimulate a rational economy. Indeed, a "natural order" connected the Caribbean islands with the continent. Hurting the colonists' and the Americans' interests did not benefit the metropoles but only served the colonial merchants, an "intermediary class" that interposed itself between consumers and producers. The protectionist system prevented foreign consumers from buying commodities at their fair price and diminished national growth for which the "jealousy of trade" was the worst enemy. Conversely, the colonies should be granted an "entire liberty of commerce" while "taking financial responsibility for their own protection and administration." Instead of "enslaved provinces" (*provinces asservies*), colonies were to be regarded as "friend states (*etats amis*), protected, if you want, but foreign and separate." The slavery metaphor, inspired by the American revolutionaries' rhetoric against Britain, helped clarify the stakes. The metropole had to achieve a voluntary division leading to a new form of political association, grounded on a federative link, not a relationship of dependency and domination—a kind of Commonwealth.[11]

The creation of the United States raised questions that went well beyond what Vergennes was imagining. The new country necessitated the transformation of colonies into "allied provinces," and the alliance implied the establishment of a treaty acknowledging the existence of two different and asymmetrical polities. This legal connection would be based on a contract within a new constitutional framework. The nature of these new states remained somewhat unclear, however, with no historical precedents. In fact, Turgot might have reiterated some of the arguments that the American envoys had tried to advance at the beginning of the imperial crisis in London, when the secession was not unavoidable.[12]

Although Turgot's view did not prevail and remained unpublished for a long time, the memorandum was widely discussed by economists, philosophers, colonists, public officials, and lawyers. Even Vergennes, through Dupont de Nemours's mediation, came around to adopting elements of it when negotiating a free-trade treaty with Britain in 1786. The significance of Turgot's report has been in part overshadowed by Adam Smith's *Wealth of Nations*, published the same year and translated into French almost immediately. Smith employed quasi-similar words to denounce the British monopoly on the colonies. Like Turgot, he decried a "nation of shopkeepers" bent on an Act of Navigation that deeply hurt the British economy. Like Turgot, he thought that the colonies should be granted a liberty of commerce and full independence, imagining a British-American treaty that would transform the Americans into "the most faithful, the most affectionate, and the most generous allies." Like Turgot, he had no real hope that the metropolitan authorities would approve such a deal. Smith was indeed one the few mavericks who contested the profitability of the imperial project, which galvanized much public support otherwise. *Wealth of Nations* would become the catechism of free-trade liberalism for centuries to come, but Turgot's pamphlet remained a landmark of colonial thinking throughout the French revolutionary sequence. Dupont de Nemours, Turgot's faithful disciple, would have the report published in 1791 to call for the implementation of its reforms in a context of increasing colonial tensions within the French Empire. Slaveholders and abolitionists would repeatedly try to make Turgot's ideas their own.[13]

The Liberty of the Seas

During the war, the king did not make any definitive decision regarding the liberalization of trade between the islands and the United States. In December 1775, secretary of the navy and colonies, Antoine de Sartine, who had no intention of disrupting the colonial monopoly, had gathered deputies of merchants and colonists to reach a more effective implementation of the prohibitive system. All along, he followed an indecisive policy, alternating between emphasizing the necessity of provisioning the French colonies, addressing the complaints of the Chambers of Commerce (commercial institutions located in cities throughout France), and responding to Vergennes's secret attempts to supply the American patriots with weapons and ammunition. Famous writer and businessman Pierre Caron de Beaumarchais played an important part in the schemes designed by the Ministry of Foreign Affairs. While Beaumarchais's firm provided much needed guns to Americans, the colonial government in Saint-Domingue helped Congress's envoy to Cap-Français, Stephen Ceronio, provision the United States through the Antilles. Yet France's secretary of the navy opposed any long-standing commitment with North Americans, before the conclusion of a formal alliance with the United States. Even after Turgot's dismissal, the State Council remained highly divided, and a number of players on the ground seized this opportunity to serve their own agenda.[14]

The treaties concluded on February 6, 1778, did not really clarify French policy on the exact nature of the relationship desired between the continent and the colonies. Through the "treaty of alliance" France acknowledged "the liberty, Sovereignty, and independence absolute and unlimited of the United States, as well in Matters of Government as of commerce." In exchange, article 11 stated that the United States would commit to guaranteeing the French possessions in America. The United States was therefore imagined as a future military rear base of the French colonies. Given the weakness of the US Navy at the time, this clause was more prospective than anything else. In terms of trade, the treaty of amity and commerce did not go very far. The key element was the principle of "the most favored nation" according to which the partner would immediately benefit from any advantage granted to a third party, but France granted this privilege to all its allies in Europe. More specifically, one article proclaimed that several free ports would be open to US trade in Europe. For the Caribbean, the king did not make many promises other than to stipulate that "the free Ports which have been and are open in the French Islands of America" were to be preserved. These provisions, by sanctifying previous relaxations on the colonial monopoly, rebuffed the metropolitan merchants, but the king did not bind himself to further liberalization of the colonial trade. In Congress's views, the agreement, albeit disappointing, left the door open to further relaxation.[15]

This ambiguity did not escape French officials in Saint-Domingue who adopted the most extensive interpretation and legalized the trade with Americans as soon as they received the texts on July 20, 1778. The metropolitan state's understanding of the treaty left much space for circumstantial adaptations. Sartine, under increasing pressure from metropolitan merchants, zigzagged between firmness and tolerance; he opened the neutral trade on March 30 before officially closing it again in September, while condoning the informal admission of foreign ships. At the same time, the French government satisfied requests made by metropolitan merchants for financing a number of expensive convoys from Europe to provision the colonies.[16]

The French policy reached new levels of ambiguity when the war came to be fought in the name of the liberty of the seas and, consequently, of the liberty of commerce, leading to a collision between colonial law and neutral rights. Article 23 of the Treaty, a victory for American commissioners, achieved a breakthrough in the history of international law by officially acknowledging neutrality. After a century-long legal debate on neutrality, a major European imperial power adopted for the first time the principle that "free ships made free goods." The new law meant that commodities produced or bought in enemy territories would take the nationality of the neutral flag. The king's ordinance of July 26, 1778, underscored this new stance when it "prohibited to arrest and to drive neutral vessels into ports of the kingdom, even if they were leaving or heading to enemy ports."[17]

If the proclamation of these principles was radically new, the legal doctrines that buttressed them had longer historical roots. The French had long embraced Hugo Grotius's principle of *mare liberum* according to which all nations were entitled to navigate the seas—a theory advanced by the United Provinces (the Netherlands) in the seventeenth century while confronting an expanding British Navy. Conversely, the British, who had adopted their own form of colonial monopoly in 1651, the Act of Navigation, usually brandished Selden's theory of *mare closum*: nations had a right to claim domination on parts of the sea. During the Seven Years' War, Versailles had taken up the position held by the Dutch and depicted "Albion" as a "Nation of filibusters" pointing to universal dominance of the seas. The former minister of the navy, Choiseul, had even orchestrated a propaganda campaign against the maritime tyrannical power, which had authorized a capture of two French vessels before any official declaration of war in 1755. When France proclaimed the "liberty of the neutrals" and the "liberty of the seas" in 1778, it was to clearly differentiate itself from Britain and, even more, to entice possible European allies into an alliance against British thalassocracy. Vergennes's strategy aimed to isolate Great Britain and create a great coalition with northern powers, including Russia, Sweden, and Denmark—countries forming a league of armed neutrality to defend themselves from the British Navy. The French government also hoped to draw the United Provinces into the war. This is why the top counselor in the Ministry of Foreign Affairs, Mathias Joseph Gérard de Rayneval, kept denouncing the British for claiming they possessed the "supreme and exclusive faculty of prescribing arbitrary laws contrary to the navigation and the commerce of all nations and of insulting all flags with impunity—in a word, of regarding the sea as its exclusive domain."[18]

At the same time, the British line of conduct had a regenerative effect on French propaganda. The British stuck to the self-proclaimed rule of 1756, designed during the Seven Years' War to prohibit the provisioning of the French Antilles through Danish and Dutch vessels. This was a principle that justified the legal capture of vessels destined for colonial ports that were ordinarily closed to foreign trade in peacetime. French West Indian ports prohibiting the admission of foreign vessels before the war were not entitled to admit foreign vessels during the war. Moreover, according to the "continuous voyage" rule, if a French vessel had made a stopover in a foreign colony, its cargo remained French and subject to British seizure. The most dramatic outcome of this policy was the brutal looting of Saint-Eustatius, the hub of Dutch smuggling, in December 1780. When Britain revealed little concern about respecting neutral rights, France gained much leeway in championing the liberty of the seas in order to seduce the United Provinces, Denmark, and Sweden, which coalesced with Russia to form the League of Neutrals. The creation of the United States connected the stakes of colonial commerce with those of European trade and diplomacy.[19]

The topic was not confined to legal disputes between lawyers and diplomats; it was also a major inspiration for authors and artists who took part in the patriotic mobilization, with the encouragement of the foreign ministry. Among these writers was Jean-Baptiste Coeuilhe, the main librarian at the Bibliothèque Royale, whose poem entitled "The Liberty of the Sea" won the Marseilles Academy literary contest in 1781. In this piece, Coeuilhe reproduced two commonplaces: the natural right of navigating and the denunciation of the English despot on the seas:

> Liberty, liberty on the Empire of the Seas,
> This is the wish, this is the right of the Universe....
> A people however disregards this law.
> Only one people said: No, the Sea belongs to me.
> I am the sole Sovereign there, & deserve to be....
> In their pride, those Insulars speak this way,
> Haughty as much as reckless navigators,
> Great disturbers of human tranquility,
> Free in their homes, Tyrants everywhere else.

Coeuilhe underscored the civilizing virtues of commerce and navigation, which, he insisted, needed protection from the assaults of British brigands. Conversely the free circulation of vessels would engender a universal citizenship, in the messianic perspective of *doux commerce*. The liberty of the sea was a prelude to a more global regeneration. Although Coeuilhe won an award for this poem, he did not stand out for his originality: the theme was central to French monarchical propaganda.[20]

The *Affiches américaines*, the official newspaper in Saint-Domingue, unremittingly repeated this refrain in justifying French involvement in the war. The paper, which was both an organ of propaganda and a public forum for colonists, had followed closely the development of the British imperial crisis in the American colonies, from the Stamp Act Crisis to the Declaration of Independence. New political ideas circulated widely. The colony was directly involved in and affected by the war in myriad ways. Troops of people of color from Saint-Domingue were central to the siege of Savannah in 1779, and the military experience acquired by some of these officers, such as André Rigaud and Jacques Beauvais, would later prove essential to the Saint-Domingue revolution. But commerce, given the significance of the New England trade in the economy, was the most urgent concern. Celebrating the peace in 1783, *Affiches américaines* praised Louis the XVI for "giving liberty to an immense country and restituting freedom to commerce." It glorified the king who had fought for "the particular liberty of a people and the general liberty of the seas."[21]

The theme of the liberty of the seas provided much inspiration to metropolitan artists as well. In *France Offering Liberty to America* (1784), painter Jean Suau depicted the connections between US independence and commercial revolution. The American, represented as a Native American, is gratefully kneeling in front of his liberator, with two massive ships in the background and people carrying various goods on the sides. Artists also glorified the French Navy. The preponderance of naval battles distinguished the American Revolutionary War from previous global conflicts. In contrast with 1763, France, thanks to its alliance with Spain, had successfully managed to thwart British maritime dominance, warranting the celebration of French victories on the sea. Jean-François Hue immortalized the achievements of Admiral Charles-Henri d'Estaing in Grenada in 1779 in two paintings that were exhibited at the 1784 Salon. Facing growing discontent at home, the king commissioned Auguste-Louis de Rossel de Cercy to produce eighteen paintings representing the most important naval battles of the war and designed to show Louis XVI as the great protector of the seas. De Rossel, for instance, immortalized the battle of Hispaniola in the painting depicting the heroic defense of the smaller *Scipion* against the much larger *HMS London*. Louis Roger's print, entitled the "Independence of the United States," clearly synthesized how the government shaped the ideological meaning of the French intervention: the creation of the United States and the defense of the liberty of the seas. On the central column was Louis XVI's portrait crowning portraits of Franklin and Washington. "America and the seas, O Louis, recognize you for their liberator," wrote Roger.[22]

Figure 1.1 Le combat du *Scipion* contre le *HMS London*, le 18 octobre 1782 au large de Saint-Domingue by Auguste Louis de Rossel, 1788. Musée de la Marine, 3 OA 17, painting 112 x 163 cm.

But what did this propaganda mean for the regime of the French colonial monopoly, the *exclusif*? Was it possible for the monarchy to herald the liberty of the seas, on the one hand, and uphold the colonial monopoly, on the other? Vergennes's advisor, Rayneval, responding to Edward Gibbon's indictment of France at the beginning of the war, had a hard time distinguishing maritime stakes from colonial issues. He was intent on making clear that the liberty of the seas did not entail the abolition of prohibitive laws. Referring to international norms, he established as a European law "that the trade with colonies was exclusive, meaning that no foreigner had the right to take part in that trade." Rayneval, quoting former treaties between Spain and Britain, buttressed his argument with the distinction between coastal seas, where coast guards were entitled to seize foreign vessels, and high seas, where this should be prohibited. Yet this distinction, elaborated by Cornelius van Bynkershoek in *De Domino Maris Dissertatio* (1703), was not universally accepted. As historian Lauren Benton has demonstrated, even Grotius's stance on the liberty of the seas entailed regulations that warranted sea captains' intervention in repressing piracy.[23]

Rayneval's argument echoed a long-standing legal debate. A number of lawyers had claimed that the liberty of the seas had nothing to do with

INDÉPENDANCE DES ÉTATS-UNIS.

Figure 1.2 Indépendance des États-Unis, by Louis Roger, 1786. Bibliothèque nationale de France, Collection de Vinck, 1204, aquatint, 13.5 cm.

the liberalization of colonial trade. Danish thinker Martin Hübner, writing during the Seven Years' War, had already asserted that the provisioning of the colonies by neutrals did not subvert the colonial monopoly. Political economist François Duverger Véron de Forbonnais, a staunch defender of the prohibitive regime, favored the admission of foreign vessels to neutrals in times of war and fashioned himself as the champion of the liberty of commerce—a characterization that physiocrats would in no way endorse. This confusion stemmed from a wide use of the same phrases—namely, the liberty of commerce or the liberty of the seas—by antagonistic legal thinkers and political economists. Nonetheless, Rayneval's rhetorical acrobatics, destined to justify the French foreign policy and alleviate metropolitan merchants' concerns, engendered growing expectations for North Americans and planters alike. All parties would want to take advantage of the confusion unleashed by the monarchy's contradictory discourse.[24]

Colonial Enlightenment, Free Trade, and American Patriotism

The revolutionary crisis in North America, along with the dual language of the French government regarding the liberty of commerce, galvanized the debate on colonial identity. Chambers of Commerce argued that granting further commercial freedom to the French West Indies would endanger the very sovereignty of France over its colonies. A major source of anxiety lay in the nature of the planters' attachment to the metropole beyond strict commercial regulations. The colonists' patriotism was all the more suspicious as Guadeloupe and Martinique had voluntarily surrendered to the British during the Seven Years' War. The public spirit of the colonies, their capacity to subsume their particular interests to the common good, was thus under scrutiny. Furthermore, the cultural reality of a single French people including all inhabitants within the empire was put into question. This debate was part of a broader intellectual context marked by the explosion of patriotic publications. It is therefore reductive to view the controversy through an anachronistic opposition between liberalism and protectionism. As historian Paul Cheney explained, physiocracy decontextualized the economy from its social, geographic, and "climatic" environment, while the "science of commerce," steeped in Montesquieu's philosophy, rejected this kind of disconnection.[25]

All these strains in political economy and international law produced the state of intellectual tension that surrounded the publication of *abbé* Raynal's *Histoire philosophique et politique des établissements et du commerce des Européens dans les deux Indes* in 1772. The first edition was followed by two others in 1774 and 1781, in which a number of authors debated and even disagreed about a variety of heated topics. A major bestseller of its time, this colonial encyclopedia was copied, imitated, and refuted repeatedly, becoming the essential starting point for all discussions on the French Empire. Less known than this "literary monument" but also highly influential was the work of two itinerant, transatlantic pamphleteers—Michel-René Hilliard d'Auberteuil and Pierre-Ulric Dubuisson—who, like Raynal, both published extensively on colonial Saint-Domingue and proffered advice for enlightenment reform. Both also wrote contemporary histories of the American Revolution, which they connected explicitly to Saint-Domingue. These writers understood the events in North America through a Caribbean prism; their point of view was not purely European. Each of them served the monarchical state, and each enjoyed uneven success.

While the debates were animated by intrigue and violence—Dubuisson was even suspected of having poisoned Hilliard d'Auberteuil—the participants shared a number of common premises that placed the colonies in the foreground.

Raynal collaborated with the influential Victor-Marie Malouet, a former public official in French Guyana and a landowner in Saint-Domingue, to publish an additional pamphlet on Saint-Domingue in 1785. Hilliard d'Auberteuil, with the support of physiocrat Lemercier de Larivière, was part of the official committee that drafted a set of unsuccessful legal reforms for the colony. Dubuisson was hired by Sartine's successor at the Ministry of the Navy, Charles Eugène Gabriel de La Croix, marquis de Castries, to refute Hilliard d'Auberteuil's theses. The wealthy and powerful native of Martinique, Jean-Baptiste Dubuc, who had managed almost singlehandedly to shift France's commercial policy after the Seven Years' War, remained highly influential in the corridors of Versailles. None of them invented the notion of "American patriotism," but each of them contributed greatly to the elaboration of the idea in the light of the American Revolution. Both Hilliard d'Auberteuil and Dubuisson agreed that Saint-Domingue was in fact the real stake behind all the debates surrounding the French-American alliance. The Pearl of the Caribbean, far from being on the distant periphery of France, was actually the wealthiest province of the kingdom and, as such, deserved favorable treatment instead of discriminatory regulations.[26]

For Hilliard d'Auberteuil, there was no doubt that the question of free trade involved the broader question of the colonial identity of Saint-Domingue. Depicting himself as a "true patriot," he formed the wishes of a "real citizen," moved by "the love for the patrie . . . the country where one lives, the society of which one is a member." Drawing inspiration from Montesquieu, he insisted on the difference of climates, customs, and enterprises between Saint-Domingue and "domestic France." The colonial link assembled two discrete societies forming a "union" between equal parts. Rejecting the colonial subordination to metropolitan commerce, he maintained that Saint-Domingue and the metropole were locked into a contractual relationship. Like Rousseau, although in support of the interests of a slave-holding society, Hilliard d'Auberteuil resorted to a historical fiction to shed light on the origins of inequality between the colony and the metropole. The pamphleteer rejected the claim that the colonies had been created by and for metropolitan merchants, who unduly identified themselves with the state and the public good. Building on a piratical myth, the colonist contended that Hispaniola, the island of filibusters, had incurred no debt toward the metropole. The first European inhabitants of the island were part of a cosmopolitan world, composed of shady Dutch, British, and French adventurers who understood the universe "according to their particular interest, enfranchised from any personal allegiance." These "brigands" had struck a defensive alliance with the monarchy against Spain. The treaty acknowledged the rights of Saint-Domingue by creating its own legal space: the colonial specificity could not be reduced to any kind of provincialism. Free-trade cosmopolitanism, rooted in contractual legalism, was therefore at the core of a Saint-Dominguan identity steeped in "commercial patriotism." Inspired by the events in North America, Hilliard d'Auberteuil set the stage for a theory of commercial republicanism, interweaving mercantile interests and political regeneration.[27]

One of Hilliard d'Auberteuil's central targets was the *exclusif*, sustained by the "ingratitude" and the "greed" of metropolitan merchants—the ultimate illustration of "commercial tyranny." The metropole exerted a hegemonic domination on the colonies when it derived its wealth and its power from these islands, foremost from "the most useful and the wealthiest," Saint-Domingue. Hilliard d'Auberteuil subverted the commonplace idea put forward by the merchants: Saint-Domingue, although deprived of French provincial privileges, was the real center and the metropole the periphery, because economic power was all that mattered. To make it blossom, free competition had to be put in place. A fair price had to be set for commodities. Opening the market to foreigners was a decision that should be made at the colonial level, not by the metropole. Rewriting the history of Saint-Domingue, he asserted that the colony had decided on its own to abandon its rights to foreign trade through a treaty signed in 1671 when Colbert was minister of the navy. Thus, Saint-Domingue had historical claims to rescind this policy. Yet Hilliard d'Auberteuil's most forceful argument was more pragmatic, echoing Turgot's previous warnings. The government would always prove unable to counteract the "reciprocal interest of cultivators and smugglers," only depriving the state from possible duties. What would not fuel imperial revenues would be spent in bribes, feeding a corrupt colonial justice. A helpless metropole needed to accept the new realities of the times; with the emergence of the United States, Saint-Domingue found itself on higher ground.[28]

By forcefully asserting Saint-Domingue's commercial power, Hilliard d'Auberteuil suggested that the antagonism between colonists and planters foreboded an "imminent separation" if nothing changed. Writing in 1777, he hinted at how deep and transformative the effects of the American Revolution could be for any understanding of the colonial relationship between France and Saint-Domingue. The geopolitical circumstances, under which the natural interdependence between Saint-Domingue and North America could evolve, made it necessary to reform France's colonial policy. The "greed" of the merchants was only to blame for the obstacles to the further development of the Saint-Dominguan economy. Hilliard d'Auberteuil thus reprised and mixed arguments already articulated by Vergennes, Turgot, and other physiocrats, but he was reformulating them with the colony as the real center of decision-making.

The allusion to a possible colonial secession was highly provocative. Rival pamphleteer Dubuisson was outraged at the way Hilliard used the United States to threaten the French government. He laconically exclaimed: "No, the colony is French, it is peopled with French inhabitants." More convincingly, he pointed out the flaws of Hilliard d'Auberteuil's critiques, as the binary opposition between the "planter" and the "merchant" overshadowed the complexity of local configurations. Dubuisson clarified to his readers that many plantation managers in Saint-Domingue also acted as business commissioners, having "two faces" and serving two "contradictory interests." Most colonists, however, chose to ignore this socioeconomic complexity by denouncing the tyranny of the exclusif and equating their cause with that of the thirteen colonies. The struggle of the American patriots inspired the white colonists' fight for commercial equality within the French Empire.[29]

The 1781 edition of *Histoire des deux Indes* elaborated on Hilliard d'Auberteuil's point, although this new version completely recused it at the same time, with Denis Diderot's scathing intervention against slavery and the slave trade. The progressive inclusion of the American Revolution into the colonial encyclopedia explored the possible analogies between the thirteen colonies and the French West Indies. Diderot interpreted the creation of the new state in a messianic way, an event at the crossroad of cosmopolitanism and patriotism that made the regeneration of the colonies possible. The cosmopolitanism derived from the admission of foreigners to American markets; the patriotism thrived thanks to a true "naturalization" of colonists who therefore could nurture genuine connections with the places where they would eventually settle. The migration to far distant lands had been the original sin of the colonists, whose national character dissolved in their quest of personal enrichment. The colonists had neither been the "most useful citizens" nor the "promoters of civilization"; instead, they had completely lost their humanity as extreme capitalist agents. In the final chapter of *Histoire*, Diderot lambasted "a new species of nomadic savages," who "cross so many countries that they do not belong to any." These individuals were the dark side of the globalization.:

> They take women where they find them, & take them only for an animal need: of these amphibians which live on the surface of the waters; who only go ashore for a moment; for whom any habitable space is equal; who really have no fathers, mothers, children, brothers, relatives, friends, or fellow citizens; in whom the sweetest & most sacred bonds are extinguished; who leave their country without regret; who only come in with impatience to get out; & to whom the habit of a terrible element gives a fierce character.

This passage, leading to a famous condemnation of the slave trade, pointed to the inherent and nefarious ambiguity of the colonial situation that transformed the colonizers into animals, driven by their greed for riches and sexual desires, by their self-interest in its crudest form. These people from nowhere, going to nowhere, needed to settle down, to get a real nationality with which they could relate. That was why Diderot advocated the generalization of US nation-state-making as a remedy for colonial corruption. In Diderot's view, the liberty of commerce was nothing but a preamble to a much broader liberty—the liberty of national subjects and, more strikingly, the liberty of the enslaved.[30]

The wide circulation of Hilliard's *Considérations* and the formidable success of the *Histoire's* third edition, both censored, boosted the expectations of all interested parties: US statesmen and merchants, Dominguan planters, metropolitan traders, and government officials. All believed that the general peace would bring about significant changes in the French colonial system. The very nature and the identity of colonies were subjected to scrutiny, for another reform of the exclusif, now unavoidable, would highlight the ambivalence of wobbly arrangements. The state council had now to define the meaning of the "liberty of commerce" through a legislative act in which many placed conflicting hopes.

The Making of the August 30, 1784, *Arrêt*

The negotiations to end the American Revolution that led from Yorktown in October 1781 to the treaty of Paris in September 1783 took a long time and were punctuated with spectacular moments of reversal. The great number of players involved and the to-and-fro among London, Paris, and Philadelphia, where domestic issues often collided with peace talks, contributed to this complexity. Meanwhile, public officials in the French West Indies took local initiatives that contradicted the orders coming from the metropole, without any coherence among colonies. In Saint-Domingue, public officials restored the exclusif as soon as they heard about the conclusion of peace. Conversely, on July 23, 1783, the colonial government in Martinique reduced duties imposed on American vessels, justifying this decision by the promise of "a reciprocal advantage between both Nations." The peace treaty, which turned out to be a diplomatic defeat for France, did not settle the conversation but instead opened up broader discussions. The king published the *arrêt* (ordinance) on August 30, 1784, only after sixteen months of dispute.[31]

It was even unclear who should be in charge of the reform. In 1767, the Ministry of the Navy and the Colonies had taken full responsibility for the first mitigation of the exclusif; but after 1778 the legal regime of the colonies was involved in the treaties with the United States, making it a diplomatic issue as much as a "domestic" one. The legal form of the new arrangement was also uncertain: should there be a new treaty with the Confederation, with the Ministry of Foreign Affairs as the major player, or would it only require a royal ordinance with the Ministry of the Navy as the principal architect? This jurisdictional uncertainty boosted the rivalries of ministers who were always prone to inject personal animosity into the language of political economy. The secretary of the navy, *maréchal* de Castries, appointed in October 1780, resolved to hold his ground against Vergennes, whom he accused of having handled the war very poorly. When Charles-Alexandre de Calonne, another very strong personality, became Contrôleur general in late 1783, the ministerial squabble grew even more intense. Calonne claimed that the divide between "external trade" and "domestic trade" was arbitrary and outdated, reprising a physiocratic point that was already commonplace. Yet two men did their best to navigate the intricacies of ministerial bickering: Vergennes's senior advisor, Rayneval, who had played such an important part in the French propaganda during the War of Independence, and Turgot's disciple, Dupont de Nemours, who exerted a heavy influence on both Vergennes and Calonne. Dupont, who was the "last real physiocrat," became a general intendant of commerce and was appointed director of the Bureau de la Balance du commerce, a major service of the Contrôle général. Fascinated by the United States, he would push for an extensive free-trade agreement.[32]

Many others sought to make their voices heard. The colonial office, within the Ministry of the Navy, the trade office within the Contrôle général, and the French diplomatic personnel in North America gathered a number of reports from all kinds of lobbyists, merchants, and planters. Self-proclaimed representatives of the United States, like Gouverneur Morris, issued their opinions in anxious letters and reports. More than fifty pieces of writing dealt with the connected issue of the French-American relationship and the reform of the *exclusif*. All of them were mobilized by government officials to produce no fewer than twelve drafts of what would be known as the arrêt of August 30, 1784. All these reports were circulated from one ministry to another, with an increasing number of annotations. As such, the ministerial memorandum is a literary genre in its own right. On the one hand, it has a clearly defined recipient whom it seeks to convince. On the other hand, contrary to a printed text, whose form is already more fixed, the memorandum is full of annotations and erasures by different hands. In some cases, the text is divided into two parallel columns—on the right, the original memorandum, on the left its commentary, or even its refutation, paragraph after paragraph. Moreover, many authors cannot be identified, as many of the comments are anonymous. But the signature itself was no proof of authorship, as Gilbert du Motier de Lafayette's memorandum perfectly illustrates. The popular hero of the American Revolutionary War had easy access to Versailles and particularly to Castries who hosted him for several days at his own house. Lafayette, at the heart of the network of patriots in Paris, was also determined to plead for the strengthening of French-American connections. Franklin thought Lafayette's voice would be much more compelling than his to promote the liberalization of trade between the French West Indies and the United States. Lafayette, who was in no way versed in the "science of commerce," agreed to make Franklin's memorandum his and signed a text that he had not drafted. It is possible that other memorandums also had fake authors. The various interpolations in these apocryphal writings gave shape to a transatlantic political discourse that defined the French Empire and its relationships with the wider world.[33]

One of the issues at stake in the debate was the question of what kind of knowledge would be legitimate enough to be a basis for the law. Who was best positioned to conceptualize the reform? Planters who knew the "realities" of the colonies, seaport merchants involved in the long-distance trade, US diplomats, or government officials balancing competing interests in the corridors of Versailles? A Bordeaux merchant, in the name of the "speculative science of commerce," stated that the "commercial law ruled the world," that "it was the only one that did not need commentaries, because it drove men by a natural interest to the greatest interest possible." The rules of commerce spoke for themselves and could not be debated: businessmen were to rule. This line of argument was echoed by a trader from Marseille who opined that the merchant joined "the subtle perceptions of the interest" to the "principles of a scientific theory." The "Chamber of agriculture" in Cap-Français objected by arguing that the "particular interest" of merchants hurt the universal good of France. According to the minister plenipotentiary to the United States, however, both parties were equally biased, forcing the government to rise above rival interests.[34]

In spite of this contention, all these writings shared a common concern: how to adjust the existence of an allied independent state with the colonial system? This question could not be confined to technical and quantifiable considerations about imports of cod or exports of molasses. The corpus addressed a number of theoretical points, but unlike most dry ministerial reports, the style of many memorandums was very literary and full of metaphors. The family romance of the French Empire was a recurring leitmotif: the metropole was the "mother" or the "father," and the colonies its "children"; but the parents should not become tyrannical, as all "children, however well-born, struggle with the chains with which paternal solicitude envelops them." These stylistic efforts, far from being solely rhetorical tools, testified to the difficulty of imagining a new kind of system. With the creation of the United States, what would the French Empire become? Could the United States be part of the French colonial family?[35]

The British Empire: A Model?

To resolve this conundrum, most of the reports turned to foreign models, especially to the British Empire, following a long tradition of harrowing fascination. The question of opening the ports of the Antilles to the Americans cannot only be understood in strictly bilateral terms, as it was fully embedded in a trans-imperial game. The policy of France was not only modeled according to its re-lations with the United States but also depended on the British imperial policy toward the new state. With that global perspective in mind, it is misleading to try to separate the American stakes from European matters. The peace negotiations re-shuffled the cards along a dual logic of rivalry and cooperation, since this mo-ment also marked the first stage toward the rapprochement between France and Britain.

The reports on the reform of the exclusif reflected the ambiguous relationship of France with the British Empire. Since the time of Colbert, the rising tide of Great Britain had sparked the worried attention of administrators, philosophers, and economists. The "political economy of the French decline" was a common theme, and its treatment by figures such as William Petty, Josiah Child, and Charles Davenant attracted much attention from French thinkers in the mid-eighteenth century. Voltaire, the most famous of those Anglophile flatterers, no-toriously contended that there were intimate links between commercial power and the grandeur of a free state. Some memorialists pushed further the analysis of the foreign imperial models, reflecting on diverse types of government, social structures, and the role of commerce in political systems—what Montesquieu concretized with his "science of commerce." Yet the physiocrats had been more skeptical of the British commercial policy. Far from sharing the Anglomaniac enthusiasm of the time, Dupont de Nemours continued to warn against the attractions of Great Britain which, barricaded with customs duties, saddled with debts, close to bankruptcy, and torn apart by factions, was the paragon of cor-ruption and protectionism in every sense. In this respect, all the reports, letters, and memorandums of 1783–1784 were undoubtedly the heirs of those debates on political economy, which aimed at identifying national coherences.[36]

But so labile a reference was the British Empire that it could just as easily serve the cause of free trade as it could that of protectionism. Indeed, Scottish thinkers David Hume and Adam Smith or liberal conservative Josiah Tucker were no more quoted than Josiah Child, who theorized the legitimacy of the British Navigation Acts that were issued in the mid-seventeenth century and adapted for decades that followed. During most of the eighteenth century, the protectionist conception was routinely brandished by the French Chambers of Commerce in order to denounce any softening of the prohibitive regime. However, at the end of the American War of Independence that argument seemed clearly more fragile. Not only had England just been defeated, but the Act of Navigation had been the major motive for an uprising in the thirteen colonies. Moreover, the nomination of William Petty, Count of Shelburne, as prime minister in July 1782 seemed to announce a total upheaval of Britain's co-lonial policy. It was well known that Shelburne, a warm proponent of free trade, stood for an accommodating policy with the United States and the opening of the British West Indian markets to American produce. Until Shelburne's government fell to the Fox-North coalition in February 1783 and to the Order in Council of July 2, which excluded the Americans from the West Indies, the imperial model across the Channel could only be ambivalent, for the outcome of the British debates regarding its colonial trade with the United States remained eminently uncertain. Thanks to the press and correspondence, these polemics echoed across the continent, contributing to what historian Manuela Albertone defined as a "three-way interrelation."[37]

The commissioners of the United States, Franklin, John Adams, John Jay, and Henry Laurens, for whom the opening of the West Indian market had become a diplomatic priority, took advantage of those uncertainties to push France to reform its colonial system altogether. With Britain, the negotiations got off to an excellent start. Shelburne, determined to put an end to the French-American alliance, offered to establish a vast free-trade zone including the British Empire and the United States, even if it led to suppressing customs duties altogether. He also wished to create a new form of privileged link between England and its former colonies by enacting the mutual naturalization of British subjects and American citizens. This, he believed, would create a new form of political status and international cooperation. The peace preliminaries concluded between the United States and Great Britain on November 30, 1782, to the detriment of France, followed the same approach but did not yet settle a matter that was ultimately the responsibility of Parliament. The project prepared for the Board of Trade by the pro-American John Pownall was submitted to the House of Commons on March 7, 1783. This text, which entitled the Americans to the same rights as the British subjects, was supported by a section of the West India lobby who forcefully asked for the restoration of the old commercial routes. The arguments of those lobbyists were similar to those developed by the spokesmen of the French planters, who believed that the United States was essential for supplying the islands. Yet it was on this occasion, as historian Andrew O'Shaughnessy highlights it, that the "West India Interest" was cornered into a defensive mode. Great Britain could still count on the loyalty of continental colonies, which were supposed to replace the thirteen colonies. Not only were Canada, Nova Scotia, and Newfoundland allowed to provide for the West Indies; they were also to be rewarded for not having supported the United States during the war. The rapprochement plan, although approved by Charles Fox and Edmund Burke, collided with the staunch opposition of the representative William Eden. Any suppression of the Act of Navigation would lead to the decline of the manufactures, the drastic downsizing of seamen, and the end of British power in the world. Eden convinced the House of Commons to reject the bill. But by April 1783, Fox had sent David Hartley to Paris to negotiate a new arrangement on positions similar to those of the Pownall project. At the same time, Franklin was organizing leaks so that those new negotiations might be known in France in order to exert pressure on Versailles. Penetrating the British West Indies would force France and Spain to follow suit.[38]

The negotiations between the United States and Britain created much skittishness among French metropolitan merchants who feared that their constant praise of British commercial superiority would create a backlash. The great trader Jean-Stanislas Foäche, who was at the head of the biggest slave-trading firm in Cap-Français, articulated his anxieties in a report addressed to the secretary of the navy. Until then, Foäche had pressed the government to emulate Britain but he instead tried to demonstrate that "England, having always managed everything in favor of its navigation and its commerce, could now admit the American flag into her isles with no inconvenience, while with this very admission, France would ruin its navigation and commerce." Foäche subtly argued that the very success of the British Navigation Act henceforth enabled England to relax its system, but France was not in such a position yet. He also pointed out that the consumption of sugar in Great Britain exceeded the production of the islands and that the tafias and syrups were inferior in quantity and in quality to those of the French Antilles. Jamaica would serve as the base of American contraband into the French possessions, to the benefit of England. Foäche certainly knew what he was talking about; after all, he had himself made much of his fortune from smuggling slaves sold by British traders in Saint-Domingue.[39]

However, with the failure of the Hartley negotiations, confirmed by the order in council of July 2, 1783, excluding US vessels from the West Indies, the British Empire regained its appeal for those who supported the colonial monopoly. From then on the traders could again reframe their argument around British superiority. Quoting Josiah Child and the Act of Navigation—described as *magna charta maritima*—one memoir mentioned that the English had "for a long time and with reason passed as the most enlightened people regarding Commerce." France, despite its defeat, continued to draw inspiration from an empire that remained the epitome of commercial power. The French consul general in the United States, François de Barbé-Marbois, confided: "The Act of Navigation of England, unjust and unpolitical towards the whole nation in general, has nevertheless proved prodigiously advantageous to the commerce and navigation of this kingdom." With another commercial war at hand, fighting on equal terms was necessary. This changing tone did not escape the US commissioners whose diplomatic defeat in London almost jeopardized their cause in France. In a desperate attempt to thwart the argument, Gouverneur Morris now invited the French to stop regarding the British as "their masters in the science of commerce."[40]

From a geopolitical and political economy point of view, the birth of the United States complicated the role of England and France in Europe and the Americas. According to one report, American independence produced an absolute revolution that "changed the state of all and everything. It changed the state of our islands in regards to America, and reciprocally, it changed this very state regarding us. Lastly it changed it in our relation to England which we must keep in mind in all our operations, and who, like us, have possessions in this hemisphere." Along those lines, independent America had indeed become a "secret" opponent of France for its colonies, which shared with "England an interest of common conservation." This called for "a system of union, which did not exist, and far from it, in the former state of affairs." Despite the imperial rivalry, England and France had common interests against the United States, for both countries stood up for a territorial and colonial model endangered by the very existence of the confederation. England was losing her quality of "natural enemy" and becoming a "natural ally."[41]

Along with the negotiations regarding the East Indian trade and the creation of the new East India Company in 1785, this analysis is the key to explaining the development of diplomacy from the War of Independence to the Eden-Rayneval treaty of commerce of 1786, destined to create a French-British free-trade zone in Europe. This liberalization paralleled a strengthening protectionism in the American periphery all in the name of a form of imperial solidarity. Indeed, both sides of the Channel feared American ambitions to seize the reexporting trade of colonial commodities. Lord Sheffield's pamphlet on the necessity of preserving the Act of Navigation, excluding the Americans whose market was captive, was, from the start, well known and quoted in France, even before a translated edition of his work was published a few years later. According to Sheffield, Britain would win back American trade without having to open its West Indian colonies. In a report prepared in Paris, Eden, who had opposed the opening of British colonial markets to the United States, wrote just before the conclusion of the treaty with France in 1786:

> There are strong appearances of a disposition to believe that Great Britain and France ought to unite in some solid plan of permanent peace: and many of the most considerable and efficient people talk with little reserve of the dangers to be apprehended from the revolted colonies, if they should be encouraged to gain commercial strength and consistency of government.

The French Chambers of Commerce rebuked this free-trade plan with Britain, but Vergennes, always in favor of defending the balance of powers, was worried about the increasing influence of the United States in the Americas. The alliance with the United States led to a protracted ideological struggle over the meaning of the French Empire, which left many of these contradictions unresolved.[42]

Saint-Domingue, "Point of Reunion" Between France and the United States

The war and the Treaty of Paris had offered no mutually agreed-upon answer to this basic question: how to reconcile the existence of an independent state in the Americas with the need to preserve the colonial interests of France? According to many, this "revolution" was a formidable opportunity for the kingdom. On military terms, "our dear allies" would prove essential to the looming war against England; peace, it was generally understood, was only an interlude. By supplying the colonies in this future war, the United States would tip the balance in favor of France. But the American advantage was also viewed in commercial terms. The tantalizing image of French vessels sailing into an American market aroused the greed of the Chambers of Commerce. The traders of Le Havre and Nantes, who had provided the insurgents with food and weapons during the war, pushed the government for the creation of an independent state. A united America, they insisted repeatedly, would consider France to be her "metropole of adoption." The lexicon of economic dependence was transformed into a colonial language that made it hard to imagine the existence of an independent entity with full and absolute sovereignty in America, notwithstanding the treaties of 1778. The Confederation, which was yet to be regarded as a state of its own, was to remain intrinsically—and indefinitely—subordinate to European powers.[43]

The merchants' expectations were soon to be greatly disappointed. The business of French metropolitan commerce in the United States proved to be catastrophic, as suggested by the chorus of recriminations against "American ingratitude" that flooded the public sphere. All the gold and the rivers of blood that had flowed in the effort to nurture and protect the independence of the young republic had resulted in this shameful, appalling scene of Americans dismissing French commodities and refusing to give France any special favors, opening their market to the whole "universe," without committing to any European power. The French merchants, who had been accustomed to the exclusivity of a captive colonial market were forced to enter an arrangement in which the only rule was the rule of competition. The Anglophile prejudices of the Americans, who kept favoring British manufactured products and relying on British credit, doubled the force of this indignity. Gone were the days when the Americans would buy French goods and ammunition. In accordance with Lord Sheffield's predictions, Britain could pursue its economic domination without having to finance the administration and the defense of its former colonies. It did not even have to legalize the trade between the United States and its colonies in the Caribbean. The commercial subordination to Britain, they insinuated in different keys, thwarted this nation's so-called political independence. Metropolitan merchants expressed the most violent frustration at the failure of their struggle to "accustom" the United States to regarding France as their "adopted metropole."[44]

What remained perfectly natural was the link between the French Antilles and the United States, grounded as it was on the self-evident economic interdependence of the islands and the continent. Contrasting with the poor success of metropolitan commodities on the American market, French colonial goods were very popular. In the United States, sugar, coffee, and cocoa were not luxury or even semi-luxury products but affordable by nearly all sectors of society. This democratization had particularly impressed Barbé deMarbois, who explained the phenomenon:

> The customary consumption of sugar is becoming always more general. The use of tea and consequently sugar extended as far as the countryside. Servants and even negroes in some families have tea in the morning and at night. Many laborers add sugar to the grog they drink; the use of coffee has even become more general in the past few years, and many people have substituted it for tea. Cacao gets daily more fashionable: proportionally, the United States consumes a greater quantity of these objects than Europe

This vivid and exaggerated picture of a country defined by consumerism hinted at the subversive potential of trade, reminiscent of the boycott that started the American Revolution. Barbé de Marbois, like Lafayette and Franklin, advocated legalizing trade with the United States under the French flag, even if this meant imitating the British Navigation Acts and excluding American vessels. Reprising Hilliard d'Auberteuil's stance, they warned that "refusing honest liberty might bring about general abuse." Contraband would be inevitable in the event of a general prohibition. Smugglers, stimulated by the mutual needs of consumers and producers, would flout any restrictive law. Besides, American foodstuff should be imported so as to replace subsistence crops with lucrative commercial cultures. A proactive state could take action by preventing the Americans from reshipping colonial goods to European markets and thus effectively pulling the rug from under the feet of French metropolitan merchants. The laws of consumption would shape the connection between the French West Indies and the United States.[45]

For metropolitan traders, the mere existence of the new country produced a whole new world of risk. According to one member of the colonial office, the "frightening vicinity" of the United States caused a "great danger" for the interests of the Crown. Like Dr. Frankenstein, France had created a country that was subverting the system from which it was made. In fact, the North American continent "endowed by nature to become promptly the mightiest power on land and sea" could not be fixed in the servitude demanded by the metropole. This is an image that evokes Thomas Paine, although its history can be traced through the rhetorical machinery of French diplomacy, the endless memorandums of American commissioners, and Thomas Pownall's *Memorial Between the Old and New Worlds*, which was instantly translated into French. For Pownall and others, the new context had fundamentally transformed the importance and the scale of smuggling, which was actively supported by a government. France needed to brace itself for facing "the most startling rivalry" from "American provinces now governed by themselves and for themselves." The realization led to a particularly disturbing conclusion: if there was something increasingly "natural" about the relationship between the continent and the islands, then the link between metropoles and colonies was that much more artificial. It seemed unlikely that the French state could count on the gratitude of the United States. In fact, as Lafayette acknowledged, that feeling of gratitude "from state to state gives in with time to that of suitability and greater national advantage," for "mercantile interest withholds impartiality." Thus, the true allies of the united America would be "those Nations with which it would make more profit." Only the "union of interests" would establish the foundations for this new association. This community of interests was in contradiction with the political and moral community of the colonial order.[46]

The prospect of a new treaty with the United States was another major blow of confusion for the colonial categories that *l'Histoire des deux Indes* had already severely fractured. The distinctions between metropole, colonies, and foreign land appeared terribly problematic. The first object of contention was the specificity of the American alliance. The guardians of conservatism boxed the United States into the all-encompassing category of an "alien" nation—one that could only be considered a rival power and, by extension, one that was increasingly seen as a smuggler. Only by viewing the "united America" as a "stranger" could the French have any chance of revitalizing the "true principles" that had presided over the "foundation" of their colonies. Merchant lobbyists insisted on the importance of going back to the "origins" in order to grasp the "destiny of the colonies." A mere territorial expansion had never been the main reason for the conquest. Developing agriculture and nurturing industries was the goal of colonial expansion. The metropole founded the colonies and needed to barricade them against rival powers.[47]

The nature of the French-American alliance meant examining the colonial system itself. Mobilizing familial and sexual metaphors, several memoirs highlighted the many contradictions created by the partnership. The Americans were recast as "lovers" and reimagined as the "vulgar rich who, looking down on the rest of America, already saw their continent as the husband of all women, placed by convenience most closely to other regions which were nonetheless the wives of all husbands." The economic convergence could only bring about an "illegitimate union." The desperate quest for profit drove the French colonies just as much as their old American counterparts, so much so that common interests necessarily led to a common identity and a shared destiny. The Americans of the "North" and those of the "South" were "brothers." They had had to overcome the same migratory tests. Both embodied a "spirit of enterprise" that would eventually push the colonies to revolt against their "homelands."[48]

It was in this context that the Martiniquais Dubuc suggested another definition of what was called a "colony," creating a mid-way status between the foreign and the national. He cunningly borrowed his arguments from the "speculative science of commerce" to turn them back against the traders. Dubuc was thus siding with the "true interest" of the metropole, defined as a power confronted with the competition of "rival nations." The essence of colonies was to replace the "foreign consumer" with the "consuming colonist," and the "colonial goods" with the "national merchandise." This way those establishments had to be recognized as "national for their products and foreign for their consumption." The language of patriotism could, by extension, be harmonized with that of the market, and the internal border between the metropole and the colonies could also be redrawn by the pens of men like Dubuc.[49]

The Colonial Chamber of Agriculture in Cap-Français, growing worried over the tone of the debate, offered a possible solution to this controversy. The French colony of Saint-Domingue, they argued, could resolve all the contradictions of the alliance. The Pearl of the Caribbean was to become the "*entrepôt* equally useful to [French] commerce, to the colony and to the Americans." Versailles had to contemplate that Saint-Domingue would emerge as the "gathering point of trade between both nations, crushing both Jamaica and Cuba." Saint-Domingue should be regarded as the true center of the alliance, an alliance that promised to achieve both French imperial supremacy and the expansion of the United States. The maintenance of the *exclusif* could only spur the "most general revolution with nefarious effects." The threat of contagion was all too real, but in the planters' views, this looming revolution involved free whites only, as slavery was barely mentioned other than as metaphor.[50]

The French West Indies were at the heart of debates regarding the alliance between France and the United States. Official advisors, philosophers, colonists, merchants, French, American, and British contributed to a controversy about the creation of the United States and its implications for the French political community. Could the colonies be the laboratory of a free-trade experiment? Was the United States an ordinary country, an incipient imperial power, or an unprecedented political entity that threatened to shatter the European colonial system altogether? What were the colonies for the metropole within the French Empire? What became increasingly important, for writers across the political spectrum, from monarchical propagandists to Enlightenment philosophes, was a particular vision of free trade in which the convergent histories and complex entanglements of Saint-Domingue and the United States pointed to a political theory that is best understood as a commercial republicanism with colonial roots. The new discourse of commercial republicanism illuminates the varied schemes and proposals that emerged to accommodate the meaning of the American Revolution to French imperial interests in 1783.

The conclusion of this debate might seem rather disappointing. When the Castries, the Secretary of the Navy and the Colonies, eventually arbitrated on August 30, 1784, he opted to preserve the "true destiny of the colonies" by just mitigating the exclusif again. Instead of two, seven ports of entrepôt—among them, three in Saint-Domingue—were instituted in the West Indies; the trade of a few more commodities like salted beef and coal was legalized, but the most lucrative output, colonial goods and flour, remained within the French monopoly. Castries's compromise was intended to be consensual and moderate along rather protectionist lines. The ministry expected the Americans to complain, as Jefferson was appointed the new ambassador to Paris, but the secretary at any rate did not concede to "offer the kingdom in sacrifice" to a losing alliance. The "very nature of the colonies" subjected them to the "rigors of prohibitions," he explained. He also brushed aside the suggested analogies between the United States and the French West Indies for, according to him, the "spirit of independence would not carry its effects onto the slave colonies in the tropics." The burden of slavery, a topic barely touched on in the debate, was supposed to be an obstacle to Turgot's revolutionary contagion model: planters' inner enemy demanded the protection of the metropole, and the metropole was to rule. This view was indeed part of a wider ambition of Castries's ministry, which planned on reasserting metropolitan authority in all kinds of areas, including the regulation of slavery and the rights of free people of color.[51]

If Castries was anxiously awaiting the grievances of US diplomats, he was caught off guard by the general revolt of the Chambers of Commerce. Paradoxically, the decree, destined to safeguard the prohibitive regime, was interpreted as the colonists' victory and the next stage toward the complete liberalization of colonial trade. French merchants organized an unprecedented lobbying campaign against the new law and coordinated an effort to dispatch extraordinary deputies to Versailles. Dupont de Nemours, as the head of the office of the balance of commerce, wrote in 1786 that the commercial lobbies pleaded their cause "in front of the tribunal of opinion," flooding Paris with "memorandums, observations, requests on the *arrêt*." The debate was not confined to the corridors of Versailles, as a number of philosophers, including Turgot, expressed their skepticism about the constitutional form of the new American republic. While a fertile imagination had fueled earlier debates, the controversy grew increasingly simplistic and binary, pitting merchants against colonists. Both groups mutually rejected each other outside the "national community," as agents of foreign interests, with the United States regarded as British satellites. Merchants viewed the decree as the "triumph of rival nations" and "colonists' greed," when colonists regretted they had to wrench themselves from "monopolists' jealousy." And all in the name of the nation.[52]

All came to the conclusion that the French nation, under the pressure of the United States, needed a regenerated empire, more fully centered on its core, Saint-Domingue. Dubuisson could not be clearer: "if the matter was about the preeminence between integral parts of the Empire, I would not flinch a second to assign it to the Colonies." In the current state, Saint-Domingue, "the wealthiest province in the empire," could legitimately be tempted to ally with "an active, industrious and trading people, neighbor to the French Colonies."[53]

An Inexhaustible Mine of Wealth, 1784–1788

The astonishing growth of the French colony of St. Domingo is such
that it promises to be very soon the most important distant possession
in the world, and to exceed greatly the value of Mexico and Peru.
South Carolina Weekly Gazette, August 28, 1784, 2

In the wake of the American Revolution, the US press observed the spectacular
progress of Saint-Domingue with intense interest. Indeed, the period from 1783
to 1789 was one of unprecedented expansion in the history of French colonialism.
Production of sugar, cotton, and, above all, coffee skyrocketed: in 1789, France
imported 230 million *livres* of produce, two-thirds of which were then exported
to European countries; 40 percent of sugar and 60 percent of coffee consumed in
Europe came from the French colonies. Thanks to Saint-Domingue, the French
balance of trade was positive by 80 million *livres tournois*. This monumental success came with extreme suffering. Nearly 200,000 enslaved people were deported
to the colony during this period, a staggering 36 percent of the entire Atlantic
slave trade at that time. By comparison, Jamaica, the second-largest slave colony,
accounted for only 13 percent. On their way to Saint-Domingue, at least 27,000
enslaved people died on the Middle Passage crossing the Atlantic. This figure
did not even account for those who were illegally "smuggled" from Jamaica and
other British and Dutch islands. Those who survived to reach the plantations
were subjected to atrocious working conditions, disease, injuries, and very often
an early death. Hard labor on almost 800 sugar plantation factories, along with
3,000 smaller artisanal coffee and cotton *habitations* (the word for plantation in
the French West Indies), took the lives of enslaved people at an unprecedented
level, despite their ongoing efforts to resist or merely survive.[1]

The United States took advantage of and participated in the colony's expansion, with Saint-Domingue emerging as the second most active trading partner of

Entrepôt of Revolutions. Manuel Covo, Oxford University Press. © Oxford University Press 2022.
DOI: 10.1093/oso/9780197626382.003.0003

the early republic after Great Britain. The spectacular development of the colony would not have been possible without US trade, which supplied the colony with timber and foodstuffs. At no time in its history did Saint-Domingue have to assimilate so many people in so few years. In 1789, estimates place between 450,000 and 550,000 enslaved people in the colony, along with around 30,000 free people of color—those who had been emancipated or were descendants of emancipated slaves—and roughly 40,000 resident white colonists. With the soaring influx of residents, all of whom needed to be fed, there was little time to increase local food production, already disrupted by hurricanes, earthquakes, and droughts, while the metropole, suffering its own period of demographic stress, was unable to provide adequate help. Cattle were imported from the Spanish part of the island, but almost everything else came from the United States. The dramatic growth and survival of Saint-Domingue was an indirect but major consequence of the American Revolution and the Franco-American alliance. Yet this collaboration aggravated metropolitan merchants, who pushed for a strict implementation of the *exclusif* despite their inability to supply the colony.[2]

The French government attempted to integrate the United States into a triangular trade that would benefit the metropole. The *arrêt* of August 30, 1784, was intended to balance contradictory interests by extending the system of the *exclusif mitigé*. The government established seven *entrepôts* in the French Antilles, including three in Saint-Domingue (Cap-Français, Port-au-Prince, and Les Cayes-St. Louis). Foreign vessels were allowed to bring timber, cattle, cured meats, hides, furs, resins, tars, rice, corn, vegetables, and salted fish into these ports and could export syrups, molasses and goods from France, paying a 1 percent duty. Foreign trade in sugar, coffee, cotton, indigo, cocoa, and flour remained prohibited. The arrêt accomplished its objective, enabling the colony's economic expansion while protecting metropolitan firms' interests. However, the integration of the United States into the French imperial system turned out to be rockier than anticipated. Rival tensions crystallized around US involvement in the contraband trade. This is a term that covers not only a range of realities—from customs fraud (smuggling of products subject to duties) to actual smuggling (introduction of prohibited products)—but also refers to a plurality of perceptions. The legality, illegality, and legitimacy of trade was a contentious issue that became increasingly politicized.

The Politics of Contraband Statistics

How substantial was trade between Saint-Domingue and the United States in the aftermath of the American Revolutionary War? Did official numbers provided by the French government reflect the reality of that traffic? The legal ambiguity of US trade gave rise to fantasies and concerns among merchants, planters, and government officials. Exchanges were legal if conducted through one of the seven designated entrepôts and US captains paid customs duties, but trade in the most lucrative commodities was forbidden, and Americans could not engage in the slave trade with Saint-Domingue. It was obvious that traders, American and French, were trafficking colonial commodities and flour, but to what extent? How could the entirety of trade between Saint-Domingue and the United States be evaluated?

These questions were raised as soon as the king enacted the new legislation. Metropolitan merchants believed smuggling was spiraling out of control and that authorized trade constituted only a fraction of traffic. Government officials were fully aware that fraudsters were bribing customs officers, who were often incompetent or indifferent. Ambroise Arnould, head of the Bureau of Commerce, knew official figures were undervalued and addressed the subject in his three-volume report on France's foreign trade. In an attempt to counter inaccuracies, Arnould created his own scientific method by integrating a contraband parameter, "weighing all the circumstances of prohibition." The result was "two extreme points, in the middle of which lies the probable." Arnould's assessment of US trade with the West Indies was intended to be reassuring. Between 1786 and 1788, lawful trade by the Americans accounted for nearly 4 million livres tournois. He surmised that the balance was paid in "commodities whose extraction is not permitted" but only to supply the American market, and he believed that sugar imported into the United States amounted to 6 or 7 million livres tournois, half of which may have come from the French West Indies. This represented a tiny fraction of the 230 million livres tournois of colonial produce imported into metropolitan France, since French colonies were "an inexhaustible mine of wealth."[3]

The fact that Arnould minimized the extent of contraband was no accident. To prepare his report, he relied on annual memos commissioned by the secretary of the navy and produced by the Bureau de la Balance du Commerce. These texts, far from being neutral, were intended to prove that the arrêt of August 30, 1784, was not prejudicial to metropolitan trade and that the financial hardship merchants were suffering was unrelated. Statistical interpretations either ignored contraband entirely or dismissed its impact as residual. These statistics had high political stakes: the ministry wanted seemingly hard data to deflect protests from the Chambers of Commerce, which lambasted the United States for looting their colonies. A New Jersey newspaper provided accurate testimony when it reported that "the liberty the king of France has given to the Americans to trade to his West-India islands has greatly disgusted many considerable bodies of men in his Kingdom." The government needed to find ways to appease this

disgust and demonstrate that it was protecting and promoting the national interest. Since Contrôleur General Jacques Necker published the official accounts
of the monarchy, the best-selling *Account to the King*, the public report of the
monarchy's budget, the "tribunal of public opinion" expected more than speech;
it wanted figures and percentages. Statistical evidence and numerical data could
placate growing mercantile discontent.[4]

The US market was a laboratory of French political economy, a space where
new theories would be tested. To carry out further reforms, the bureau needed to
frame smuggling as contained and harmless. The comptroller-general of finances
created a bureau entirely devoted to trade with the United States. This commission, which convened from February to May in 1786, was charged with analyzing
the potential effects of admitting American whale oil, creating free ports on
mainland France, and ending the monopoly on tobacco imports. Among the
members of the committee were Lafayette, spokesman for the Americans, plus
all the directors of the Bureau of the Balance of Commerce. Meanwhile, Thomas
Jefferson, then ambassador in Paris, was pushing to advance his compatriots'
interests. The committee issued briefs that minimized the difficulties faced by
colonial administrators in containing smuggling.[5]

A report written a few years later by Claude-Corentin Tanguy de la Boissière
took a very different stance, declaring that contraband trade had indeed been
out of control. The author had been a lawyer in Saint-Domingue before starting
a new career as a journalist and political agitator versed in the science of political economy. Having fled the Saint-Domingue Revolution to the United States
in 1793, Tanguy was commissioned by the French ambassador in Philadelphia
to write a report demonstrating that the young republic had taken advantage
of France's generosity without returning the favor. In a radically different context, marked by a crisis in Franco-American relations and rapprochement with
Great Britain, Tanguy's historical account of trade relations focused on the nine
years of peace between 1784 and 1792 and was a diatribe against US mercantile
policy. Although the author presented numerical arguments to support his "scientific" analysis, the pamphlet was nothing but propaganda. The war had cost an
astronomical sum, which Tanguy estimated to be 4,103,890,000 livres tournois,
and France had been duped by her allies, who had willfully submitted themselves to the economic domination of Britain. Taking up the classic arguments
fostered by the Chambers of Commerce, he accused foreigners of plundering
France and claimed the arrêt of August 30, 1784, had delivered the French colonies to the Americans. Not only was the fundamental right of Europe dismissed
by granting favors that no other imperial power would envisage, but France was
also exposing itself to unfair competition, since French merchants, unlike the
Americans, were subjected to heavy taxation.[6]

Table 2.1 **Legal and Illegal Imports into the French Colonies of America, 1784-1792**

	Legal Trade		Illegal Trade	
	Quantity	*Value*	*Quantity*	*Value*
Cod	1,397,781	24,652,854	952,173	17,139,114
Marinated Fish	137,196	3,085,461	142,146	3,127,212
Salted beef	120,348	4,274,199	1,296,189	45,366,615
Flour	124,649	6,088,194	4,170,816	160,461,890
Manufactured Goods manufacturées				6,561,000
Slaves			24,614	34,459,600
Total				267,115,431

Source: Tanguy de La Boissière, *Mémoire sur la situation commerciale de la France*, tables F, I, and N. Quintals for cod; barrels for marinated fish, salted beef, and flour; value in *livres tournois*.

To prove that the arrêt had been detrimental to French interests, Tanguy challenged the statistics presented by Arnould and intended to reveal discrepancies between the figures produced by French and US Customs. He also drew on the investigations of Tench Coxe, former deputy to Alexander Hamilton at the American Treasury and author of prodigious studies of the early republic's economy. Tanguy differentiated the legal trade measured by Arnould from illicit trade calculated using US sources. To do this, he delineated two types of fraud: (1) the systematic under-valuation of lawful goods in captains' declarations, and (2) smuggling, namely, the introduction or "removal" (*enlèvement*) of prohibited commodities. Tanguy alleged that the United States exported illegal flour valued at around 160 million livres (about 25 percent of the amount the metropole exported to the colonies), and 276 million pounds of sugar and coffee (31 million pounds per year). Illegal trafficking accounted for almost 85 percent of imports and 90 percent of exports, while the main commodities legally introduced to the colonies (cod, marinated fish, and salted beef) constituted less than 17 percent of all trade. As Arnould had not taken fraud or smuggling into account, Tanguy claimed that his data were worthless.

To assess the overall shortfall for France, Tanguy also monetized indirect damage on the French economy: 10,641,632 livres tournois should have been collected from all import and export commodities; 34,860 sailors had gone unhired due to US competition, which he equated with a loss of 56,361,050 livres; and as France was reexporting to Europe the vast majority of colonial

Table 2.2 **Legal and Illegal Imports from the French Colonies of America, 1784–1792**

| | | Legal Trade | | Illegal Trade | |
	Goods	Quantity	Value	Quantity	Value
Legal	Syrup	409,356		?	?
Goods	Rum	34,776		?	?
	Taffia	8,532	33,879,735	?	?
Prohibited	Sugar	67,041	1,887,165	3,219,165	156,203,739
Goods	Coffee	30,717	2,047,590	1,497,789	120,011,859
	Cotton	3,870	408,204	135,900	27,308,232
	Cocoa	180	5,994	115,695	21,983,454
	Indigo			35,271	34,126,650
	Goods from France		6,606,468		
	Total		44,835,156	5,003,820	360,133,434

Source: Tanguy de La Boissière, *Mémoire sur la situation commerciale de la France*, tables F and P. Barrels for syrups, rums, and tafias; quintals for sugar, coffee, cotton, cocoa, and indigo.

goods unloaded in the metropole, production taken away by the Americans had hit the country's trade balance by about 26 percent of the surplus. Exports of West Indian products in 1789 should have amounted to 195 million livres, 50 million more than Arnould had calculated. Tanguy set these considerable losses against the cost of French participation in the American war, concluding that the French had not just squandered their money, but they had also wasted their blood.

However, Tanguy's assessment of contraband trade was considerably exaggerated. His single goal was to demonize Americans for their ingratitude and rapacity, and despite an appearance of precision, his number-crunching was based on false premises. Although Tanguy claimed to have consulted the US Customs archives, he had access only to figures produced after 1789, since no general statistics existed in the American Confederation era (1776–1788). Moreover, Tanguy had extrapolated figures based on the data of 1789–1792, a period during which the exclusif had been suspended. After 1789, the colonial government temporarily authorized the importation of flour and the export of colonial commodities; therefore, a substantial amount of the goods he classified as illicit were provisionally legal. Tanguy believed political economy was a tool that should serve a nationalist agenda, as he summarized in the conclusion of his pamphlet: "May from now on the government destroy this treacherous and fatal system of a blind infatuation, for all that is not self, for all that is not French."[7]

At the same time it produced propaganda, the French government was also attempting to accurately determine the extent of illicit trade. Thanks to the Treaty of Amity and Commerce of 1778, the secretariat of state to the navy had new agents to accomplish this mission: French consuls in the United States. As guarantors of French maritime and commercial interests, they were critical to imperial policymaking in economic matters. A legacy of Italian medieval cities, the *ancien régime* institution of consuls had been adopted by all European states, but the French government imagined a modernized role for their agents in the United States. In particular, the consuls were to carry out an economic information mission aimed at the North American market, regarded as the laboratory of a renewed political economy. They were to examine the circulation of vessels in American waters and monitor illegal traffic with the French West Indies. The Ministry of the Navy would use this information as a counterpoint to observations by colonial officials. Article 12 of the arrêt of August 30, 1784, stipulated that ships from the French colonies could only enter ports with resident French consular agents.[8]

Posted in Boston, New York, Philadelphia, Baltimore, Norfolk, Charleston, and smaller ports, these agents were intended to assess the effectiveness of the crackdown on smugglingin the West Indies, control their administrative counterparts, and ensure that all imperial agents were fulfilling their duties. Their tasks were rather contradictory: they were to both observe and suppress contraband trade; however, these actions incentivized smugglers to avoid their observation. As the consuls could not base assessments on the sea captains' manifests, they needed to find other sources of information, such as local gazettes and customs archives, but even these were a poor reflection of reality. So great was the "neglect" and disorganization of US customs that French agents concluded even Versailles had a more accurate knowledge of US trade than local port-cities. In fact, the customs officers—many in league with the smugglers—did what they could to conceal their records and the activities of traders. "Customs, coffee houses, and merchants are so perfectly intertwined that we cannot see any facts," lamented the French consul in Philadelphia. Since the export of flour and the importation of colonial commodities was lawful in the United States, US customs officers believed it their patriotic duty to protect the clandestine practices of American traders. Claiming full sovereignty for the new nation, including administrative and commercial independence, they endeavored to counteract any form of interference, even from a so-called ally.[9]

French consuls would certainly not have found the "truth" in the documents produced by customs officers, traders who misrepresented the nature and volume of their cargoes, or ship owners who wanted to avoid US tariffs. Aware of the surveillance they were under, captains often claimed to come from neutral islands, entrepôts where trade in colonial goods was legal: the Dutch islands of St. Eustatius, Curaçao and Saint Martin; the Danish and Swedish islands of Saint Croix and Saint Barthelemy; or British islands with specific status, such as the Turks and Caicos Islands. With the exception of Saint Croix, these tiny islands generated almost no colonial produce but had long been hubs of cross-border smuggling. A French merchant settled in Saint Eustatius described the small island as "the general entrepôt for all the other colonies and consequently open to general competition of all nations." Sea captains often loaded commodities produced in Saint-Domingue, Jamaica, or other colonies in those entrepôts; in other cases, they merely stopped there for shipping certificates; occasionally, they abstained from this process altogether and simply obtained forged papers claiming a false port of origin. As the Philadelphia merchant Stephen Girard, who owned three vessels and specialized in Saint-Domingue trade, explained to his brother and accomplice at Cap-Français, a ship's captain must say "he was going to St. Eustatius but that, having fallen to the wind, and that his schooner was too heavy, he had decided to enter the first port of St. Domingue to sell his rice, in this way to alleviate his vessel." Every now and then a ship owner would coordinate multiple shipments from islands belonging to different empires. For example, Baltimore merchant Samuel Smith ordered his captain to go to Curaçao, sell his cargo of foodstuffs and buy 200 Spanish leathers, then head to Les Cayes in Saint-Domingue to load sugar before heading back to Baltimore. In the merchants' minds, the "Pearl of the West Indies," the heart of the French Empire, was just one major piece in a larger Caribbean puzzle.[10]

These practices did not fool the French agents. Consuls kept registers of the data they collected but were also skeptical of their own statistics. As one observed, it was "impossible to give a somewhat satisfactory approximation on the trade of the French Antilles." Often, they had no choice but to base their evaluations on rumor. Assessments were contradictory between consular posts and quarters. This almost groundless information was nevertheless accepted by colonial officials who attempted to evaluate the effectiveness of controls by examining prices of colonial commodities on the US market. Administrators in Saint-Domingue were anxious that sugar "has a moderate price in the great cities of the United States, and this price proves that [French sugar] is in a sort of abundance"; yet they still surmised that Saint-Domingue contributed "less than in the past and most of it is imported from Jamaica and other English, Dutch or Danish islands."[11]

The consuls attempted to determine the best multiplier for calculating real traffic from legal trade. Should they add 50, 75, 100, or even 200 percent to the figures they had? The Boston consul proposed studying consumption to circumvent the shortcomings of customs data. He estimated that a family of seven consumed a pound of sugar each day. He then declared that based on the population of Massachusetts, 172,500 quintals of sugar had been imported from the French West Indies; however, the consul had not consulted any significant reports on the amount of sugar consumed in the state. This number is all the more unconvincing as many inhabitants in that part of the world preferred maple syrup to sugar. The document the Boston consul produced is practically a blueprint for constructing statistical illusions on false premises, but it does reveal the government's fetish for numbers. The consul's reasoning went as follows:

> The population of Massachusetts is estimated at 350,000, and I have divided this population into a family of seven, including the servant, which has produced 50,000 families. I then calculated that at a pound of sugar a day in each family, consumption rose to 365 pounds of sugar, annually per family, which multiplied by 50,000 families gave me 172,500 quintals including 110,556 quintals contributed by 141 vessels from the French islands and 61,944 quintals contributed by 79 vessels from foreign islands, which 1,725,000 quintals to 35 francs the quintal, proportional price of sugar sold in Boston at different prices according to its quality, gave me 6,037,000 francs.

Between the fantasy of universal smuggling and its outright negation, contraband trade was simultaneously a statistical construction, a legal object with uncertain contours, and a terrain of political confrontation.[12]

A Prosperous Legal Trade.

Attempting to establish an accurate assessment of smuggling would only be done in vain. However, it is possible to reach an approximation of the legal trade between Saint-Domingue and the United States. Traffic increased during the American Revolutionary War, but the ties uniting New England with the French West Indies had a longer history. Since the end of the seventeenth century, the ports of Massachusetts, Rhode Island, and Connecticut had exported dried cod for taffia (an alcoholic syrup made from sugar cane) and molasses, which in turn fueled the many distilleries in the region. At the time of the American Revolution, an increasing number of ports on the Atlantic seaboard became involved in this trade, with commodities varying according to the region: New England continued importing molasses and exporting fish and timber, Mid-Atlantic states mainly exported flour, and the South's major export was rice. The undervaluation of volumes of exports would be at its highest in Philadelphia,

New York, and Baltimore, because, unlike rice and fish, importing American flour into the French Antilles was prohibited by the exclusif.[13]

In Boston, 20 percent of total maritime traffic came from the French West Indies in 1786 (104 vessels and 7,762 tons). This figure does not account for vessels that stopped over in another US port (such as Norfolk or Charleston) before reaching New England. In New York, the French West Indies accounted for only 6 percent of total traffic, but this figure was distorted by the exclusif. In fact, coffee and sugar from Saint-Domingue passed through the Dutch colonies of Curaçao and St. Eustatius, with which the trading community of New York had strong ties.[14]

Although imports from Britain were disproportionately more valuable than goods exchanged with the Caribbean, trade with the French West Indies made up a significant share of total trade. Many vessels from the French West Indies landed in the largest US port-cities but also stopped in many secondary ports. For instance, in 1788, 108 vessels—among which 73 were solely bound for Saint-Domingue—officially shipped from Connecticut's 9 small ports to the French West Indies. The port of Middletown shipped 48 vessels (3,200 tons) in 1788; New London, 28 vessels (1,883 tons), and New Haven, 16 (1,001 tons). In fact, as Connecticut was rich in goods sought after in Saint-Domingue, such as timber, cattle, and horses, some New York cargoes were diverted to these small ports. The main reason for this, however, was that these locations were exempt from direct supervision by French consular agents. Jean Girard suggested that his brother specify tiny Williamstown and Burlington as ports of origin on official expedition papers. As he explained, the only name the Admiralty Court in Cap-Français was on the watch for was Philadelphia, the capital of flour smuggling.[15]

The main distinction between these various US ports lay in their respective share of the Lesser Antilles and Saint-Domingue trade. In this regard, New England's profile was very different from the profile of the rest of the Atlantic seaboard. The French consul at Boston recorded the delivery of all passports issued to sea captains destined for the French West Indies, giving a sense of the breakdown of shipping. In Massachusetts, the Lesser Antilles—particularly Martinique—took the lion's share, while Saint-Domingue dominated the Mid-Atlantic states. Historic connections between Martinique and Massachusetts, based on the distillation of French molasses, partly explain this discrepancy. Moreover, the diet of the enslaved in the Lesser Antilles was distinct from that of Saint-Domingue: whereas dried cod was a fundamental protein in Martinique, this was not the case on the larger island. For Mid-Atlantic and Southern ports, Saint-Domingue was the major West Indian market and accounted for a half to two-thirds of Caribbean traffic.[16]

Breaking down the maritime movement of various states, trade with Saint-Domingue was dominated by Massachusetts, which alone represented one-third of US shipping. By compiling data from Saint-Domingue's newspaper, *Affiches américaines*, the distribution of vessel entries from the United States can be constructed for the three entrepôts during 1788. While New England was the commercial engine, with the combined trade of Massachusetts, Rhode Island, Connecticut, and New Hampshire accounting for over half of the total, other states, including Pennsylvania and the Carolinas, also had significant trade.

Between 1784 and 1787, forty-four to fifty-two vessel entries into New York City (an average of 5,055 tons over four years, about 7 to 8 percent of the total traffic) officially originated from the French Antilles, but neutral islands were more significant (an average of 6,184 tons). However, from 1789 on, with trade in Saint-Domingue partially legalized, these figures were reversed: produce from the French Antilles almost doubled to nearly 11 percent of total tonnage in 1791, while trade from the Dutch and Danish islands declined. This shift is illuminating: rather than making false statements, sea captains could reveal the real source of their cargo without risk.[17]

Legal imports from the United States to the French West Indies were substantial in the 1780s, amounting to 13,065,000 livres tournois in 1786 and 12,069,000 in 1788. Legal exports of molasses and syrups were significantly less valuable, amounting to just 10,730,000 livres tournois in 1786 and 5,772,000

Table 2.3 **Origin of US Vessels Entering Saint-Domingue Harbors in 1788**

State	Number of entries	Percentage of the total
Massachusetts	169	29.1%
Connecticut	71	12.2%
Pennsylvania	60	10.3%
Rhode Island	47	8.1%
South Carolina	46	7.9%
North Carolina	36	6.2%
New York	35	6.0%
Virginia	35	6.0%
Georgia	34	5.9%
Maryland	22	3.8%
New Hampshire	15	2.6%
New Jersey	6	1.0%
Delaware	5	0.9%
Total	581	100%

Source: Created from data in *Affiches américaines.*

in 1788. The foreign trade of Saint-Domingue was overwhelmingly directed toward the United States. In 1788, 93 percent of foreign imports to Cap-Français and 98 percent to Port-au-Prince came from the United States. A temporary admission of the foreign slave trade in the Lesser Antilles meant that Martinique and Guadeloupe traded with a greater variety of foreign partners. In Saint-Pierre, only 42 percent of total foreign imports originated from the United States, while exports did not exceed 16 percent. In contrast, Le Cap-Français emerged as the crossroad of US trade and French metropolitan commerce in the region. In 1788, 61 percent of legal US trade in the Caribbean concerned Saint-Domingue, a figure that increased to 63 percent in 1789. The Port-au-Prince traffic, although more modest, resembled that of the island's economic capital. Only the port of Les Cayes was visited by a significant number of vessels from the neutral islands, mainly Curaçao and Saint-Eustatius.[18]

Several observations can be drawn from this analysis of legal trade between the United States and Saint-Domingue. First, all US ports on the Atlantic, not just New England, were involved in trafficking with the French West Indies. Yet Massachusetts—with its adjunct, Maine—was the largest exporting and importing state, due to a long-standing trade and the importance of molasses to the local economy. Imports of sugar and coffee were distributed between US ports, with the redeployment of Saint-Domingue trade toward the central states beginning in the late 1780s. Small ports also played an essential role. But what was the precise value of this trade? To what extent did it drive local expansion? These are questions that no historian can answer.

How to Contain Endemic Smuggling?

Traders were highly creative in finding ways to obtain colonial produce and import flour. "The enterprising spirit of the Americans is exhausting the means of evading

Table 2.4 **Shipping in Entrepôts, 1788**

Port of Entry	Number of vessels	Port of departure	Number of vessels
Le Cap-Français	416	Le Cap-Français	399
Port-au-Prince	224	Port-au-Prince	198
Les Cayes	98	Les Cayes	99
Jacmel	2	Jacmel	1
Total	740	Total	697

Source: Created from data in *Affiches américaines*, 1788.

the laws of Europe," observed the disillusioned consul at Charleston. False shipping declarations were a common and convenient way to escape repression, and merchants cheated on their manifests in many different ways. A common strategy was to lie about the cargo, presenting prohibited commodities as lawful goods. The captain of *La Tempête*, for instance, put "sugar at the bottom of the cellar" and "covered it under mahogany planks." Another technique consisted of transferring American flour into barrels made in France. In Saint-Domingue, smugglers unloaded cargo at night or in poorly accessible coves, while small local coasters with knowledgeable crews could easily dodge coast guards and carry shipments out to sea. This trade was public knowledge, as a French merchant described with disgust: "I saw the harbor of Cap-Français covered with American ships. I saw 75 enter in the space of 18 to 20 days. I saw their flours publicly transported in the streets. I saw it boarding and landing at night."[19]

The most common smuggling technique was that of false forced release (*relâche forcée*). Captains would sabotage their own ships to be permitted to land in the United States or Saint-Domingue, where they could legally sell their cargo. In a secret—but typical—letter, the firm Marie & Cie recommended that Stephen Girard have his captain report a leak before approaching Port-au-Prince. In Philadelphia and Charleston, consuls counted ten suspicious forced releases for the years 1784–1785, and eight in Massachusetts, Rhode Island, and New Hampshire between 1784 and 1787. Although, the consuls commissioned experts, such as carpenters, to assess damage, sabotage could almost never be proven. Such an investigation was carried out in New York on the ship *L'Italienne* of Marseille, coming from Port-au-Prince on September 22, 1785. Captain Reybaud, anticipating an inspection, had previously transported 98 bales of cotton and 75 sacks of cocoa to the stores of a French merchant. In this case, as in most, the captain was given the benefit of the doubt and released.[20]

Unsurprisingly, confidentiality was at the heart of smuggling practices. The main worry was betrayal by sailors, as merchant Samuel Smith explained to his sea captain: "Secrecy and avoiding all conversation on the subject either on board or on shore is necessary." Talkative sailors posed a grave threat and in most cases were the only reason French customs officials were able to arraign smugglers. The tensions inherent in life at sea, such as unpaid wages, physical abuse by captains, and navigational conflicts, could lead disgruntled sailors to report on captains who were smuggling, leading to confiscation of goods as well as indictments. The share of condemned cargoes granted to whistleblowers was also a powerful incentive. The Boston consul managed to prosecute the captain of the brigantine *Union* because of testimony from Antoine Blanc, a sailor who deserted the ship after a forced release on August 8, 1786, with "a cargo composed of ninety barrels of raw sugar, one hundred and forty quarters of sugar and seven thirds of raw sugar, eight bales of cotton, eighty-nine bags of cocoa."

Blanc declared that after a few days at sea, "Captain Prudent Bevier summoned all the sailors to his room and told them: my children, I am not going to Le Havre but to New England. For that purpose, he promised them twenty gourdes each. To which each one having consented, the vessel proceeded for Salem." Madame Robert Coëls, a passenger on the ship the *Bien-aimé*, who left Les Cayes in June 1786 bound for Nantes, paid the price for one of these cover-ups, since the ship's real destination was Boston. Rather than heading for France, this Saint-Domingue inhabitant and her five children were forced to spend the winter in New England. She initiated legal proceedings against the captain, who had used her as a living alibi.[21]

Another commonplace method of fraud was to use a French flag when reaching Saint-Domingue and a US flag when landing in North America because consular jurisdiction could only be exercised on French subjects and French vessels. Several legal ordinances defined the conditions required to enjoy the privileges attached to French vessels: not only the ship owner but also the main officers and two-thirds of the crew had to be French. As smugglers could easily deceive the consuls, the nationalities of ships were in constant flux. For instance, Stephen Girard, then still called Etienne, originally from Bordeaux, had settled in the United States in 1776 to flee his creditors and, with the cooperation of his brother, constantly changed the nationality of his vessels. In July 1785, the brigantine *The Two Brothers* left Philadelphia with two captains on board, one French (Carbonel), the other American (Hart). At Cap-Français they remained some distance from the coast until a message was received from Jean Girard, telling them whether the ship should enter the harbor as an American or a French vessel. In some cases, smugglers altered the crew by bringing French seamen on board to reach the two-thirds threshold. Ships generally took on a French identity on arrival in Saint-Domingue and were Americanized for the United States.[22]

French officials attempted to impose national frameworks on seasoned cross-border activities but quickly realized that regulations required modernization to contain the flow of illegal trade. The integration of the United States into a reorganized French Empire made it possible to create peripheral communication networks between consuls and colonial administrators. This was facilitated by the fact that all state agents were under the tutelage of the Ministry of the Navy. The careers of these agents overlapped significantly: civil servants could successively occupy the post of consul in North America and then become a colonial administrator in the islands. A number of families had one foot on the mainland, another in the colonies: François Barbé-Marbois was appointed consul general in the United States before becoming the last *intendant* of Saint-Domingue in 1785; his brother, Etienne, replaced him as vice-consul in New York. Anne-César de La Luzerne had been the first French ambassador in the United States;

his brother held the prestigious post of general governor of Saint-Domingue before reaching the culmination of his career as minister of the navy. These state agents, who augmented their official relations with family ties, embodied the imperial agenda of tethering the United States to France.[23]

The minister of the navy asked his agents to maintain constant correspondence in order to expose smugglers and intercept fraudulent cargoes. The consul general relayed the minister's instructions by harassing his subordinates in US port cities, but communication between the mainland and the islands proved particularly difficult. Ship captains could refuse to take official mail or dump it overboard, so colonial officials were often reduced to receiving consular information from the United States via offices in Versailles. These letters always arrived too late, giving smugglers more than enough time to disappear or change their names. These communication problems between imperial peripheries highlight the mismatch between the intended project of generalized surveillance and the paucity of resources available to the French state to effect this surveillance.[24]

A major hurdle for consuls was the inability to control vessels leaving a US port under the US flag. Therefore, on March 31, 1786, the Ministry of the Navy decreed that consuls would issue passports to Americans destined for the French West Indies; they would record the name of the vessel and the captain, the tonnage, the number of sailors, and the nature of the cargo. This visa would be a prerequisite for admission to the colonies. Although control of maritime movements in the French colonial territory had a long history, this was a particularly significant innovation; consuls had been specifically prohibited from issuing passports since Louis XIV. This reform was part of what historians have called the long "identification revolution" of the eighteenth century. Surviving registers reveal that consuls abided by the regulations scrupulously. At the same time, colonial officials were introducing new administrative procedures in Saint-Domingue. The intendant explained that to control traffic, all information must be "transcribed and kept in [a] register. . . . Each vessel has, so to speak, an open account where one scrupulously knows all the movements. It also mentions all changes of captains or shipowners." Saint-Domingue's newspaper, *Affiches américaines*, which indicated precisely the maritime movement of all foreign ships and listed passengers leaving the colony, was another surveillance tool. The administrative effort required for these procedures was considerable and unprecedented; from this time forward, state agents applied imperial rules.[25]

These proceedings outraged the American public and press, which deplored legislation it deemed detrimental to the sovereignty, honor, and rights of the United States. Imposing passports was an additional attack on freedom of commerce and more generally on the natural right to circulate, a foundational principle in the creation of the early American republic. While France viewed the targeted practices as illegal, the American public fervently defended their

legitimacy, and newspaper articles repeatedly declared the French legislation "a national insult." As the trading schemes employed by merchants were
the consequences of political independence, they were deemed all the more
legitimate. Having to disguise cargoes and secure false papers were painful
obligations that ran counter to national dignity and the honor of the republic.
In a context of economic depression, the consuls' prying was unacceptable interference, appearing to disavow the capacity of US Customs to produce official
documents. In sum, France was claiming an *imperium in imperio*. One anonymous pamphleteer urged the federal government to "immediately remonstrate
against this new procedure with that manly dignity and spirit which actuated us
while struggling for and finally hath given us, a rank among the nations of the
earth." The legislation particularly hurt the commercial interests of specific states
such as Georgia and North Carolina, where no French consul officiated. The
country as a whole, merchants argued, was to be treated on equal terms. The "nationalist ferment" the new procedures caused helped to stimulate constitutional
thinking on the Union's regulating powers.[26]

From the point of view of French officials, the universal registering of traders
and ships appeared to have failed. Although consular reporting complicated the
smugglers' hide-and-seek games, illegal traffic did not cease. As Portsmouth
vice-consul Armand Ducher remarked, "What can be said in these letters? that
such vessel is in contravention; but the French or American ships shipped from
the United States for our colonies are all in contravention." Frustrated in their
efforts to identify individual smugglers, consuls targeted suspicious groups, defined from their own prejudices. They accused the Creoles of Saint-Domingue,
white people supposedly born on the island, of being responsible for the
smuggling: the consuls believed these people had no loyalty and changed their
nationality at will. The prejudice also fed off the widely held belief on "degeneration" that American conditions caused on minds and bodies. These Creole
"cosmopolitans" would be described today as globalists: "They go and come to
those states and from these states to the French Isles." These devious migrants
who refused to settle down and whose origins were uncertain made convenient
scapegoats. A "Mr. Guyon," for instance, had no roots anywhere: "This Planter
coming from the Arcahaye Plain, Isle St. Domingue, to Philadelphia, New York,
New London, and Boston" was illegally importing sugar. A community of rest-
less adventurers was blamed for its connections with American merchants: the
uprooted colonial, the overseas vagabond, described as "Creole" with contempt,
stole French national wealth.[27]

Unsurprisingly, consuls connected this denunciation of cosmopolitan Creolism with antisemitism: Jews and Creoles were supposedly in ca-
hoots with American captains. Abraham Sasportas, the "representative" of all
Charleston Jews, in concert with his cousin in Cap-Français, was blamed for

exhibiting "fraud and double flags." Unable to identify smugglers, French agents stigmatized specific groups as excessively greedy and, therefore, "false French". All Jews were designated targets. Consuls even combined these various smuggler identities to define the US national spirit. The consul in Boston reported this questionable and telling joke to the minister of the navy: "Someone testified to his surprise that in a country of tolerance there was no Jew; an American of good sense answered, they would die here of hunger, for we ourselves are all Jews." Administrators castigated a marginal class of smugglers as "adventurers," "creoles," and "Jews"; these stateless people, they believed, revealed the unfinished character of the American nation, a collective of rootless migrants.[28]

This demonization of smugglers was not incompatible with debates over the relevance and enforceability of the French exclusif. The colonial government in Saint-Domingue tirelessly denounced the corruption and laxity of admiralty officers. "We have changed them several times," the intendant noted, "but they almost all become corruptible after a few months of service." He was right. Jean Girard, for instance, relied on signals from the admiralty clerk to avoid coast guards near Cap-Français, while some vice-consuls were themselves involved in sugar trafficking. The representative of France in Maine was suspected of smuggling coffee between Falmouth and Port-au-Prince. Even when not violating the law, consuls often turned a blind eye, believing that assisting smugglers, or at least allowing them to pursue their trade, was serving France's national interest. French officials were neither passive implementers nor totally corrupt and complacent individuals. Many felt that application of the law as it stood was contradictory to the true national interest, of which, in their view, they were better judges than the ministerial bureaus in Versailles. While abiding by the central guidelines, most insisted that the law be revised. The Boston consul emphasized "that it is the EXPERIENCE to show the changes to be introduced later in this important part of the administration." Although he quoted major thinkers of the time—physiocrats, lawyers, and free traders such as Joseph Priestley, Mirabeau, Raynal, Cesare Beccaria, and Necker—he considered his position as a practitioner an advantage over mere theoreticians; unlike abstract thinkers, civil servants were the real agents of the Enlightenment.[29]

The motives of those in favor of relaxing the exclusif were geopolitical as much as philosophical. Many officials warned the Ministry of the Navy that the harshness of repression might eventually push the Americans into the arms of Britain. Relations between the French colonial empire and the United States were perceived in the light of imperial Franco-British rivalries, and the United States, through smuggling, could be the arbiter of this rivalry in the Caribbean. Vice-consul Ducher called for French commercial legislation to respond to the way Britain had designed its own free port system; the British government had created these hubs only to encourage smuggling with Saint-Domingue in the hope of weakening France. Acting as a broker between both countries, diplomatic staff also adopted US rhetoric on free trade. Copying what they read in local newspapers, they put forward the principle that "unlimited extraction of colonial produce" constituted a "natural right." Létombe, the consul at Boston, explained that smuggling in the American world could not have the same status as in Europe, as contraband trade was "a real offense against the Sovereign and the Nation. But with this difference that this crime owes its existence to law; since the forbidden commodities are of primary necessity here, the temptation to smuggle is invincible." Going beyond the notion of provisional tolerance toward illegal trade, he made a bolder statement of political economy, connecting the issue with the larger debate on luxury. Without citing his source, Létombe quoted verbatim a sentence from legal theorist Beccaria's *Crimes and Punishments*, a bestselling book and major legal reference at the end of the eighteenth century.[30]

Officials on the islands and in the United States favored legalization of trade as long as it was conducted on French vessels; if they could not prevent fraud, at least French people rather than foreigners should benefit from the shipping industry. British legislation appeared more realistic and profitable, since it did not admit US ships to the West Indies but allowed British ships to export sugar, coffee, and cotton to the continent. The exclusif mitigé, the consuls warned, boosted the American Navy while hurting French maritime interests. West Indian traders had no choice but to resort to American shipyards to buy new vessels. As metropolitan supply was not able to meet the demands of colonial shipping and the timber came from New England, the Frenchification of vessels was difficult to regulate. A new policy would require the state to draw a clearer line between French and foreign ships. Some consuls campaigned for a legal crackdown; the one in Charleston suggested that all crew be French and that the French should be prohibited from flying foreign flags. New certifications were required for individuals, boats, and goods; national identity was to become immediately visible and unalterable. Writing in South Carolina, the consul even suggested "the masts of the constructions be stamped," taking inspiration from the cruelties inflicted by planters on enslaved people to identify their "property" in case they ran away. The many institutions associated with slavery framed the ways in which consuls approached commercial regulations.[31]

Who Were the Smugglers?

In the eyes of French officials, smuggling was an "American" activity, a "Creole" or "Jewish" business, and an occupation of untethered adventurers and outlaws devoid of any patriotism. They also believed that smugglers were spearheading

US penetration into French imperial space, despite the Treaty of 1778 being intended to facilitate conquest of the American market by France. They wrote that they were helplessly witnessing the commercial invasion of Saint-Domingue, thus enabling an informal mode of economic colonialism. However, the contribution of "adventurers" to this trade was only the most obvious element of an economic activity that shaped port societies of the early American republic and French colonies. Far from being exceptional, marginal, or picturesque, smuggling was part of everyday life. The livelihood and capital of several hundred sea captains, several thousand sailors, and a few dozen ship owners derived from this trade. On the continent as well as the islands, people consumed smuggled goods without necessarily knowing or caring about the legality of the merchandise.

The image of US merchants invading Saint-Domingue's market is also misleading: French merchants were actively collaborating with Americans within transnational multi-centered networks. The high mobility of traders and ships integrated the colony into a Caribbean world that included North America. Merchants moved constantly from one place to another, founding commercial companies in the United States, then in the French West Indies, before resettling on the continent. Trade relationships were not only bilateral but were part of a complex Caribbean infrastructure. Curaçao, Saint Eustatius, and other "neutral" entrepôts were smuggling crossroads crucial to the existence of US-Saint-Domingue trade. Vessels would make multiple stops on a circuit that involved several intermediaries. A maritime venture had many stakeholders: the ship owner(s), the owner(s) of the cargo, the captain(s), at times the supercargo (a merchant on the ship responsible for buying and selling), and the consignee(s). The consignee was often a *commissionaire* established in the corresponding port. For instance, a ship owner in Philadelphia could ship goods from Cap Français to Charleston where a consignee would forward part of the cargo to another US port. In Cap Français, merchants often outfitted brigantines to Port-au-Prince, Les Cayes, or other islands in the West Indies before redirecting them to the United States. The ships and the goods were circulated from one commissionaire to another following a chain of trust. The financial connections, based on personal credit and bills of exchange on various European places, added additional layers of complication.[32]

Contrary to a cliché from political economy literature in the 1780s, planters were rarely in direct contact with American captains, instead resorting to intermediary merchants. It is true that ship owners sometimes commissioned sea captains to buy and sell cargoes themselves, but the latter were often young men deprived of capital making their first steps into the business world. Bestowing control of mercantile operations on captains only happened in cases where the ship owner had no connections in corresponding ports. As captains were unlikely to have all the skills required to conduct successful business (including navigational abilities, a command of foreign languages, and an ability to assess the quality of goods and negotiate prices), this practice was likely to be unprofitable. Sea captains were certainly ill-equipped to deal directly with French planters. The hardships experienced by Henry Packer Dering, a captain operating for a merchant living in Sag Harbor (New York) and sent to Les Cayes in 1787, perfectly illustrate the problem. Packer Dering's personal diary opens a window on his daily activities as captain/commissionaire. He received the brigantines *William & Mary*, the *Hampton*, and the *Polly*, and their cargoes of herring and horses, but he was unable to sell the goods. Summing up his frustration with a pithy phrase, he recorded "Disappointment upon the back of disappointment." The despondent captain undertook an exploratory trip in Saint-Domingue's hinterland, hoping to find new suppliers. Traveling from plantation to plantation, he met many inhabitants and socialized with French colonists who offered him lodging and food. However, Packer Dering, who spoke very poor French and did not know the country well, came to rely on a certain Stupuy, a commissionaire established in Les Cayes. It rapidly became clear that the commissionaire was defrauding Packer Dering, who visibly lacked connections and know-how. In a world where cash was scarce and credit-relationships governed, a foreign sea captain subject to discriminatory laws was in a weak position to negotiate.[33]

Was this trade dominated by American adventurers? In US ports, many traders—prominent merchants, small ship owners, and even lowly sea captains—were engaged in the Saint-Domingue market. Such an adventure required little capital and immobilized funds for a far shorter period than transatlantic commerce, especially the slave trade. A modest brigantine or schooner (60 to 90 tons), possibly chartered, with a small crew (from 5 to 9), could perform fast rotations. Between New York and Saint-Domingue, depending on the weather and the pilot's skills, a trip would take between eight and thirty days, on average twenty-two. Several vessels did up to four roundtrips a year. The Saint-Domingue market was therefore favorable to newcomers, the best example being Stephen Girard. Having previously chartered ships, Girard purchased his first brigantine *Les Deux Frères* in April 1784, followed by the *Kitty* in 1786 and the *Deux Amis* in 1787. His fourth ship, the *Polly*, cost only 7,000 livres. Thanks to the Saint-Domingue market, Girard emerged as one of Philadelphia's leading merchants and went on to trade in Marseilles and East Asian ports. As Saint-Domingue was an essential part of the broader West Indian trade, powerful merchant families were also involved. In Baltimore, for example, the most substantial commercial firm, John Smith & Sons, was also one of the first to outfit vessels for the French West Indies. In New York, Governor & Kemble, Lynch & Stoughton, Gelston & Saltonstall, and the Mumford family—whose network covered the small ports of Connecticut—all owned numerous vessels specializing in the Saint-Domingue market.[34]

Stephen Girard was not the only successful ship owner of French origin in the United States. Many had moved to North America during the War of Independence to take advantage of opportunities presented by the destabilizing of British-oriented commercial networks, including Sasportas in Charleston, who like Girard came from Bordeaux. Others decided to stay after taking part in the war, such as Paul Bentalou from Montauban, a small town in southwestern France, who went on to found a major firm in Baltimore. Many took American citizenship, benefiting from state-specific legislation, such as in Maryland, where skilled immigrants were welcomed. Peace attracted new Francophone players, including the merchant Etienne/Stephen Dutilh, who settled in Philadelphia in 1783 and became one of Girard's main competitors in the Saint-Domingue market. About one-third of shipments destined for the French island were sent by these newly established Frenchmen in Mid-Atlantic ports. In many cases, the United States was only a stopover in their career. Abel Hamelin special-ized in importing syrups from Saint-Domingue, first to Philadelphia, then to Charleston. One of his friends asked this revealing question: "How are things going in Philadelphia? Have you made a living there good enough to live off your annuities in Nantes?" The letter-writer strongly believed that Pennsylvania was only a transitional step, not a new homeland. He expected Hamelin to return to France, as merchants usually returned to the metropole after making a fortune in the islands. As such, the United States played the same role as Saint-Domingue for these individuals in search of fortune.[35]

The US market also offered new opportunities for traders in Saint-Domingue. After the war, several firms specializing in North American trade emerged in Cap-Français, Port-au-Prince, and Les Cayes. Often a parent com-pany located in a US port would back the creation of a branch in the colony. Typically, these were family-run businesses, with one brother directing trade on the continent while another was the consignee on the island; this was the case for Etienne and Jean Girard, Etienne and Jean Dutilh, and James and Thomas Perkins. Just like French merchants, Americans hoped to make their fortune on the island before returning to the continent. Out of sixty Cap Français merchants and shipping companies in 1784, nine were shipping, re-ceiving, or selling ships and cargoes from the United States. Saint-Domingue merchant houses specializing in the US market were smaller than those dealing with the metropole and had a rather short life expectancy of between three and five years. They were often liquidated before maturity, resulting in an intense renewal of firms. It was not uncommon for traders to change partners and found a new company conducting the same business.[36]

The market was not exclusively driven by US nationals. On closer inspection, even so-called American business houses were not very "American." Most were in fact binational; for instance, Jean-Gabriel Tardy of Charente partnered with Samuel Wall of Boston "for the purpose of transacting French & American business." In contrast to the prejudiced caricatures circulating in the consuls' correspondence, traders identifying as Jews were not common: only the Frères Molines firm and Séguineau frères were part of the Judeo-Portuguese community. The biggest firms in Cap-Français, such as Furtado frères and Nonès Lopez & Cie, were connected to big business in Aquitaine and not involved in the US market. In other words, the US trade of Saint-Domingue was no more "Jewish" than the national Atlantic trade, despite Les Cayes having a sizable Jewish-Dutch community with connections to Curaçao and Saint-Eustatius. While a few merchants were born in Saint-Domingue, many were the offspring of established traders in metropolitan France and had started

Table 2.5 **Major Firms Conducting US Trade in Saint-Domingue**

Firms involved in the US trade 1784–1785	*Port-city*
Ceronio & Nicolleau	Le Cap-Français
Tirel & Ravy	Le Cap-Français
Wall, Tardy & Cie	Le Cap-Français
Estansan & Raybaud	Le Cap-Français
Brassier & Faurès	Le Cap-Français
James Dennie	Le Cap-Français
Moline frères	Le Cap-Français
Girard & Hourquebie	Le Cap-Français
R. Marie & Cie	Port-au-Prince
Jean & Jean-Baptiste Barrère	Port-au-Prince
Séguineau frères	Port-au-Prince
Jean Lafargue	Port-au-Prince
Louis Lafosse	Port-au-Prince
Gérard Mallenon	Port-au-Prince
Étienne Patot & Cie	Port-au-Prince
Mumford & Rodman	Les Cayes
Formon, Leclère & Cie	Les Cayes
Adelon & Marsan	Les Cayes

Sources: *Affiches américaines*; ANOM E 346, "Mémoire sur le commerce étranger" by Raybaud.

their careers as sea captains. Most came from Bordeaux, but there were also some Bayonnais, such as Joseph Cassarouy, who embarked for Cap-Français in 1769, and Pierre Adelon, who had initially been a privateer captain during the war. The mass influx after 1783 of Frenchmen in search of fortune had resulted in a flood of clerks on the labor market. Many of these young men then looked for opportunities to start a business, while the more entrenched firms attempted to impose a monopoly. The United States acted as the safety valve for a saturated market and, to some extent, became the commercial periphery of Saint-Domingue.[37]

Despite cutthroat competition, the market was large enough for a variety of firms to exist. The most robust were formed during the American War of Independence and adopted an economic strategy that integrated production with distribution. The firm Séguineau frères, for example, owned a store and warehouses in Port-au-Prince and Saint-Marc, a large coffee plantation in Fond-Baptiste worth 447,790 livres tournois, and a smaller one at Fond-des-Nègres estimated at 30,000 livres tournois. Séguineau frères directly exported the coffee produced on their own plantation and provisioned surrounding plantations with North American foodstuffs. By reducing the number of intermediaries, this mode of operation facilitated smuggling, diminishing the inherent risks. Their case was not unique. For instance, Choffart, Cottineau & Cie in Port-au-Prince, in a business relationship with Paul Bentalou and Monbos Latil & Cie in Baltimore, exported produce from the Cottineau sugar refinery.[38]

One of the leading merchants in the market was named Gérard Mallenon. The son of a Bordeaux merchant, Mallenon had moved to the colony in 1760. During the American Revolutionary War, he laid the foundations of his business through privateering, outfitting no less than twelve ships in his own name and for various shareholders. When the war ended, he expanded his trade in the United States by building up his existing mercantile networks. At the time of his death, he was the consignee for Vanuxem & Lombart of Philadelphia, as well as eleven ship captains from New England, selling cod, salted beef, flour, timber, and candles on their behalf for a commission of 2.5 or 5 percent. In return, Mallenon loaded these vessels with syrup. He became the owner of a distillery in which six enslaved people worked on syrup production. Wishing to import North American distilling techniques into Saint-Domingue, he had appointed a New Englander named John McInery as head of the distillery. Mallenon owned significant commercial vessels, including the massive 300-ton *Betsy*, worth 14,000 livres, the 80-ton brigantine *Actif*, worth 4,500 livres, and the 180-ton *L'Espérance*, worth 3,600 livres. He was also the proprietor of four sites in Port-au-Prince valued together at 85,000 livres, and he claimed ownership of twenty-two enslaved people, worth 63,325 livres, most of whom were stevedores to load and unload his ships; this was a rare number for a merchant without a plantation.

Mallenon's fortune exceeded 250,000 livres, certainly far less than the major sugar planters, but matching that of an average coffee planter.[39]

Mallenon navigated a fine line between the legal and illegal. Although exporting syrup and importing foodstuffs was legal, Mallenon's business aroused the suspicion of the French consul in New York. On June 13, 1785, sailor Joseph Guérin denounced the sea captain of Mallenon's *Port-au-Prince*, for changing flags when entering the port. On another occasion Jean Guichard, Mallenon's nephew, executor, and former captain, had been involved in a suspicious forced release in Charleston. Yet there was apparently no follow-up to these cases, and Mallenon's social position on the island was undamaged. Indeed, Mallenon, who was close to the colonial government, was selected by the traders of the capital city to supply Port-au-Prince with rice and other edibles after the scarcity of 1786. Considered a "solid trader," he struck a major deal with intendant Barbé Marbois, worth 120,000 livres. The merchant also pledged to double that amount through an advance on his own funds, a clear sign that Mallenon had extensive credit. Mallenon's profile and social standing contrast sharply with the typical smuggler as depicted by French officials. He and other well-established merchants/smugglers branched out into real estate and production. Far from being mere consignees, men like Mallenon were autonomous ship owners looking toward the United States, not France.[40]

The characters described by the consuls were newcomers who entered the market later. A better example of this type of individual would be Laurent Faurès. Following the traditional training of an apprentice trader, Faurès became a bookkeeper in the Pascaud and Faurès firm, formed in September 1779 in Cap-Français. As was often the case in the West Indies, Faurès's first employment was in a family company, in this case, that of his uncle, an established trader in Cap Français who shared his Bordeaux origins. The firm did not last long and dissolved, presumably after bankruptcy. Faurès then moved back to Bordeaux in August 1781 before returning to Cap-Français in April 1783, where he founded a new company with his brother Bruno and Antoine Marcorelles. Marcorelles and Bruno each staked 25,000 livres in the startup while Laurent acted as manager. The purpose of the firm was to take advantage of the Franco-American Treaty of Amity and Commerce. The founding act specified that one of the partners would be required to travel regularly to North America. This was a very modest company compared to the big firms in metropolitan France or slave-trading firms in the colony. In comparison, the capital of Foäche, Morange & Cie, the main house of commerce in Cap-Français, was valued at 1,627,208 livres tournois in 1786, more than seventy times the worth of Faurès and Marcorelles. Scheduled to last five years, the Faurès company was terminated before expiry on May 29, 1784: with the restoration of the exclusif, it had lost "its raison d'être." Faurès's marriage to the daughter of an Acadian refugee, Sophie Elisabeth Pigeot from

Louisbourg, in February 1786, restored his credit as his wife brought with her a small coffee plantation in Plaisance valued at 26,910 livres. Faurès then formed two new companies with another partner under the name Brassier & Faurès (July 5, 1786, and May 18, 1787), once more specializing in the US market. As well as being the consignee for US merchants on the island, he started a distillery. Faurès, like Mallenon and many others whose cases are less well documented, played a double game, trading legal syrups and exporting sugar and coffee when in a position to do so. To compensate for initial capital weakness, the main asset of these firms was their ability to adapt, resulting in permanent circulation. Only this mobility made it possible to circumvent prohibitions and monopolies.[41]

Outlaws?

Although they were smuggling goods, these traders did not hesitate to use the law for their own benefit when they saw fit, often taking the judicial route to resolve conflicts. Mallenon, for example, filed sixty-six suits in the Admiralty Court and the Civil Court (*sénéchaussée*) in Port-au-Prince against ship captains, bakers, and various merchants. The Massachusetts consul reported that "there were eighteen lawsuits in the Supreme Court sitting in Boston, seven of which were between Frenchmen." Smugglers knew how to take advantage of the legal differences between the United States and the French colonies. They also used the law whenever their reputation was at stake, anxious to defend their credit as trustworthy merchants. On August 18, 1790, Jean Girard brought legal action before the Civil Court of Cap-Français against the merchant Jacob Mayer, with whom he had formed a short-lived firm. Mayer was accused of spreading rumors in Philadelphia about Girard's supposed financial hardship. The plaintiff prevailed, securing compensation of $100, having his "honesty" recognized, and once more enjoying "public esteem." Among the witnesses were Étienne Dutilh and James Perkins: all four had been involved in smuggling cases, but apparently this did not affect the value of their testimony or prevent Girard from deserving "public esteem." Girard obtained a notarial act certifying his good credit, endorsed by the consul in Philadelphia.[42]

With well-to-do merchants participating in smuggling and an administration overwhelmed by a proliferating contraband trade, was the colonial exclusif a void and outdated legal framework? French officials, discovering transgressions everyday certainly had a sense of permanent failure, and offenses led to confiscation and fines in only a few cases. However, it would be misleading to believe that commercial laws had no impact simply because they could be violated. Traders' perceptions of the situation were diametrically opposed to those of the consuls. Business correspondence of the time regularly reveals feelings of being systematically thwarted, despite inventive ploys. Jean Girard described the "tyranny" of Barbé-Marbois, and the colonial intendant's "hatred of the Americans." Dutilh shared his concerns: "It seems to us that at this moment most people are afraid to send ships to you, especially because of the rumors spread that the entrance of American vessels was becoming more and more difficult in the French islands and that several were arrested and confiscated." Another merchant lamented, "Things are getting worse and worse through the government's hindrances, based on the most damaging system that can ever be formed for the colony," while Baltimore merchant Samuel Smith described the trade as "a scene of loss, detention and disappointment." In June 1789, Perkins, Burling & Perkins, the main American firm in Cap Français, abandoned contraband trade; while it was possible to evade the law, the need to bribe customs officers—at times unsuccessfully—weighed heavily on the profitability of maritime ventures. Traders also worried about being denounced by their competitors working for firms in the metropole. Tellingly, the company Mesnier frères blamed Dutilh, who had made the mistake of offering his services from Philadelphia and resented American flour crushing "the trade of the most beautiful province of France." According to the company, it was "not natural for foreigners to ruin our navigation and our manufactures."[43]

The major issue for traders was not seizure of their ships or confiscation of cargoes but the effects of smuggling on their business relationships. Without recourse to the law they were exposed to the possibility of being cheated by partners. Smuggling weakened trust and made ship owners particularly vulnerable. Once legally disarmed, merchants were at the mercy of their confidants. Even Stephen Girard's brother, Jean, threatened to denounce him to customs officers to obtain the sum he believed he was owed. In blackmailing his own brother, Jean hoped to extort money using the law he had flouted on a regular basis for years.[44]

Ironically, smugglers did not hesitate to bring their counterparts to court, but they rarely won cases. Paul Bentalou described such an event in his diary. With Francis Casenave and Thomas Burling, Bentalou had bought a vessel from the US government, the *Washington*, in 1784. Casenave was instructed to conduct a smuggling circuit between St. Thomas, Curaçao, Jamaica, and Cuba. In 1785, Bentalou loaded the *Washington* with flour for Port-au-Prince and had Casenave charter a second ship, the *Flying Fish*, headed by Captain Dumeste. The captain played the role of middleman with Alexander Lindo of Kingston and Choffart, Cottineau & Cie of Port-au-Prince. The intention was to transport flour while also smuggling enslaved people into the colony. The scheme, however, was financially disastrous. Once in the colony, Casenave, with the complicity of a "housewife" whose name we do not know but who was probably one of the many powerful free women of color in Port-au-Prince, appropriated all profits and refused to repay advances granted by the firms in Saint-Domingue and Jamaica.

In 1788, Bentalou received claims from the first firm for 13,101 *livres coloniales*, and from the second for 4,261 dollars. The Baltimore merchant appealed to the French consular jurisdiction for arbitration, but as his agreement with Casenave had no legal value, he lost the case. The situation took its toll on Bentalou over the years, leaving his mind "in a constant agitation between hope and fear."[45]

Powerful Salem merchant Elias Hasket-Derbie, owner of the first New England vessel to trade directly with China, underwent a similar experience. His commercial operations in the West Indies were immense, but he was dependent on untrustworthy business partners. Hasket-Derbie filed a complaint against the Port-au-Prince merchants, Jean-Baptiste Barrère and Alexandre Lemaire. In July 1786, the captain of the *Betsy*, Ichabod Nichols, had already sold some of his cargo in Curaçao and Saint-Pierre when he disembarked in the capital of Saint-Domingue. He then contacted the two merchants and sold them his remaining goods. In order to pay the captain, who had orders from his shipowner not to accept credit, the two Dominguan merchants offered sugar for transportation to Inagua in the Bahamas, but this solution proved impracticable. They then suggested Frenchifying the vessel under the name *Neptune* and sending it to Nantes loaded with colonial goods, a French captain, and letters of recommendation for firms in metropolitan France. This proposal was accepted by the captain who entrusted one of his two vessels to a French captain, named Levavasseur. However, the new captain admitted to the forged French papers in court. As an informer, he was entitled to a share of the seized cargoes, which promised to be far more profitable than a sea captain's wages. Hasket-Derby pleaded good faith and claimed ignorance of his captain's intrigues, but this failed to prevent Barbé-Marbois from confiscating the cargo. There are countless similar stories in the archives, demonstrating that the exclusif, although flawed, did have force and affected merchants' behaviors and strategies in complicated ways.[46]

US trade played a crucial role in the unprecedented expansion of Saint-Domingue during the 1780s. Without US logistical support and food supplies, it would have been impossible to accommodate the rapidly increasing labor force of enslaved Africans. American goods had deeply infiltrated colonial society: all inhabitants, as consumers, depended on them in one way or another. Whites, free people of color, and the enslaved consumed goods from the United States and, consciously or not, engaged in these global flows. However, merchants back in the metropole did not understand commercial exchanges in these terms, and, far from acknowledging mutual benefits, they saw only the risk of a US invasion.

True, illegal trafficking was a common practice and made some merchants a fortune, but it was not necessarily profitable and could prove immensely risky, as reflected in the decrease in trade between the United States and Saint-Domingue in 1788. Although the colonial monopoly could not eliminate smuggling, it was a huge disincentive for merchants who did not conduct business on behalf of metropolitan firms. State officials, consuls, and colonial administrators were aware of these conflicting interests and attempted to maintain an unstable equilibrium in the service of French sovereignty. Their ambiguous relationship with smuggling reveals the complexity of this political negotiation. The smugglers challenged the authority of the central state but also contributed to the colony's growth. Although lambasted as marginal outliers, they were unavoidable and legitimate players in the Atlantic world economy. When the metropolitan grain crisis took effect in 1788, this situation became untenable. The time for shaky compromise had ended; insurrection began.

The Whole and the Parts, 1789–1790

In the Middle Ages, "liberty took refuge in the lagoons of Venice and on the rocks of Genoa. These two republics invited Commerce and the Arts; they became rivals in power and happiness." The anonymous author of *Reflections on Commerce* contended that the analogy between Italian maritime republics and France was appropriate after the National Assembly had issued the Declaration of Rights of Man and Citizen. Colonial trade buttressed state power and liberty, he insisted. France, engaged in a process of regeneration, should get inspiration from the commercial republics of the past, then enlightened by merchants in an age of darkness. The Assembly should keep systemicism and metaphysics at bay and listen to those who had experience in trade. His assumption was that "Commerce" would speak with one voice, but this proved to be unfounded. If slavery was consensual among mercantile elite, the colonial exclusif turned out to be immensely contentious. Debates on this policy were so ferocious that in January 1790, the US *chargé d'affaires* to France, William Short, who followed parliamentary debates closely, commented that the "two parties of merchants of France and deputies from the islands are so violent that the members of the assembly who acknowledge their ignorance of colonial matters fear to meet the question in front." This conflict did not remain at the rhetorical level and rapidly escalated to armed revolt in Saint-Domingue and Martinique.[1]

The revolutionary exclusif debate has been relatively neglected by historians. At best, it has been credited with preparing the terrain for "veritable issues," a point of entry into matters unrelated to the years 1789–1790. At worst it has simply been ignored. In most accounts, dissent surrounding the exclusif was overtaken and subsumed by the confrontation between advocates of slavery and abolitionists. But this reconstructed hierarchy does not reflect contemporary experiences and the representation of gradual colonial revolution—from the exclusif, to the rights of free people of color, to slavery—fails to account for how these various issues were interconnected, crossing lines between metropole

Entrepôt of Revolutions. Manuel Covo, Oxford University Press. © Oxford University Press 2022.
DOI: 10.1093/oso/9780197626382.003.0004

and colony and challenging national identity, the Franco-American alliance, and imperial dimensions of France in the throes of revolutionary regeneration.[2]

Would these regenerative endeavors be applied to colonial commerce and, as a result, to the colonies themselves? And in what sense would this be regeneration? The debate over the colonial exclusif crystallized the anxieties articulated by patriotic writers in the eighteenth century. As historian John Shovlin demonstrated, those writers "combined calls for an expansion of national wealth with attacks on the deleterious effects of money on social, political, and cultural life." They also believed that "moral qualities were crucial to the regeneration of France, and that wealth, in the hands of the wrong people, produced in the wrong way, or used perversely, might destroy those qualities." The revolutionaries, although committed to regeneration, clashed over the risks associated with the moralizing of trade, on the one hand, and the necessity of reasserting commercial sovereignty at the international and imperial levels on the other: the exclusif lay at the intersection of these concerns. The eighteenth-century debate over the relevance of the colonial monopoly reached its climax in 1789.[3]

It is important to bear in mind that significant events were not restricted to Paris. News of what took place in the colonies would take at least a month to reach France and therefore largely escaped supervision. Communication between the metropole and colonies—haphazard under the old regime—became even more chaotic after 1789. Initiatives did not always originate from the metropole, politics within the French Antilles often being the engine of change. Throughout the colonies, the exclusif mitigé—as redefined by the arrêt of August 30, 1784—was producing local antagonism. In Saint-Domingue, only the three ports d'entrepôt—Cap-Français, Port-au-Prince, and Les Cayes—were open to foreign trade, hampering the development of many secondary ports. The system was also unpopular on an international level, with the British Empire and the United States, which, despite the Treaty of Amity and Commerce of 1778, had no advantages over other nations. Although the most lucrative products were excluded from legal commerce, smuggling had prospered to the point that Saint-Domingue had become the second largest commercial partner of the early republic.

Focusing on the exclusif illuminates the complex interaction between tensions of empire and revolutionary dynamics. This conflict was not confined to a contest of ideas, a battle between integral protectionists and orthodox free traders, but became an authentic political struggle at a time when France was experimenting with democracy for the first time. As parliamentary life and procedures were being developed, political strategies, clandestine arrangements, and pressure exerted by a variety of lobbies shaped the power balance in and beyond the National Assembly. The cracks in the political economic system that developed as an experiment in the wake of the American Revolutionary War reached a crisis when the political divisions in Saint-Domingue moved to Paris and met the French Revolution in explosive ways.

"Revolts Under the Tropics"

Tensions had been rising since reform of the exclusif in 1784. The Chambers of Commerce in metropolitan France were apprehensive. Particularly since the unpopular Franco-British Eden-Rayneval free-trade treaty of 1786 had been ratified, exasperated merchants believed they had been ignored by the monarchy. Colonial spokesmen were equally on edge: fearing a repeal of the arrêt, they were pushing for additional reforms. In 1788, the situation reached a crisis point in Saint-Domingue as the colonial administration collapsed, preceding revolutionary events in the metropole by months. Although a certain amount of dispute between the colonial governor and the *intendant* was expected, irreconcilable differences between governor Marie-Charles du Chilleau and intendant Barbé-Marbois incited the collapse of executive power on the island long before news of the storming of the Bastille arrived. A site of encounter between imperial tensions and the French Revolution, the "last white revolt" of the ancien régime also constituted the first phase of the revolution of Saint-Domingue, so much so that its effects continued to be felt well beyond 1789.[4]

These events originated in the harvest failures of 1788. It is generally accepted that a rapid escalation in food prices was a significant driving force in the French Revolution, but the scarcity of flour in Europe also had devastating effects on colonists, as import levels from the metropole plummeted. The significance of flour did not reside exclusively in its nutritional qualities: it also played a major role in the cultural imagination of the ancien régime. In the colonial context, from Louisiana to the West Indies, the consumption of bread was saturated with meaning, producing a common cultural identity for the metropole and the colony. Food was a symbol of resistance to "savagery" and barbaric practices. To eat bread, and demand the right to do so, was to activate a sense of Frenchness. The consumption of flour was also designed to distinguish the alimentary regime of the colonists from that of the enslaved, who relied on the local production of sorghum, yam, and banana: neither the *grand blanc* (literally the "great white," that is, a wealthy planter) nor the *petit blanc* (the poorer "small white") could openly consume African products without endangering their status. While it is highly likely that colonists violated these rules in private, the composition of public meals fulfilled an essential sociopolitical function. Moreover, contrary to legal regulations, people did not always set aside plots of land for food crops. The fact that Bordeaux was a main supplier of these products explains why, on April 30, 1789, an explosive situation resulted from the Parliament of Guyenne—the supreme court in the province—responding to the metropolitan grain crisis by prohibiting the export of flour. Hispaniola was already experiencing unrest, however, before this news reached the Americas.[5]

In a serious crisis, the exclusif mitigé regime allowed for the suspension of prohibitive laws. During natural disasters such as hurricanes and earthquakes, or wars, the governor and intendant could permit the importation of flour from North America. This common practice tended to make the "exception" the norm. In 1789, the flour crisis was judged serious enough for the possibility of implementing this suspension to be considered. As events unfolded, the governor and *intendant* clashed over how to proceed; Du Chilleau wanted to open the ports to foreign trade; Barbé-Marbois did not.

This opposition sets into sharp relief two different conceptions of the empire as well as two distinct career strategies. Barbé-Marbois had been specifically appointed as *intendant* to ensure the arrêt of August 30, 1784, was strictly enforced, and he had secured this highly coveted position through his expertise in American affairs. As French consul general to America he had raised questions about Virginia to Thomas Jefferson, inspiring the latter's famous *Notes on the State of Virginia*. Having married the daughter of the governor of Pennsylvania, Barbé-Marbois had procured the consulate of New York for his brother. He personified the new category of administrator that emerged in the aftermath of the Seven Years' War and for whom service to the state appeared irreconcilable with local concerns. As Barbé-Marbois believed the law of the king and thus of the metropole had to be strictly applied, he was a highly unpopular intendant. The arrival of the Marquis Du Chilleau at the end of 1788 marked the return of a state official who evidently conformed to a traditional model. A veteran of the American Revolutionary War, Du Chilleau was determined to push aside the long-established intendant, placate the colonists and, perhaps, preserve his own economic interests. He was embedded within Saint-Dominguan society and, like many other colonial officials, a landowner through his wife. Colonists had petitioned Du Chilleau before his departure from Paris, pleading the case for free trade and the needs of planters. On his arrival in Saint-Domingue, the governor began to utilize colonial networks and turn public opinion against the intendant while mobilizing the Chamber of Agriculture, which acted as an informal opposition body. The two men's diametrically opposed interests sustained a debate of political economy that was not without its paradoxes: the modern statesman, Barbé-Marbois, defended the most traditional doctrine, and the more traditional figure, Du Chilleau, embraced new ideas.[6]

To enable the colonial government to maintain control over imports, both in terms of quantity and price, Barbé-Marbois suggested employing official Saint-Domingue vessels to bring flour from the United States. The intendant also planned to commission a number of merchants to supply the island. Du

Chilleau denounced these ideas, however, arguing that utilizing coast guard vessels in such a way would allow smuggling to flourish. Moreover, the selected traders would be regarded as privileged beneficiaries of an arbitrary power. The governor went beyond these pragmatic considerations and made an explicit appeal for free trade, at least in the short term, in line with "economist" thinking of the 1760s. Du Chilleau believed opening the flour trade to foreigners would avoid monopolistic agreements that hindered competition: "thus allowing the Americans to contribute to this introduction, it is at the same time introducing abundance, without harming the merchant or the consumer." Barbé-Marbois finally yielded to his colleague's resolution, and the importation of flour through all ports—not just the three ports d'entrepôt—was authorized by an ordinance passed on March, 30 1789. While for the intendant this was a regrettable but necessary development, for the governor it was merely the first step in a far more radical project.[7]

Having visited the underdeveloped Southern Province of Saint-Domingue, Du Chilleau became convinced something had to be done to revitalize the region. The province had been relatively neglected by both the French slave trade and American merchants, partly because of restrictions on access. To remedy this, Du Chilleau signed an order on May 9, 1789, opening three ports—Les Cayes, Jérémie, and Jacmel—to practically unrestricted foreign trade for five years, replicating legislation already in force in Martinique and Guadeloupe. In addition, arguing over the shortage of cash, he wanted to allow US exports of sugar and coffee, but only up to the value of the food imported by the Americans, passing the relevant legislation on May 27, 1789, against Barbé-Marbois's advice. To the intendant, a connoisseur of smuggling practices, these measures signified total removal of the exclusif and, therefore, destruction of the French empire. So vehement was Barbé-Marbois's opposition that on the day Du Chilleau passed the relevant legislation, he presented a long speech to the Sovereign Council of Port-au-Prince (the equivalent of a colonial *parlement*, the highest court of justice and political arena of the ancien régime) denouncing the absurdity of introducing the measure while Britain retained its prohibitive system. "These generous principles," he argued, put France at the mercy of other nations, "attentive to our errors, to our slightest faults, ready to take advantage." The governor, unaware of the impending danger, had single-handedly ratified the orders in defiance of colonial law. This conflict between the two men, which was also between two contrasting models of administration and political economy, would trigger a full-fledged pre-revolutionary crisis.[8]

Once public, the conflict spread, dividing the whole of white society into two fiercely opposed factions. This was no longer a simple personal feud but a symptom of a deep colonial crisis, a central element of which was the substantial debt planters owed to traders in France, as Barbé-Marbois emphasized:

> Within three days this beautiful colony will be like St. Barthelemy or
> St. Eustatius, a universal *entrepôt* for all commercial people: the French
> nation is not excluded; but she will be least favored because she is cred-
> itor of the colony for huge sums, and all newcomers will be preferred.

If unrestricted trade was open to foreigners it would be too easy for planters to
ignore the claims of French creditors. The price of flour was far from the only
issue. Barbé-Marbois managed to rally a significant number of Le Cap's urban
elite against Du Chilleau, the base of his support including *commissionnaires* of
the recently created Chamber of Commerce. Due to an economic boom the socioeconomic composition of Saint-Domingue's colonial elite had evolved since
the 1760s. Through a strategy of land investment and vertical integration, and
thanks to the debts owed by many planters, traders had acquired more and
more plantations in Saint-Domingue. Moreover, many *commissionnaires* managed them in lieu of absentee owners, who surmised they were being swindled.
A planter even published a whole statement of grievances to complain about
how his commissionaire conducted a reckless business without any "power of
attorney." The increasing influence exerted by such merchants also explains why
the majority of colonists supported Du Chilleau. Heavily indebted to French
merchants, many found the American alternative appealing. Nevertheless, support for the governor was not restricted to privileged grands blancs: the more
modest sections of the white population, designated the petits blancs, were well
aware of the difference in price between American and French flour. The resulting
"clamor" for free trade with America ran contrary to the expectations of political
rhetoric in the metropole, where moral economy involved tighter regulations on
the market. In contrast, petits blancs were demanding "less intervention."[9]

Du Chilleau, aware that Barbé-Marbois had denounced him, decided to
pre-empt the recall he believed imminent and left for France on July 10, 1789,
intending to justify himself in front of the Ministry of the Navy. Despite his
departure, Du Chilleau was regarded by the Saint-Domingue colonists as the
champion of their cause. The planters, who had begun to appropriate "patriotic" slogans from the metropole and adapt them to their own agenda, regarded
Barbé-Marbois as the epitome of "ministerial despotism." When news of the
storming of the Bastille reached Saint-Domingue, colonial authority had already
been substantially weakened. Revolutionary events in Paris were reinterpreted
in the light of this home-grown conflict and became the pretext for revolt against
this "ministerial despotism," a popular denunciation in France, most often aimed
at the Finance Comptroller General.[10]

The white colonists, inspired by the American model and galvanized by the
Parisian patriots, wanted to follow in the footsteps of the 1776 insurgents while
remaining in a "regenerated" imperial framework. On September 23, 1789,

an angry crowd in the Northern Province burned an effigy of the despised intendant. By October 26, demonstrations in Cap Français were so violent that Barbé-Marbois was forced to flee on a ship bound for the metropole. Although this uprising was in many ways a continuation of the white revolts that had punctuated the colony's history, the revolutionary dynamic changed the political stakes decisively at a time when new sources of political legitimacy were surfacing. Attributing the events entirely to rejection of the exclusif would be excessive, as numerous grievances against the intendant had accumulated. A scrupulous official in favor of financial austerity, Barbé-Marbois had exacerbated the grounds for discontent. Advocating centralization, he had suppressed the Sovereign Court in Le Cap in the name of administrative rationalization. He had also obstructed planters' endeavors to be represented at the Estates General. But according to the intendant himself, the insurrection was first and foremost a revolt against the exclusif; everything else was a smoke screen. In a document justifying his conduct, he explained these "revolts in the tropics."

> It is because I did not wish to contribute to the admission of foreigners; it is because I have made every effort to prevent the execution of this design, and I would say that, thanks to my care, it has only been fatal to me, if I could find something fatal in events which were the necessary consequence of my attachment to my duties: in a conduct which I believe to have been useful to six million of my fellow citizens.

According to merchant lobbyists and many planters, 6 million people were employed by the colonial economy. Beyond this clash between the two representatives of the French monarchy in the colony, cracks within Saint-Dominguan society broke open in the summer of 1789. It was in light of this conflict that the fate of the colonies would be debated.[11]

Colonial Lobbyists Confront the Constituent Assembly

When news of Du Chilleau's actions reached France, the Chambers of Commerce railed against the governor, accusing him of destroying the entire French economy. When Du Chilleau docked on August 23, 1789, he arrived in a country that had abolished the nobility's privileges and feudal rights almost three weeks earlier. In response to the demands of many merchants, he was imprisoned in Nantes before being recalled to Paris. The governor's arrival placed the exclusif issue in the spotlight: colonial tensions were shifting from the colony to the metropole, where the stakes would be transformed in the context of revolutionary Paris.[12]

Despite the strenuous demands of planters, as a colony Saint-Domingue could not secure legal representation at the Estates General. Nevertheless, a small number of prominent planters, mystified by Louis XVI's reluctance to recognize their status, had met in secret, listed their grievances in *cahiers de doléances*, and elected a deputation of thirty-one members, half of whom—mostly absentee planters who owned more than twenty-five slaves each—resided in Paris. A majority of Saint-Domingue's deputies were of noble lineage, and three-quarters owned sugar plantations. A lobby group calling itself the "colonial committee" had been created in Paris around Louis-Marthe de Gouy d'Arsy, initially to protest the abolition of the Sovereign Court in Cap Français. The group then attempted to negotiate inclusion in the Estates General. Saint-Domingue's lobbyists were indignant that "these islands whose trade had doubled Nantes, enriched Marseille, La Rochelle and Le Havre, made Bordeaux one of the most flourishing cities in Europe," would not be represented, leaving "their enemies without opponents." They also argued that representatives of Saint-Domingue should be counted among the nobles since many counts and knights owned plantations in the colonies. "Blood relationships," they claimed, united "the nobility with Saint-Domingue" to the point that the "Court had become Creole by alliance." Although the king rejected their request, they did manage to secure the admission of six members to the National Assembly. Reform of the exclusif held a prominent position in their cahiers de doléances (list of grievances). Two points were considered indispensable: perpetuation of the introduction of foreign flour and the admission of foreigners to all ports in the colony.[13]

In response to these demands, the metropolitan ports' Chambers of Commerce presented themselves as a body, one distinct from the Third Estate and the nobility, and therefore capable of steering future reforms. Essentially, they saw themselves as a fourth order to lead the way. The king rejected their demands as well. The ports' cahiers wanted to abolish the 1786 free trade treaty with Britain and replace the decree of August 30, 1784, which they considered too lax, with a total exclusif. Interpreted as a concession to the United States under the 1778 Treaty, the law was believed to greatly penalize French interests. According to the Chambers of Commerce, not only did the French fail to penetrate the US market, which was monopolized by the British, but the United States had also seized a large part of the colonial market through smuggling. This failure could be explained by economic factors but at the time was understood in moral terms relating to American "ingratitude" and therefore justified the refusal of any new concessions. Fifty-nine merchants petitioned Louis XVI, calling for liberty and protection, compatible with privileges the merchants intended to reform among themselves. The colonial exclusif was one of these priorities, and since the king did not accede to their requests, it prompted the dispatching of the "extraordinary deputies for manufacture and trade" (*députés extraordinaires des manufactures et du commerce*) from the colonial ports to Versailles. The Chamber of Guyenne called on the merchants to join together "to form a mass of enlightenment and activity capable of counterbalancing the efforts which the deputies of the colonies, admitted to the National Assembly, would not fail to do in order to escape the prohibitive regime to which they were subjected." Their long-standing lobbying experience enabled them to organize effectively and form a merchants' committee, which, despite assuming a national dimension, represented only a fraction of French commerce in the port cities.[14]

The conflict between Barbé-Marbois, considered in the metropole as the savior of the maritime provinces, and Du Chilleau, champion of the colonists, was supposed to become the final battle in a long controversy that had started decades earlier. Nevertheless, the existence of La Société des Amis des Noirs (Society of the Friends of the Blacks) created by Jacques-Pierre Brissot and Etienne Clavière in February 1788, radically transformed the political landscape. This society, which included among its members patriotic deputies such as Lafayette and Honoré-Gabriel Riqueti de Mirabeau, in coordination with the British Society for Effecting the Abolition of the Slave Trade, aspired to immediately prohibit the slave trade and improve the lives of the enslaved in the short term, while gradually implementing full abolition. Initially the society included slaveholders interested in new economic ideas, such as Charles-Malo and Alexandre de Lameth, but these veterans of the American war left as they began to understand the philanthropists' ultimate goal and later became fierce adversaries of the society. Although the objectives of the society may seem rather moderate in retrospect, they were deeply unnerving for colonists and merchants in the revolutionary context of the time.[15]

From these concerns another lobby group emerged, holding its first meeting on August 20, 1789, at Hôtel Massiac in Paris. The group consisted of some of the richest colonists, such as the Marquis de Gallifet, and merchants, including the immensely wealthy Stanislas Foäche from Le Havre. Several colonial societies based in the Atlantic ports of Bordeaux and La Rochelle also affiliated themselves with the Parisian group. Club Massiac sought to bring colonists and traders together to defend a white-only plantation economy. Some large landowners— mostly absentees, some of whom had never set foot on Saint-Domingue—were willing to make concessions on a commercial level. But in November 1788, the former colonial official, planter, and political theorist, Pierre-Victor Malouet, who would become a prominent member of Club Massiac and an influential deputy in the Constituent Assembly, had warned against demands for freedom of trade. In his eyes, the colonists would always be "unfavorably viewed by the public and the government when [they] would ask, as has been done so far, for connections that are directly contrary to the interests of the metropole." Club Massiac was intended to advance imperial interests that far exceeded the particular interests of colonists or traders. Their political economy standpoint emphasized the intimate connections between "Agriculture, Manufacture, and Trade." More circumstantially, these imperial agents worried that the panic unleashed by the Great Fear (the period of panic by peasants in the summer of 1789) and revolutionary enthusiasm would derail the French colonial system. During the night of August 4, a few liberal nobles had come close to throwing slavery away, along with most feudal rights, and Club Massiac did not want such an event to happen again. The Declaration of Rights of Man and Citizen posed an acute threat but also could be weaponized against abolitionists through articles 2 and 17, which sanctified property rights. From the outset, the group was concerned about the colonial narrative to be submitted to the National Assembly and the response this would receive from journalists and the French public, so it was intent on actively silencing disputes over colonial matters by interceding in quarrels between colonists and merchants.[16]

At first, rich planters of color tried to join together with Club Massiac. Although they were fighting the racial discriminations they suffered in West Indies, many also saw themselves as slaveholders who had shared interests with white colonists. In early September 1789, Vincent Ogé, one of their main spokesmen, addressed Club Massiac in a speech emphasizing their commonalities. He wanted to contribute to the "conservation of our properties" and insisted that free trade should be granted to Saint-Domingue. This attempt failed, however; the white colonists wanted to treat rich planters of color as subalterns and argued they formed a necessary "intermediate class" between them and the enslaved. The rebuke prompted influential free people of color to organize and create the Société des Citoyens américains, spearheaded by lawyer Etienne Dejoly and powerful planter activist from the south of the colony, Julien Raimond.[17]

Connections between these lobbies and Saint-Domingue varied considerably. Although most members of these pressure groups belonged to the economic and noble elite, they were part of divergent colonial networks and defended opposing agendas. The deputies of the colonies regarded themselves as agents of the *habitants*, who lived off the products of their own plantations. By contrast, Club Massiac consisted mostly of absentee planters—French residents with colonial plantations and metropolitan feudal properties, many of whom were also involved in trade. The Chambers of Commerce considered the prohibitive regime to be as essential to the survival of the colonial economy as the slave trade itself. For the merchants' committee, it was a question of "presenting a great measure of resistance to the torrent of new opinions and to the influence of the Americans"; colonial deputies were no less their enemies than the Société des Amis des Noirs. Merchants utilized a variety of recently published books celebrating the British imperial political economy to support their argument, recycling the British proslavery rhetoric and translating pamphlets that praised the triumphs of the British Navigation Act. At the same time, they claimed that the Amis des Noirs were complicit with a British conspiracy aiming at destroying the French colonial trade, the nation's power, and its revolution.[18]

In a way, contrasting "colonial" and "anticolonial" groups is misleading. The Société des Amis des Noirs should be considered a colonial lobby group. Brissot and Clavière shared economic ideas that were readily hostile to the exclusif with Saint-Domingue representatives; as founders of a Gallo-American society, they had even written a renowned pamphlet on Franco-American trade. This philanthropic society considered the colonial system as much—if not more—in terms of economic efficiency, from a perspective inherited from the physiocratic school, as by moral principles. In his 1786 book, *The Influence of the American Revolution on Europe*, Enlightenment philosopher par excellence Marie Jeanne Antoine Nicolas de Caritat, the Marquis de Condorcet, praised the French government's liberal policy that favored the early American Republic. According to Condorcet, the opening of trade had ensured peace in the region by prompting the United States to renounce territorial expansion. On this subject, Condorcet, who had attacked the institution of slavery in his *Réflexions sur l'esclavage des nègres*, was an ally of the colonists against the merchants. Moreover, planters referred to the same intellectual authorities; colonist Jean Barré de Saint-Venant, for instance, drew heavily from the books of Adam Smith when defending the decree of August 30, 1784. In 1789, although hostile to the admission of colonists to the National Assembly, Brissot justified smuggling between the Americans and the planters, because "the irons which Europe impose on them are against the nature of things." He also condemned the "contract of slavery" imposed on the colonies by the metropole.[19]

In 1789, there was no single colonial lobby group but instead several parties with their own agendas, although fragile alliances were emerging. All these groups had deputies at the National Assembly, published multiple pamphlets, and submitted petitions. Adding to the cacophony, the US minister at the Court of Versailles—homas Jefferson, and his successor, William Short—were also working behind the scene, pushing for a relaxation of the prohibitive regime.

Revolutionary Rhetoric: How to Regenerate the Colonies?

Despite Club Massiac's insistence, Saint-Domingue's deputies refused to abandon their demands for trade reform. Confrontations between representatives of the colonists and the merchants in the National Assembly were extremely hostile. These discussions did not take the form of one long debate but occurred during many heated exchanges, often accompanied by pamphlets published by the various groups involved. Together they present a good case study of the transfer and adaptation of colonial questions to the context of revolutionary Paris.[20]

The arguments deployed by the different parties changed over time. The colonists endeavored to present themselves as the apostles of liberty by employing physiocratic considerations and the rhetoric of natural law, popularized by the philosophes. Like the economists, the colonists claimed to be fighting against monopolies that benefited only particular interests, as insisted by Deputy Jean-François de Reynaud de Villeverd, a former governor in Saint-Domingue:

> France has no interest in the flour trade with the Colonies, that it is a real monopoly, not as the traders were adroitly slipping in favor of the state, but in their favor only, and even to the detriment of the state.

The deputies opposed the despotism of the minister of the navy who had "refused the aid of humanity, commanded imperiously by NATURAL LAW; he had set against this irresistible law the PROHIBITIVE LAWS which condemned the colonies to famine." At a time when the American example was constantly invoked in debates and when the French Revolution appeared to bring two countries labeled "friends of freedom" closer, Nicolas Robert de Cocherel and Reynaud systematically referred to the United States, while traders spoke of the "foreigner," alluding to the English enemy. In short, the colonists appeared to be saying nothing more than the patriotic representative Jean-Paul Rabaut-Saint-Étienne: "Like the Americans, we want to regenerate ourselves."[21]

In a more precarious manner, the colonists also used the philanthropic argument employed in 1783: to refuse the American supply was to condemn the enslaved to death. The deputies went so far as to claim that the annual deaths of 13,000 enslaved people in Saint-Domingue were due to the colonial exclusif rather than any ill-treatment. The colonists were utilizing liberal rhetoric, Americanophilia, and philanthropy, concepts intended to position them among the "patriots" of the Assembly and that formed the basis of arguments by the Société des Amis des Noirs. Lafayette and others were responsive to economic arguments; yet their approval remained unspoken. Admission of colonists to the National Assembly, in spite of vehement opposition from Mirabeau, had angered the Société des Amis des Noirs. Presumably, the colonists were not addressing their outright enemies but the many deputies who had little knowledge of colonial and economic issues. Saint-Domingue's deputies, who believed they could find their labor force from the British anyway, went so far as denouncing the atrocities of the slave trade and requesting that the issue of abolition be debated.

They unabashedly contrasted the horrors of deportation with the good treatment supposedly received by Africans on the plantations.[22]

This ploy proved extremely dangerous. The traders countered the colonists point by point. Like their opponents, they cast themselves as true "patriots," as the merchant elite had done in the provinces, notably by leading municipal revolutions at a local level. In their pamphlets, the traders portrayed planters as rich aristocrats concerned only with their own interests. This tactic was made all the easier as every one of the colonial deputies was noble and wealthy. In addition, the merchants borrowed from the Société des Amis des Noirs' rhetoric the hateful image of an ever more insatiable colonist. They pointed out that flour was not part of enslaved people's diet, which consisted mainly of cassava, yams, and bananas grown on plantation plots reserved for that purpose. The merchants contrasted the lives of the white planters, this privileged few, against the "six million Frenchmen," workers, and manufacturers that the end of the exclusif would throw into misery and onto the streets. Consequently, France appeared dependent on the various elements of its colonial economy: the slave trade and the prohibitive regime.[23]

Beyond political rhetoric, the colonial framework endured a frontal challenge. On one hand, planters demanded the colonies be associated with "regeneration," thus guaranteeing them the political and economic rights enjoyed by citizens of metropolitan France. On the other, they pleaded for the maintenance of their specific regime: the preservation of slavery and discrimination against free people of color. Saint-Domingue deputy Gouy d'Arsy, following in the footsteps of Hilliard d'Auberteuil, repeatedly claimed the colony—which contributed the most to France's economic prosperity—was the most significant province in the kingdom. The mythical donation with which the colony allegedly gave itself to the monarch marked the existence of a formal contract anticipating the regeneration of the nation. Early settlers had "founded, cleared, and cultivated the largest, most beautiful, most productive Province of France." Deputies also explained that they shared the same "French blood," which had not "degenerated" in America. They also frequently utilized a family metaphor to establish an analogy with Corsica, the political representation of which did not pose the same problems. Saint-Domingue belonged to the "ENTIRE FAMILY"; "The islands of America were the SISTERS of Corsica, which had the right to be represented; Saint-Domingue was ultimately the ELDER and CAPITAL of the colonies." Planters even lamented their "enslavement" to commercial interests, using a striking metaphor in the context of the plantation complex.[24]

Resistance to these demands by merchants radicalized the colonists' agenda. As positions hardened, new theorizations of the French empire emerged. "If Saint-Domingue is not a French colony, it is even less a French province . . . and the only denomination that suits it is that of the French American province," explained Cocherel, who cited Montesquieu to resolve contradictions within his argument. The metropolitan constitution could not apply to Saint-Domingue, because the "province" was the fruit of a "mixture [of] diverse peoples, ... some French, Spanish, English, Dutch by birth, ... the others snatched from the burning climate of Africa." Given the cultural differences in this combination, a "mixed constitution" was needed to justify the colonists' demands. Cocherel solicited a "decision on the question of prohibitive laws," which he deemed to always be prejudicial. He also consented to "the abolition of the slave trade ... if it was the wish of the National Assembly." He was thus ready to sacrifice the French slave trade, believing that the British could advantageously substitute for Nantes, Marseilles, and Le Havre merchants. This speech demonstrated that planters and traders were still at odds. It also raises a larger issue: as the nation was being regenerated, what did it mean to be a colonist and a French citizen?[25]

Responding in the name of port merchants, Pierre François Blin defined the aims of the colonial project: colonies should be considered less as subject entities than as a "species of allied powers, federative parts of the nation." Yet he concluded that they should not be represented in the National Assembly and that the colonial link must be ensured by the executive power of the king himself. The word colony, as he later explained, was almost synonymous with "monopoly":

> For if we suppress the monopoly, colonial relations can no longer exist; if there are no longer any colonial relations, there are no more colonies. The countries bearing this name become independent powers, for which it would be absurd for the nations of Europe to pay protection costs.

Distance and the absence of territorial continuity justified the existence of such a coercive system. This was one of the reasons that Saint-Domingue could not be assimilated into either a province or a *département*, a designation created in December 1789 to avoid territorial inequalities in the metropole. In this sense, the prohibitive regime was not a mark of subjection; it was merely a tax paid to the nation; a tax levied by the mother country. Mercantile elites in French metropolitan port-cities echoed the same arguments and orchestrated a campaign against free trade and abolitionism. Rouen's municipal council warned in a letter addressed to the National Assembly that once entry into the colonies is "open and free, these are not colonies anymore; this is then the market, the common property of mercantile nations." Repealing the exclusif and the slave trade, they argued, would sabotage the wealth and power of the French nation, undermine the influence of the French government on the "political system of Europe," and help Britain attain global hegemony.[26]

The saying "Un bon averti en vaut deux"—a French adage meaning someone who has been warned and is on his guard becomes formidable to his enemies—summarized the dilemma the National Assembly had to resolve. Four allegorical women and one man, depicted as the Greek God Hermes, represented different aspects of the complex equation. The woman described as "the colony" occupies the center of the print and looks toward the woman representing "France." That woman holds a shield where the new motto of Revolutionary France is inscribed: "the Nation, the Law, the King." Hermès, the messenger and the god of trade, whispers warnings in France's ear: "Do not think you can deceive me, do not think you can escape me on earth and on the waves. My power extends to the end of the world. My vengeance awaits you." On the left side of the print, the United States seems skeptical of the interaction while England (on the Leopard) is offering wealth to the French colony. In the background, ships emphasize the trading stakes of the decision the National Assembly has to make. The colony is certainly drawn to France's promise of extending freedom, but her right hand, concealed, is also holding England's note. The author of the print suggests that the independence of the United States and British imperial greed threaten French sovereignty over its colony, which is in the position of making its own choices.

The exclusif debate touched on something deeper than the mere legality of foreign trade in the colonies: it fundamentally questioned the compatibility of nation-state building with the maintenance of a colonial empire. Raynaud, another colonial deputy, cited the liberal economist Anne Robert Jacques Turgot and argued that within a confederal framework, colonies were equal to the metropole and should be allowed to trade with foreign powers. *Abbé* Sieyes himself, who had inspired the beginning of the Revolution with his publication *What Is the Third Estate?*, shared this opinion, although he viewed national unity as sacred: France was and should be "a single whole, subject in all its parts to a common legislation and administration." He also stated that the "islands of America and other distant possessions . . . should have a representation within them; and only a federal deputation to the metropole."[27]

The confrontation between Cocherel and Blin, against a backdrop of the campaigning Société des Amis des Noirs, thus laid the foundations for a debate over the need to adopt a confederal regime, with stakes that went beyond slavery. The ideal of a federal republic had already been championed by a body of doctrines in the 1770s: philosophers Claude-Adrien Helvétius, Paul-Henri Thiry Baron d'Holbach, and Gabriel Bonnot de Mably, along with lesser known authors such as Jean-Dedieu Raymond Boisgelin de Cucé, had enthused over this political model. The idea materialized during the grandiose celebrations of the Federation on July 14, 1790: the unity of the nation was to emerge from its parts. A backlash against the confederal idea would arise later, when

Figure 3.1 Un bon averti en vaut deux. Anonymous, 1790. Bibliothèque nationale de France, collection Hennin, 10894; collection De Vinck, 1206, etching, 9.5 x 14.5 cm.

départements were regarded as potential counterrevolutionary forces, working against the nation's will. The notion of the "one and indivisible Republic" developed progressively, through parliamentary debate, territorial reforms, and political clashes. From this perspective, the colonial question was at the same time in contradiction with and central to the "political matrix" constitutive of national sovereignty.[28]

Being intertwined with notions of personal freedom, the very definition of "liberty of commerce" in the colonial context endangered the slave trade. The Assembly charged a special committee with presenting a report to the deputies on this issue. The text they produced fully justified the concerns of Club Massiac. The authors emphasized the countless contradictions in the colonial debate:

> [The colonists] ask for this liberation in the name of the liberties which have just been born among us, but which they surely hoped did not resound too strongly: in the midst of these brilliant houses which owe their full value to the entire enslavement of those whose work makes it prosperous and rich. Thus, by one of those moral contradictions so striking but so common, what Commerce calls abuse, and the colonists the use of liberty, is claimed by those whose entire fortune rests upon the maintenance of slavery.

The report did not pursue this logic any further but indicated how much the exclusif debate and reciprocal attacks—each side accusing the other of being aristocratic—threatened slavery following the Declaration of the Rights of Man and Citizen. As stated in a pamphlet published by Antoine Bonnemain, there could not be any colonial regeneration without the abolition of slavery. Since the text benefited neither colonists nor merchants, it is easy to understand why the Assembly did not discuss the ad hoc committee's report. Club Massiac was relieved. Reassuring its affiliated society in Bordeaux, lobbyists pronounced that "the quarrel has remained at the beginning of a trial which will most probably end without judgement."[29]

As the merchants were preventing the National Assembly from ruling, the colonists were gradually losing ground. Club Massiac, determined to bury the exclusif debate, strove to negotiate alliances with the merchants' delegates. The Chamber of Commerce of Nantes was pleased with the rapprochement made by the merchants and the "colonists of Paris" (Club Massiac), who were far more conciliatory than the "colonists of Versailles" (Saint-Domingue's deputies). The representative of La Rochelle distinguished between the party "attached to the deputies who are in the national assembly, the least numerous, fortunately, but the most dangerous by its principles of independence" and the "committee which desires a meeting and conciliation with commerce, the most consider-able in the number and importance of the owners who compose it." Many dep-uties, alarmed at the risk of bankruptcy, felt uncomfortable disrupting the most significant branch of external trade. The US chargé also believed the repeated argument that 6 million French depended on the exclusif was particularly com-pelling. They "know that the superior orders must necessarily be dissatisfied. They will not take the risk of alienating the popular layers." The deputies under-stood the situation not only from the point of view of Saint-Domingue but also by analogy with the pressure coming from people in the streets of the metropole. The decisions they would make were intended to placate Parisian and provincial public opinion. A merchant from Le Havre named Bégouën rebutted the dual challenge of the slave trade and the exclusif, arguing that not only "merchants and capitalists" would lose "400 or 500 million livres they are due," but "through an uninterrupted chain" the "innumerable class of workers of all kinds" would also be condemned to "idleness and misery." Traders, by posing under a banner of progressivism, had managed to present the colonists as a privileged elite. Just as the storming of the Bastille had been reread in the colonies through the prism of local conflicts, the exclusif controversy was reinterpreted in light of the met-ropolitan economic crisis.[30]

Saint-Domingue was not the only engine for colonial change. Rumors of revolt were also emerging from the Lesser Antilles. On December 3, 1789, Martinique's Colonial Assembly had not waited for metropolitan guidelines to end the entrepôt privilege enjoyed by Saint-Pierre and had opened all of its ports to foreign trade. Five days later, Guadeloupe's Assembly placated tensions between Basse-Terre and Pointe-à-Pître by granting the status of entrepôt to both port-cities. These decisions and the rumor of slave revolts in Martinique led the National Assembly to decree the formation of a committee specializing in colonial affairs, charging it with drawing up a specific constitution for the colonies. The plantation complex was so threatened that on March 1, at the Société des Jacobins, amis de la liberté et de l'égalité, Mirabeau argued powerfully in favor of abolition of the slave trade. In response, Club Massiac monopolized debates on the subject within the newly created Committee. As no members of the Société des Amis des Noirs had been appointed—although two colonists and two merchants were included—this was easy to achieve. Antoine Barnave, linked to the world of planters through his friends, the Lameth brothers, and a nephew of the Saint-Dominguan military officer and leader Jean-Jacques Bacon de la Chevalerie, was the most influential personality on the Committee and played a decisive role in drafting the report that would set the political tone of the Assembly. The appointment of a prominent speaker from the Constituent Assembly, a progressive patriot who wanted to make the Declaration of Rights of Man and Citizen the "national catechism," pleased both Société des Amis des Noirs and the left. Barnave, however, was sympathetic to the Chambers of Commerce's agenda. In the decisive report he presented on March 8, 1790, Barnave repeated the arguments advanced in 1784. Against "the great philosophical principles" and "the ingenious speculations," he maintained that "all parts of social existence are intimately bound and combined with the possession of a great trade, with that of our colonies." Saint-Domingue had somehow colonized the metropole and continued to energize it: "The value of production, the activity of manufactures, transport, internal trade are, for the most part, the effect of our relationship with them." In this way, national independence was irreducibly linked to the colonies, for without them "the English would gain unimpeded superiority over all the seas," and the Spanish allies would be condemned to give up their American possessions. Barnave adapted the argument developed under Choiseul and Vergennes to establish the paradox of linking the French Revolution to the maintenance of colonial rule. Any questioning would undermine the foundations of the economic and military power of France, which would present favorable grounds for a counterrevolution. In sum: without the exclusif, no colonies, and without colonies, no revolution.[31]

Although firmly committed to the principle of national unity, Barnave justified a legal dualism based on differentialist theories: the colonies, not included in the "provinces" yet forming "part of the empire," had to benefit from a specific constitution reconcilable with their "places," "manners," "climate," and "productions," namely, the institutions of slavery and color prejudice. But the report was also a straightforward justification of both the slave trade and the prohibitive regime, presenting these as essential ways of enabling France to accomplish its natural destiny as a great commercial power. "The prohibitive regime was, undoubtedly, an essential condition for the union of the metropole and the colonies; it [is] the foundation of the interest it has [in] their preservation, it [is] the compensation for the costs it was obliged to support to protect them." A draft decree, adopted without discussion, proclaimed that the Assembly had never planned to include the colonies in the constitution of the kingdom, yet consecrated the exclusif and the slave trade. Article 6 stated that the Constituent Assembly "had not intended to innovate in any of the branches of commerce, direct or indirect, of France with its colonies," even if the colonial assemblies should "express their wish that modifications be made to the prohibitive . . . regime."[32]

The committee had successfully evaded the main issue while reaffirming the legitimacy of the merchants' demands, both colonialist and protectionist. The deputy of La Rochelle explained: "Without naming things by their real name [the decree] upholds the slave trade, slavery, and the prohibitive regime." Pending the petitions developed in the French West Indies, the Constituent Assembly had merely extended ancien régime legislation. Institutional strategies, which had given the merchants and their influential spokesman, Barnave, the upper hand had prevented the colonial deputies from securing a repeal of the exclusif. While internal customs had been abolished, the Constituent Assembly did nothing to liberalize colonial trade, even consolidating the principle of the exclusif by positioning it as central to the French Revolution's success. The decree of March 8, 1790, presaged the decisions made on the East Indian Trade with the continuance of a privileged Company in the name of national sovereignty. These debates, however, had exposed a breach in the imperial framework of the ancien régime.[33]

Colonial Patriotism Between Revolution and Counterrevolution

As the colony remained in the throes of revolutionary turmoil, legal continuation of the prohibitive regime did not translate into practice. The new governor of the island, Antoine-Thomassin, Comte de Peynier, extended the sanctions granted by Barbé-Marbois, with one restriction: Americans were authorized to import flour and export colonial produce only through the three major ports d'entrepôt: Le Cap Français, Port-au-Prince, and Les Cayes. Although this distinction was insignificant from a French metropolitan perspective, as the geography of the island meant these ports were widely dispersed, it aroused strong hostility within the colony.

Figure 3.2 Portrait présumé de Barnave by Joseph Boze. Paris musées/ musée Carnavalet, D 4365, painting, 61 x 49.5 cm.

The colonists intended to take their part in patriotic regeneration. The patriotism of the white planters favored a free-trade policy combined with the political exclusion of free people of color. Despite the complacency of the Constituent Assembly, local assemblies had declared themselves revolutionary, regardless of decisions made in Paris, and organized their own elections to form a Colonial Assembly. One merchant noted the dangers this Colonial Assembly could pose to metropolitan commerce and "viewed the planters as in competition with the merchants of France." The first Colonial Assembly, held in the city of Saint-Marc on April 14, 1790, drafted a constitution for Saint-Domingue that included plans to end the exclusif. The elected president, Bacon de la Chevalerie, set the tone in his opening speech, promising to open ports to foreign trade and replace French commissionnaires with genuine local merchants. He drew on Hilliard d'Auberteuil's historical argument, according to which Saint-Domingue, a society of pirates, had allied itself with France and could recover its rights. The radical members of the Saint-Marc Assembly always denied wanting to secede from France, yet they supported bills on foreign trade that were regarded with suspicion in the metropole. The Colonial Assembly's policies were also controversial within the colony itself. One plantation manager, for instance, was concerned that Saint-Domingue would be forced "to claim the protection of another power of which they would soon become prey and who would exercise the prohibitive laws that primarily affect all minds with equal despotism."[34]

On May 28, 1790, the Saint-Marc Assembly, on its own initiative, enacted a constitutional principle that recognized Saint-Domingue's right to override the exclusif. The "preponderance of the French empire in the European political system," the colonial deputies justified, relied on the island's prosperity. Three weeks later it opened all colonial ports to foreign trade. Bacon de Chevalerie, utilizing powerful populist rhetoric, attacked the "odious source of monopolization, the matter of mercantile speculations that turn only for the benefit of some capitalists they enrich at the expense of the foreigner who sells as well as the farmer who consumes." Taxation on produce brought by foreigners was to back bounties for local merchants who would import foreign goods. This reform was both an end and a means: a means of securing a supply of arms in case of conflict with the governor and of asserting the political autonomy required to maintain discrimination. Since 1763, colonial society had witnessed the remarkable rise of an elite among free people of color, whose plantations in coffee, cotton, and indigo were flourishing. Julien Raimond, who had made a fortune in the southern part of Saint-Domingue, had become much more vocal about obtaining equal rights in the 1780s. White colonists were highly concerned about how this would be affected by the politics and attitudes of the metropole. There was also a social factor for this confrontation with the Constituent Assembly. The General Assembly consisted mainly of small coffee plantation owners who were commoners, unlike their "delegates" in Paris. Many did not feel represented by these counts and marquis they had fled from in order to resettle in a colony emancipated from ancien régime constraints.[35]

The situation between "patriots" and "loyalists" became explosive, with a local polarization reflecting extremely divergent interests. The division of the colony was reminiscent of the conflict between the governor and the intendant that had occurred just one year earlier. A composite coalition formed around the governor to protest against "abuses" committed by the Colonial Assembly. The exclusif was one of the factors driving the formation of the coalition. The Provincial Assembly in the north called on the governor to suppress the General Assembly. Its most radical members were at Saint-Marc and its president, who was from Le Havre, shared the concerns of Le Cap's merchants. Decisions made in Saint-Marc not only threatened the integrity of the transatlantic trade but also challenged local interests. The coastal captains of Port-au-Prince wrote to Peynier asking him to "prevent the execution of the decree [that] authorized the entry of foreigners into all ports." The "party of the governor" (also called the "white pompoms") was heterogeneous, with many free people of color rallying behind Peynier as the governor appeared to offer some level of protection from the discriminatory intentions of white planters. Conversely, Saint-Marc obtained assistance from the Western Assembly in Port-au-Prince, which advocated the rights of the petits blancs. The planters who lived off the produce of their own land and viewed the wealthy Parisian colonists with suspicion supported the Assembly's radical program. These divisions rapidly took a violent turn: on Peynier's orders, Colonel Thomas-Antoine de Mauduit du Plessis dissolved the Western Assembly on July 29, 1790, in fighting that resulted in around ten deaths. The General Assembly was suppressed and, on August 7, eighty-five of its most radical members embarked for France on the *Léopard*, earning them the name, the Léopardins. The exclusif shared the governor's victory, but as much as white planters had hated intendant Barbé-Marbois, the resentment they felt toward Governor Peynier increased. Retaliation came in March 1791, when Mauduit du Plessis was brutally assassinated.[36]

The former members of the Saint-Marc Assembly arrived in the metropole in September 1790, intending to plead their case and justify their actions. "The merchants in the three entrepôts," they argued, "monopolized basic necessities and sold them at a usurious price." However, their opponents in the Northern Assembly followed suit: the exclusif controversy yet again took center stage. Events in the Antilles threatened the alliance between colonists and merchants that Barnave and Club Massiac had worked so hard to establish. Barnave, fully aware of how the crisis had begun in 1788, wanted to stifle the matter as soon as possible and avoid any new discussions about the colonies. In his report of October 12, 1790, the speaker of the Colonial Committee attempted to prevent another debate by unilaterally condemning the Colonial Assembly and "sanctifying" the colonists' property—that is, slavery—but neither the risk of slave revolts nor Barnave's efforts could prevent another controversy. The recently arrived colonists resumed their campaign against the prohibitive regime, targeting Barnave, who embodied the great colonial trade, and flooding Paris with their publications. Thomas Millet blamed the merchants for "starving" the Antilles with a bogus account of Saint-Domingue's supposed flour scarcity. Mahy de Corméré insinuated that merchants, "attached to the sweet habit of an oppressive monopoly," had distorted the Colonial Assembly's policy. The colonists wanted to prove they were better Frenchmen than the merchants suspected of working for foreign interests. One of the Léopardins published a pamphlet in which he condemned Barnave and patriotically denounced the smuggling practiced by French slave traders. Metropolitan merchants were accused of trading "negroes brought by the English . . . as if they had brought them themselves," for whom they had only paid "half-price." The Léopardin attacked the "misguidance of merchants" that, by leading a fratricidal war against the colonies, gave credence to the erroneous idea that Saint-Domingue aspired to independence.[37]

The extraordinary deputies of Commerce replied to these accusations. The representative of the Nantes Chamber of Commerce condemned the "offensive abuses against trade," and claimed the only real concern was the considerable debt accumulated by planters. The lobbyist, though, did not want to revive old quarrels. It was necessary, he proclaimed, to "gather colonists and traders, but also the colonists between them, divided between several factions, strategies, and interests." At the same time, Club Massiac set up a "general commission" to bring together spokespersons from the different interest groups, hoping to find common ground and prove that "the systems of the *Amis des Noirs* and supporters of people of color" had caused the 'troubles." This commission held twelve meetings at the Hôtel Massiac between January 19 and April 3, 1791, but the attempt at reconciliation failed, with the exclusif once again being the stumbling block. The Ministry of the Navy had decided to activate the prohibitive legislation even though shipments of flour from France to the colonies were insufficient. In other words, nothing had changed; the same conflicts were repeated and the legislation remained in place.[38]

———

In general, colonial policy did not alter during the first eighteen months of the French Revolution. Slavery, the slave trade, and the political exclusion of free people of color remained intact. The Constituent Assembly, although generally labeled liberal, also consecrated the principle of the exclusif. Deputies dismissed the multiple free-trade reforms launched under Louis XVI's government and did not follow the US model, despite constant praise for the American Revolution. Concerns over commercial sovereignty trumped attempts at change. This conservatism and the failure to repair the cracks of the French-American alliance in Saint-Domingue were decisive factors in the unrest among white colonists.

The sequence of events between 1788 and the first half of 1790 can be characterized as a serious revolt in favor of free trade. The colonists, however, never forgot their numerical inferiority to the enslaved and did not imagine themselves capable of imposing colonial order without the support of a powerful army and navy. They started to envisage cession of the colony to the British, or even to the Spaniards, but they knew themselves to be too militarily weak to embrace independence and face so many domestic enemies alone. Furthermore, both the metropole and the colony were undergoing interconnected revolutions: the Saint-Domingue revolution took place in Paris as well as in Cap Français. This produced many discrepancies. The Constituent Assembly sanctified commercial legislation that contradicted measures taken in Saint-Domingue. In the name of patriotism, colonist deputies attempted to participate in the national regeneration that other patriotic colonists in the Antilles were revolting against. The debate over ideas became extraordinarily complex due to constant political readjustments. Divided into cliques, economic interests, and diverging political options, the white society of Saint-Domingue fragmented to a point that no unity was ever feasible. The exclusif may have been the first bone of contention, but the issue of race was even more divisive.

An Empire of Liberty? 1790–1793

> Our islands must have relations with the United States, it is the wish of
> nature; we must be bound with them by a treaty of commerce, it is the
> wish of our propriety, and that of our principles. To the league of kings,
> we must oppose the league of free peoples.
>
> Jean-Baptiste Boyer-Fonfrède, *Archives Parlementaires*,
> t. LIX, 16 (February 19, 1793)

When Girondin deputy Jean-Baptiste Boyer-Fonfrède advocated abolishing
the *exclusif* and opening the French Antilles to US trade on February 19, 1793,
he endowed a decree celebrating links between the American and French
Revolutions with anticolonial and anti-monarchist meaning. By decolonizing
the economic relationship between the French West Indies and the metropole,
he made Saint-Domingue the counterintuitive pinnacle of a republican project
based on international law and commercial diplomacy. Adopting this new legislation, the National Assembly proclaimed the creation of a new "empire of liberty," with Saint-Domingue at the center of the French-American relationship.
This new kind of empire was to establish a cosmopolitan order emancipated
from British despotism and colonialism, but the relationship between the "free
peoples" was still founded on the existence of racial slavery. This "liberty of commerce" remained very much compatible with personal unfreedom because the
sovereignty of the republic was prioritized over the extension of citizens' rights,
at least in the short term.

Boyer-Fonfrède's speech and its ensuing resolution—which proved to
be provisional—were the culmination of a particularly tortuous journey.
Between the Constituent Assembly reaffirming the principle of colonial monopoly in October 1790 and his speech in February 1793, four events of immense magnitude had redefined the colonial stakes of the French Revolution.
First was the revolt by mixed-race people demanding equal political rights,
initiated by the wealthy Vincent Ogé and Jean-Baptiste Chavannes. The

Entrepôt of Revolutions. Manuel Covo, Oxford University Press. © Oxford University Press 2022.
DOI: 10.1093/oso/9780197626382.003.0005

debacle resulting from this revolt and the cruel and prolonged executions of Ogé and Chavannes at Cap-Français in February 1791 brought the race issue to the fore, sparking extensive debates in the Constituent Assembly on the rights of free people of color. Second, the largest slave insurrection in world history erupted in August 1791 on the northern plain of Saint-Domingue, fulfilling the worst fears of planters and merchants and putting the entire colonial system at risk. The third event took place in the metropole on August 10, 1792, when the Insurrectionary Parisian Commune overthrew the monarchy: the National Convention established the République française the following month. Not only had the entirety of colonial society revolted, but the very nature of the empire's political system had also been transformed. Finally, Louis XVI was guillotined in January 1793, and France was on verge of global war with Britain and Spain.

In this explosive context, free trade seems to be a matter of secondary importance, but in reality the issue continued to shape the French colonial debate in Saint-Domingue, the metropole, and the United States. The free-trade controversy, while not taking precedence over the future of slavery, had become entangled with wider political, racial, and social issues. Debates relating to the colonial monopoly were not racially neutral, as they raised questions about aspects of citizenship, the contours of which had been redrawn within a republican framework. The exclusif not only enforced protectionism in economic terms; as a legal exception, it also created second-class citizens and second-class territories. If the principle of equality was to triumph, commercial restrictions imposed on the colonies had to be lifted. But at a time when the republican revolution blurred the markers of national loyalty, the exclusif tied the colonies to France. Therefore, the debate spurred a series of new imperial anxieties: in a political community without a king, what tied the colonies to the metropole? Was it commerce? What was the significance of this commercial relationship if the colonies could trade on the same footing as everyone else? Did racial identity ensure the durability of this bond? And what was the political meaning of trade? Should foreign trade be confined to republics and forbidden with monarchies? The main players employed commercial republicanism as an instrumental set of arguments, exhibiting striking inconsistencies and trying to build fragile coalitions. Yet clashing and constantly shifting political and economic positions gradually solidified. Contradictions were exposed and quickly became untenable under the fast-evolving circumstances. The vision of an empire of liberty led by sister republics—with Saint-Domingue at the center—was an impossibly paradoxical vision and bound to explode. The cauldron of racial and imperial war made that explosion take on a world-historical scale.

Race and Revolutionary Political Economy

Vincent Ogé, born around 1756 at Dondon in Saint-Domingue, was an affluent, free-born man of color. Apprenticed as a silversmith in Aquitaine, he had returned to the colony in 1776 and established himself as a merchant in Cap-Français. Having traveled to the metropole to settle a court case in 1788, on September 7, 1789, he unsuccessfully sought support from the Club Massiac for political equality between whites and free people of color. Two days later he joined the Society of American Colonists and Citizens of Color, participated in the drafting of their *cahier de doléances* and, alongside Etienne Dejoly and Julien Raimond, spoke on behalf of free people of color before the Constituent Assembly. On March 28, 1790, the Colonial Committee granted voting rights to all property owners aged twenty-five and over, without explicitly mentioning free people of color. Ogé returned to Saint-Domingue to ensure that this legislation was executed, but in October 1790, frustrated by the intransigence of white planters and unable to solidify a coalition of slave owners across the color line, he led an armed insurrection with fewer than 300 men alongside the so-called quadroon Jean-Baptiste Chavannes. Despite initial successes the insurgents were soon outnumbered by government reinforcements and forced to take refuge in the Spanish part of the island, Santo Domingo, in November 1790. Ogé and Chavannes were handed over to the Dominguan authorities, broken on the wheel—a horrific torture technique—and beheaded in Cap-Français on February 23, 1791.[1]

This gruesome punishment had considerable impact in the metropole and gave rise to two significant Constituent Assembly debates on the rights of free people of color in May and September 1791. The topic proved extraordinarily divisive. While Antoine Barnave, the former chair of the Colonial Committee, and his partisans were ejected from the Jacobin Club for their hostility to the rights of free people of color, the most progressive patriotic deputies, such as Abbé Grégoire, Maximilien de Robespierre, and Jérôme Pétion de Villeneuve, were furious with planters who opposed any reform. This debate, however, was not marshaled along emerging party lines.[2]

Merchants were particularly divided. At the beginning of the French Revolution, traders had been quite unanimous about the economic potential carried by the "national regeneration" and had taken the lead in the municipal revolutions that rocked maritime port-cities. Their confidence had also grown with the confirmation of the exclusif and the failure of the Amis des Noirs to effect regulations on the slave trade. Yet the coalition of business interests fractured over racial issues. In February 1791, Saint-Domingue's deputies wrote to forty metropolitan Chambers of Commerce and asked for their unconditional support for white supremacy and the political exclusion of free people of color. Nantes, Rouen, Dunkerque, Le Havre, and Abbeville enthusiastically responded while most other cities remained silent, and a couple of Chambers of Commerce vocally dismissed the deputies' strategy as counterproductive. A controversy crystallized in the clash between two major metropolitan ports: Bordeaux and Le Havre. Bordeaux, which derived much of its wealth from direct trade with the West Indies and exports of colonial produce to other European countries, was the wealthiest French port with a diversified trade. Its economy depended less on the slave trade than its competitors. The city also became a political hotbed of the French Revolution. Several new institutions and committees, including the Directory of the Department, the National Guard, the Jacobin Club, and the Chamber of Commerce of Bordeaux, mobilized by revolutionary activists who would later become the Girondin faction, supported the extension of po-litical rights to free people of color in the belief this would restore order in the Caribbean: the sine qua non of resuming business. According to Bordeaux officials, since the National Assembly was determined not to challenge slavery or the exclusif, an alliance with slave-owning people of color should be considered. However, merchants of Le Havre—the third most important French slave-trading port—rebuked the Bordelais and emphasized the colonial necessity of the "prejudice of color." Le Havre merchant Stanislas Foäche, a prominent member of Club Massiac and the backer of the greatest slave trading firm in Cap-Français, voiced his concerns on behalf of West Indian planters.[3]

On the other side of the Atlantic, white planters in Saint-Domingue viewed Bordeaux as a major threat to their interests. Bordeaux had already infuriated white activists by unambiguously condemning the "spirit of independence" dis-played by the first Colonial Assembly in 1790. A year later, the port of Gironde offered to send its own national guard to enforce the law on free people of color. In the eyes of many planters, this decision revealed the alignment of the city with the agenda of Amis des Noirs. At the festival of Federation organized by white colonists in Port-au-Prince to commemorate the storming of the Bastille on July 14, 1791, a replica of the Arc de Triomphe built for the occasion singled out Bordeaux as a "crying woman" among the geniuses of Le Havre, Nantes, Marseilles, and Dunkerque. A few months later, the municipality of Port-au-Prince accused Bordeaux of being responsible for "all the misfortunes that afflict this colony." The planters were enraged because Bordelais sea captains had called for racial equality between masters to present a united front against insurgent enslaved people. Some were also accused of trading with Black revolutionaries, "buying at a low price the goods they had looted from [the] plantations, and giving them in exchange ammunition to fight against the colonists." This trade is not utterly implausible, although for it to have been restricted to sea captains from Bordeaux is questionable.[4]

In metropolitan France, the clash over the rights of free people of color intermingled with debates about the colonial exclusif, but it took a turn that was less ideological than political. Bordeaux blamed the colonists for trading with foreigners, while supporting the rights of free people of color. More surprisingly, the Amis des Noirs, who had always expressed themselves in favor of free trade, started opposing the repeal of the exclusif. This reversal can be explained by analyzing abolitionist publications and speeches. Swiss banker and revolutionary Etienne Clavière, co-founder of the philanthropic society and a friend of its more famous leader, Brissot, published a controversial treatise in support of free people of color intended to break the alliance between white planters and merchants. He denounced the planters' secessionism and what he deemed to be the illegal opening of ports by the first Colonial Assembly. Although his tactics appeared to support the exclusif, this was not Clavière's intention at all: he rejected the measure's method and its political significance. By opening trade to foreigners, the Colonial Assembly had usurped the legislative initiative that should only be held by the true legislative body, the National Assembly.[5]

The issue was not free trade per se but national sovereignty. A colonist argued in a pamphlet that since the French did not take full advantage of the American Revolution, Saint-Domingue should become "the arbiter of a new treaty between North Americans and France." From his perspective, planters were entitled to negotiate free-trade agreements with Philadelphia and ignore Parisian supervision. This policy, which was enacted a few months later in the context of the slave insurrection, was exactly the point Clavière and other supporters of Brissot disagreed on. Like the planters, the Swiss banker praised free trade, citing the extremely wealthy island of Dutch Curacao as an exemplar, the *entrepôt* that attracted ships from across the world. The regeneration of the empire required this liberalization, but the measure had to originate from the metropole, not white supremacists in the colonies. The apparent contradiction illustrates the Amis des Noirs' dilemma, torn between their economic convictions and political tactics. Legislative unity had to be preserved to ensure the political rights of free people of color and, more broadly, national sovereignty.[6]

In fact, Clavière found much of his inspiration in the pamphlets of Raimond, the main spokesman for free people of color in the early stage of the French Revolution. Raimond had advocated abolishing sumptuary laws that prevented mixed-raced colonists from buying luxury goods. He regarded this discriminatory rule as "the most unpolitical ordinance since this destroyed a branch of metropolitan industry." Traders had more to gain if free people of color could buy these products. Elaborating on Raimond's point, Clavière viewed free people of color as the greatest citizens, truly emotionally attached to France. Citizens of color were considered to be appreciative consumers of French products, primarily luxury goods, and Clavière recycled the unfounded and racist cliché of the "mulatto" as a great lover of sophisticated ornaments, jewels, hats, and tunics. If the National Assembly extended political rights beyond the color line, the colonial exclusif would become unnecessary, as opening the colonial market would stimulate the economic growth of Saint-Domingue.[7]

The fraught colonial debate in May 1791 excited passions among Parisians. On the streets of the capital, white colonists attempted to intimidate supporters of free people of color, while pro-Jacobin crowds threatened to "loot" and "hang" colonial aristocrats. In this context, political economy arguments mixed with larger considerations of human rights and so-called racial science. Some deputies argued that the National Assembly needed to recognize free people of color as full citizens/consumers if it wanted to "regenerate" the empire. Trade relations should shape a national identity that benefited from what Abbé Grégoire termed "the mixture of races." The abbé argued that free people of color were superior because they combined European and African qualities. Raimond got his voice heard as well. Other supporters of citizens of color justified their legal and political integration with references to the circulation of French blood on both sides of the Atlantic, a metaphoric evocation of the circulatory phantasmagoria that pervaded the political economy at that time. In this sociopolitical imaginary, economic motives and racialized conceptions were mutually nourished. Frenchness, whiteness, and the colonial monopoly raised interconnected questions about national regeneration. Journalists on the left asked whether associations between colonies and metropole were "rights" or "purely and simply commercial relations"? "Were the colonies French, yes or no?"[8]

Deliberations on the rights of free people of color in the spring of 1791 crystallized colonial opinions and intertwined economic, political, and racial issues. Opposing the Jacobin left, the far-right Abbé Jean-Sifrein Maury presented a speech that encompassed the entire colonial system. On this occasion, colonial "resistance" was consistent with the counterrevolution, and it is not surprising that Maury emerged as its herald; he had already extolled the usefulness of local particularism because, in the logic of Old Regime Parlements, he believed privileges were a check on monarchical despotism. His speech, both long and complex, received impassioned applause, so much so that the National Assembly had his opinion printed and widely distributed. Its importance lay in Maury's attempt to link all the system's elements and demonstrate a coherent imperial imaginary. Building on the massive literature produced by white colonists justifying the "prejudice of color," Maury drew a distinction between the "free negro" and the "mulatto." In Maury's eyes, the former was far more "interesting" because "by his good behavior" and "work" he had secured his manumission; the "mulatto" was merely the "shameful fruit of libertinage," a "culpable mixture" engendering "an intermediate race." Rejecting "metaphysical constructions," Maury used foreign examples, employing the United States as a counterrevolutionary model: neither Virginia nor North Carolina had granted rights to the manumitted. He further noted that "naturalized" people in England did not enjoy the same rights as the English by birth. The racial question was therefore intertwined with a theme of national belonging: the "mulatto" could only be considered a naturalized foreigner. By maintaining family ties with the enslaved, the "mulattoes" presented a grave danger, and if they were awarded political rights, the white colonists—the "only ties with the mother country"— would be inclined to proffer themselves to England. The theory of colonial "degeneration," explored at length by eighteenth-century naturalists such as Georges-Louis Leclerc de Buffon, made its way into the Assembly's debates.[9]

As the colonies were indispensable to the economic power of the nation, Maury explained, the exclusif must therefore be maintained. Rebuffing the "heresies of the economists," who, since Anne-Robert-Jacques Turgot, had claimed that colonial independence would have little consequence, Maury suggested that suppression of the colonial monopoly and the ensuing secession "would sacrifice the entire kingdom." In his conclusion Maury declared that the whiteness of active citizens guaranteed the national belonging of the colonies and the commercial power of the nation. While France was confronted with internal and external enemies—the English and the Africans—whose alliance could subvert the kingdom, the exclusif preserved the national, economic, and racial border. Maury's intervention clarified and synthesized colonial thinking that redefined the line of demarcation between the metropole and the colonies, between whites and non-whites, between the national and the foreign. The deputy did not prevent a number of rights being granted to a small group of free people of color on May 15, 1791, but the printed speech circulated widely among planters in Saint-Domingue and became a kind of colonial manifesto, the catechism for opponents of the National Assembly's legislation.[10]

A reaction against awarding rights to free people of color arose swiftly in the French West Indies. Defeated on the slavery issue, the Amis des Noirs had only secured a precarious half-victory for free people of color born of free parents, people genealogically further removed from the stigma of slavery. Yet it was an already excessive concession to Saint-Domingue's white planters who immediately revolted against the National Assembly's new laws. They refused to regard mixed-race people as their equals and quickly mobilized their forces, persecuting, harassing, and even lynching anyone who would challenge their supremacy. Saint-Domingue's explosive situation coincided with the crisis that followed the king's failed flight in metropolitan France. Indeed, the kind had tried to flee France and gather foreign troops against the National Assembly in June 1791. The combined effects of both events incited a schism within the Jacobin Club. Barnave, a steadfast supporter of Louis XVI, came to embody both the monarchy and the colonial reaction.

Meanwhile, criticism of the United States was also growing, fueled by metro-politan merchants. The new republic was suspected of encouraging smuggling in the West Indies, and many French deputies felt the need to prevent any "increase in power" of such an ungrateful country, which aimed to "strip" France of its colonies. During the debate on free people of color, when Dupont de Nemours pleaded for liberalization of Saint-Domingue trade in favor of the United States, he was alone. This free-market rhetoric was out of touch with the mood of the Assembly. In a commercial report on September 22, 1791, François-Pascal Delattre, a member of Club Massiac, advocated the implementation of a French Navigation Act and denounced the "dangerous doctrine" of the "indefinite com-mercial freedom" demanded by "men of system, cabinet speculators, abstract theorists." Delattre recommended the English model, which had brought the "science of commerce to the highest degree of elevation that can be attained." England was "armed with prohibitions"; the "prohibitive regime" was therefore salutary. To furnish France with the economic power that suited its demographic weight and natural resources, it was necessary to exclude all foreign and parasitic carriers. Colonial trade was "the most precious of all for France" and required the "absolute exclusion of foreigners." Hostile economic protectionism abroad and racial discrimination were part of the same national security policy.[11]

This report paved the way for a major speech by Barnave on September 23, 1791. Taking the intangible nature of the colonial monopoly for granted, the deputy described a coherent colonial system. Contrary to the advice of French economists, the deputy asserted that the interests of merchants were "the interests of France itself." Barnave made the case that the kingdom was under threat in two ways: colonists might refuse to accept Assembly legislation and aspire to self-determination for their own preservation; and free people of color—who, as they had been "born there"—were devoid of the "spirit of re-turn" to France, had "no kind of connection with the mother country," and "would become truly by their spirit, by their instinct and by their feelings, ab-solutely foreign to France." White citizens, Barnave claimed, "never cease to be-lieve themselves children" of France. This analysis was based on racial prejudice, since many free people of color had spent a large part of their lives in France. To Barnave, the colonial exclusif, like racial discrimination, was part of the same policy, designed to ensure the loyalty of colonies he had always regarded as sus-pect. The line of demarcation between the national and the foreign, conceived in constitutively economic, social, and racial terms, was thus clearly drawn. Barnave's martial speech was accompanied by apocalyptic prophecies of the po-tential collapse of France. The Assembly, under the pressure of white planters, followed the deputy's lead and annulled the meager concessions extended to free people of color. The so-called disaster, however, had already begun: a slave insurrection had taken place in Saint-Domingue the previous month, and it was the white colonists, not free people of color, who were planning to deliver the colonies to their powerful British neighbors.

The Slave Revolution and the French-American Commercial Diplomacy

In Philadelphia, Thomas Jefferson could hardly contain his exasperation at the Constituent Assembly's procrastination on the free-trade issue. The secretary of state had many reasons to think that Dominguan planters shared a common interest with the United States. Since 1789, trade with the French colony had increased to unprecedented levels: more than ever Saint-Domingue was crucial to its economy. US merchants pressured the federal government to keep this major market open for their exports of flour, wheat, vegetables, and meats. Although Jefferson believed his desire for a thriving independent farmers' society was dependent on this commercial relationship, he remained cautious. There is no evidence that he intended to act on a threat of military intervention. Any such impulses would certainly have evaporated once the slave insurrection began. From that time on, Jefferson's main concern was how Britain might take advantage of the crisis. He also understood that the revolution could threaten slavery at home and the federal constitutional compromise of 1787. Access to the French colonial market remained one of his goals but could no longer be his main priority.[12]

Faced with Jefferson's reluctance to pursue the issue, the French colonists decided to take action themselves. In Saint-Domingue, a new—all white—Colonial Assembly met in August 1791 and developed an autonomist agenda at odds with the National Assembly's policies. The small concessions made to free people of color in May and the slave insurrection three months later goaded deputies into considering a "call to the English," an invitation to Britain to occupy the colony. There was nothing new about this idea. Guadeloupe's planters, for instance, had welcome the British occupation during the Seven Years' War. At the request of its president, Marquis Paul de Cadush, the Colonial Assembly raised the black cockade, a monarchist symbol, and proposed handing the colony over to the extraordinary British commissioners dispatched from Jamaica. But the call was not a success. Not only were British emissaries less than enthusiastic, but many French colonists also resented this "Creole" radicalism, believing Saint-Domingue needed France more than ever. These ineffective steps toward a rapprochement with the British were framed as an expression of "island patriotism," engendered by the "colonial spirit" of the eighteenth century. As historian David Geggus has argued, the act itself is difficult to interpret: it may illustrate desires for autonomy, royalism, separatism, or merely some degree of safety. The decree annulling the concessions made to free people of color issued in Paris on September 24, 1791, certainly went some way to appeasing anger among the planters. Any "foreign alliance" with Britain (or Spain) would remain a poorly crafted project until the end of 1792.[13]

The terms of the offer to Britain also demonstrate that local interests took precedence. The Colonial Assembly would recognize foreign tutelage only in exchange for self-government and free trade with the United States. Even the slave revolt did not prevent the colonists from making free trade one of their primary goals. As well as soliciting the English, emissaries were sent to Havana and Philadelphia requesting ammunition and troops. M. Roustan, a member of the Colonial Assembly, sailed to North America bearing the title of "deputy of the colony of Saint-Domingue near the United States" in order to negotiate directly with Congress and the federal government for arms and food. One of his colleagues, Doctor Jean-Louis Polony, undertaking a similar strategy with the state of South Carolina, galvanized solidarity between the southern and the Saint-Domingue planters but could not convince Carolinian lawmakers to provide troops. Roustan did manage to secure provisions, although Philadelphian abolitionists refused to help those inflicting the "most atrocious slavery" in Saint-Domingue.[14]

The French ambassador in the United States, Jean-Baptiste Ternant, found himself in a tricky situation. His primary duty was to ensure the security of the French West Indies, but he was also required to block any attempt at colonial independence under the *guise* of "Franco-American friendship." Taking charge of negotiations, he swiftly annulled the title the assembly had unconstitutionally conferred on Roustan, since a "colonial mission independent of the legation of France" could not exist. Roustan's "letter of credence" emphasized the "relations which have long existed between these states and Saint-Domingue, their fraternal attachment." This statement was all the more alarming to Ternant as the "general government of the United States could probably not have been more eager to seize this opportunity to secure the recognition of a colony, whose ambition it is to trade, and which since its new organization began to have some sort of political existence, though subordinated to the wish of the mother country."[15]

Roustan, far from being the last Dominguan emissary, was the first of a long series of colonial envoys to the United States. A few weeks later, Ternant had to deal with two new commissioners appointed by the Colonial Assembly on October 11, 1791. Tellingly, their interpreter was Laurent Faurès, a merchant who had tried to make a fortune in the US-Saint-Domingue trade. The ambassador had written to inform Governor Philippe François Rouxel de Blanchelande that such proceedings would be illegal, but his letter reached Saint-Domingue after the two new delegates had been dispatched to Philadelphia. Once again, they asked for arms and provisions; they also announced that the Colonial

Assembly had requested the governor to grant an exequatur, a written official recognition authorizing a US consul in Cap-Français, a position that had not previously existed. Ternant immediately voiced his opposition: such a consul, whose function was primarily commercial, could easily become an unofficial ambassador. The establishment of quasi-diplomatic relations was a kind of coup intended to consolidate Saint-Domingue's autonomy and commercial sovereignty. The emissaries also attempted to carefully negotiate directly with the US Congress and federal government. The president of the Colonial Assembly had stated that Saint-Domingue was "part of France" and that the request was being made solely in the name of Franco-American friendship. Ternant, having no official instructions, attempted to secure new funding and demanded the informal ambassadors be recalled.[16]

Hoping for a federal loan, the colonists may have even offered to mortgage Saint-Domingue to the United States, a proposal that cast doubt on their claims of loyalty. Ternant, who had also heard of the talks with British representatives based in Jamaica, believed Britain was covertly attempting to monopolize commerce with Saint-Domingue. Jefferson refused to grant ambassadorial status to the two envoys for fear the British Empire would benefit from the weakening power of France in the Caribbean. However, in spite of his assurances to Ternant, he did agree to meet the colony envoys, forwarded their letter to Congress, and conveyed to them the sincere attachment the US government felt toward France and her "possessions." As Saint-Domingue held a special status in that relationship due to its "common interests" with the United States, these two entities were impelled toward some form of "Union." Jefferson also reminded the emissaries that he had no desire for the colony to secede. This tactic was intended to put pressure on the French ambassador, with whom he was about to negotiate a new treaty of alliance and commerce. The slave insurrection had enabled this new diplomatic game, one of its many unexpected repercussions.[17]

These diplomatic maneuvers in Philadelphia reverberated in Paris, where the incident was reinterpreted against the tense atmosphere of fall 1791. A month after the constitutional decree had withdrawn rights from free people of color, news of the insurrection reached the metropole. Under these new circumstances, the Parisian political situation was turned upside down: Barnave's influence had waned and the Amis des Noirs had entered the new Legislative Assembly under Brissot, yet the emotion caused by the Caribbean news immediately put "philanthropists" on the defensive. The colonial lobby continued to condemn the "négrophiles" in the metropole. On November 30, the leader of a colonial deputation, Thomas Millet, held forth on the lengthy "atrocities in Saint-Domingue" before the Assembly. Millet ended with a violent diatribe against a "treacherous" society secretly inciting revolution by seeking destruction of the colonies. The deputy explained that the "call to neighboring powers" had been nothing but a request for help, not a declaration of independence, and was justified by the circumstances. The colonists had demonstrated their attachment to France and were better citizens than the "deceitful" philanthropists, who, he claimed, conspired with Britain to dismantle the French empire.[18]

The Jacobin Brissot had minimized the scope of the slave insurrection in his journal, the *Patriote français*, and claimed "royalists" were manipulating the insurgents to provoke a counterrevolution in the Caribbean. Confronted with Millet's report, his project of gradual abolition was compromised, and he faced the accusation that "philosophy" could only lead to slaughter. Brissot's response the following day was extremely long and received frequent applause. By presenting a history of the revolutions in Saint-Domingue and Martinique since the Estates General had first assembled, Brissot intended to provide a completely different interpretation of events. He blamed the explosion of violence on "the great dissipating white colonists" and "the little colonists, adventurers, men without principles and almost all without morals" who haunted the den of corruption in colonial cities. The honest white colonists, the merchant creditors, "attached by their interests to France," and the people of color in particular, who paid their dues promptly and whose "African blood" mingled with "European blood," were the only ones loyal to the mother country. Brissot's political and sociological outline established a classification based on three interrelated criteria, the combination of which determined loyalty to the nation: race, solvency, and morality.[19]

Brissot was particularly concerned with the secessionist plans of the white planters and the "independence system" devised by "vicious colonists." According to him, the call to Jamaica betrayed their desire to deliver the colony to England, while the colonial mission in the United States, the "Quakers' country," served only as an alibi. What the colonists sought above all was "to evade commercial laws" and thereby nullify the debts binding them to French merchants. Metropolitan traders had previously been deceived about the true interests of the colonists, but Bordeaux had raised the veil. In debt, and corrupted by the slave system, the planters would embrace anyone who could help them escape their commitments. In response to requests from the Chambers of Commerce, Brissot proposed a stricter mortgage law that would enable courts to seize the property of colonists. The deputy emphasized the commercial significance of Saint-Domingue to the French economy by referring to the 6 million Frenchmen whose employment derived from colonial prosperity, an intentional appropriation of the rhetoric of his colonial opponents.[20]

Brissot's speech appeared to legitimize the exclusif. Three factors explain this complete reversal. Since 1791, the leader of the Amis des Noirs had come to fear that foreign trade might lead to colonial independence and undermine the political dominance of metropolitan authorities at the expense of free people of color.

Moreover, the deputy's allies, the merchants of Bordeaux, were for the most part reluctant to repeal the colonial monopoly: they had considerable commercial interests in Saint-Domingue. The main representatives of the port strongly supported relaxation of internal trade but were far less enthusiastic about the liberalization of foreign trade. Brissot's strategy was an attempt to destroy the fragile coalition between various colonial pressure groups by securing support from merchants, who were particularly keen to continue Atlantic trade; whether their commercial partners were whites or "mulattoes" was immaterial.[21]

On the other side of the Atlantic in Saint-Domingue, the policies followed by the Colonial Assembly were becoming strikingly incoherent. Although the slave insurrection was threatening to the entire plantation system, colonists were spending a great deal of their time debating the abolition of the exclusif and whether their assembly should be entitled "colonial" or "general." When welcoming the first civil commissioners sent from the metropole to pacify the colony, the president of Saint-Domingue's Assembly greeted them as the "dear allies" of the "Creole nation" and infuriated the loyalist delegates. In response to the diplomatic failures in the United States and Brissot's rebuke in France, Saint-Domingue's colonial debates grew particularly heated in December 1791. The colonial representative Thomas Millet aired his frustration at a commercial "corporation which always confuses the interests of the merchant with the interests of commerce, which sees in the prohibitive laws the surest guarantee of its particular successes." He claimed metropolitan merchants had infiltrated the National Assembly and were dictating French trade policies. However, this speech showcased the deep divisions over the future of revolutionary Saint-Domingue within the white society. The "East side of the Assembly" proved to be more loyal to the metropole, while the "West Side" advocated autonomist policies. Some deputies, like Millet, rejected the very word "colony" as a feudal notion, an illegitimate and outdated form of subordination in an age of revolution. Loyalists, however, won the debate.[22]

In a spectacular reversal, the Colonial Assembly began to support the exclusif legislation and repealed all previous measures in favor of free trade. On December 30, 1791, the assembly armed two light vessels to prevent food from reaching smaller ports in the Western Province—Saint-Marc, Petit-Goave, and Léogane—where it would become "prey to the fury and brigandage of men of color who had become the new masters." Indeed, at its request, a frigate was dispatched to Léogane in January 1792 to remove three US vessels from the harbor. Stewart & Plunket, a Baltimore firm, had sent produce on the schooner *Port-au-Prince* to Saint-Domingue under the direction of Captain Levin Jones in December 1791. The capital of the colony being well supplied with flour, the provincial assembly had initially authorized Jones to unload cargo at other small ports on the coast, but to the Colonial Assembly's horror, the captain had sold his goods to free people of color. Six other American vessels were seized in the harbor of Saint-Marc as well. The exclusif had become the legal basis for maritime intervention.[23]

The white planters who had constantly demanded the legalization of foreign trade appeared to have turned into monopolists. This radical transformation had a local cause: the Western Province was in the grip of a civil war between urban whites and a coalition of people of color and former supporters of the governor, known as the Croix-des-Bouquets confederation after the parish in which the rebels' headquarters were based. The exclusif had become a weapon of war, a means of cutting off supplies to the "insurgents." The municipality of Léogane, whose mayor, Labuissonière, was a person of color, complained: "These laws having been made for a quiet state can no longer be the rules of an authority wisely dispensed and that according to our internal situation which you are well acquainted with, far from being wise and having good effects, they are only a source of abuse and calamities." The decree on the exclusif of August 30, 1784, diverted from its original function, was enforced to serve a new military purpose.[24]

Decisions made in metropolitan France—or rather the absence of reform relating to the exclusif—and the failure of diplomatic negotiations in Philadelphia, had produced a completely unexpected outcome. New local circumstances changed the meaning of imperial policies. The political game in the colony grew yet more confusing, as American merchant Nathaniel Cutting related in his diary: "The Politics of the different Parties in this Island are dark & intricate; puzzled in mazes & perplexed with errors, my understanding traces them in vain and I must confess is lost and bewildered in the fruitless search."[25]

Republican Political Economies

In the metropole, maintaining or repealing the "prohibitive regime" was more than a mere choice between free trade and protectionism. The exclusif illuminated the legal contradictions of colonial arrangements envisaged by the Constituent Assembly and generated a major theoretical debate about the nature of empire and revolution. In the second French National Assembly, the Legislative Assembly, which came together in October 1791, two delegates supporting Brissot—Armand-Guy de Kersaint and Jean-Philippe Garran de Coulon—took up the fight. To them, abolition of the exclusif went hand in hand with the republicanization of the regime and the extension of political rights to all free people of color.

In November 1791, naval commander Kersaint, a veteran of the American Revolutionary War, sent a memorandum to the Colonial Committee of the

National Assembly on ways to restore order and peace in the colonies. Following Brissot's line of argument, the naval officer claimed to have "lived a lot in the colonies" and "owned black slaves"; he was a colonist, even though he did not share the opinions of the Club Massiac. Kersaint attempted to explain the causes of the troubles and the remedies that could ensure "the generous interests of the motherland and those more particular of our traders." According to Kersaint, the three main causes of the conflict were "greed," the desire to "get rich through foreign trade"; "aristocracy," the determination to "overthrow the French constitution"; and "the love of independence in slaves." These three "feelings" generated three evils: colonial independence, royalism, and slave revolts.[26]

Because colonies were properties of the Crown, they presented a counterrevolutionary threat to France as a whole. Kersaint linked the colonial question to the burning question of relations between the executive and the legislative, crystallized in the metropolitan debate on ministerial responsibility and the royal veto. The amount of power held by the king had been central to the heated debates following Louis XVI's failed flight in June 1791. Given these circumstances, Kersaint believed that "the absolute independence of the colonies is preferable to their independence from the legislature," which could lead to the colonies becoming a springboard for British-led counterrevolutionary movements. In other words, constitutional monarchy, as established in the constitution, was an obstacle to the legal integration of the colonies. Kersaint suggested that the republic alone could ensure the equality of national rights between the metropole and colonies.[27]

Representative Garran de Coulon elaborated on this argument in a text read before the National Assembly on February 29, 1792. He approached the colonial question in its entirety as he denounced the constitutional dualism created by the Constitution of 1791. This speech can be considered the first legal assimilationist program. Garran de Coulon rejected colonial "independence within the Empire." He pointed out that maintaining a colonial exception after the abolition of provincial privileges and formation of the eighty-three departments represented a serious threat to the rights of the nation. Granting the colonies independence could solve this legal contradiction. Moreover, the secession of the thirteen colonies had not harmed Britain's interests in its trade with the United States. Independence, however, albeit potentially desirable from an economic point of view, was in fact unrealistic. According to Garran de Coulon, the colonies had proven their need for the motherland's protection. The "plots of independence" had been conceived by a "colonial aristocracy," determined to subjugate people of color. The deputy rejected the analogy of the colonial revolt with the American Revolution that white planters used as a "scarecrow." The federal government's conduct toward Saint-Domingue demonstrated that the United States did not recognize itself in "these denatured children" who seek independence "only to escape metropolitan regeneration." Regeneration should include the colonies: all discrimination against free people of color should cease, and the exclusif should be abolished. Even before the overthrow of the monarchy, Garran de Coulon was laying the foundations for an assimilationist republican political economy.[28]

Kersaint and Garran de Coulon, along with the entire "Brissotin" (later Girondins) political group met with strong opposition from supporters of the colonial status quo. The Brissotins demanded complete equality between free people of color and whites. With the intensifying civil war in Saint-Domingue and the need to contain the slave insurrection, the Amis des Noirs eventually convinced a majority of deputies that France should alter its policy altogether. Legislation was passed on March 28, 1792, granting equal rights to free people of color. A civil commission with dictatorial powers was to be sent to Saint-Domingue to implement this policy, restore order, and repress the insurrection. As far as the exclusif was concerned, the legislation did not specify that the colonies would enjoy free trade with the United States: the decree actually made the payment of debts by colonists mandatory and reasserted the political and commercial sovereignty of the metropole. Deputy Mathieu Dumas lamented that colonial turmoil had "a lethal influence on commerce and the national navigation," with foreigners "invading the part that was exclusively reserved to our ports." If foreign trade was not circumscribed, France could "save the remnants of the colony but we will lose it in fact by losing its commerce."[29]

Two major events would transform the terms of this debate: the birth of the French republic and the Declaration of War on Great Britain. In the aftermath of the fall of the king on August 10, 1792, the new executive council included a number of fervent *américanophiles*, all of whom attached immense importance to colonial issues. Among these were the minister of foreign affairs, Pierre Lebrun-Tondu; and the minister of finance, Étienne Clavière. A few months earlier, Clavière had called for a "triple alliance" between Britain, the United States, and France, in which free trade between the three nations would underpin civil liberties. He dreamed of a geopolitical reversal, a British alliance and dissolution of the "family pact" with Spain, a country he, like many other French economists of his time, deemed backward and monopolistic. However, the new government was unable to strike a deal with Britain; war was imminent. Under these conditions it was unclear how and to what extent free trade could be implemented in the West Indies.[30]

A rather obscure character, Armand-Guy Ducher, played a crucial role in these debates. Having served as vice-consul in Portsmouth, New England, Ducher was an expert on political economy and American affairs who published countless newspaper articles calling for a republican association between France and the United States. The former consul advocated the establishment of a "new alliance" in *The Moniteur,* in which he claimed that implementation of a double navigation act would guarantee the opening of Antillean ports to the Americans. Not only were France and the United States characterized by a common political identity and shared commercial interests, but they were also exposed to similar counterrevolutionary threats. Ducher advocated the creation of a Franco-American union, comparable to that achieved by the Constitution of 1787 in the United States: a "national pact, to secure territory, independence, republicanism and trade." Reframing the debate of 1783 in different terms, he raised concern over how to integrate the United States into a republican colonial system.[31]

In an article following his reflections on the "removal of the barriers between France and its colonies," Ducher also contributed to the issue of conciliating the principles of unity and indivisibility of the kingdom and the existence of colonies. He pleaded for the rewriting of colonial commercial laws. By establishing a "protective system of the parts" and ensuring the "prosperity of the whole," the colonists could be dissuaded from becoming sovereign. Ducher believed it was "politically and commercially absurd to allow a wall of separation to remain between members of the same family. All relations between them, between sections of the same body politic, should not be more embarrassing than circulation of the blood." Reform would result from a national unification project by eliminating internal customs. Given the economic importance of Saint-Domingue, "this superb enclosure which has for limits two seas & the Alps & the Pyrenees, France," could be equivalent to three-fifths of global trade. Integration of the colonies, an alliance with the United States, and targeted protectionism against monarchical rivals were thus placed in the service of republican economic nationalism.[32]

These ideas were at the heart of Edmond Charles Genet's embassy in the United States. The new executive council that replaced the monarchical government was preparing for an inevitable confrontation with Britain and had selected an enthusiastic revolutionary to represent the French Republic in Philadelphia. Genet's primary mission in the United States was colonial. The new French ambassador was to secure military and food supplies for Saint-Domingue, still suffering from its civil war and threatened with foreign invasion. The role of strategic support devised by the Count of Vergennes in 1778 was to be enacted. Reform of the colonial exclusif was central to the Executive Council's "economic and trade pact with the United States of America." France was to have only one "ally" in the world, the "only free people on earth" which was to be offered a "kind of exclusive right." Genet was to reach an agreement with the United States through a "national pact in which the two peoples merge their commercial interests with their political interests and establish an intimate concert to favor in all respects the extension of the empire of liberty . . . and to punish the powers which still hold exclusive commercial and colonial systems." The liberation of Spanish America, prophesied by Anne-Robert-Jacques Turgot in 1776, would follow. In Brissot's eyes, an exclusive American alliance would be the fulcrum for a Pan-American Revolution in the context of global war. The National Assembly addressed the United States Congress along these lines on December 22, 1792. "Healthy policy," it explained, would be based on trade and not "exclusive interests": the colonies, "far from being eternally subjected to rivalries and wars" would become a tie "between nations." Making Saint-Domingue the link between the United States and republican France would revolutionize the world.[33]

Jean-Baptiste Boyer-Fonfrède, a representative from Bordeaux and supporter of Brissot, drafted a decree to open colonial ports to the Americans and guarantee the provisioning of the French West Indies. The deputy had become a member of the General Defense Committee, created on January 1, 1793, to oversee all military operations. The colonies needed to prepare themselves for a new maritime war with Britain and Spain. The contents of the decree were largely ideological. As Boyer-Fonfrède explained, diplomacy in both the new republican France and the colonial system were to be transformed:

> To satisfy the greed, the interests of some men who defile that of the country when they invoke it, to increase some fortunes in France, we have reduced more than once the colonists to devouring one another; our trading system must change as does our political system. . . . The colonies were declared integral parts of the French Republic, when all the others enjoy the unlimited freedom of trade, the colonies are excepted from the common law and subjected to oppressive regulations.

Boyer-Fonfrède's speech was a radical condemnation of the colonial idea. The circumstances that had made this measure possible had also convinced many members of the National Assembly that suspending the exclusif made sense. At the same time an authentic commercial republicanism had emerged that was intended to rebuild the international order while laying down the principles of popular sovereignty.[34]

A month later, another deputy on the same committee, Bertrand Barère, enumerated the reasons that France should declare war on Spain. The Spanish Monarchy wanted the "annhiliation of our liberty and the consolidation of royalism," he explained. It is striking that Barère did not first mention French grievances against Spanish designs in Europe. Instead, he blamed the Spaniards for "instigating the revolt of the Negroes in Saint-Domingue . . . by trafficking, . . . by exchanging arms, cannons, munitions of war and mouth, against the silver and the gold, the precious furniture and the foodstuffs." The deputy blamed the Spanish in the eastern part of Hispaniola for their counterrevolutionary trade with Black insurgents, then regarded as royalists' puppets. The

Assembly concurred that this bartering stood in stark contrast with French-US commercial republicanism.[35]

But did the republic "assimilate" the colonies, or was the maritime war the major factor in this transformation? The answer to this question is crucial. If the former, reform would be maintained once peace returned and the legal status of the colonies would be radically altered. If the decree was only a reaction to circumstances, however, it could be a temporary measure. This ambiguity explains why those metropolitan merchants who supported the colonial monopoly immediately took action to limit the impact of the decree. A report on the "mode of execution of the decree of February 19th," presented by the Committee of Commerce on March 12, 1793, disputed Boyer-Fonfrède's analysis and highlighted the notion of "reciprocity." France had given much to the United States without ever receiving anything in return. In the face of "American ingratitude," the Assembly could demonstrate goodwill by exempting from duty foodstuffs introduced into the colonies; but the "flow of colonial products" had to be carefully curtailed or the colonies would become the "exclusive property of our allies." As such, only imports of foodstuffs (not manufactured goods) were to be allowed, and the export of sugar and coffee restricted to "one-tenth of the tonnage" of American vessels, provided these ships had entered the ports of the republic with a quantity of edibles corresponding to at least "two-thirds" of their cargoes. Even though these figures were based on the French consuls' deeply flawed analysis, the restrictions were intended to limit the volumes of sugar and coffee exported in the quantities needed to supply the US consumer market. The Committee of Commerce wanted to prevent American traders from taking over the reexport trade to Europe.[36]

The decree could not be more ambiguous: it granted a significant duty exemption, was presented as a favor, but at the same time reaffirmed principles in opposition to any deregulation of colonial trade. The foreign ministry explained to Genet that the ambassador could use this uncertainty to his advantage while negotiating with the US government. The law "could be suspended if French captains did not benefit from a perfect reciprocity." Brissot and his Girondin allies, far from being utopian revolutionaries, were ready to employ every diplomatic tool to found their "empire of liberty." They certainly believed that the political revolution would stem from a commercial transformation, but they would twist as many arms as necessary to implement their chosen policies.[37]

The phrase "empire of liberty" is usually associated with Jefferson's vision of American expansion. As historian Peter Onuf wrote, by "banishing metropolitan power from the New World, Jefferson imagined a great Nation, a dynamic union of free peoples." This union was based on a republican political economy that regarded free trade as the driving force behind the construction of a cosmopolitan world. Political entities would have equal rights; domination of one nation over another would end. A republican understanding of commerce as a challenge to the colonial system was communal to many revolutionaries on both sides of the Atlantic. Brissot and his Girondin allies shared an intellectual commitment to a commercial revolution that was comprehensively political. Shaping a new republican alliance with the United States and placing Saint-Domingue at the center of this pact was intended to have universal consequences in favor of equality and freedom from monarchical tyranny.

Yet the revolt of free people of color and the largest slave insurrection the world had ever witnessed transformed the meaning of what this "empire of liberty" could become. The debate over free trade could not be disentangled from Saint-Domingue's racial context. Under these circumstances, the colonial and revolutionary politics of the early 1790s were at odds with the philosophical standpoints of all the actors involved. Merchants from Bordeaux fought the traders of Le Havre over the rights of free people of color; colonists in Port-au-Prince demanded that the exclusif be applied to cut off all supplies to mixed-race insurgents who traded with Americans; Jefferson refused to deal with Saint-Domingue's emissaries for fear of US slave revolt and British commercial hegemony; the Girondins themselves condemned the opening of colonial markets to foreign vessels, dreading that planters were planning a colonial secession in favor of white supremacy. This game of entangled revolutionary politics could not be boxed into simple ideological controversies. But merchants on the ground saw an unprecedented opportunity in the chaos created by the French and Saint-Domingue revolutions.

The Best of a Bad Bargain, 1789–1793

On November 3, 1791, after a forty-eight-day voyage from Le Havre, the ship *Défenseur* reached the French colony of Saint-Domingue. On board was Nathaniel Cutting, a New England commissioner employed by the French-American merchant house, Swan & Dallarde. Cutting was already familiar with the "Pearl of the Caribbean," having previously brought captives across from the coast of Guinea, and was expecting to make a significant profit from his cargo of muslins. Only on arrival in Saint-Domingue did the merchant learn of the widespread insurrection, which had been unfolding for over a month. Cutting described his concerns in a diary: "I fear this time the Colony is ruined by mistaken politics. A most unfortunate time for my affairs! I must make the best of a bad bargain." Cutting was determined to tweak his commercial strategy to the circumstances of the insurgency, limit his losses, and perhaps even make a profit. He was not alone; American traders viewed the revolution as both a considerable risk and a new world of opportunities.[1]

This chapter explores the mercantile understanding of this defining moment and shows that trading practices on the ground reshaped the politics of the French-American alliance more significantly than the lawmaking of the National Assembly in Paris. Although the perpetuation or cancellation of the colonial *exclusif* was the subject of intense political conflict between 1789 and 1793, a formidable commercial expansion was also taking place in the Caribbean. US exports to the French Antilles increased to nearly 20 percent of total US foreign trade. Imports of molasses, sugar, and, increasingly, coffee reached unprecedented levels. Not everyone benefited from these economic transformations; some lost a great deal of money. Cutting, for example, sheepishly left the colony after seven months of unsuccessful attempts to sell his merchandise. For other traders, the French flour crisis and the slave insurrection created new paths to fortune. From this perspective, the immediate aftermath of the insurrection was certainly not an "econocide." Although some insurrectionists endeavored to systematically destroy the sugar plantations—a practice that historian Johnhenry

Entrepôt of Revolutions. Manuel Covo, Oxford University Press. © Oxford University Press 2022.
DOI: 10.1093/oso/9780197626382.003.0006

Gonzalez has described as a form of colonial luddism—the devastation was not universal. Even more significantly, many merchants successfully adjusted to the new configuration in a way that planters did not. The event accelerated the massive redeployment of commercial and financial circuits already under way in the Atlantic world.[2]

The expansion of US trade had considerable political impact. Merchants' networks not only had notable adaptability but also redefined revolutionary and counterrevolutionary dynamics in both direct and indirect ways. Far from passive, traders became enmeshed in the colonial economy's military defense, used their smuggling acumen to devise new slave-trading systems, secured substantial provisioning contracts in Cap-Français, Paris, and Philadelphia, and took on official functions. Yet the ensuing financial tensions created by this revolutionary bubble had dramatic consequences and played a fundamental role in the transformation of the French empire.

The Flour Fever of 1789

The opening of Saint-Domingue's flour markets in 1788–1789 generated a considerable influx of US vessels. At first, the commercial export of flour was more significant to US traders than the imports of sugar, coffee, cotton, indigo, and cocoa. Ship owners no longer had to fear competition from the metropole, and the needs of the colony were immense. The lifting of prohibitions provided Saint-Domingue with a competitive advantage over Jamaica, Cuba, and the Lesser Antilles. Indeed, with the British regulations of 1786 and 1787 making access to their West Indian market more complicated and Spanish trade restrictions also posing many obstacles for foreign traders, Saint-Domingue was playing the role of a Caribbean suction pump. American exports in particular experienced notable growth, with volumes of US flour entering Saint-Domingue equivalent to what had been annually shipped to the French West Indies from Bordeaux in the 1780s. The flour trade energized the export of other commodities: in 1790, the French Antilles received 29 percent of legal US exports of flour, but also 68 percent of pork, 78 percent of beef, and 80 percent of fish. Conversely, 52 percent of the sugar, 58 percent of the coffee, and 84 percent of the molasses imported into the United States officially came from the French West Indies. In Pennsylvania, 84 percent of coffee was imported from the French islands and amounted to almost 1.2 million pounds in volume. These figures do not include significant portions of undeclared goods: in 1791 it was still "customary" to report only half or a quarter of total cargoes. Four US states were particularly dependent on this trade: Massachusetts (whose distilleries badly needed molasses), New York, Pennsylvania, and Maryland. The number of US vessels

Table 5.1 **Entries of Vessels from the United States in 1789**

Entrepôts	Vessels	Tons
Le Cap	385	27,176
Port-au-Prince	193	14,817
Les Cayes	68	5,078
St Pierre	147	30,772
Basse-Terre	227	14,955
Total	1,407	99,955

Source: ANOM, F2b 13, no. 40.

entering Saint-Domingue's ports multiplied in 1789 and 1790. Although this growth was genuine, part of the preexisting illicit traffic had also become apparent through the temporary legalization of foreign trade, with sea captains no longer having to lie about their ports of origin.[3]

After years of increasing smuggling suppression, Saint-Domingue emerged as an El Dorado for American traders. In February 1789, a merchant from Port-au-Prince had warned that "bringing in flour" was not "practicable" because of the "hindrances experienced by our coasters, who are visited at all times." "As for smuggling," he cautioned, "don't think about it." Everything changed when colonial authorities granted temporary permits for the import of flour and *intendant* Barbé-Marbois was chased out of the colony in October 1789. Information spread rapidly, first in business correspondence and then the press. The subsequent windfall was such that many merchant houses redeployed to take advantage of the boon. Benjamin Mumford of Norwich, Connecticut, sent his son to Les Cayes-Saint-Louis in 1789 to establish a new commission-based business and coordinate imports of flour. Trader James Morphy created a merchant

Table 5.2 **US Exports to the French West Indies in Value**

	In million dollars	% of Caribbean trade	% of US exports
1790	3.2	51.5	16.3
1791	3.4	56.3	19.7
1792	3.7	52.1	18.1
1793	5.0	56.3	19.6

Source: John H. Coatsworth, "American Trade with European Colonies in the Caribbean and South America, 1790–1812," *William and Mary Quarterly* 24, no. 2 (April 1967): 243–66.

house in Cap-Français specializing in US trade. Etienne Dutilh himself left Philadelphia to settle in the colony's main port, conceding that, in contrast with Saint-Domingue's limitless prospects, it was not possible to "make a fortune among the Anglo-Americans." Dutilh's goal was to spend two years in the French colony accumulating substantial capital before returning to Philadelphia. These newcomers joined the many firms already in existence.[4]

The French flour crisis was also timely for non-political reasons. The climate was favorable, as a winter drought meant Saint-Domingue planters had begun "to run out of food for their negroes" and were searching "everywhere for old flour to convert into biscuits." Meanwhile, the United States "had never had as good a grain harvest as the last and had never had such a high price."[5]

However, the mercantile influx did not mean all traffic was profitable. It is easy to assume that trade volumes reflect market demand and therefore translate into profits. Take the example of Brown & Benson based in Providence, Rhode Island, which had invested in the Caribbean markets for generations and whose distilleries relied partly on molasses imported from Hispaniola. The firm's activities were more diversified than others, trading with merchant houses in many parts of the world, but with a strong focus on Surinam. Yet, like most of its competitors, the firm rushed to Saint-Domingue during the early stage of the French Revolution. Brown & Benson instructed Captain Munro on the brig *Commerce* to "embrace the first fair wind and proceed with all possible dispatch to Cape François and there dispose of your cargo for the highest price you can obtain and invest the Neat proceeds in good Mollasses it being for our own Distillery." After a ten-day voyage, on September 10, 1790, captain Munro encountered "a market as completely glutted with American Produce as he ever saw in any life, it is judged here is 25, 000 barrels of flour in stores and vessels coming in daily." This testimony was in sharp contrast with white colonists' grievances in Paris. Due to the abundance of flour and the "amazing scarcity and high price of the produce of the island," the captain explained, the voyage was "ruinous." Three or four US ships were entering the harbor every day. "Wherever the Americans go, they crowd in and hurt each other in the markets," commented the French consul in Boston: "American traders say here that the markets of our West Indies barely pay them the cost of shipping."[6]

Why, then, did merchants act as they did? Their decisions were actually informed by previous experience of Caribbean trade. Brown & Benson interpreted the events of 1789 as just another temporary crisis: hurricanes, earthquakes, and slave revolts regularly suspended monopolies, opening up brief windows for free trade, and local decisions not validated by central metropolitan authorities were regarded as provisional. Although the colonial government confirmed these exceptions on a regular basis (on April 1, August 10, and October 21, 1789, and April 21, 1790), traders acted swiftly, anticipating an imminent enforcement of the monopoly. While the 1789 crisis may appear to be the "end of the *exclusif*," this does not take into account how merchants at the time interpreted and responded to events. As historian Pierre Gervais has demonstrated, traders did not think of profit strictly in accounting terms. Economic choices, founded on imperfect information, were not made on the success or failure of isolated business ventures but were part of a development trajectory within networks of trust. Merchants seized opportunities to expand and exploit their networks even if they knew that sales might not be profitable in the short term. Having seen "with pleasure" that permission to sell foreign flour had been extended, Stephen Girard sent his ship captain brother "immediately with eight hundred barrels of this commodity to continue until we are refused entry to the harbor." Similarly, Baltimore trader Samuel Smith, "hearing of Cape Francois being open for flour till the 1st October next with liberty to bring back coffee or sugars there for those articles" resolved to dispatch a vessel for Saint-Domingue. More than any other parameters, opening of the market justified shipment. Yet merchants were also willing to mitigate the risks associated with possible legal reversals and prepared smuggling operations.[7]

Sales of these shipments were erratic, with abundance preceding scarcity, and profits fluctuating immensely from week to week. Within poorly coordinated markets, prices did not function as efficient indicators: the mismatch between supply and demand was constant. As Cap-Français had been inundated with American flour, ship captains redirected their cargoes to Port-au-Prince, causing a shortage and subsequent inflation in the main port. The consul general of France noted that "the measures of the administrators made food of all kinds flock to the colonies," and "flours, cured meats and cattle were cheap there." Retail prices also suffered as, despite the political rhetoric of scarcity, bakers in Cap Français were in a strong position to negotiate with US merchants. They questioned the quality of American flour, stating that the superfine flour Dutilh sent made "bread too dark," while Cares brand flour produced "very bad bread." Although shipments did not necessarily result in lucrative sales, ship captains improvised stalls at the town's bustling urban markets. "For business, long live Le Cap Français," exclaimed one trader; "we don't need to hire people to buy, they come to you and it's to take or not to take, we buy and sell in two words."[8]

How US Merchants Viewed Saint-Domingue's Revolution

An increasing number of American traders settled in the port cities of Saint-Domingue, from where they closely observed the political events of 1789 and 1790 but did not see any need to fundamentally change their business plans.

Metropolitan resistance to abolishing the exclusif confirmed that the Saint-Domingue market would not be open forever. In the eyes of most merchants, this was the main consequence of the colonial crisis unfolding in Cap-Français and Paris. Conflict between autonomists and loyalists and the revolt of free people of color were viewed with detachment and perplexity. Commercial correspondence of the time displays little political reflection, focusing rather on market prices, quality of goods, and the comings and goings of vessels. The letters do not usually demonstrate merchants distinguishing between periods of acute crisis and those of great calm, apart from a few incidental and often exasperated remarks breaking the monotony. Most traders were particularly careful to reserve judgment as correspondence could flow from hand to hand and even be published in newspapers, potentially damaging business reputations. In Cap-Français, commissioner Aubert explained he was doing all he could not to compromise his name in the "rebellion." He believed people of color were far too "arrogant" but that he should remain a "bystander" in a revolution "like this." Another merchant later commented that "although there is a real persecution against our color, we do not believe that it can extend to us, because we are never involved in any political affair. . . . [W]e limit ourselves to taking care of our particular affairs." Given such political instability, engaging in politics could prove perilous, and the majority of traders turned a deaf ear to the debates raging within the Colonial Assembly and on the streets of Port-au-Prince.[9]

However, there were exceptions. Within the body of mostly insipid and standardized merchants' correspondence, that of the Girard brothers is astonishing. Their close relationship provided immense freedom of tone, blending commercial language with intimate and political reflections. Although Jean mostly rambled about his personal problems, his fragile health, and his failing finances, political issues repeatedly arose in the letters of the merchant in Cap-Français. The two men were not in agreement: while Stephen held strong patriotic feelings for their native country, Jean had become disillusioned with the French Revolution due to events in Saint-Domingue. Jean's language was unapologetically racist and similar to that of most white planters at the time. Although cohabiting with a mixed-race "housewife," he abhorred abolitionists and "mulattoes," deeming them responsible for all of the colony's ills. Scandalized that "officers of the infamous caste, incendiary and murderers who deserved to be broken on the wheel, commanded the whites," Jean Girard believed the real patriots were the Spanish. He also expected the English to take over the colony and intended to welcome them "with open arms."[10]

Traders were more split than planters on their views toward free people of color. Many interpreted events in the same way as Jean Girard. Cutting—who was Thomas Jefferson's main source of information—believed mixed-race people rather than Black enslaved people "had committed immense devastation—burning habitations and destroying all before them." But this anti-mulatto prejudice was not shared by all traders. François Belon in Léogane argued in favor of a rapprochement between white and free people of color and was horrified by the white planters' violence. Pragmatic Etienne Dutilh was relieved "that we armed the free mulattoes and negroes to defend our lives and common properties. We started here to take this side without which I assure you we would have been here in a much worse position than we are." Dutilh's firm had a lot at stake: no fewer than seven of his ships were constantly traveling between Philadelphia and the colony.[11]

Once the insurrection was under way, colonists fluctuated between hope for a swift victory and fear of total destruction. While most ports remained in the hands of elites—either white colonists or free people of color in places such as Léogane or Saint-Marc—rural revolutionaries threatened to overwhelm urban spaces. Many planters and managers left their estates with their families and Black servants to take refuge in congested cities on the brink of explosion. From August 1791 to June 1793, Cap-Français was under siege while insurgents were occupying the northern plain. Colonists worried that urban enslaved people would join forces with fieldworkers and burn the city to the ground. Cutting reported in his diary that "tubs of water are placed at the corners of every street to be ready in case of fires, and a sentinel likewise is placed at the intersection of every street during the night to keep order." Isolated incidents caused mass panic, violence, and lynching. Enraged white residents murdered a Black man discovered on a small boat in the middle of the night. The mob did not give him the opportunity to explain himself.

> The poor devil would dive and swim underwater like a wild duck, but when he arose to the surface someone would be sure to discover him and the boats continued their pursuit till with the strokes of their oars and boat hooks they killed him. Then the intention of his midnight expedition is probably buried with him.

It is not implausible that the man plotted to sabotage a vessel where colonists stored weapons and ammunition, but he might also have been attending to mundane, innocuous business. The profoundly biased sources say less about his doings than about the whites' outbursts of violence and panic.[12]

Fear coexisted with a strong belief the colonists would eventually triumph, a conviction steeped in long-held white arrogance. One planter observed that the number of insurgents "decreases every day by the advantages we have over them, and we are hopeful of overcoming it." Another was delighted to announce that "we couldn't be happier in the pursuit of rebellious negroes." The conviction that France would provide military resources boosted confidence. The arrival of any ship from Nantes, Bordeaux, or Le Havre created an emotional roller-coaster for colonists. Claims circulated that France was organizing a retaliatory expedition, 10,000, sometimes 20,000 strong, but this was systematically refuted by facts. French armed forces did not arrive until September 1792, but the 6,000 soldiers who accompanied the civil commissioners, lacking immunity and falling ill, were not the mighty troops the whites were hoping for. Colonists could be optimistic one day and deeply despondent the next; often they had these contradictory feelings at the same time. But traders did not live in a perpetually agitated state. Cutting's diary exhibits the contrast between the exceptional nature of the insurrection and the mundane nature of their everyday life. The New Englander could be horrified at witnessing the heads of defeated insurgents on spikes or could be protesting against massacres committed by whites, yet a few hours later enjoy a nice walk or the beauty of moonlight or "amuse himself" playing pool and reading newspapers from Philadelphia and Baltimore.[13]

Americans, however, did not remain passive spectators of the uprising. They signed up to protect the cities, transport troops, and even participate in military expeditions against the revolutionaries. The Cap-Français National Guard assigned police functions to the American guardhouse whose commander, James Perkins, was authorized to arrest any unidentified individuals who defied a curfew. American traders spent many nights on guard duty, lamented Dutilh, who took part in daily patrols and led, in his own words, a "dog's life." Some, such as James Meyers of Philadelphia, volunteered to attack insurgents in the countryside. James Perkins's partner, Thomas Burling, participated in several military expeditions accompanied by three clerks. The merchant incurred a serious thigh injury, while one of the clerks "took sick with the fatigue and hardships that he underwent and died three or four days after his return." Samuel Otis, part of the Otis & Mackay firm and son of the secretary of the US Senate, "made a sortie . . . from Haut du Cap in order to scour that part of the Mountains back of the Town toward L'Acul." Sea captains actively helped colonial authorities hire thirty American sailors as "gunners," and US ships transported colonial troops at the governor's request.[14]

For traders, political events were first and foremost factors in the success or failure of their speculations. For them, market prices rather than radical slogans or military skirmishes, were the most salient aspect of the ongoing revolution. As historian Alec Dun has shown, US newspapers published so many detailed accounts of colonial massacres provided by sea captains that "news from Le Cap penetrated daily life in Philadelphia." Yet descriptions of atrocities took a back seat in commercial correspondence as the merchants primarily understood the uprising as a price shock, which they viewed as a possible "revolution." Writing to a colleague in Marseilles, Girard related that "the distressing news that we have just received from St. Domingue has brought about a great revolution here in the foodstuffs of the Isles, particularly in the raw sugars which have risen to 14 *piastres*." A New York company, alarmed at the stagnation of sales and the extreme uncertainty plaguing American markets, declared that "should the destruction of the plantations be general . . . no one can say to what price sugar and Molasses will rise." A month after the insurrection, "nothing [was] sold, raw sugar [was] extremely rare" in Cap-Français. Some traders felt it necessary to wait before selling any goods, believing prices could "only go up." An American captain returning from the port of Saint-Marc noted that "every article of produce has lately taken an amazing rise in the price." But in the medium term, the revolt could provide a formidable commercial opportunity. A Connecticut trader, having just learned the country was "wholly in the power of the Blacks," concluded that it was a good time to speculate in Saint-Domingue's goods, "as the chief supply we have come from Hispaniola."[15]

Merchants spent a vast amount of time ruminating on how the uprising might affect their trade. Would rising prices benefit American traders or their metropolitan competitors? Some speculated that the "misfortunes that come to this country" would "cause furious bankruptcies in France." Many commissioners for French merchant houses, rather than waiting for the arrival of massive vessels from Bordeaux or Nantes, hastily loaded colonial goods onto small US brigantines to avoid looting. At Léogane, Belon, the agent for a major Nantes merchant, noted that he had "a large sum of produce from the colony" and proposed shipping it "to the United States of America, by dividing our consignments to Boston, New York, Philadelphia and Baltimore." Although Belon's partner did not follow his advice, others displayed more foresight. For example, the firm Girault Frères, fearing the spread of unrest and "the risk of losing everything," implored Sanderson & Hall in Les Cayes to load sugar on their schooner. Some planters sailed with their families to the United States, taking everything in their stores with them. Believing the move temporary, they hoped to sell sugar, coffee, and cotton to support themselves and prepare for their return. Mr. Gobert, whose sugar had burned, took "a few coffees" with him "while waiting to know how everything will turn out on this island." With the number of migrants increasing, prices plunged several times. Coffee imports exceeded the US consumer demand, causing French consuls to worry that Saint-Domingue commodities would be reexported to Europe on US vessels.[16]

While the commercial operations of merchants and captains depended on the preservation of plantations and continuity of production, they had only a limited view of what was taking place in rural areas. What was the extent of the damage? Which plantations had been spared? Which had been set on fire? Who among the enslaved had joined the insurrection? Who had stayed to work? How many were in hiding? The accounts of American captains going from port to port were listened to with great interest. "Many gangs of slaves are kept to work upon the plantations in that quarter" of Fort-Dauphin, indicated one captain in April 1792. Another related that "devastation in the Southern department is not nearly so general and important as we have hitherto been taught to believe." In Port-au-Prince, they rejoiced that business was "going on as briskly as possible." Cutting repeatedly attempted to quantify the cost of the damage in his journal, and his evening activity in Cap-Français consisted of observing the smoke originating from the plain, giving a sense of the extent of devastation. He understood the insurrection was not following a linear course. While many enslaved joined leaders Jean-François Papillon and Georges Biassou, some chose to flee and others took up arms before returning to work on the plantations. It was hardly a secret that some revolutionaries traded mules for food and arms with the Spaniards, who were indirectly supporting the insurrection. Nobody knew what the outcome would be. As the insurrection leaders unsuccessfully attempted to negotiate with the Colonial Assembly between December 1791 and January 1792, troops on both sides were exhausted.[17]

Merchants, who obtained some harvested raw sugar and coffee, were fully aware of these ambiguities and hesitations and kept on plying their trade. Traffic stopped completely only when the Colonial Assembly enforced a provisional embargo in the fall of 1791; an "extremely bad policy," according to the Baltimore merchant Samuel Smith. After that date the number of vessels from Saint-Domingue docking at US ports such as New York and Baltimore rose significantly despite monthly fluctuations and spikes due to weather. Traffics were not as massive as during the 1789 boom, but in Philadelphia, the volume of imports from Saint-Domingue increased by almost 30 percent between 1790 and 1792, from 11.1 thousand tons to 14.7 thousand (around 15.6 percent of total entries in Philadelphia). Massachusetts imported produce worth 2.4 million *livres tournois* in 1791 (20 percent more than in 1788). Incoming vessels entering the state from the French West Indies numbered 182 (18,076 tons)—not only from Saint-Domingue but also from Martinique, whose planters profited from the crisis in Hispaniola. Different parts of the colony were not equally affected by the destruction. In the first half of 1793, Port-au-Prince alone exported produce to the United States valued at 4,639,774 *livres coloniales*, including 2,055,564 in coffee, 1,438,845 in raw sugar, and 853,430 in molasses. These exports far exceeded the 2,330,704 livres coloniales of foodstuff, timber, livestock, clothes, candles, and tobacco legally imported into the capital city. In May of that year, thirty vessels left Saint-Domingue's capital city with official cargoes of 6,937 quintals of sugar and 1,008,309 pounds of coffee.[18]

almost a month in Cap-Français. As a result, the legal slave trade to Havana increased by 335 percent from 2,500 in 1790 to 8,500 in 1791 and 1792. The peak in 1791, far from being marginal, shaped Cuba's economic future. From 1793 to 1800, these figures averaged almost 4,000, although it is harder to ascertain the origin of the captives. An official table recorded the duties on exports of "French goods" made by US merchants in the first half of 1793. Two hundred eleven enslaved people had been deported from Port-au-Prince since the beginning of the year, a number that did not even take into account all those described as "passengers."[27]

The Business of "Unprincipled Rascals": Provisioning Contracts

The uprising not only opened markets for the intercolonial slave trade. Merchants immediately understood that colonial authorities, responsible for supporting troops and feeding refugees fleeing the countryside, would have to establish lucrative provisioning contracts with well-positioned firms. Cities were overcrowded with people whose supposed wealth had become meaningless. Planters and managers had flocked there with their families and Black servants who, for the most part, had been forced to accompany them, and an increasing number of widows and orphans were dependent on public help. Crops produced beyond the urban stockades were inaccessible. One merchant predicted that "good newly arrived flour will sell very well." Given price volatility and the uncertainties surrounding Saint-Domingue's harvests, signing a provisioning contract with the government appeared the safest way to profit from the revolt.[28]

Some of these contracts were implemented within Saint-Domingue. One of the firms that was the greatest beneficiary was the French-American merchant house, Zacharie, Coopman & Cie. Originally from Lyon, Etienne Zacharie and his partner, Jean-Baptiste Vaucher, had settled in Baltimore in the 1780s, while Francis Coopman, a native of Flanders, had moved to Saint-Domingue at around the same time. Their Cap-Français merchant house was the first to sell US food-stuff to the colonial government in October 1791, and it went on to secure a succession of increasingly lucrative contracts. On February 16, 1792, the house undertook to deliver $201,000 worth of edibles in five months. Etienne Wante, a special envoy from Saint-Domingue to the United States, struck two new contracts with Zacharie at the Consulate General in Philadelphia in November 1792 and January 1793. At this point, the colonial government owed the firm 3.5 million livres coloniales, a truly enormous amount. But the success of the firm is slightly surprising as the prices it offered were 50 percent higher than the current market rates and the company lacked the logistical means to fulfill the contract. Zacharie, who was not among the most prominent ship owners in Baltimore, had to outsource the shipments to larger trading houses.[29]

While traders continued demanding the implementation of free trade and abolition of the exclusif, they also sought to monopolize the market, resorting to techniques that had nothing to do with invisible market forces. Zacharie Coopman's commercial strategies perfectly illustrate this point. The firm received support from the colonial administration, which relentlessly demanded that payment to this merchant house be a priority. Wante, the official envoy to the United States, was not a disinterested official, having many friends among Cap-Français's trading community. Zacharie was hosting Wante's wife in Baltimore at the time Wante was negotiating contracts on behalf of the colonial administration; Zacharie was even a witness at Wante's second marriage to a refugee from Saint-Domingue, Marie-Rose Dubreuil, which took place in Maryland. The second witness to this marriage was Yves Bizouard, treasurer of the colony, who validated appropriation of the funds. In other words, supply contracts were made with friends and, according to Zacharie's many enemies, involved bribery. The vice-consul in Baltimore even denounced the French consul general for receiving payoffs from the shady firm. The controversial contracts became more politicized when Saint-Domingue's Colonial Assembly accused the government of corruption and conflict of interest, but as the company ceased to exist after the burning of Cap-Français, the affair went no further.[30]

The merchant who benefited most from the revolt never set foot in Saint-Domingue. Throughout his career, illustrious Boston merchant and financier James Swan wanted to be part of something noble and important, while deriving wealth and prominence from his political standing. The embodiment of commercial republicanism in the revolutionary era, this Scottish native had been brought to New England at age eleven and went on to distinguish himself during the American Revolution: a member of the Sons of Liberty during the Boston Tea Party in December 1773 and on the Massachusetts Board of War. Swan established his fortune by marrying a rich heiress from New England and speculating on the properties confiscated from loyalists in Virginia, Pennsylvania, Maine, and Boston. The debt crisis of the 1780s, however, wiped out his newly built wealth, prompting him to seek new business opportunities in France based on wartime connections with senior figures in the entourage of Admiral Charles Henry Hector d'Estaing and Jean-Baptiste Donatien de Vimeur, comte de Rochambeau. With this strong backing, Swan traveled to Rouen and Le Havre, a booming slave-trading port during the 1780s. He prepared a memorandum explaining why the metropolitan French trade had failed in the United States and made recommendations. This was translated into French by Philippe Joseph André de Létombe, the Boston consul and dedicated to Lafayette. In Paris, Swan met with Pierre Gilbert Le Roy, baron d'Allarde (then Dallarde), an influential member of the Constituent Assembly, whose famous decrees of March 2 and 17, 1791, suppressed corporations. At the end of the legislature the two men joined forces to create Dallarde, Swan & Cie.[31]

Saint-Domingue's turmoil would be a formidable commercial springboard for the new firm. Swan, who was also a friend of Jacques-Pierre Brissot, addressed a memorandum to the Colonial Committee of the Legislative Assembly in which he presented a general supply plan for the colony in a time of crisis. He recommended funding this from the balance of American debt contracted during the American Revolution and insisted that someone such as himself, with connections on both sides of the Atlantic, was in the best position to provide for the colonies' needs. His lobbying proved effective. On November 2, 1792, the firm secured a significant contract with the Ministry of the Navy in Paris. For a 5 percent commission—2.5 percent was the norm—Swan undertook to supply US foodstuffs to all the French colonies between December 1792 and February 1793. Salted meat and fish were at a fixed price, paid in London via bills of exchange and abandoned at Swan's peril. The French consuls, who were to verify the quality and "loyalty" of the goods, diligently supervised the operations.[32]

The monthly consumption of sea and land troops employed in Saint-Domingue was 5,000 barrels of flour and 1,000 barrels of salted beef. Swan, who remained in Paris, delegated the shipments to ship owners from Boston and New York. In early 1793, just before the French National Assembly declared war on Britain, fourteen ships set out with Dallarde, Swan & Cies' cargo. The success of this venture gave Swan's career a formidable boost. In April, Swan secured another, even more ambitious contract with the ministry for provisioning colonies in the entire empire, including the Mascarene islands and Senegal. The sum of 2,218,000 livres was immediately made available, to be converted into pounds sterling for "purchases, charters, cancellations and insurance."[33]

It was on the strength of his successful colonial shipments that Swan emerged as a prominent partner with a new public body created by the French revolutionary government: the Subsistence Commission. The firm submitted bids to supply not only the colonies but also the metropole. It secured substantial contracts to import into France 30,000 tons of vegetables and 60,000 quintals of rice from the United States, 100,000 ox leathers from Libourne, and 250,000 quintals of wheat from Cadiz. On 29 Messidor Year II (July 17, 1794), Swan was appointed agent of the French Republic in the United States and awarded a 5 million livres monopoly contract to ensure supplies to the metropole. Swan's firm reached its peak. By the decree of 6 Pluviôse year III (January 25, 1795), the Committee of Public Safety delegated the balance of the public US debt to Swan in order to benefit from his credit. He was commissioned to negotiate directly with the Department of the Treasury to liquidate French claims, as the federal government wanted to repatriate its funds from the Dutch banks. Swan was in

Figure 5.2   Colonel James Swan by Gilbert Stuart. Museum of Fine Arts, Boston Swan Collection—Bequest of Miss Elizabeth Howard Bartol 27.538, oil on canvas 73.66 x 60.96 cm.

charge of a credit line worth 11,156,473 livres tournois. The national bank put up for sale 5.5 percent interest on US government debt so it could provide cash to Swan. Many of these titles were in fact sold on the London market. The Swan affair anticipated the financial management of a "cashless state," mortgaging its assets to supplier-bankers. James Monroe, the new US ambassador in Paris, was horrified by this development, complaining to his friend, James Madison, that Swan was a "corrupt unprincipled rascal," yet "by virtue of being the Agent of France" had "a monopoly of the trade of both countries." Swan's rise to prominence was directly connected with Saint-Domingue's revolution.[34]

Food and Public Debt

On the ground, however, procurements from Zacharie Coopman and Swan could not meet the colony's vast and pressing requirements. The government needed to tender contracts to a multitude of smaller merchants,

despite lacking the financial means to do so. In 1788, the colonial government had spent 11 million livres coloniales and earned around 14 million in
tax revenues. From October 1791 to May 1792, Saint-Domingue's Northern
Province's expenses more than doubled these amounts to reach 23.3 million
livres coloniales, while revenues plummeted. More than 40 percent of these
expenses were related to food provisioning. The US and Spanish sea captains
who brought flour, salted goods, and fresh meat demanded payment in cash,
but as Cutting reports in his diary "there is little or no specie in the Treasury
here" and "the Capitalists are not inclined to advance any Cash to Government
at this Critical moment."[35]

A scarcity of coinage existed before 1789, fueling constant debates within
Saint-Domingue's learned societies. François de Neufchâteau, then a public official in the colony, had published a *Memoir on the scarcity of cash*, in which he
suggested freeing Spanish trade from all prohibitions in order to stimulate the introduction of precious metals. Indeed, as historian Robert Lacombe explained,
"Saint-Domingue's membership in the French monetary system" was "theoretical"; "its true monetary unit was the piastre, or 'coin of 8', struck in Mexico
City or in Peru." Neufchâteau's recommendations, however, were not heeded.
Although the problem was not new, due to the monetary crisis affecting the metropole, where the French Revolution had prompted an unprecedented flight of
gold and silver, it took on a greater significance.[36]

The creation of paper money made it possible to compensate for the lack of
circulating coinage and could offset the financial deficit caused by the insurrection. *Assignats*, paper money designed by the revolutionaries to save France
from bankruptcy and backed by confiscated church property, had served such a
purpose in the metropole. Local administrators also issued a multitude of local
currencies termed "patriotic bonds." In December 1791, the main financial officer in Saint-Domingue proposed issuing such "cash vouchers" worth 4 million livres coloniales. These vouchers were bonds that could be reimbursed in
cash after six months: they were delivered to suppliers and were intended to become commercial paper. Unlike the assignats, however, they were not backed
by national property but by the promise of forthcoming taxes. The administration hoped that "before this term the revenues will increase, and the expenses
decrease." Rebuking these unconvincing talking points, colonists and traders
strongly rejected a new paper money intended to create colonial public debt
and subject to speculations. "Money schemes have been agitated in the Colonial
Assembly," Cutting warned, and "if it was to be carried into effect, in my humble
opinion it would put the finishing hand to the ruin of this Colony."[37]

Without cash and paper money, the main means of payment consisted
of drafts on the French National Treasury, which represented two-thirds of
public expenses made in Saint-Domingue. Merchants were unenthusiastic and

negotiated an acceptance of these drafts against reinstatement of the courts to compel debtors to pay what they owed. The assembly authorized debt proceedings, with the exception of those concerning foodstuffs purchased after the beginning of the insurrection. In return, payments were to be made in devaluated drafts on the National Treasury, thereby erasing part of the debt. Traders with the best connections employed other means of credit in their private transactions, particularly bills of exchange on London, since French bankers were deemed unreliable. However, the colonial government repeatedly forced the purchase of commodities in drafts on the treasury.[38]

These measures provided short-term respite but also amplified distrust and speculation. Transactions were carried out with the discount of bills at 55 percent or 60 percent of losses. Moreover, the situation rapidly spiraled out of control as officials in the south provided such drafts without the consent of Saint-Domingue's main authorities. In the metropole, the National Assembly, which had not assigned these funds from the colonial budget, rejected requests for payment. The financial problem soon collided with the political question: the colonial question. Representatives of the colonists had been constantly requesting help, but Brissot and the Girondin deputies blocked financial aid, fearing these funds would be used with secessionist intent. The political polarization explains why exceptional funds were not allocated until March 27, 1792, and even then were limited to a fairly small amount. Although financial expert and deputy Pierre-Joseph Cambon deemed that 80 million livres tournois were necessary to provide Saint-Domingue with adequate help, the decree extended only 6 million livres tournois for disaster relief. This impasse, created by tensions between the National Assembly and the Colonial Assembly, continued until 1795. The decree of March 27, 1792, was only the first in a long series relating to Saint-Domingue drafts, and the issue returned again and again to the National Assembly. Between each decree, the payment of bonds was suspended. As funds proved to be insufficient every time, the Assembly was repeatedly confronted with the acceptance or refusal of drafts arriving in the metropole. These constant equivocations exposed the fissures of the imperial state and undermined the public credit of Saint-Domingue.[39]

This was not the only financial problem merchants faced. A substantial part of the relief awarded was assigned to US debt contracted during the War of Independence. In March 1792 this was valued at 29 million livres (on an initial loan of 34 million livres, plus interest). The main part of this sum was used to supply France. After the outbreak of Saint-Domingue's uprising in August 1791, the French ambassador to the United States began to negotiate payment of an advance on the monthly repayment of the debt. The plan was to immediately finance shipments of flour and ammunition destined for Saint-Domingue. In September 1791, he secured an advance from Washington and Hamilton of $40,000 (about 220,000 livres) and in March 1792 a payment of $400,000 (2.2 million livres) was made in four installments of $100,000, but these sums quickly proved insufficient. Colonial authorities, however, paid American captains in bills of exchange on Philadelphia, with the hope that the ambassador could secure other advances.[40]

At the end of 1792, bills amounted to 3,286,183 livres tournois, well in excess of the available funds of 48,903 livres. Increasing numbers of American traders were provided with unpaid bills. Some suppliers received a combination of drafts on the French General Consulate in the United States and the National Treasury, which were also rejected. With the arrival of Ambassador Edmond-Charles Genet in Philadelphia, the situation worsened, as colonial authorities started paying their suppliers with anticipations on the payment of US debt. Genet thought this technique would put pressure on the US federal government, but in fact, it merely increased distrust toward the French. A wide variety of commercial paper was in circulation, disrupting Saint-Domingue markets. In most cases, the colonial administration bought goods by combining drafts on the treasury, drafts on Philadelphia, and, the best option for merchants, cash or colonial commodities. Traders swiftly realized that all these bonds were bad debt, dubiously guaranteed by France's claims on the United States. James Swan took advantage of Saint-Domingue's financial chaos as he took on the US debt to France in 1795. In the meantime, however, the situation deteriorated and contributed to one of the most significant events of Saint-Domingue's revolution.[41]

The Commercial Origins of the Battle of Cap-Français

Trade tensions created by the speculative bubble, the financial crisis, and Saint-Domingue's food needs escalated dramatically in the days before the battle of Cap-Français. On May 24, 1793, the new governor appointed by metropolitan authorities, François-Thomas Galbaud, landed in the colony. He invited Cap-Français's merchants to deliberate on urgent measures to "fly to the aid of public affairs." Galbaud deemed it necessary to immediately provide for the troops defending a city under siege. As Britain had entered the war on February 1, 1793, almost no shipments were arriving from France, and British privateers had already flocked to Saint-Domingue's coasts. Only the United States could supply the colony. Faced with the risk of shortages and solicited by forty-four US captains, Galbaud summoned the various bodies representing the political, military, and economic powers of the colony: all major officials, prominent planters, traders, and American sea captains.[42]

The government, it was decided, would borrow colonial commodities from French traders and barter these with US captains for foodstuff. Rather than receiving drafts on the National Treasury, American merchants were willing to swap their goods for sugar and coffee, and they lobbied the governor for "produce from the country according to a tariff drawn up for this purpose." Circumstances were favorable: over a hundred French ships loaded with colonial goods were gathered in Cap-Français harbor, waiting to cross the Atlantic as a convoy. Acquiring these goods promised to be more profitable for the American merchants than the government's bad debt. French and American traders negotiated prices for the commodities "with all the loyalty and frankness which characterize two free nations and imbued with real republican sentiments." The transaction, staged with pomp, fulfilled a quasi-diplomatic function: the traders represented two allied republics and friendly nations. This commercial operation, carried out within the framework of a republican ceremony, signified a regenerated form of alliance.[43]

The facts, however, provide a scathing rebuttal to this language of commercial republicanism. The unity celebrated by official voices obscured the disagreements and frustrations that quickly emerged during deliberations. Some French traders were indignant that the price of American flour exceeded offers made to them in earlier, private transactions. Merchant M. Paouilhac accused the commissioners Jean-François Crevon, Jouves, and Aubert of lacking "patriotism." One merchant mentioned that his firm had enemies "whose number is . . . great" and who would use any "means to send traps." Galbaud scared many traders when he proclaimed that property rights "were illusionary and meaningless when the Republic is in danger." The government itself displayed little trust in American merchants. "Foot and horse patrols" inspected stores to "prevent the transport from one house to another of all kinds of provisions." Ultimately, American traders provided goods for a value of 671,385 livres coloniales. The "French," however, defaulted, refusing to deliver the promised colonial commodities.[44]

Commercial frictions between US and French merchants merged with Saint-Domingue's fractious politics. The encroachment of US commerce into the colony had far-reaching consequences and contributed, albeit unwillingly, to the watershed events that reshaped the history of the French empire. Although Galbaud was the new governor, he was supposed to obey the civilian commissioners, Léger-Félicité Sonthonax and Etienne Polverel, who had been sent by the National Assembly to enforce the rights of free people of color and quell the slave insurrection. However, planters and sailors incited Galbaud to defy the commissioners. Sonthonax and Polverel had been away from Saint-Domingue's main port for some time and, on their return, were horrified by Galbaud's policymaking. On June 13, 1793, they dismissed the governor and ordered him back to the metropole. French traders viewed this power struggle as an opportunity to escape their debts, and they turned to Sonthonax and Polverel. On their request, the civil commissioners denounced the "illegal" assembly of May 24, which, according to them, had resuscitated the "corporations" of the ancien régime. However, to ensure "public faith" and the "credit of the administration," they ordered that the Americans be "paid without delay in money or colonial supplies." Uncooperative French merchants would be forced to deliver these goods by any route within three days or be imprisoned. On June 17, the commission announced charges against twenty-seven requisitioned firms. Some had to pay up to 36,000 livres coloniales in coffee, sugar, cotton, and molasses. Yet the French merchants continued to resist, even concealing the commodities on their vessels.[45]

According to merchant Samuel Perkins, the squabbling was one of the catalysts for the outbreak of hostilities in Cap Français. Infuriated American merchants—who had formed an effective lobbying group—spent the day of June 18 "hunting up the delinquents." But the latter either "absolutely refused to do anything" or "kept themselves out of [the Americans'] reach." As a result, the committee of American creditors went to the court of justice to demand punishment be implemented. Samuel Perkins recalled the day of June 19 when they took this radical step:

> Returning home they found the stores everywhere shut. The most gloomy silence prevailed in the streets, and the inhabitants, who were collected at various places in small knots or groups, eyed the committee as they passed, and showed evidently that they were speaking of them or their measures. . . . [A]t my house I was called up into the balcony, and a spy-glass was put into my hand. "See," said my partner, "the ships of war are getting springs on their cables, have brought their broadsides against the town; what can all this mean?"

The battle of Cap-Français began the next day. This five-day conflagration reduced the largest port in the French West Indies to ashes, sparked the influx of thousands of refugees to the United States, and ultimately resulted in the abolition of slavery.[46]

Although Perkins had "no other evidence than the circumstances themselves," the Bostonian never had "the slightest doubt" that the French traders acted in response to the American creditors' move and switched their allegiance back to Galbaud to counter Sonthonax and Polverel, who planned on coercing them to pay their debts. It is certainly true that sailors and planters targeted free people of color who they believed threatened the foundations of colonial society. It is also true that French traders, responsible for the vessels anchored in the harbor, had a lot at stake and a major voice in the matter. Pierre Guymet and Pierre Gauvain, who were among the main "instigators" and "accomplices" of Galbaud, had just been been heavily fined for not delivering their sugar and coffee to the US traders. By standing behind the governor, the French merchants were supporting the racist project he embodied and hoped to escape their debts to the Americans. The burning of Cap-Français fulfilled their wish: they never paid back the 670,000 livres they owed. Yet the US captains did not lose everything. Taking over the city, the Black revolutionaries were more than eager to trade not only the merchandise they had found in abandoned warehouses but also goods they brought from the plains. They were willing to make deals with Americans, who, although whites, were deemed "better" than the French. The haggling, occurring in the middle of a battlefield, was inventing a new kind of commercial republicanism, a truly revolutionary one.[47]

From 1789 to 1793, commercial republicanism, the aspiration that trade could effectuate a newer kind of international relations on equal terms, both flourished and collapsed. During those four years, the US trade in Saint-Domingue refashioned the French-American alliance in the context of entangled insurrections. Merchants were geopolitical actors in their own rights, following their own interests and logics, which at times intersected with the governments' stated intents, and at times contradicted them. At any rate, they did not remain passive victims of revolutionary events. On the one hand, they fought to preserve the economic model of Saint-Domingue and creatively speculated on flour, sugar, coffee, cotton, molasses, and other commodities. They even expanded the scope of the slave trade, decisively contributing to Cuban expansion. On the other hand, trade paradoxically and indirectly influenced political developments, not by spreading a liberal discourse of civilization, but by producing explosive conditions. American traders led the market to saturation and ferociously competed for sizable public contracts. Uneven growth and mounting competition caused friction between "French" and "American" merchants, which intersected with Saint-Domingue's racial politics and boiled over in June 1793.

The destruction of Cap-Français shook the commercial world of the Antilles to its foundations. While only a few traders lost their lives in the battle, many more lost their account books, merchandise, and warehouses, or at least claimed they did. A number of enslaved people who used to serve them in Cap-Français also joined the insurgents: Cupidon, Azor, Robin, George, and Congo started new lives when they refused to accompany Jean Dutilh and Etienne Soulier who fled the city in flames for Baltimore.[48]

In this context the Black revolutionaries in the northern plain aptly exploited the many divisions of the colonial elite, exposing the cracks of French-American commercial republicanism. They played the leading role in Saint-Domingue's abolition of slavery, inciting Sonthonax and Polverel to proclaim general freedom as a consequence of the battle. Their acts also made clear that the Saint-Domingue revolution was not the logical continuation of an Atlantic revolution spreading universal and homogenous ideas. The island's events were driving the French Revolution away from the American Revolution. The French-American alliance nonetheless provided the logistical conditions for imperial emancipation. When the Black deputy Jean-Baptiste Belley, the mixed-race deputy Jean-Baptiste Mills, and the white deputy Louis Pierre Dufay left Saint-Domingue to carry news of abolition abroad, they embarked on a vessel intended for the United States, to avoid crossing the Atlantic on a French ship vulnerable to British privateers. The United States, a necessary stopover on the way to Paris, would play a role in the history of French republicanism, just not the one imagined in 1789.

6

The Atlantic Politics of Commercial Republicanism, 1793–1794

> On September 21, 1792, the National Assembly proclaimed the freedom of France, or rather that of Europe. That same day, on September 21, 1793, the Assembly must proclaim the freedom of commerce, or rather that of the seas. It is not enough to found the political republic, it is necessary to found the commercial republic.
>
> Bertrand Barère, *Archives Parlementaires*,
> t. LXXIV, 597 (September 21, 1793)

It was in these terms that Bertrand Barère, on behalf of the Committee of Public Safety, solemnly celebrated the first anniversary of the French Republic. In the eyes of the prolific speaker, nascent republicanism could not be defined in exclusively political terms. If the republic was the expression of popular sovereignty and was opposed by nature to the monarchy, it should also be endowed with a maritime and commercial dimension that would give meaning to the liberating role of France on the global scene. That is, it should extend to peoples united by the reciprocal interest of economic exchanges who were fighting a coalition of kings tied by kinship. The expansion of the republican transformation should be institutionalized in a French "Navigation Act," inspired by the British Navigation Act but based on "democratic" values. Beyond intellectual theorizing, republicanism must be put into practice through a new form of commercial diplomacy, a political culture that reconciled virtue and private interests, cosmopolitanism and patriotism, defense of the community and market values. The Franco-American alliance, the growth of West Indian trade, and the prohibition of British vessels from that trade could regenerate the world and free the seas from naval tyranny.

This stately proclamation, with its extremely lofty ambitions, is generally missing from the grand narrative of the French Revolution. The thundering speech, given as a vulnerable republic teetered on the verge of collapse, was

Entrepôt of Revolutions. Manuel Covo, Oxford University Press. © Oxford University Press 2022.
DOI: 10.1093/oso/9780197626382.003.0007

decidedly untimely and quickly disappeared from the annals of history. Battling almost all of Europe, France was also in the midst of a civil war, with insurgencies taking place in many cities and provinces, especially in the western region of Vendée. Intended to mobilize a fragile republic, the speech proclaiming the "commercial constitution of the French Empire" would not be alone in the cemetery of projects imagined by the National Convention. Moreover, its celebration of liberty was in stark contrast with a revolutionary government breaking away from the ordinary rule of law. The democratic constitution approved by universal suffrage in June 1793 had been abandoned. Under pressure from the Parisian sans-culottes, the Convention adopted increasingly repressive measures against an expanding number of vaguely defined political opponents. From an economic point of view, with grain prices being regulated under the Law of the Maximum, it appears unlikely that any ambitious position would be taken in favor of free trade. However, it is precisely the historical focus on the "Terror" that has made a speech belonging to a longer imperial history incomprehensible.[1]

This chapter explores the global genesis and disintegration of the "commercial Republic," a French colonial empire regenerated by the Franco-American relationship and the freedom of the seas. Barère's announcement illuminates an aspect of French republicanism often overlooked, an aspect traversed by transnational tensions and marked by significant ambiguities. What did Barère actually mean by "liberty of commerce"? In times of war, the freedom to trade related less to the commercial regime of colonies, such as the colonial exclusif, than to the right of neutrals to trade with the enemy. In 1793, a heated debate was taking place over the definition and acceptance of US neutrality in the global conflict between France and Great Britain. At issue was whether French law should reaffirm the so-called modern definition of neutrality as established in the 1778 Treaty of Amity and Commerce, according to which "free ships make free goods," or a return to earlier practices. Britain had rejected the principle of neutrality and with the Rule of 1756 legalized the seizing of cargo destined for colonial ports closed to foreign trade in peacetime. Should France appease neutrals in the context of the country's diplomatic isolation from an almost united Europe? Or was it necessary to copy the British model in order to weaken the enemy?[2]

Debates about neutrality not only called the meaning of French republicanism into question but also placed Saint-Domingue at the center of lawmakers' concerns. However, it was not France taking the initiative but Britain, which, at the request of Saint-Domingue colonists, was wielding its maritime power. Discussions in London about the legality of US trade in the Caribbean preceded the debates over France's commercial policies. In Paris, confrontations between a variety of opposing pressure groups made the French Navigation Act incoherent. Eventually, Barère's grand vision foundered on the political realities of the early American republic, shaken by the repercussions of the French and

Haitian revolutions. Far from consolidating the unity of revolutionary republics, the "liberty of commerce" revealed an insurmountable diversity.

The British Initiative

In the early 1790s, the British Empire was going through its own massive identity crisis. The loss of the thirteen American colonies, expansion in India, the abolition debate, and the double impact of the French and Saint-Domingue revolutions gave way to what historian Abigail Swingen calls "competing visions of empire." Trade with the United States had been tightly controlled under the British Navigation Act; in the aftermath of the American Revolution, legislation was made even more stringent. The Order-in-Council of July 2, 1783, which prohibited vessels under the US flag from entering West Indian colonial ports, was renewed each year and, in 1788, became law. The West India Lobby vainly attempted to combat this restrictive policy. Jamaican planter Edward Long, for instance, wrote a pamphlet praising the French exclusif legislation (the arrêt of 1784) and emphasized the inability of mainland British colonies (Canada, Newfoundland, and the Northwest Territory) to provide the same goods as the United States. Another prominent Jamaican planter, Bryan Edwards, argued that the exclusion of US shipping made British goods less competitive than those of Saint-Domingue, the jewel of a "rival and enemy" France. Countless newspaper articles made the same point. Interest groups defending the position of American merchants added to this chorus of condemnation. The government itself was highly divided on the issue. Prime Minister William Pitt, an admirer of Adam Smith's political economy, believed a policy inclined toward free trade would benefit the empire. Nevertheless, despite support from Edmund Burke and many Whig representatives, West Indian planters failed to reform the Navigation Act.[3]

Supporters of the colonial monopoly dictated British policy. Following in the footsteps of Lord Sheffield, American loyalist George Chalmers published several important pamphlets on the Navigation Act, which earned him the position of first clerk on the Committee for Trade. Chalmers challenged US claims on West Indian trade by asserting the right of every independent state to regulate its trade. But the most prominent defender of the Navigation Act was Charles Jenkinson, known as Lord Hawkesbury, the indefatigable president of a revitalized Board of Trade from 1786. Convinced that Cromwellian legislation had established British supremacy, Hawkesbury came to embody the Navigation Act as the guarantor of its perpetuation. Thanks to the exclusion of the Americans, in Hawkesbury's view, British shipping was more prosperous than ever, now boasting a tonnage of 110,000, up from 94,000 before the

American Revolution. As he summarized in a landmark statement: "Though we had lost a dominion, we might almost be said to have gained an empire." Rather than the futile conquest of infinite territories, maritime and commercial power were the real foundations of empire.[4]

Hawkesbury did not reject all reform. The new Board of Trade, anxious to modernize some aspects of commercial regulations, conducted numerous inquiries, inviting key stakeholders to express their opinions. Hawkesbury strongly supported extending the free port system in the Caribbean and in 1787 added two new ports that could legally admit certain commodities produced in the West Indies. Noting that cotton production in the British colonies could not meet the needs of Manchester textile manufacturers, the board encouraged importation of produce from Saint-Domingue while ensuring that British commerce would profit: US ships were prohibited, not US goods. This reform was not inspired by a dogmatic free-trade ideology but a "science" of regulation; a permanent adaptation to the commercial and political context.[5]

Hawkesbury, however, did draw a line in the sand: US vessels should never be permitted to enter the West Indies. A report on American-British trade submitted by the Board of Trade on January 28, 1791, made this perfectly clear. As this policy had proved such a success, materializing in a substantial increase in British commerce in the Americas, the report concluded that the government should uphold this legislation, the heart of imperial identity. The "public law of Europe" had established that metropoles had exclusive control over the commercial regulation of their colonies. Moreover, Britain had to reject the "modern" neutrality law championed by France in 1778. Hawkesbury proclaimed that "any Article, allowing the Ships of the United States to protect the Property of the Enemies of Great Britain in time of War, should on no account be admitted." The United States, much more than Denmark or Sweden, posed a serious threat to the vital interests of the empire. "From their Situation," he warned, "the Ships of these States would be able to cover the whole Trade of France and Spain with their Islands and Colonies in America and the West Indies." William Grenville, foreign secretary, belabored a similar principle: "Free ships do not make free goods." Although the contraband trade with the United States in the Caribbean would never be eliminated and local officials continued to suspend the Navigation Act in times of crisis, the metropole clung to its claim of sovereignty over colonial commerce.[6]

With the onset of the French and Saint-Domingue Revolutions, the British government was forced to reconsider this policy. At first, Britain was reluctant to become enmeshed in any part of the turmoil. Although some planters expressed concerns that the Saint-Domingue uprising might have repercussions in other parts of the Caribbean, Pitt was not displeased that the French were experiencing such colonial chaos and that many Jamaican planters were profiting from the crisis as French competition waned. The prime minister also believed Britain would benefit from the turbulence in Europe; he avoided involvement in the conflict between France and Austria that began in April 1792. As the economy began to flounder, however, Pitt was drawn into war. Believing the revolutionary contagion might cross the Channel, the government became anxious that British radical clubs on the "Jacobin model" could proliferate. Pitt was particularly alarmed when the French Republic was proclaimed in August 1792, fearing that revolutionary armies might invade the Netherlands. The French decree on November 19, 1792, promising "fraternity and help to all peoples who [would] recover their freedom" could subvert the entire continent. The beheading of Louis XVI was the final straw. At that point, war became inevitable.[7]

Since Pitt was mostly concerned with European affairs, why did he focus British military might on conquest of the French West Indies? In fact, Saint-Domingue colonists played a crucial role in shaping Pitt's Caribbean strategy. Envoys from the French West Indies had sought protection from Britain since the slave insurrection of August 1791 but only secured the ear of British authorities at the end of 1792. Many were absent proprietors and former members of Club Massiac who had left France for London in August of that year, the day after the fall of the monarchy. The four leading negotiators were the adventurer Pierre-François Venault de Charmilly, who had started talks in the summer of 1791, and three former members of the French Constituent Assembly: Louis de Curt for Guadeloupe, Arthur Dillon for Martinique, and Pierre-Victor Malouet for Saint-Domingue. Although they offered to deliver the colonies to Britain, promising to actively support British occupation in order to preserve slavery and the "prejudice of color," they fiercely debated the terms of British intervention. They successfully convinced the prime minister that France's power derived largely from Saint-Domingue's wealth.[8]

The commercial regulations Britain intended to enforce in the occupied French island were contentious from the start. Unsurprisingly, French colonists remained as divided on the issue as they had been since the onset of the grain crisis in 1788. Venault de Charmilly made the case that the real threat to British interests in the Caribbean was not France but the young American republic, "the eternal enemy and the most dangerous rival for England." Exploiting the argument articulated by Anne Robert Jacques Turgot in 1776, he warned Pitt that the "North Americans" would "turn their eyes to the sugar islands and Spanish possessions" and "carry the torch of freedom that the Creoles are awaiting so impatiently." Chalmers echoed this by expounding on US threats to British commerce in the West Indies. However, some colonists refused to exchange the exclusif for the Navigation Act, conditioning their support for British intervention with the right to admit US vessels to the French West Indies.[9]

The Board of Trade had no definitive stance on a subject that came under meticulous scrutiny. De Curt met Lord Hawkesbury twice in December 1792 to convince him that Britain should at least endorse the *exclusif mitigé* and allow the United States to engage in some level of trade with the islands. His partial success enraged British planters and customs officials, who resented the preferential treatment enjoyed by the French Antilles. Transfer proposals were submitted to the Government for the Windward Islands on February 19 and for Saint-Domingue six days later. Article 10 of the Saint-Domingue proposal stipulated that import and export duties for European goods should be "settled on the same footing as in the English colonies"; but Article 13 stated, "Until the devastated areas are repaired, navigation will be free with the United States." Venault de Charmilly forwarded this set of rules to the Jamaican governor, Adam Williamson, and to the white Saint-Domingue colonists who recognized it as the legal basis for their "capitulation" in September 1793. Article 12 stated that "the importation of food, livestock, grain and timber of any kind from the United States of America shall be permitted in Saint-Domingue on American vessels." This compromise was intended to reconcile the interests of French colonists and British merchants, whose financial support was essential for military success and the restoration of damaged plantations. Through this clause, the Board of Trade had provisionally relaxed trade restrictions without challenging the core principles of the Navigation Act. After all, tolerating temporary foreign trade was part and parcel of British imperial governance.[10]

The real issue was not the legalization of American shipping to occupied Saint-Domingue but US neutrality in Europe and the Caribbean. Determined to avoid the mistakes made during the American Revolution, when the fleets of France, Spain, and the Netherlands aligned against the Royal Navy, the British government intended to employ its formidable maritime power to starve the isolated French enemy. The 1756 rule prohibited trade between neutrals and enemy ports that were closed to foreign trade in peacetime (in other words subject to the *exclusif*). The Order-in-Council of June 8, 1793, extended this to authorize privateers to capture any neutral vessel destined to supply France and laden with corn or flour, defined as contraband goods. This regulation—limited in scope since it did not apply to other kinds of foodstuff—provoked the ire of the United States. But the British position continued to harden, with Pitt launching a vast maritime expedition to occupy part of the French Antilles during the winter of 1793–1794. In order to prevent the mass arrival of Saint-Domingue commodities in Europe and to assist the naval campaign, Grenville adopted the brutal Order-in-Council of November 6, 1793. This went far beyond the 1756 decree: any ship, whatever it may be, could be captured if it were loaded with French colonial commodities. Prepared in the greatest secrecy, the order was interpreted by the governors of the West Indies in the most all-embracing way,

launching the privateers of Jamaica, Bermuda, and the Bahamas onto unpre-
pared American vessels. The results were spectacular: in less than four months,
250 US vessels had been captured in the Caribbean.[11]

While the British government ignored the ensuing outcry by US merchants,
it did take heed of the response to this maritime chaos from French colonists. At
a meeting of the Board of Trade on January 6, 1794, De Curt effectively proved
that Britain had contravened the law of 1756. Giving a detailed description of the
French commercial regime in the Caribbean, he demonstrated that according to
the exclusif mitigé French ports had been open to foreigners in peacetime; therefore, it was unlawful to prohibit US shipping to Saint-Domingue. His exposé
prompted the Board of Trade to recommend an immediate repeal of the order of
November 6, 1793. The new order, on January 8, 1794, rejected "modern neutrality" but circumscribed the legal perimeter of privateering. More goods were
defined as contraband: cargoes of foodstuff produced in the French colonies and
destined for Europe, shipments of French property, cargoes heading for ports
under siege, and war material. Nevertheless, direct trade between neutrals and
enemy islands was lawful once again. As long as the policy guaranteed successful
conquest of the French West Indies, Hawkesbury was open to a degree of flexibility. This legislation skillfully placated West Indian colonists, applied pressure
on US traders, and violently attacked French economic interests.[12]

Claiming sovereignty over the "Pearl of the Caribbean," the British governor
of Saint-Domingue, Adam Williamson, made the ideological meaning of this intervention clear: to consolidate the tenets of European colonialism and counter
the republican contagion in all its forms, including its commercial dimension.
A colony is not established to become "the theater of republican virtues, nor of
the development of human knowledge," he stated. Rather, the island's "true property is to make a lot of commodities, and the goal of the metropole is to export
the most with as little expense as possible." From this perspective, the expansion
of US trade and the Franco-American alliance were as treacherous a threat to
colonialism as the slave insurrection.[13]

The French Revolutionary Politics of Neutrality

The outbreak of hostilities with Britain compelled the French Republic to define
"freedom of the seas" and "neutrality." In 1792, the National Assembly had raised
the possibility of equating privateering with piracy and banning "private maritime warfare," but a majority vote could not be secured and no law materialized.
Many questions remained unanswered. Would French privateers have the right
to attack neutral ships conveying provisions to enemy ports? How would the
few French allies respond to a possible crackdown on neutral trade? In short,

the Franco-American treaty of alliance was to be put to the test. At the domestic level the issue was controversial. The year 1793 was marked by a clash between the Girondins, who, at this point, wanted to stop the French Revolution, and Montagnards, the most radical members of the Assembly, unrest in many provinces and cities during the "Federalist revolt," and the so-called Terror. But opinions on American neutrality did not neatly follow the divide between right and left. In fact, the issue became a flashpoint in revolutionary committee rivalry, a feature that had plagued the early stages of the French Revolution. In 1793, a tug of war began between the Naval Committee and the Committee of Public Safety, which was charged with overseeing the war efforts and ensuring the republic's survival. Rival factions competed over the Assembly's regulations without knowing the outcome of Edmond Charles Genet's mission to redefine the Franco-American alliance. Power struggles devolved into confusion and misunderstandings.[14]

Barère, an intransigent spokesman for the Committee of Public Safety who derived his colonial ideas from a geopolitical analysis of the balance of power between France and Britain, was a major protagonist in this confrontation. A diligent reader of Montesquieu's *Spirit of the Laws*, Barère firmly believed in economic bonds between republics and reproduced Gaspard Joseph Armand Ducher's pamphlets on "commercial diplomacy." On May 3, 1793, Barère offered to reimburse all expenses spent on outfitting neutral ships in order to prevent capture by the British. Inspired by the precedent of the American Revolution, he wanted to bring neutral powers together behind the banner of a "league of armed freedom." According to Barère, the Assembly should strengthen their alliance with the United States and endeavor to design a "French-American Navigation Act." Since trade was inherently political, France should grant privileges to countries that were authentically republican. Commerce would be the backbone of a global republican alliance based on popular sovereignty.[15]

Far from bringing the discussion to a close, Barère's statement incited furious responses from the backers of French privateers. Numerous pressure groups rebuffed the deputy's stance and strove to undermine the "Americanists," inundating the Naval Committee with petitions. As the Assembly debated whether the seizure of enemy cargoes on neutral vessels should be legal, the Naval Committee repudiated Barère's lead and, even before hearing the United States' response to the French-British war, championed the rights of ship owners. The Naval Committee's rapporteur, Charles-Louis Antiboul, presented a decree on May 9, 1793, intended to outline French policy on neutrality. France would attack Britain and force her to admit the principle of "freedom of the seas." This goal and the British "acts of inhumanity and injustice" justified suspension of the principles set forth in the 1778 Treaty. Looting of American, Danish, German, and Genoese ships by the British had already violated the "rights of the people."

Antiboul believed it was no longer possible to "fulfill, vis-à-vis all the neutral powers in general, the wish ... for the full and complete freedom of commerce and navigation." The decree of May 9, 1793, declared that enemy cargoes seized on neutral vessels could be legally confiscated.[16]

However, the US ambassador to France, Gouverneur Morris, intervened, highlighting the contradictions within the decree. Addressing a formal complaint to the minister of foreign affairs, he pointed out that Britain was in a far better position to retaliate than France and that the decree would only incite the British Empire to embrace the Rule of 1756. Given Britain's naval superiority, republican defeat was inevitable. Morris demanded that Article 23 of the 1778 Treaty be respected and convinced the Committee of Public Safety to make exceptions for countries that had treaties with France.[17]

From then on, the National Convention became a battleground for the two committees, eliciting four legal reversals in less than two months. The legislative whirlwind is hard to follow. Although the expulsion of the Girondins took place during the insurrections of sans-culottes on May 31 and June 2, this pivotal moment in the national narrative had little impact on the debates. The Committee of Public Safety successfully defended the principle that the early American republic should be exempted from restrictions on neutral rights and a decree to that effect was presented on May 23, 1793. Five days later, however, a deputy demanded the decree be suspended and a new report be drawn up by the Naval Committee. Morris reiterated his complaints to the new minister of foreign affairs. The Committee of Public Safety reengaged with the issue on June 30, and the following day Barère presented a report declaring the United States deserved "all the more respect as they [have become] the breadbasket of France." Barère drafted another decree through which the Convention, "wishing to maintain the union established between the French Republic and the United States of America," would exclude US ships from "the provisions of the decree of May 9, in accordance with article XVI of the treaty passed on February 6, 1778." The Convention appeared to bring the debate to an end by confirming the exemption on July 1.[18]

But the struggle was far from over. Three weeks later, Gouverneur Morris complained that a court in Le Havre was postponing making a decision about a US vessel seized by a French privateer. His informants told him the French captain was in touch with two members of the Naval Committee: Jacques Delacroix, a deputy of Eure, and Jacques-Louis Taveau, deputy of Honfleur, a port city on the Channel where the privateers had outfitted their ship. The tribunal members, aware that the Naval Committee was preparing a new decree, were stalling. In fact, Taveau wrote a report duplicating requests made by the privateer owners, members of the Jacobin Club. The minister of marine and colonies, Jean Dalbarade, a former corsair himself, supported the move. On July 27, the Naval Committee passed a decree that once again exposed American vessels to French privateering: Honfleur's local interests had prevailed.[19]

This succession of legal reversals illuminates important features of French revolutionary politics in 1793. The Committee of Public Safety was not an all-powerful warmongering institution. On the matter of neutrality, it proved far less hawkish than the Naval Committee, which eventually claimed victory. It could even be argued that a pressure group from a small provincial town had greater influence than the Committee of Public Safety. The usual divide between left and right, Girondins and Montagnards, or radicals and moderates, sheds little light on the more complex politics of lobbies and special interests.

The Commercial Constitution of the Empire

Debate about "the freedom of the seas" shifted to another, connected subject: the Navigation Act, through which Barère sought to circumvent the new neutrality laws on US shipping. The deputy resumed the project defined earlier by Ducher and unsuccessfully submitted to the Constituent Assembly in 1791. Barère believed the act would provide new military resources for the fragile republic. France must brace itself for a major trade war. Ironically, Barère, one of the most outspoken Anglophobes in the National Convention, praised the British model.[20]

The 1793 revolution was not constitutively anti-commercial and did not specifically oppress merchants. Under relentless pressure from the group called the *enragés* (Enraged), ultra-revolutionary activists who associated "hoarding" with "moderantism," the Montagnards paid lip service to the denunciation of *négociantisme* (mercantilism), but the general political perspective was ambivalent. Part of the sans-culotte discourse maintained that a trader could render a "public service" and act as a "public servant" working for the government. However, the sans-culottes did distinguish between the "patriotic" merchant and the disreputable "speculator" and "hoarder." The privateer, by conciliating private interests with the common good, embodied a regenerated form of trade, and his profits were also those of a republic at war. This ambivalent rhetoric partly explains why merchants faced negligible persecution during the revolutionary decade.[21]

Barère depicted trade as a powerful weapon in the global conflict. While violently denouncing Britain, he also wanted the French empire to "anglicize." His speech of May 29, 1793, on the state of the republic at war concluded that the Act of Navigation was urgently needed to create a "naval army." "Manufacturers and commercial establishments" would multiply and France would become a "maritime nation," able to thwart the ambitions of the "tyrant of the seas" and

Figure 6.1 La Liberté des mers by François Godefroy, c. 1794. Collection Hennin, 12276. Bibliothèque nationale de France, etching, 12 x 14 cm.

restore "freedom of trade" and "the right of nations." National trade, in a "patriotic" sense, should be distinguished from that of the "cosmopolitan" merchants, the "speculators." The reform would glue "the colonies to France" through their "own interests," based on "absolutely duty free" trade. This act would also inaugurate a new "commercial diplomacy" with all nations. This call revealed French maritime vulnerability. What had made the French Navy so effective at countering the Royal Navy during the preceding war was the Spanish alliance, but now France was alone. Despite French efforts in shipbuilding, Britain had twice as many ships as France in 1793. In this context, expanding the commercial fleet and favoring neutral powers such as the United States and Genoa were the only viable options.[22]

It is, however, difficult to know to what extent this imperial demand challenged the "colonial system" in its entirety and therefore slavery. A few days later the Jacobin Club and the Paris Commune associated with publicist Claude Milscent, deputy abbé Grégoire, and a few spokespeople for free people of color, petitioned to abolish slavery, making an argument based on political economy and geopolitics. A delegation led by Pierre-Gaspard Chaumette, leader of the

Paris Commune, and a Black woman Jeanne Odo, "aged 114," presented the petition to the National Convention on June 4, 1793. Signatories insisted on the better efficiency of waged labor and on the need to expand the French army in the Caribbean. Yet the only consequence of this event was the cancellation of the premiums granted to the slave trade on July 27. The Convention was far from being unanimous on the issue of abolition, and the "imperial revolution" imagined by Barère did not annihilate the old regime legacy. The priority was to restore France's maritime power.[23]

On July 3, 1793, deputy Pierre Marec from the port-city of Brest presented a first draft of an Act of Navigation in three articles. The act was intended to establish, alongside "the political constitution of the empire," the "first base of its commercial constitution," destroy "the intermediary of all indirect navigation in the maritime transport system," and "stop the intermediate coastal trade" that made France "dependent on the maritime powers of Europe." "Unlimited freedom" was a utopian idea that would never materialize and merchants and sailors could become the "true sans-culottes." Marec demanded that a national divide between French and foreign navigations be clearly established. He also believed the exemption granted to neutral and allied powers would strengthen republican bonds. In response, Deputy Joseph Delaunay claimed that France, dependent on Holland for its supply of goods from the North Sea, could not enact this first draft. The metropole had never been able to fully provision Saint-Domingue, even in peacetime.[24]

Revolutionary-minded Americans living in Paris often tried to influence decisions made by the National Assembly. The most prominent among them, Thomas Paine, who had been granted French citizenship and elected to the National Convention in September 1792, contacted Barère. Responding to pleas from the American captains stranded in Bordeaux by the embargo, the author of *Common Sense* lobbied the Committee of Public Safety on behalf of US trade. He wrote a twenty-page memorandum in which he called for the creation of a new French commission to the United States and suggested that neutrals could play a truly cosmopolitan role by organizing a far-reaching international conference to establish peace. Paine's efforts were not in vain since Barère included some of these ideas in a memorandum he submitted to the Committee of Public Safety.[25]

At the same time, lobbyists for the Saint-Domingue colonists, officially converted to republicanism, plotted behind the scenes. With the preservation of slavery their primary objective, Pierre-François Page and Augustin-Jean Brulley maneuvered themselves closer to the Montagnard ruling elite, benefiting from the expulsion of the Girondins, including the leader of the Amis des Noirs, Jacques-Pierre Brissot. Page and Brulley were in constant contact with the Committee of Public Safety through deputy Louis-Antoine Léon de Saint-Just, the young Montagnard leader and Robespierre's friend, whom they met with seventeen times between the beginning of June and the end of September as he prepared a report on the colonies. They also enjoyed the confidence of André Jeanbon Saint-André, the Committee of Public Safety member responsible for naval and colonial issues, who served as president of the Convention in July. Page and Brulley met Barère only later, but they visited Ducher at home. The Saint-Domingue commissioners were feigning support for the Navigation Act policy, a tactic that would make them appear to be "republicans" and convey the message that they opposed colonial independence. They also took up the American merchants' cause, demanding the Bordeaux embargo be lifted and utilizing their contacts in the Ministry of the Navy and the Naval Committee to that end.[26]

Supported by the Saint-Domingue colonists and advised by Paine and Ducher, Barère implemented his "commercial republic" project in September 1793. The new economic and political regime should reflect the national sovereignty of a republican people, and in the name of the legal equality of persons and territories, Barère sought to bring down the "great barrier" separating the colonies and the metropole. There should be no duties on goods circulating among them. The "colonists [were] also French" and must be treated as such since internal customs between French *départements* had been repealed in 1789. This principle went hand in hand with the desire to ensure the self-sufficiency of a regenerated national empire.[27]

The purpose of the Navigation Act was to regulate trade within a large economic zone; the law was not anti-liberal and even less anti-commercial. The first objective, nationalist and protectionist, was to seal the border between the British and French. The act was also intended to rally neutrals behind France, which presented itself as guarantor of their freedom and independence. Barère appropriated an ancient syllogism—"without navy, no colonies, and no colonies, no commercial prosperity"—but republicanized this through the legal "assimilation" of the colonies into the nation and the Franco-American alliance. Article 3 of the draft decreed that French vessels could export colonial cargoes to the United States, while US vessels would be allowed to introduce goods produced in the United States to the colonies. However, this conciliation of economic power and republicanism rested on ambiguity. The "freedom of the seas" relied on restoration of the French colonial monopoly—albeit in a modernized form, that is to say, "anglicized" and "nationalized"—and the recognition of neutrality. The imperial republic was a powerful republic, capable of defending its independence through commerce and naval power.[28]

The Navigation Act had the status of a "commercial constitution" and was therefore limited to six articles, but the practical details needed clarification. Ducher himself drafted the additions in forty articles, which Barère then submitted to the Convention on 17 Vendémiaire Year II (October 8, 1793); they were adopted ten days later. In fact, Ducher had practically copied the United States Navigation Act—enacted on July 20 and September 1, 1789—hoping this would prevent a commercial invasion of the colonies by the United States. Ducher warned that France would "lose its colonies" if the "Anglo-Americans" had access to unregulated trade, as they would "import the goods of their manufactures, of England, of the Great Indies, and . . . export sugar, cotton, indigo from the French West Indies into all the ports of Europe directly and without coming to France." "We will have no more colonial trade; we will have to sell or burn five thousand ships," lamented Ducher, adding that Saint-Domingue was "worth more to France than the most beautiful port of the Mediterranean."[29]

This law, albeit long-awaited, did not have the impact that Ducher and Barère expected. The press took little notice, reflecting a perhaps unsurprising lack of public interest in such matters during a time of Terror and global conflict. The advent of the "Commercial Republic" was devised by experts in the intricacies of maritime law. The new Maximum law on the other hand, regulating grain prices and wages, had tangible effects on the everyday lives of the French people. Moreover, the meaning of the Navigation Act remained obscure even to some members of the Committee of Public Safety. Saint-Just himself, who abhorred "the violent laws on trade" and believed "freedom of commerce was the mother of plenty," asked the Saint-Domingue colonists: "what should be done with regard to the Americans?"[30]

The proliferation of decrees and proclamations in response to changing circumstances, contradictory motivations, and an unstable political landscape had made France's policy virtually illegible. The message for the United States was blurred, particularly since the multiple texts, preceded by rumors, took months to reach America, by which time the political context had already changed on both sides of the Atlantic. For example, when the French ambassador received his orders, specified by a Girondin minister, the Montagnards had already eliminated their rivals. At times, news never reached its destination, and when it did, the text was often so unclear that French diplomats could ignore it or interpret it at will.[31]

On paper, the French Revolution engendered a commercial and imperial republic, a republic destined to ensure the liberty of the seas and protect the interests of less powerful nations. France was republican because a constitution defined the colonial relationship in legal terms. The regenerated nation proclaimed a global alliance between modern republics threatened by British thalassocracy. Since political sovereignty was officially associated with economic sovereignty, this was a commercial republic. It was also *puissante* (powerful), a key notion in the French imperial imagination. Yet the theory, vague and muddled as it was, had only limited resonance. In fact, the project broke down in the United States, the alliance between the two sister republics ending in spectacular failure.

The Impossible Commercial and Political Pact

Official policy was based on the hypothesis that the United States would support the French Republic against Great Britain. The Committee of Public Safety counted less on the military help of the young republic, which was devoid of a powerful war fleet, than on its logistical support. First and foremost, the United States was to provision the French colonies and provide a hinterland for French privateers. At the very least, the allied country was to terminate trade with the British enemy. However, Genet's mission to North America, intended to make the project a reality, proved a fiasco, following a series of events that played a crucial role in the political history of the United States.

The young minister arrived triumphantly in Charleston on April 16, 1793, to wide popular acclaim. Despite crowds flocking to Genet's meetings, his reception from the federal government, wary of becoming enmeshed in a European war, was decidedly cold. The French ambassador then proceeded to make innumerable diplomatic blunders: he outfitted American private vessels without consent from the US government, publicly attacked Alexander Hamilton, secretary of the treasury, for his supposed Anglophilia, and, catastrophically, antagonized the Francophile secretary of state, Thomas Jefferson. In addition, the Haitian Revolution fatefully disrupted Genet's endeavors. Not only did the ambassador face a massive influx of refugees from the French colonies, but he was also confronted with one of the most important events in the Age of Revolution: the abolition of slavery in Saint-Domingue, an event to which he had to respond with no guidance from the oblivious French metropolitan authorities.[32]

Even before these unpredictable events occurred, Saint-Domingue had been central to Genet's mission to Philadelphia. His instructions specified that the protection of French islands by the United States must be ensured. He was to remind the government that the "great commerce" of the colonies would very generously compensate the Americans' efforts. Yet, embarking on the countless other projects attached to his mission, Genet lost sight of this central goal. His duties included outfitting French privateers from US ports; liquidating American debt; reuniting the "beautiful star of Canada to the American Constellation"; nurturing "the principles of freedom and independence in Louisiana"; and dispatching "agents to Kentucky" to spread French revolutionary influence. Genet added his own whims to this list, including preparations for an expedition to Louisiana and Florida. The French Consul in New York became exasperated by the ambassador's constant and fruitless agitation: "What does it matter to you that you dreamed Canada and Florida! We had to send shipments and the convoy."[33]

However, the federal government had anxiously anticipated France's requests. The French Revolution, initially greeted with unanimous enthusiasm throughout the United States, had become highly controversial. Not only had the massacres of aristocrats and priests in September 1792 and the execution of Louis XVI in January 1793 divided public opinion, but the Haitian Revolution was also raising concern among white people while inspiring the enslaved to be more assertive about their rights. The Federalists believed that revolutionary radicalization threatened the solidity of the American Republic, and anti-Jacobinism became an important marker in the definition of political identities within the Union. Conversely, Jefferson and the Republican-Democrats viewed revolutionary violence as a "necessary evil" and acknowledged that the French Republic was struggling for independence and survival in a global war led by the "conspiracy of kings."[34]

Jefferson and Hamilton fiercely debated whether the federal government should officially recognize Genet, the first representative of the French Republic. Washington accepted the diplomat's credentials but refused to implement Article 11 of the 1778 Treaty, according to which the US was obligated to "guarantee" French possessions in the Americas. On Hamilton's recommendation, Genet opted for a "proclamation of neutrality," which he published on April 22. Yet, far from fading out, the bipartisan confrontation between Federalists and Republican-Democrats ignited in August 1793 when news circulated that Genet was appealing to the American people directly to overturn US neutrality. Reasserting their confidence in France while distancing themselves from Genet, James Madison and James Monroe responded to the Federalist attack by publishing their "resolutions on Franco-American relations." They feared a gradual dissolution of the bond between the two countries would lead to a rapprochement with Britain and believed increasing Anglophilia was a result of machinations by the "fiscal" party (i.e., the Federalist Party), which discreetly strove to root out "monocratic" and "aristocratic" tendencies in the early republic. Throughout the United States, Republican-Democratic societies were emerging in support of France and popular sovereignty. The French Revolution had rekindled the spirit of 1776 and had the potential to deepen the democratic gains of the American Revolution.[35]

In this explosive context, Genet hoped once more to gain the confidence of Jefferson, pleading for global regeneration through free trade and claiming that only a Franco-American alliance could bring about commercial republicanism at the global level. He penned an ode invoking the glory of *doux commerce*, which "binding all the scattered men on the globe should make them part of one and the same family perpetually animated by the exchanges which their reciprocal needs require." Genet decried "tyrannical" commercial laws through which the people were "victims of fiscal greed" and the "artificial barriers" created by monarchical governments. In the name of a shared enlightenment, the Franco-American relationship should be exemplary. The new pact between the two countries would unite two peoples "according to the laws of nature" and break with cabinet diplomacy for good. Genet, however, qualified this generous declaration with a series of reproaches. The ambassador complained that the wealth of Saint-Domingue fueled US trade with the former motherland. Because Britain clung to its "exclusive trade" and tyrannical ambitions of "universal empire over the seas," France would have no choice but to imitate the enemy. In return for the great benefits that France extended to its ally, the French Republic only asked that the United States buy "their sheets and their wines."[36]

Jefferson ignored the ambassador's overtures as well as the offer from "the most powerful nation on earth." Genet was actually in no position to strike a new treaty. Discredited by scandal in the United States after he had outfitted privateers despite Washington's prohibition, he had also lost all support in France, where those who had sent him across the Atlantic had been guillotined in October. Genet had been receiving diplomatic instructions in the fall from a now dismissed foreign minister, and the Committee of Public Safety ordered his recall on October 11, 1793. Genet described the possibility of France applying pressure on the United States as "illusory." The commercial openings he could offer to the federal government were incidental: necessity was law, and France, yielding to the principle of reality, made no concessions by admitting the Americans to her islands. Famine was looming in the French West Indies and there was no alternative source of supplies. "The islands of America," he philosophically observed, "will become what nature wanted them to be, independent of Europe and under the protection of the peoples of the continent from whom they were detached." This revolution was "inevitable," and "consistent with the immutable laws of nature of which the most powerful peoples are only the blind instruments." Re-reading Anne Robert Jacques Turgot's 1776 prophecy in the light of Saint-Domingue's revolution, Genet foresaw the independent future of the Americas. His naturalistic providentialism was also an admission of helplessness and failure.[37]

The Trade Wars of Commercial Republics

In the fall of 1793, British privateering in the Caribbean, the French military debacle in Europe, and the abolition of slavery in Saint-Domingue reset the charts. A series of cataclysmic events took place: British expansion threatened the United States with commercial strangulation, at a time when the French ally was flailing; the destruction of Cap-Français, Saint-Domingue's buoyant port, materialized in the mass arrival of refugees in US cities during the summer; a few weeks later, news of Saint-Domingue's emancipation proclamation spread across North America; in September, the British invaded part of the colony, along with the entirety of the French islands of Tobago and Martinique; and five days later, the newspapers reported that royalists had delivered Toulon, a major port in the south of France, to the British. This cavalcade of news from Europe and the Caribbean felt ominous, as if the French Republic were perhaps living its final days.[38]

The situation was also serious for the future of the United Sates. Genet implored Jefferson to intervene and implement Article 11: Saint-Domingue needed help, and the United States needed Saint-Domingue. "Sir, this colony in which a decree of the National Convention has just admitted your vessels under the same conditions as ours," he reminded Jefferson, "this colony, which for ten years has been the mainstay of your agriculture and navigation; this colony, finally, which furnished you with the means of financing your European trade, is close to being lost for you as well as for us." Genet did not shy away from the abolition of slavery, ratifying the proclamation without waiting for permission from the metropole. A new France was emerging in the Gulf of Mexico, he explained: new Black citizen-soldiers who "owed" the French Republic their freedom would definitively embed the French presence in the Caribbean. The United States should embrace this "philosophy" or at least accept the "empire of circumstances," as "the new people who are forming on this island could become a useful friend or a dangerous neighbor."[39]

In his attempt to convince Jefferson, Genet engaged in a political economy analysis. First, he made the case that republican and abolitionist Saint-Domingue could thrive without slaves and contribute to US prosperity. Paying wages to new citizens and dividing plantations into small plots would energize the production of coffee, the principal US import. This could have been a compelling argument: as historian Ashli White has demonstrated, beyond the rhetoric of fear, southern planters had prodigious confidence in the institution of slavery, to the point of continuing to import "French Negroes." The early American republic could tolerate the existence of an allied abolitionist colony without weakening its social fabric. Second, Genet emphasized that whereas France was embarking on a colonial revolution by opening its ports to its republican ally, Britain had started an all-out trade war on the United States. The Jeffersonian society of small landowners, whose livelihoods depended on commercial opportunities in the global marketplace, was under threat. The British Order-in-Council of June 8, 1793, brutally thrust the young American republic into the colonial world. The British Empire was spearheading an Atlantic counterrevolution, both commercially and politically.[40]

Crucially, Genet asked Jefferson to protect the "tricolor" delegation of deputies from Saint-Domingue (black, mixed-race, and white) conveying the emancipation proclamation to Paris. The three men—Jean-Baptiste Belley, Jean-Baptiste Mills, and Pierre Louis Dufay—were making a stopover in the United States before embarking on their transatlantic voyage, but enraged white Saint-Domingue refugees in Philadelphia had heard about their mission and attempted to lynch the deputies, who managed to escape only thanks to the support of the mayor. Jefferson could not stay away from the crisis and had to take a stance. Thanking Genet for information "on the present state of the French islands in the West Indies," he agreed that "their position must always be interesting for the United States, with whom nature has united them by the powerful link of natural needs." the secretary of state refrained from glossing over the invocation of Article 11 and did not wish to elaborate on Saint-Domingue's emancipation proclamation before its ratification. Exasperated by Genet's ineptitude, Jefferson had no patience for his challenge to the legitimacy of the federal government and, as a southern planter, he was also concerned about how the revolution in Saint-Domingue was developing. Yet, at this point, Jefferson still believed the greatest threat to the existence of the United States was British hegemony. Receiving protection from the secretary of state, the tricolor deputation made it safely to the French metropole, where their arrival heralded one of the most significant events in the Age of Revolutions: the abolition of slavery throughout the French empire on 16 Pluviôse Year II (February 4, 1794). Despite his "proslavery" policy, his racial thinking, and his opposition to immediate abolition, Jefferson played a reluctant part in this world historic event.[41]

Jefferson's reasoning was that expansion of the British Empire posed the primary threat to the security of the United States and the preservation of popular sovereignty. In collaboration with Madison, the leader of the Democratic-Republican party in Congress, he launched a broad legislative response to the British maritime attack. He claimed that not only had the time come to implement retaliatory tariffs on the former motherland, but he also convinced Washington to denounce Britain more forcefully than France in his presidential address on December 2, 1793. The president made a distinction between the behavior of Genet, which was indefensible, and that of France. Two weeks later, the United States Trade Report that Jefferson sent to Congress outlined a plan of attack. The secretary of state had prepared two earlier versions that, conceived in peacetime, were intended to secure the admission of American vessels to West Indian ports. Jefferson was convinced that republican virtue could only be consolidated if the United States had access to the global market, and the measures he suggested were the master tools of his "commercial diplomacy." Although Genet misunderstood Jefferson's caution, the report made the case that France behaved better toward the United States than Britain did. In order to shatter the British system of "prohibitions, tariffs and regulations," the United States had to oppose "counter-prohibitions, tariffs and regulations" since the route of international treaties had proved impracticable. Jefferson and Madison made a strategic choice, resulting from a calculated assessment of geopolitical forces. This commercial retaliation was intended to reveal the commercial dependence of European empires on the United States and compensate for the military weakness of the young republic.[42]

On January 3, 1794, Madison presented recommendations for implementing this policy to Congress. He called for retaliatory tariffs on powers not contractually linked with the United States. Despite Hamilton's opposition, Madison held all the cards and appeared bound to succeed. Republican-Democrats had just won elections in the House of Representatives, Genet's blunders were fading from public memory, and pro-French support was growing more vocal every day. Political societies, those "laboratories of democracy," had proliferated since the summer of 1793 and were proclaiming the French Revolution to be a continuation of the American Revolution. For these diverse popular societies, composed mainly of artisans and shopkeepers but also a significant number of traders, the future of the young republic depended on the outcome of the French-British war. A pro-French republican press repeatedly hammered this point home, prompting Federalists to demonize the "demagogues" attempting to "manipulate" the masses. Journalists, they claimed, were endangering a constitutional edifice based on representation by election.[43]

The Saint-Domingue refugees who arrived en masse in US Atlantic ports in 1793 joined the conversation. Many were publishing their own newsletters, and activist clubs were formed in Philadelphia, New York, Charleston, Boston, and Baltimore. They communicated with each other, organized their own celebrations, and petitioned the federal government. Yet Saint-Domingue's politics remained controversial in the United States. In opposition to these outspoken refugees, "Jacobin" popular clubs materialized in many port-cities, formed by immigrants of French origin, mostly sailors, from very different walks of life, who showcased connections between the American and French revolutions. On November 23, 1793, the Society of Friends of Liberty and Equality celebrated the anniversary of the British evacuation of New York, calling for a similar outcome in Toulon. In Philadelphia, a patriotic society affiliated with the Jacobin Club steadfastly supported Genet's boldest undertakings. The vice-consul of France in Boston, Antoine Charbonnet Duplaine, one of these clubs' hotheads, demanded implementation of the Navigation Act while denouncing the actions of the Federalists. "Although enemies of prohibitive laws," he explained, "we feel that as long as other governments are not changed into republics founded on reason and philosophy, it is absolutely necessary to take the most effective measures to encourage our commerce and our navigation; and that if we do not employ all the means which are in our power, the other nations will regulate them according to their convenience and interests." The French Navigation Act and

Madison's resolutions were part of a common arsenal to protect republicanism from maritime despotism.[44]

However, Congress faced a genuine dilemma. While the British metropole was the largest European market, the French West Indies provided the main outlet for the US goods in the Caribbean. Exports of French colonial commodities to Europe, particularly coffee, were also a promising new branch of trade. But neutrality was still a contested principle and the United States had to make a decision. The House of Representatives was transformed into a battleground in which political economy arguments were the order of the day. This dispute has often been reduced to a struggle between an "idealistic" Francophilia and a more "pragmatic" Anglophilia, with Republican-Democrats blinded by desire for revenge on Britain and their democratic naïveté. This characterization is deeply misleading. Rather, the rich debates that took place displayed a variety of arguments grounded in international law theory, backed up by empirical data and statistics. Two assumptions were open to debate: the United States was in a position to force Britain to back down, and France was on the verge of definitively abandoning its "colonial monopoly." Only the latter condition could support the principle of republican solidarity and make retaliatory tariffs on Britain economically reasonable.[45]

In fact, Madison's Achilles heel was the illegible politics of the National Convention: the French legislation of 1793 was a knot of contradictions. French procrastination over acknowledging neutrality had compromised the political advantage the National Assembly could hope for from opening its West Indian ports to American trade. All of Madison's opponents utilized this argument. South Carolina representative William Loughton Smith, a close friend of Hamilton, pointed out that "the commercial regulations of France during the period of the Revolution have been too fluctuating, too much influenced by momentary impulses," and "too much manifesting an object of the moment, which cannot be mistaken to consider them as a part of [the] system." Smith concluded that the United States should base its policy on French commercial legislation prior to 1789. The only decree representatives should take seriously, he contended, was that of August 30, 1784, and even this suffered from two intrinsic weaknesses: it did not support a free-trade ideology and did not grant privileges to Americans beyond those enjoyed by other foreigners. While Britain had proved to be a "selfish rival" power, the "machinations of an insidious friend" could be as dangerous.[46]

Lawmakers did not regard the French Navigation Act as a commercial revolution. Worse still, they had a hard time making any sense of the French law. A representative of Maryland, William Van Murray, situated this reform in the long colonial history of France. Since Jean-Baptiste Colbert, the prime minister of Louis XIV, laid the foundations of French colonial policy, he explained, France had founded its "maritime grandeur" on the wealth of the West Indies: no less jealous than other powers, it had always manifested "a spirit of monopoly." The republic, through its Navigation Act, seemed to "adhere to its colonial system," since the Americans were prohibited from taking part in the reexport trade. Fleeting "circumstances" drove "temporary" alterations, without any major change of "principles"; such a transformation was unlikely, as the French Republic would base its policy on its own national interest. France was profiting from the colonial monopoly and would not give this up out of idealism. The merchant Samuel Smith, a new representative from Maryland, pushed the argument by quoting Montesquieu: "Republicans know their interest better than monarchs. . . . France, regenerated France, will never admit you freely into her West Indies." Contradicting Tom Paine's commercial utopia, Smith delivered an eye-opening speech arguing that the republican revolution would not inaugurate the era of doux commerce.[47]

By demonstrating his expertise on French colonialism, Samuel Smith managed to sway his colleagues. As a merchant engaged in legal and illegal trade with Saint-Domingue, he had mastered the intricacies of Caribbean commercial laws. He also conducted business with the British in Europe. From this angle, Smith embodied the Atlantic trade of the early republic. As a patriot and a republican, he leaned toward solidarity with France, but it appeared to him that the French Republic had not given up on the "colonial system"; it was not in the country's interest to do so. Smith opposed Madison's proposals by pointing out the contradictions in Barère's speech of September 21, 1793. The British Navigation Act did not prohibit imports of American flour as long as they were loaded on British ships, while the French granted only temporary exceptions. "The result of these observations," he concluded "is that, the general colonial system of Europe is to monopolize to the Mother Country all the supplies it is capable of making, and particularly the carrying trade." In short, colonialism took precedence over transatlantic republican ties.[48]

Congress had asked this simple question: could colonial republics be as protective of their monopolies as monarchies? The answer was a resounding yes. The commercial interest of the United States clashed with French colonial greed. Federalists seized this opportunity to underscore how different the French Republic was from the American Republic. Richard Bland Lee, a representative from Virginia, insisted that the political institutions of a country were adapted to particular "circumstances," that each state was in accordance with the interests of a particular people and the American and French republics were more dissimilar than ever. These two different conceptions of the republic were incompatible: "Their Republic is one and indivisible; our Republic consists of sovereign States . . . having a diversity of laws and interests." The French republican model, unsuited to local circumstances, could not spread across the Atlantic. "Is every part of the United States in a situation to extend the idea of equality as far as it has been carried in France?" Lee asked, adding that he believed "no gentleman" would say it was. "The conflagrations, the desolations, and the bloody scenes of St. Domingo might also then be exhibited on our peaceful and happy plains." The Haitian revolution, widely understood as a consequence of the French Revolution, was the foil the Federalists needed.[49]

Ironically, Madison's failure in January 1794 was partly the result of debates based on obsolete information. A growing number of stories in the newspapers reported British attacks on US trade in the Caribbean, but the representatives were not acquainted with the Order-in-Council of November 6, 1793, a lack of intelligence that fatefully damaged the French alliance. Two months later, when this news eventually reached the United States, Madison's recommendations seemed extremely feeble. Many of the representatives who had opposed his proposals called for a general embargo in the Caribbean. Samuel Smith, whose ships had just been captured, challenged Federalist moderation: it was necessary to prepare for war and sequester British debts. All the rules of law had been flouted, the rights of the people trampled, and the American nation was being humiliated. Smith's furious response could have been excerpted from Barère's speeches: he lambasted that "piratical nation . . . that King of Sea Robbers—that Leviathan, which aims at swallowing all that floats on the ocean—that monster, whose only law is power, and who neither respects the rights of nations nor the property of individuals!"

The merchants who were directly affected mobilized and resumed the revolutionary tradition of forming committees and petitioning for retaliatory measures. The traders of Philadelphia, with Stephen Girard at their head, were the vanguard of the movement. Even in New York, where a strong loyalist heritage endured, the Chamber of Commerce appointed a committee to propose measures to the government, and an embargo was unanimously approved. To avoid war, John Jay was sent to London, where he negotiated a treaty that caused the most serious controversy in the history of the early republic up to the Civil War.[50]

On August 25, 1794, the chairman of the Board of Trade, Lord Hawkesbury, discovered the draft treaty that Foreign Secretary Grenville was about to submit to the United States' special commissioner, John Jay. Although many of the provisions were punitive toward the early American republic, Hawkesbury's focus was on one measure alone: the British government was preparing to admit American vessels to its West Indian colonies for the first time. This provision, destined to become Article XII in the Treaty of London of November 19, 1794, was an unprecedented violation of the Navigation Act. Believing the admission of the Americans to Saint-Domingue had caused the upheavals in the Antilles, Hawkesbury regarded this a treacherous act. "The United States will in a short Time become Master in Effect of the West India Islands," he warned, because "the Americans by having Permission to enter our Ports will have an Opportunity of instilling into the Minds of the Inhabitants of our Islands Principles adverse to the British Government. It is well known in what Manner the Inhabitants of the French Islands were corrupted in their Principles by Adventurers coming into them." As the slave revolution erupted, Hawkesbury feared the spread of insurgency less than the circulation of "American" ideas and the ensuing geopolitical turmoil in the Caribbean.[51]

The British rapprochement with the United States may have been a trap for the "European colonial system," but it also shattered the idea of a vast free trade zone that would bind the United States, France, and the French West Indies into a large anti-monarchical front. The Treaty of London concluded the first sequence of the commercial crisis that began in February 1793. Despite Republican-Democrat outrage, the treaty was ratified in Congress, and at the end of 1794, Barère's grandiose speech rang hollow. Two years of intense debate in France and the United States had not solidified an Atlantic "commercial republicanism" for many reasons. Domestic debates within revolutionary France entirely obscured the message, with the complex politics of committees and the pressure of lobbies playing a lethal role. Genet, who embodied the new republican democracy, could not implement the great "commercial and political pact." Jefferson, Madison, and Republican-Democrats in general, unable to prove that France was revolutionizing its commercial system and embarrassed by Genet's inept course of action, failed to impose retaliatory tariffs on Britain. The development of the revolution in Saint-Domingue raised new pressing issues about the future of slavery in the United States. Instead of uniting republicans, the event emphasized the diversity of republics. The French metropole did not have the manufacturing capacity of Great Britain and competed with the United States on some vital markets, such as flour; it became increasingly apparent that the commercial and political alliance could not be grounded in economic interest. Still, some idealists among French deputies hoped that one day "merchants will be [France's] only ambassadors," conducting "a peaceful trade, after having considered the destinies of the two hemispheres and assured the prosperity and the glory of their homeland." This commercial and political fantasy was simultaneously staged in Saint-Domingue. It did not end peacefully.[52]

7

The Unfree Trade of an Abolitionist Colony, 1793–1796

When the war with Britain began, the French revolutionary government hoped to implement a project conceived by Vergennes in 1778. The Committee of Public Safety, either Girondin or Montagnard, equally believed an alliance with the United States would provide both a military and an economic advantage over the British. France would benefit from support for its naval war in the Caribbean, and French vessels were supposed to trade in North American ports. The United States was intended to constitute the French colonies' hinterland, its main source of supplies. This scheme, perfect on paper, proved a failure. Furthermore, the Saint-Domingue Revolution had transformed the parameters of the alliance. The abolition of slavery prompted the partial invasion of the colony by Britain and Spain, while the majority of white planters either left for the United States, Jamaica, Cuba, and the metropole, or resettled in the areas occupied by France's enemies. The "newly free" and the "citizens of April 4" (free people of color in the old regime), while negotiating the meaning of freedom in Saint-Domingue, reframed the island's relationship to the early American republic.

This chapter argues that these intertwined events shattered the unstable balance between the French republican colony and the United States. Demands on the Saint-Domingue government proliferated under extreme circumstances: food and other supplies were needed for an army that had increased tenfold, for inhabitants accumulating in the besieged towns, and for overflowing hospitals. While demands were dramatically increasing, government resources were draining just as swiftly as the colonial state faced seemingly endless challenges: many plantations and smaller plots had been devastated and/or abandoned, there had been a drastic reduction in available labor, with many of the "newly free" drafted into the army, and the supply of flour from the metropole had ceased entirely. The civil government displayed blatant signs of weakness at a time when powerful military leaders were emerging,

Entrepôt of Revolutions. Manuel Covo, Oxford University Press. © Oxford University Press 2022.
DOI: 10.1093/oso/9780197626382.003.0008

particularly mixed-race André Rigaud and free Black Toussaint Louverture, who rallied the French Republic in May 1794. Diverse groups of "newly free" citizens, far from passively accepting decisions taken by the government, at times cooperated, at times resisted, and at times revolted. An independent democratic life and a shadow economy were emerging out of state control in the plantations appropriated by the newly free—a space defined as a "counter-plantation" by Jean Casimir. Despite that development, the colony remained, nevertheless, more dependent than ever on US provisioning. An embattled revolutionary government devised its own economic policy while receiving little guidance from Paris and facing the overwhelming constraints of global commerce. Rival agents of the French Republic were trying to accomplish two things: remedy wartime shortages while imagining a new position for Saint-Domingue and the French Republic in the Atlantic world. The contradictions between these short-term and long-term goals produced unexpected outcomes.[1]

Revolutionary circumstances overturned assumptions made by eighteenth-century physiocrats (economists), who, for the most part, ordinarily linked abolitionism to free trade. More than ideology or political agendas, the collapse of the colonial state shaped the transformation of Saint-Domingue's new society. While the period stretching between the abolition of slavery and the consolidation of Toussaint Louverture's power is often overlooked, these years are crucial to understanding how circumstantial decisions laid the groundwork for long-standing issues in Haitian history, French imperial history, and Atlantic history. The chaotic process not only redefined the relationship between the metropole and the colony, but also exacerbated international tensions with far-reaching consequences.

The Unlimited Powers of a Collapsed State

"They are on a floor strewn with corpses and debris; they reign, they make laws; it is the strangest and most limitless dictatorship," wrote the New York consul in his journal, describing the new civil commissioners who had disembarked in Saint-Domingue on September 17, 1792. The commission, composed of Sonthonax, Polverel, and Jean-Antoine Ailhaud (who swiftly left the colony), had command of 6,000 soldiers to enforce the law of April 4, 1792, ensure equality between whites and free people of color, quell the slave insurrection (in spite of Sonthonax's abolitionist sentiments), and establish a new "mixed" colonial assembly. The legal powers of the commission were considerable. They could suspend existing assemblies, were entitled to overturn their decrees, could deport opponents, and could enforce provisional regulations. All institutions were subordinated and the commissioners could declare any civilian or military body, and any disobedient citizen, a "traitor to the nation." In the face of increasing opposition, the National Assembly even expanded their authority: the law of November 8, 1792, afforded the commission "all powers," and instructions by the Provisional Executive Council on January 7, 1793, assigned oversight of the forthcoming war against Britain and Spain to it. The commission embodied French national sovereignty in Saint-Domingue. In short, it was entrusted with a "colonial dictatorship" modeled on the Roman magistracy, according to which extraordinary circumstances required extraordinary institutions.[2]

However, the commission did not have actual legislative power. The metropole retained legal control of commercial relations between the colonies and foreign countries and did not grant the commissioners diplomatic authority. It was unclear whether exceptional circumstances could legitimize decrees on international trade. Yet it was impossible for the commissioners to await directions from the government when urgent action was needed, giving Saint-Domingue, like other colonies at war, more autonomy. British privateering distorted and extended the distance between metropoles and far-flung territories, causing instructions to follow indirect routes to the colonies, assuming they arrived at all. The enforcement of laws conceived in imperial capitals increasingly depended on the will of colonial authorities.[3]

The commissioners also had difficulties interpreting legal texts originating from Europe. On the one hand, commissioners were at pains to make sense of the continually unfolding French Revolution. When they had left the metropole, Louis XVI was still sovereign; by the time they reached Saint-Domingue, the French Republic had been born. On the other hand, they had no choice but to adapt to the realities of Saint-Domingue. As obedience could not be secured through force alone, they had to strike provisional alliances with local actors. Should they abide by rules constructed in metropolitan France for a certain moment, and based on information relating to America that was already obsolete? Or was it necessary to tweak or even contravene the letter of the law in order to retain the spirit? At the very least, they were expected to follow "the direction of the Revolution," leaving the tardily apprised commissioners fearful of how their actions would be interpreted in France. Their temporary autonomy was as much an alarming condition of their governance as an opportunity.

The manner in which a metropolitan law was transmitted was as essential as its content. Information made its way across the Atlantic through a variety of channels: sailors, merchants, and passengers discussed new regulations decreed in Britain and France; vessels from the North American continent conveyed US gazettes, containing paragraphs translated and extracted from European newspapers such as *Moniteur universel*; and other printed sources were available via Cuba or Jamaica. Sonthonax learned about the proceedings of the National Assembly in the US press. Informal knowledge of a law, however, did not lead to enforcement, as the authorities were particularly wary of false rumors. Ministerial instructions certified by the executive power had a legal value that a crumpled gazette published in Philadelphia did not. Formal orders engaged the commission's responsibility as delegates of public power. Yet commissioners did take informal news into account. Flawed information could always be used to justify ex post facto decisions. Loyalty to the metropole, the nation, and the republic was an easy defense, which occupied the uncertain space separating the legal from the legitimate.[4]

Under these circumstances, how did liberty of commerce and an alliance between the two republics materialize in Saint-Domingue? Due to a shortage of food and ammunition, the commissioners considered this issue a priority. On April 19, 1793, Sonthonax and Polverel proclaimed a state of war, thereby authorizing privateering against enemy fleets from Britain, Spain, and the Netherlands. Yet they never implemented the decree adopted by the National Assembly on May 9, 1793, which partially legalized the confiscation of neutral property destined for British possessions. Only the decree of February 19, 1793, suppressing the colonial *exclusif*, had been officially received. Although the content of the law had been gleaned from American newspapers since May, the decree was only put into effect on June 12, 1793. A proclamation dated August 21, 1793, ignoring the National Assembly's prevarications, reasserted the special status enjoyed by US vessels. The commission declared that it was "in the principles of the French Republic to protect . . . the trade of its faithful allies, the Americans of the Continent." Yet Sonthonax and Polverel spoke in the name of a republic whose expressed will was far from clear.[5]

All other laws relating to this issue (those of March 26, May 9, and of the summer of 1793, as well as the Navigation Act) were never formally enforced. Sonthonax claimed ignorance: "We were deprived of all kinds of news from France in the colonies. . . . No law, no decree of the government committees, no letter, no kind of correspondence on the part of the Convention and of the agents of the French Government did penetrate the colony of Saint-Domingue." This declaration sounds somewhat excessive, as the commissioners could pick and choose the laws they deemed would serve their own policies. But Sonthonax's statement highlights the real difficulty of disentangling truth from falsehood in news supposedly originating from Europe.[6]

Sonthonax was not afraid of exceeding his mandate, as spectacularly demonstrated by his proclamation abolishing slavery in August 1793. Polverel, however, was more concerned about abiding by legal orders from Paris. The former lawyer and freemason had been a public attorney in the court of the first district of Paris in early 1791 and Jacobin Club secretary in June 1792. He had therefore fully participated in the legal culture of the Revolution of 1789, which, like Montesquieu, saw a judge as "the mouth of the law." This commitment to the "sanctification of the law" and "nomophilia" (the love for the law) explains Polverel's attitude toward US trade. Although he felt the tariffs on all non-exempt products should be scrupulously levied and accepted voluntary subscriptions in the form of a "patriotic contribution," the commissioner resolutely refused to establish new taxes, as this was the prerogative of national sovereignty alone. Polverel's unwavering stance on this caused major discord with his colleague, Sonthonax. On November 7, 1792, the intermediary commission (which had replaced the former Colonial Assembly) decided to create a new export tax, the "extraordinary subsidy," intended to end financial hardship in the Northern Province, unresolved by scarce "patriotic contributions." Sonthonax validated this move against the will of his colleague, but in Polverel's eyes the intermediary commission had outrageously overstepped its authority, for "the right to raise taxes in the colony belongs only to the Legislative Assembly of France, which is the sole representative of the Sovereign." Therefore, it was now "impossible to regard [the intermediary commission] as a true representative of the colony." Polverel banned the tax in the west and south and wrote to the National Convention to express dismay at his colleague's actions. This infuriated Sonthonax, who believed the "necessity of circumstances" justified temporarily freeing themselves from constitutional legality. "In the state where things are, it is not a question of discussing the principles," he exclaimed. "We must act, we must save the colony, and we only have this means," the "salvation of the colony is our common law."[7]

The outbreak of maritime war did not lessen Polverel's legalistic temperament. Ensuring export taxes were raised, he was anxious to respect the decree of February 19: the law allowed colonial goods to be exported by US vessels but had not expressly extended this measure to other neutrals or vessels under the French flag. In January 1794, when Les Cayes's firm Lemaitre frères proposed that in return for outfitting its vessel for New England they would supply the Southern Province, Polverel indignantly decried the "indecency" and "illegality" of the proposal, especially as the ship owner hoped to cover the true identity of the ship by hoisting a neutral flag. The Americans were no longer subject to the exclusif but the French still had to comply with the law of October 1727 and the arrêt of August 30, 1784. Again, Sonthonax proved more flexible: he allowed a certain Mayer Polony to outfit a vessel built in the United States intended for St. Thomas under a Danish flag.[8]

Yet the two commissioners agreed on one point: they never understood the decree of February 19, 1793 as a carte blanche on free trade. Sonthonax made every effort to ensure that taxes were correctly levied on American vessels, while Polverel, believing no one could ignore laws that had not been unambiguously rescinded, led a crusade against fraud. The commission exercised the highest colonial jurisdiction to rule on commercial offenses as well as cases involving seizures. In December 1793, Polverel sentenced the captain's interpreter and the consignee of the *Friendship* from Rhode Island for violating Saint-Domingue's regulations of March 24, 1781. This text forbade the sale of "edibles necessary for life . . . otherwise only three weeks after the public opening of their stores . . . so that the inhabitants have time to get what they need for their own consumption." In addition to confiscation of the relevant items, the offenders were fined 3,000 *livres coloniales* and prosecuted as "monopolists or monopoly mongers." Moreover, the commissioners required every passenger loading merchandise onto foreign vessels to carry a passport signed by the commission. Hoping to prevent the escape of royalist émigrés and the flow of French goods into British territory, they threatened to jail non-compliant American captains. The opening of ports to foreign trade did not mean deregulation but was aligned with a form of economic liberalism that combated "hoarders" and "counter-revolutionaries" and promoted the "right to exist."[9]

The commissioners, however, had few judiciary tools for their fight against fraud. They had to rely on the Admiralty courts, tribunals of the ancien régime that had not been abolished (unlike their metropolitan counterparts), to pursue maritime and commercial matters. Polverel carefully monitored the courts and customs officers to prevent spoliation of neutral ships, corruption, extortion, and neglect. The commissioners also made sure that the courts were adequately staffed. The intermediate assembly, reformed by Sonthonax and the only administrative body with authority across the entire colony, was the second degree of jurisdiction. The civil commissioners could seize a case or reverse a judgment, either in the first instance or on appeal; Polverel did this on several occasions, especially in lawsuits dealing with privateering. The entire cargo of the *Favorite*, for instance, was confiscated on Polverel's orders in January 1794.[10]

In practice, the colonial government was desperately short of the ships needed to capture smugglers. In December 1792, two coast guard vessels were outfitted to prevent "fraudulent removals" on the southern coast, but "the vessels coming from the United States, Curaçao, the Spanish Islands, and Jamaica" barely took notice. The French Navy was not only powerless to prevent illegal trafficking but was also unable to protect US ships destined for Saint-Domingue. This maritime helplessness only worsened. In the wake of the Cap-Français fire, almost the entire naval station accompanied a convoy to the United States. In the fall of 1793, "a single frigate" was "cruising at the height of Cap-Français." The *Goéland*, the *Serin*, and the *Alerte* were the only privateers to assist the frigate *Astrée* in carrying out captures of a few British, Spanish, and Dutch vessels. Naval protection of Saint-Domingue trade depended on two external privateering sources: the French Lesser Antilles and the North American continent. However, Guadeloupe's major port, Basse-Terre, was not yet the privateering capital it would become a few years later. Three ships were purchased for this purpose by the French consul in Charleston, and only twenty-five corsairs were navigating the Caribbean Sea in early 1794. On the mainland, Genet and his consuls, faced with innumerable difficulties that brought them into opposition with the federal government, could not outfit more than thirteen privateers, while the remainder of the Saint-Domingue naval station was rife with mutiny.[11]

The exponential fragmentation of the colony compounded the state's maritime weakness. Due to wartime chaos, disseminating proclamations and ordinances grew increasingly challenging. The proliferation of local conflicts shattered internal lines of communication while increasing numbers of privateer ships from Bermuda, the Bahamas, and Jamaica undercut the free movement of ships that went from coast to coast. Regions already segregated by Saint-Domingue's mountainous terrain became more isolated with each defeat of the French Republic. The British gained control of Mole-Saint-Nicolas in the North and Grande Anse in the south at the end of September 1793. This territory expanded with the annexation of Saint-Marc, Léogane, and L'Arcahaye at the invitation of free people of color. Port-au-Prince surrendered to the British on June 5, 1794, six months after Fort Dauphin capitulated to the Spaniards. The capture of Tobago by the British in April 1793 and Martinique and Guadeloupe in March–April 1794 provided new supply points for the British privateers blockading most of Saint-Domingue's ports. Formerly enslaved insurgents had also taken control of mountainous areas near Port-de-Paix and Léogane, creating maroon communities independent from European powers. The remaining republican enclaves were not only cut off from the metropole, but they were also separated from each other.

As dislocation of the colony led to the creation of separate regulations, the interpretation of commercial law, far from the lofty proclamations made in Paris, became inherently local. When Polverel was in Les Cayes, he was unaware of decisions taken by Sonthonax in Cap-Français for a month, the amount of time it took to receive news from Philadelphia. The extraordinary subsidy was levied only in the Northern Province since Polverel had prohibited its application in the west and the south; therefore the ports of this part of Saint-Domingue enjoyed a competitive tax advantage. Not all admiralty ports taxed exports in the same way. The town council of Borgne, located less than forty miles from Cap-Français, could not figure out whether US vessels should pay duties and, if so, how this should take place. In fact, a multitude of micro-regions had become economically and politically independent to varying degrees. Near the port city of Jérémie, white planters, enraged by the abolition of slavery, created a small confederation whose "executive committee" rejected the commissioners' authority and prohibited any communication beyond the borders of local parishes. The actual presence of the two commissioners, their visibility and accessibility, were essential to enforcement of their ordinances. "Only your physical person

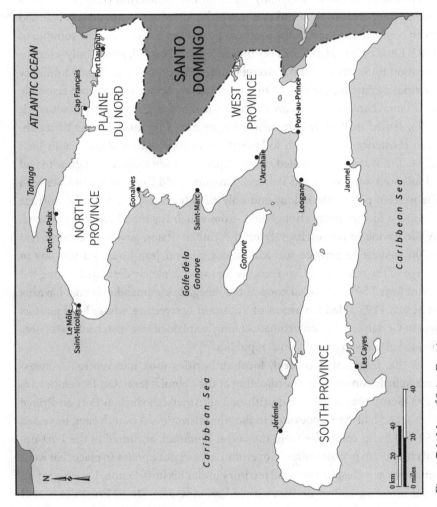

Figure 7.1 Map of Saint-Domingue

can force respect on laws and military leaders," wrote a government official. In other words, delegation of power had become virtually impossible: their authority was confined to where they could be seen. First and foremost, the commissioners' "unlimited powers" reflected the collapse of the colonial state in Saint-Domingue.[12]

The south, faithful to an old tradition, soon emerged as the most autonomous and powerful section of the colony under formal French rule. General Rigaud, a leading free person of color and a veteran of the American Revolutionary War, had taken command of most of the southern part of the colony since the summer of 1793. Little by little, Les Cayes became an informal capital, paying only selective attention to Sonthonax and Polverel's undertakings. General Rigaud's military victories against the British led to a specific commercial policy more favorable to US merchants. Etienne Laveaux, appointed acting governor on October 12, 1793, settled in Port-de-Paix, where he organized the main pocket of republican resistance in the north following the commissioners' departure in June 1794. This was an "entrenched camp" deprived of administrative staff, who had all followed Sonthonax and Polverel. Laveaux could barely communicate with the western part of the colony and only reliably correspond with the Tortuga island—a former pirate stronghold—from which Raymond Labatut operated. While having to rely exclusively on the United States, governor Laveaux had 1,700 soldiers to provide for. Mixed-race general Jean-Louis Villatte was in charge of the remains of Cap-Français, almost completely destroyed during the fire of June 1793. The failed coup of the renegade commander against Laveaux in March 1795 aided the ascent of Toussaint Louverture, whose headquarters was in Gonaives. The "unfortunate colony," explained one merchant, "was now divided into seven or eight small republics."[13]

In this fragmented context, local authorities took interventionist measures in isolation without coordinating at the colonial level. On December 16, 1793, Sonthonax forcibly requisitioned all American ships in Port-au-Prince harbor and had the cargoes sold to the administration. A month later, he seized 150,000 livres coloniales from the vessel *Bordeaux*, anchored in the Port-de-Paix harbor, to pay his troops. Governor Laveaux put a policy in place that went much further. Despite the small territory under his jurisdiction, Laveaux set up a war economy in Port-de-Paix with radical measures. On 19 Fructidor Year II (September 5, 1794), Laveaux issued an ordinance "abolishing the merchants of the city." He thus passed all commerce in the colony to the administration, prohibited private transactions, and gave the general government a monopoly on buying US cargoes to fill the general stores and feed troops. Meanwhile, Laveaux began outfitting privateer ships to force Americans to sell their foodstuff. The rhetoric of free trade was fading fast. Local circumstances dictated the government's commercial policy, whereas the National Convention's laws—whether the Navigation Act or the Maximum Law—played insignificant roles in this story.[14]

A Shopkeepers' Administration

How to abolish slavery while ensuring the supply and military defense of the colony was the common challenge faced by the civil commissioners, Governor Laveaux, Rigaud, and later, Toussaint Louverture. The colonial state needed to secure its own resources and engineer workable solutions, and attempts to create money through tax reforms did not meet government needs. The extraordinary subsidy, first conceived by Sonthonax as a forced loan from the owners, proved inadequate. Customs officers were supposed to levy a quarter of exported commodities, but the war and administrative disorganization facilitated fraud while production levels spectacularly collapsed in most of French Saint-Domingue. In the fall of 1793, the administration owned only the equivalent of 110,000 livres coloniales in sugar and coffee.[15]

The colonial government needed to find new ways of feeding and clothing soldiers and an increasing number of destitute refugees. They needed flour, cod, vinegar, and wines as well as soap, candles, timber, clothes, and shoes. In the month of August 1793 alone, consumption of essential goods purchased in Cap-Français amounted to more than 505,000 livres coloniales. In Port-de-Paix, Laveaux had to find food for his troops with "no sugar, no coffee in the warehouses," while "the hospital was deprived of everything, containing barely forty patients." Lacking protein, soldiers suffered malnutrition and fell ill. The situation was so dire that from June 20, 1793, to November 30, 1794, soldiers received no pay whatsoever. The cost of civil administration was also exceeding public resources: the commissioners needed 40,000 livres coloniales a month to compensate civil servants. The emancipation decree involved new expenses, which revealed the insufficiency of the existing tax system. The colonial state was to pay the "formerly enslaved," newly salaried employees, such as Ignace, at the general store, Herbin, a baker, Jean Louis, a carter, or Jean and Mahomet, manual workers. The new payroll cost over 20,000 livres coloniales in cash for a single month.[16]

"General freedom" raised extremely challenging questions, as all economic structures, work organizations, and property rights had to be transformed. Confronted with these monumental challenges, what were the economic options? Preoccupied with pressing matters, colonial officials were hesitant in their handling of this grand reorganization. Several strategies were possible: radically transforming the plantation complex into a subsistence economy and redistributing land to the newly free; reviving the existing plantation system, exchanging goods with the Americans and restoring Saint-Domingue's credit; or engaging the colony in full-on privateering to pillage the enemy and possibly even neutrals. Without a clear agenda they explored all these options, but with immense indecision and a lack of direction from the National Assembly.

The priority was to restart production, then sell coffee and molasses to the Americans and buy their foodstuff and ammunition. Sonthonax and all subsequent leaders were convinced that saving the colony meant restoring and reforming the plantation economy. To this end, the colonial administrators enacted work regulations (*règlements de travail*) and "rules of cultivation" (*règlements de culture*). Polverel's measures differed from those of Sonthonax, due to their complexity but also their intentions and local contexts. Polverel's proclamation of August 27 envisaged a gradual enfranchisement, based on the division of land abandoned by white landowners. The complicated, unorthodox egalitarian system devised by the civil commissioner, was similar to a modern-day kibbutz. Conversely, Sonthonax's proclamation of August 29, 1793, aimed to reconcile the interests of owners and farmers. The newly free had civil and political rights, were entitled to a third of plantation production, had escaped the dependence of the old masters, and were no longer subjected to physical punishments, particularly the whip. Attached to their original plantations and needing authorization from the justice of the peace to be able to leave, the "newly free" did not have complete freedom. "Vagrancy" was also harshly suppressed. In the views of colonial administrators, state interest called for these restrictions. Their concern, though, was less about making a profit than ensuring the survival of the colony in a context of total war.[17]

Colonial officials attempted to alleviate the colony's dependency on food from foreign trade. Because not a single US vessel entered the harbor of Les Cayes between September 1793 and August 1794, Rigaud provisionally prioritized subsistence agriculture. Sonthonax's regulations enforced the extension of provision grounds and local gardens, to which cultivators were required to devote two hours of work a day. These measures were not entirely new since the *intendant* in the old regime had attempted to force planters to implement such regulations since the American Revolution. Despite government efforts, the production of foodstuff did not dramatically increase. In May 1794, Governor Laveaux complained that "most of the inhabitants and managers have totally abandoned the culture of manioc, bananas, potatoes, yams, and maize," and "all their garden plots were devastated by their negligence." The small Tortuga island, from which owners had not fled, exported vegetables to Port-de-Paix in Saint-Domingue, but elsewhere consumption remained essentially local.[18]

The colonial government urgently needed to decide on the legal status of properties left vacant by planters. The political and social stakes could not be higher: would the newly free be small landowners or employees of large plantations? *Ordonnateur* Perroud suggested to metropolitan authorities that it would be "the wisest policy to attach to the soil of St. Domingue, as many citizens as possible," "to make owners all the individuals who breathe there, to make them true defenders of the country." "There was a lot of land that could be divided and sold to Africans," he noted. In his eyes, the military took precedence over all other considerations: the division of property into small farms would support the formation of a powerful class of citizen-soldiers who could dictate the future of France in the Caribbean and beyond. To achieve such an ambitious program, he even suggested the introduction of the *assignat*, the devalued paper money created at the beginning of the French Revolution. Instead of being backed by church estates, he argued, in its colonial iteration the assignat would make land transactions available to a greater number of players, especially Africans and foreigners. But no one took responsibility for such reform. Thus, there was no division of land comparable to the transfer of property that had taken place in metropolitan France.[19]

Through a decree on August 25, 1792, the National Assembly confiscated colonial properties of the "émigrés," the individuals who left France out of ideological hostility to the French Revolution. It also instructed civil commissioners to preserve the estates in their integrity while promptly arranging auctions. This law was adapted by Polverel in his proclamation of November 23, 1792: the civil commissioner made a distinction between the properties of émigrés, who were deprived of any claim on their property, and those of "refugees," which were placed in escrow. All commodities produced on the sequestered plantations—that is, the majority—were to be brought to the Republic's stores for sale to the Americans. The income from these properties was paid into the "Caisse de la République." Absentees could only be credited with these funds after proving they were not émigrés and demonstrating they had fled the colony in fear for their lives.[20]

"The Republic [had] become, through emigration, a great landowner." At the same time, Port-de-Paix's colonial state took full control of legal trade in the northern part of Saint-Domingue. Perroud, who had been appointed ordonnateur precisely because of his position as the "biggest merchant in Port-de-Paix," explained that he was "forced to adopt the general plan of a commercial firm." All US ship captains had no option but to sell to the colonial state and no merchant could sell to anyone else unless granted an exception. As cash was scarce and Saint-Domingue had no credit, officials bartered commodities produced on the sequestered plantations in exchange for US foodstuff. Perroud himself, believing it necessary to guarantee an adequate income, arbitrarily fixed commodity prices. The colonial state seized all economic sectors, from production to distribution, and acted both as an interested party and a commercial arbiter.[21]

This improvised program ran into several difficulties. By the autumn of 1793, colonial officials were overwhelmed by the enormity of their mission. Municipal bureaucrats, navy treasurers, and storekeepers had been instructed to monitor the application of all measures, but most staff vanished following British conquest of the colony's western region. Skilled literate men able to maintain accounts were scarce, and offices in Cap-Français were in a state of "disorganization" and "chaos." The treasury was even failing to keep track of deals struck with US merchants. On a material level the state's decline was dramatic. Bureaucrats could not locate registers, because they had no paper anymore. Perroud, who was struggling to find bookkeepers who could follow basic accounting standards, scrutinized personnel appointed at the wharves near Port-de-Paix, placing the former merchant and "friend of general liberty," Verrier, in the post of purchasing officer in Cap-Français, where communications were severely disrupted by British privateers.[22]

The most significant obstacle was the devastation of the sugar plantations, most of which had been burned to the ground in the parts of the colony under republican rule. The state did not have the resources to restore production: nails, planks, and barrels were needed to rebuild the mills, and mules had to be acquired to supply power. Human resources were also lacking; managers who were able and willing to supervise the plantations with the new labor regime in place could not be found. At the end of December 1793, sixteen out of forty-four sequestered plantations in the Port-au-Prince parish had not produced anything at all. They even owed 97,567 livres coloniales to the government. When Laveaux and Perroud left office in May 1796, they had managed to restore forty-seven plantations with 4,467 *cultivateurs* producing 1,349,707 pounds of sugar and 19,552 velvets of syrup. The government shifted their focus from sugar production to coffee, which was far easier to harvest. Since coffee did not require mills, aqueducts, or mules, coffee crops more easily reached a profitable production level. Laveaux was not abashed by the results he forwarded to the French metropolitan authorities. The level of production remained far removed from that of 1789, however, and varied immensely from one plantation to another. Vertus Saint-Louis has shown that in Borgne and Plaisance the labor force had decreased from 14,103 slaves to 7,534 cultivators. The section of Gonaïves, under Toussaint Louverture's oversight, emerged as significantly more productive.[23]

Sonthonax, Polverel, Perroud, and Rigaud were charged with assimilating the new citizens into the commercial republic, not just as employees but as consumers. This undertaking, however, required cash to be distributed in small sums to laborers. In the hope of preserving the little ready money that remained, Laveaux prohibited export of the colony's coins. Perroud forbade use of the Borgne pier in order to monitor all exchanges with US captains, fixed the price of gold to prevent depreciation, toughened penalties for smugglers, and rewarded whistleblowers. Yet the impact of these measures was extremely limited. The Americans had made off with "all the money" and "all the metals, copper, iron and lead." Scarcity prompted the creation of new paper money, but this initiative, like others, floundered in the face of trivial material realities. Perroud fantasized about a paper money bearing "general freedom" as an emblem to generate the trust of illiterate consumers, but he had to content himself with cheap cardboard and no iconography. Cultivators were unimpressed: thirty miles from Port-de-Paix, "they don't want it because the frequent rains that reign in the hills would make them lose it." The government was unable to produce solid cardboard that could withstand tropical weather, and the 280,000 livres of bills of trust (*billets de confiance*) distributed by Laveaux were little used.[24]

Most of the "newly free" wanted to work less on the plantations and to instead dedicate their energy to subsistence agriculture. In the Southern Province, the cultivateurs resisted new regulations and strove to "define their lives as free peasants ... spontaneously appropriating plantations for their personal use." Women, in particular, who made up the large majority of the fieldworkers, objected to the labor regulations imposed by Polverel in February 1794. Although there was a degree of negotiation between workers and the government, colonial officials asserted the absolute necessity of restoring crops. Polverel explained that without production the French Republic would not have the "means to defend the country and you." English and Spanish victory would mean the end of general freedom. In addition to glorifying work, Polverel commissioned inspectors to ensure that farmers returned to their plantations. In the north, Laveaux and Perroud renewed repressive measures against "vagrancy" by enforcing provisional regulations subsequently endorsed by the National Convention. The full citizenship of the newly free was in part qualified by the very designation of "Africans"—which recreated an intermediary and semi-legal status between citizens and foreign nationals. As naturalized citizens, they were subject to a number of legal incapacities that constrained their freedom, in all likelihood another remnant of the racialized old regime.[25]

In the south, legislation went even further. Long before Toussaint Louverture, Rigaud militarized labor by bringing soldiers onto plantations. Article 11 of the regulation he passed on 4 Vendémiaire year III (September 25, 1794) stated the following:

> Each plantation will be visited one day per decade, [a ten day week in the new French republican calendar] and every time on a different day, these visits will be made by a detachment of dragoons, commanded by an officer, who will draw up a report of the state of the crops and from the nature of the work in which he will find the workshop occupied

during his visit, he will arrest the cultivators who refuse to work or who disturb order and have them led in front of the military commander.

Behind declarations of ethical commitment Rigaud would also resort to privateering to expand the local workforce. He took great pride in emancipating 450 Black people on two captured English vessels and did so while proclaiming "Long live the Republic! Long live the liberty of the Africans!" Yet many such Africans were "placed on some of the best plantations, and committed to the care and attention of the overseers, who received them with a truly fraternal affection." Later, the privateer *La Française* from Les Cayes released 200 Blacks from the Danish ship *Bernstorf* while on its way to Havana from Saint Croix. Their freedom meant that more people would be able to harvest coffee and cotton. Rigaud's harsh regulations, however, did not entirely suppress the democratization of the plantations since workers could elect their managers and had a say in economic decisions. A planter even lamented that they felt they were "the true owners" of the estates.[26]

Whether in the north or south, the economic transition was extremely problematic in a crushing military and international context. The colonial state did not have the capacity to directly manage all plantations. By November 1796, 215 sugar plantations had been sequestered. Not having the means to exploit all these plantations, the government decided to take control of forty of the best ones, which would be granted all technical means and animals available, along with premiums for the farmers. The remaining 175 sugar plantations were to be auctioned as three-year leases, payable quarterly in cash. A thousand coffee plantations were also leased in this way. As no definitive list distinguished the properties of émigrés from refugees, the government was unable to sell any plantations.[27]

Resistance by the "newly free" was not limited to strikes and squatting but was also related to trade. Farmers and managers wanted to sell directly to US captains, bypassing government inspection, with good reason; it was well known that state employees were cheating the workers. A warehouse manager, for example, who delivered salt and rice in exchange for coffee from the cultivators "weighed [the bags] in a way that did not give them what they were due." Some of the newly free responded through illegal means. A few already had experience trading in the Sunday markets in Cap-Français while others had been merchants in West Kongo before being captured, deported, and enslaved. Many had been trading with the Spaniards since 1791 and already had the skills needed to trade with foreign partners. The plantations themselves turned into informal markets where the newly free would barter corn, bananas, and peas "on a daily basis." In the old regime, trading had been an important element in the lives of the enslaved. The revolution, however, offered the newly free the opportunity to scale up their business. American captains "daily unloaded smuggled flour, wine, and other items, which of course should be in the public warehouses to provide for troops, hospitals, and other rationing," while "coffees and syrups are smuggled into towns." Later, a group of Black people who had revolted against French republican authorities traded massive amounts of coffee, transported by canoe from the mountains of Port-de-Paix and Jean Rabel to Cap-Français, in exchange for ammunition. Although French officials believed this coffee had been "stolen," it was probably intentionally harvested by insurgents and therefore regarded as a legitimate property. Such informal dealings were hidden from the colonial archive so can only be guessed at.[28]

The colony was soon unable to pay for foodstuff by exporting locally produced commodities, because the value of imported goods far exceeded that of coffee, sugar, cotton, and molasses. The administration was growing dependent on and indebted to large US firms in exclusive contracts. The great trader Joshua Barney, who was a friend of Sonthonax, agreed to take on debt for the French Republic and held 833,634 livres coloniales of bonds in May 1794. With debt spiraling out of control the government started to pay with agreements based on the future productions of leased plantations. Local production, however, always fell short of expectations. Between January 1794 and 3 Thermidor Year III (July 21, 1795), Port-de-Paix purchased the cargoes of 130 neutral vessels (including 124 American) for 5.4 million livres coloniales. Laveaux reassuringly asserted that "by force of care, the country has produced enough crops to pay for the American cargoes and to make some money to give to the troops." This optimistic opinion was not shared by US captains, traders, and shipowners, who showered recriminations against Port-de-Paix in petitions and newspapers. The basis of these complaints varied, but one issue the French bureaucrats could not possibly ignore was the quality of goods. The Choiseuil Meuse plantation, for instance, yielded "very fat, not purged" sugars looking "like tar." La Petite Anse's distillery produced tafia (a cheap rum produced from molasses and inferior sugar) "so weak that it could only be considered as water . . . and could only be detrimental to the interests of the Republic." Ship captains also deplored the lengthy and expensive delays in the delivery of colonial commodities: it was not uncommon for a vessel to wait in the harbor for over five months (vessels could previously conduct a full rotation in three months), transforming an otherwise profitable venture into a loss. Captain Daniel Boyer on the *Betsey* from Boston was forced to sell a cargo of beef, pork, flour, candles, soap, cheese, bacon, and butter worth $11,250 to the administration of Cap-Français in March 1794. Waiting to be paid in produce until late May, he eventually left the harbor empty-handed. This case of economic abuse was just one among many. The government's worsening reputation dissuaded ship owners from sending their ships to the republican side of the colony.[29]

Exasperation only increased. American captains came together to address an anguished petition to the governor and forwarded this to the US government. They wanted to escalate the commercial dispute into a diplomatic crisis. "The treatment we have received from the government of the said Island," they complained "is contrary to the treaties existing between America and France and to that sacred faith which hath been pledged between the said Republics." It "has been the more unwarrantable and especially as it has been carried on under the mask of <u>disguise of a Free Trade</u> and the <u>Mockery of voluntary transactions</u>."[30] Free trade, like the Treaty of Amity and Commerce, had become empty words. Sea captains and supercargoes could not negotiate prices with the government, which fixed them unilaterally. Laveaux was even outfitting privateers from Port-de-Paix to coerce neutral vessels to sell their cargoes. Brigantines entering republican harbors were forced to unload their merchandise, even if US merchants were unhappy with government prices. When captain John Wimore attempted to sail from Cap-Français for Môle Saint-Nicolas, then occupied by the British, one of the last remaining republican frigates threatened his schooner with cannons. Some traders, however, exaggerated their losses. Baltimore merchant Samuel Smith was so delighted by the "huge profits" he made from sales of flour and purchase of Port-de-Paix coffee that he subsequently sent an even larger vessel.[31]

Still, most sea captains preferred markets in the section of the colony occupied by the British where slavery had not been abolished. Twice as many ships traveled to Jérémie as to Cap-Français and Port-de-Paix combined. In the first half of 1796, 65 percent of Philadelphia's imports from Saint-Domingue came from the occupied ports.[32]

The animosity of US captains provoked frustration and anger within the local government, whose anti-US discourse hardened day by day. These American "friends," showing little inclination toward republican solidarity, were guided by "greed" and displaying their true, "tyrannical" colors. The rhetoric of recrimination spread rapidly. An employee exclaimed, "When will we have justice from a people more interested than wise, who, for the price of blood and treasures that France has poured to help it in the conquest of his freedom only pay us back by sending us, in general, in our distress, only old cured meats, the scraps of their stores?" Beyond moral censure, Laveaux made a diplomatic argument, pointing out that American merchants were betraying the Treaty of 1778: "The United States was supposed to guarantee our colonies, and it gives the English every means of keeping them; they assert the neutrality of their flag to legitimize a trade so contrary to the treaty."[33]

The French government named the third civil commission to replace Laveaux in 1796. Its members included Sonthonax, back from the metropole after a long trial; Julien Raimond, the spokesman for free people of color at the beginning of the Revolution; Régis Leblanc, a former diplomatic agent in the United States; Marc Antoine Giraud, a deputy; and Philippe-Rose Roume, a former commissioner, who was assigned to Santo Domingo. All of them had a free-trade agenda and their intention was to break with Laveaux's interventionist economic policy. It was "essential to leave to everybody the free faculty to sell and to buy, not to make the citizens depend for all their needs on a purely mercantile administration of shopkeepers," they claimed. "It was possible," they believed, "to reconcile this freedom of commerce with the interest of the colony and the supply of its ports." These good intentions did not last long for the commissioners resorted to privateers just a few months after making this pledge. The British blockade, economic disarray, and dislocation of the colony thwarted their ideological commitment to free trade. Survival was at stake. "The commissioners seem determined to do everything in their power to ruin our trade," lamented a merchant in Cap-Français.[34]

Success or Decadence? Colonial Politics and Statistics in the Metropole

The colonial state's helplessness in Saint-Domingue was underestimated in the metropole, especially after the fall of Robespierre, as planters attempted to portray the civil commissioners as all-powerful, bloodthirsty terrorists. Metropolitan authorities paid little attention to the material difficulties faced by their envoys or the limits of abolition. Instead, they viewed Saint-Domingue as a political symbol, the laboratory where revolutionaries were experimenting with the abolition of slavery and transition to wage labor on a major scale for the first time. Therefore, measurement of US trade with Saint-Domingue became a contentious topic. Were slave-less colonies able to produce and export the lucrative commodities that had secured prosperity for French commerce in the eighteenth century? Or should they expect the ruin of the French West Indies and, consequently, that of France? Statistics were supposed to provide the answers. Assessing the volumes of colonial commodities produced since the abolition of 1793, and comparing these with figures for the period prior to 1789 should suffice. Since metropolitan imports had been disrupted by the British Navy, the quantity of foodstuffs exported to the United States from Saint-Domingue could provide solid proof of the abolition's success or failure. However, figures presented by the different parties were the subject of much controversy.[35]

On the abolitionists' side, colonial officials proved to be the principal champions of the ongoing economic transition. Their claims had two different audiences and served two distinct purposes. Downplaying the signs of a struggling economy, they wished to reassure US traders that the plantation complex was thriving, desperately attempting to entice them to ship cargoes to Saint-Domingue and supply the colony. Sonthonax, Laveaux, Perroud, and Rigaud all emphasized the restored "tranquility" and "flourishing" agriculture in memoirs or proclamations forwarded to French consuls, translated into English and published in US newspapers. "All those brave laborers have resumed their labor," they explained; "the Campaigns are constantly fertilizing under their hands." The Philadelphia newspaper *Aurora* advertised that the "situation in St. Domingo has become truly brilliant. . . . [C]ultivation and commerce flourish once again, especially since the commissioners have determined to rent out the plantations." Another article explained that "Republican virtues and close application to agriculture are the order of the day" and "the value of Colonial produce during the 5th year, has been tenfold to what it was during the course of the 4th." This marketing operation was necessary to preserve Saint-Domingue's credit as the colony was largely reliant on debts to feed itself.[36]

The colonial officials' second audience was metropolitan authorities, mainly the legislative branch and Ministry of the Navy. They needed to demonstrate their loyal efficiency and fight the campaign of denunciation relentlessly conducted by planter lobbyists. Pleas intended for government were characterized by the same rhetoric, even the same words, regardless of the author. All officials, upon their arrival in the colony or when taking up their duties, strongly emphasized the catastrophic situation in which they found the colony in order to embellish their own results. Rigaud, for example, abundantly described the deplorable state of the plantations when he took control of the southern part of the colony. "The mills," he lamented, "the buildings of 7/8 Manufactures of sugar factories had been burned in whole or in part. The sugar canes almost everywhere were ravaged by animals. . . . The coffee plantations were suffocated by creepers." Thanks to his unyielding efforts, however, the wise policy of his able government was bearing fruit. The French republican government should acknowledge him for "the progress of culture," "the emulation and zeal of cultivators," "the confidence of capitalists and speculators": in short, the "restoration of commerce." The prosperity of US trade with Saint-Domingue provided unquestionable evidence of these successes and clearly indicated the "regeneration of cultures," as "speculators, French and foreigners would not have risked their capital" otherwise.[37]

Saint-Domingue's officials had spokesmen in the metropole, who repeated or made similar remarks within the Legislative Assemblies and the press. The Parisian newspaper *Le Républicain des colonies*, published by abolitionist François Marie Bottu, elaborated at length on the economic success achieved in the West Indies. All state officials returned to the metropole, where they were accountable for the economic policies they had implemented. Returning early to the hexagon due to ill health, Giraud, a member of the Third Civil Commission, strongly defended the record of his colleagues and predecessors:

> Saint-Domingue produces nothing of what is really called necessity, neither in commodities nor in clothing. Yet there is everything, if not abundantly, at least to satisfy modest needs. The Americans who supply the flour, the cured meats, the sheets, the canvases, the hardware, do not deliver them for nothing; if they did not get returns, they would not come. What are they paid with? With colonial foodstuffs, sugar, coffee, cotton, syrup.... Despite your skepticism, the existence of the individuals who still populate this colony and the small white army that defend it do not allow any longer to doubt that there is not only a culture, but even a culture sufficient to sell, with its produce, the goods that the United States continues to bring.

Giraud exaggerated local food production levels, providing an excessively positive picture while downplaying the credit mechanisms that enabled the colony to survive. More strikingly, he remained silent on how aggrieved US merchants were with the deals forced on them by colonial officials. Beyond self-justification, abolitionists intended to prove that "the land cultivated by free men, by hands triumphant and subject to the decrees of France, will multiply its productions." Later, Toussaint Louverture would hammer the point home: as the Northern and Southern provinces each produced 25 million pounds in colonial commodities, Saint-Domingue was proving wage labor could match enslaved labor in efficiency.[38]

Their opponents, challenging the abolitionists' narrative, constantly deplored the economic decline experienced by the "Pearl of Caribbean." The deputy of Ile-de-France (today's Mauritius), Benoît Gouly, championed the white colonists in the Convention, defending their proslavery cause and relentlessly attacking the records of French officials in the Antilles. In August 1796, René-Ambroise Deaubonneau and Chotard Aîné launched a new, *Journal historique et politique de la Marine et des Colonies*, which appeared almost daily until July 1797. The journal made its theme clear by copying a motto associated with Colbert's policy: "No Colonies, No Commerce, No Commerce, No Navy." For these lobbyists, the word "colony" necessarily included slavery, for them a prerequisite for a vibrant plantation economy and maritime power.[39]

The journalists repeatedly reminded their readers of Saint-Domingue's decline since the abolition decree. They contrasted idyllic pictures of a once prosperous and heavenly colony with the brutality of its fall. Statistical rhetoric supported an emotional narrative, as they recalled that "1400 French ships and allies used to be loaded each year with the goods of St. Domingue" and France received a "real surplus of 280 million livres in colonial commodities" when "750 merchant ships were shipped from the ports of France." The colonial economy supported "20,000 sailors," they maintained, and nearly "6 million French people lived and grew rich by their relations with our colonies." Saint-Domingue used to possess nearly "8 billion livres in wealth, 1050 large plantations and a considerable number of average establishments, the revenues of which gave France more than 70 million to her advantage." But nothing had survived this past splendor. The Lefebvre plantation, for instance, "which used to make a million pounds of sugar, had last year only 67,000 livres." Cap-Français's region, the former center of wealth, had at present only eighty plantations, the produce of which amounted to 1,347,483 pounds of raw sugar. The number of blacks employed on plantations was only 4,437 and with only 1,238 mules. Numerous pamphlets authored by colonists from Saint-Domingue echoed the same talking points, employing the same statistical narrative. In *France Demanding Its Colonies*, F. Limochel concluded his call for relaunching the slave trade with a table that compared imports from Saint-Domingue in 1790 with the same metrics for 1795. The collapse looked abysmal. Journalists purposely dismissed other causes for Saint-Domingue's economic hardship; for them, abolition was the only culprit. Since "the old mode of cultivation had been abandoned, the richest cantons did not produce a tenth part of what they had produced formerly." They steadfastly ignored the administrative chaos that also affected parts of the colony under British occupation. This oversimplification of events in Saint-Domingue disregarded the crucial role played by maritime war in the extinction of official French trade.[40]

While abolitionists displayed excessive optimism, the colonists exaggerated the magnitude of the collapse. The planters and merchants who employed the vocabulary of "disaster" had a lot at stake in the matter. The crops produced in Saint-Domingue were almost never imported directly into metropolitan France. Instead they were exclusively exported to the United States—even from the part occupied by the British—and US merchants then reexported these commodities to Europe. Therefore, by basing their estimates on customs data from metropolitan ports, lobbyists provided figures that they knew to be deeply flawed. In fact, French merchants imported sugar and coffee into the metropole through the United States. The statistical rhetoric of the time must be subjected to careful analysis for the intellectual history of political economy.[41]

In Paris, lofty speeches painted in great detail how the French Revolution would engender global regeneration, a political and commercial transformation mediated by "the liberty of commerce" and the American alliance. On the ground in Saint-Domingue, events developed somewhat differently and created a striking paradox: on the one hand, liberal republicans claimed to educate and instill capitalist qualities into the newly free; on the other hand, they restricted, controlled, and monopolized their trade to ensure the survival of the colony. The French authorities adapted and sometimes ignored directions from the metropole, which were regarded as out of step with the current situation. In fact, the exceptional powers of the civil commission were a response to the disintegrating French imperial state, which was far from a well-oiled machine. In the context of foreign invasion, a multiplicity of rival institutions and agents shared the republic's territory, issuing local rules designed to cope with local crises. Plantations, transformed into insurgent camps, were sites of political autonomy and economic transformation. The militarization of government was gaining ground everywhere. Abolition involved an unprecedented economic transition at a time when the new citizen-soldiers were fighting the British, champions of the proslavery crusade. Opponents of "general freedom" in the metropole dismissed the complications of Saint-Domingue's revolutionary context to make bold claims about the colony's economic decadence. Trade between the United States and Saint-Domingue, abolitionists countered, demonstrated that "free hands" were as efficient as enslaved ones.

This, however, was a risky argument. The shock of revolution and maritime war had thrown the economic antagonism between the republics into sharp relief. Until what time could Saint-Domingue remain tethered to the United States for the benefit of the metropole? Republicans hoped that economic reorganization would overcome the provisioning hardships of the colony, the very survival of which was at stake. This illusion shattered under pressure from a double trend that escaped the notice of all, from Philadelphia to Paris. American traders were turning the failure of their commercial transactions into a diplomatic crisis, while the colonial administration was explicitly defining itself as a "large landowner" and "merchant house." The imbalance of this commercial and political partnership—replaying the traditional scheme of the debtor colony in an international context—laid the foundations for a new crisis.

8

Politicizing Merchant Identities, 1793–1798

Saint-Domingue's civil war was embedded in a confrontation involving all the European empires and most of the West Indies. Colonial societies were convulsing from local, regional, and global conflicts, and slave uprisings spread to Curaçao, Saint Lucia, Saint Vincent, and the shores of Venezuela. At sea, hordes of privateers plied the waves, while France and Britain shipped thousands of soldiers to the Caribbean, most destined to perish. This multi-faceted conflict did not annihilate maritime trade. As in previous wars, neutral ships replaced the commercial fleets of the warring nations. Yet the Dutch, Swedes, and Danes no longer had the upper hand, as the flag of the United States provided fragile security to the cargoes of sugar, coffee, cotton, timber, and foodstuff.[1]

The American federal government tried to avoid embroiling the young United States in the war by maintaining strict neutrality, despite the pressure exerted by European imperial powers. A rapprochement with Britain, materialized in the controversial Jay Treaty, offered little protection to US vessels in the Caribbean. "Every new arrival from the West Indies brings some fresh account of British insults on the American Flag" decried one newspaper. This "degradation of the national character" and the compliance of the federal government provoked a major political crisis with France in 1795. The new French regime, the Directory, emboldened by military triumph in Europe, accused the Americans of collaborating with their former metropole and decreed that neutrals would be treated "in the manner they agreed to be treated by the British." The French "commenced the exercise of their colonial despotism upon the Americans. They take all cargoes—at their own price—and pay those prices principally in promises only." Tensions between US captains and colonial officials in Saint-Domingue and Guadeloupe escalated to the point of undeclared war. But, albeit precariously, neutrality contributed to the spectacular growth of US trade, which decisively seized the reexporting (carrying) trade to the old continent formerly

Entrepôt of Revolutions. Manuel Covo, Oxford University Press. © Oxford University Press 2022.
DOI: 10.1093/oso/9780197626382.003.0009

monopolized by European merchants. The United States experienced both the promise of its commercial power and the reality of its maritime vulnerability.[2]

The conflict was not confined to international affairs and foreign commerce. A democratic crisis over the meaning of the American Revolution was also developing. The French Revolution, widely viewed as a global civil war and a struggle between democratic and monarchical forces, reignited the spirit of 1776. A mounting polarization in US public debate and increasing concern about "foreign influences" defined international commerce from an almost exclusively political perspective. Trade entangled local merchants with strangers and, in revolutionary times, these connections could not be innocuous. The conundrum for the United States was that Britain remained their main business partner in Europe, and French Saint-Domingue was the principal market in the Caribbean. Whether one sided with pro-French Republican-Democrats or pro-British federalists, trading with France could mean supporting republicanism or mobocracy, popular sovereignty or savage violence. Republican democratic public discourse declared a class conflict, accusing "stockjobbers and speculators" of insulting the "sanctuary of the national Representation" and lamenting that the enduring dependence on British credit and goods was "recolonizing the American character." From this perspective, wealthy capitalists with an aristocratic propensity backed Britain; ordinary people, faithful to republicanism, sided with France. However, the abolition of slavery had transformed the debate, as planters grew increasingly alarmed by the "contagion" permeating from Saint-Domingue.[3]

Despite the binary language of partisan politics, the trading world was characterized by a variety of behaviors and attitudes toward revolutionary events; the relationship between political orientation and economic choice was not straightforward. While it is undeniable that the majority of US merchants favored the British and leaned toward federalism, it is no less true that a minority of pro-French traders supported Republican-Democrats. Most did not want to pick a side. In fact, what was really at stake was the regulating of international trade in a context of revolutionary state-making, abolitionism, and imperial overreach.

How Refugees Helped Make Saint-Domingue the Pearl of the United States

With the war entirely isolating Saint-Domingue from European France, virtually all the colony's trade passed into the hands of US-based firms. Merchants continued exporting the same foodstuffs, such as flour, salted meats, candles, soap, vegetables, and rice. The major shift was a considerable increase in US

imports of colonial produce of which the French West Indies were, by far, the
leading suppliers: in 1795–1796, 35 percent of sugar (over 19 million pounds)
and 42 percent of cotton (1.3 million pounds) came from the French islands.
The most vibrant sector was coffee, imports of which increased by a factor of
10 between 1790 and 1795. The French West Indies alone supplied between
37 and 43 million pounds of coffee per year between 1794 and 1798; between
73 percent and 85 percent of the total imports and between 9 and 30 times more
than the British West Indies. Fifty times as much coffee was exported to Europe
in 1798 as in 1791. These numbers demonstrate that historians have exaggerated
the collapse of production in revolutionary Saint-Domingue. The United States
imported almost half of the total of coffee imports made by the French metropole in 1789. As a whole, the colony made up at least two-thirds of US trade
with the French West Indies, probably more. These numbers also include trade
with territories occupied by the British and suggest that regional variation was
far more significant than previously believed.[4]

The other main change was the significant decline of New England on the
Saint-Domingue market as most trade shifted to the mid-Atlantic port cities. In
1788, the top five US ports accounted for only 26 percent of trading volume
with the French colony; by 1794–1795, they were responsible for 70 percent of
ship entries and 74 percent of cargo value (Table 8.1). As shown in Table 8.2,
Baltimore progressively caught up with Philadelphia's trade and even emerged
as the main commercial hub in 1797, as the steady increase in overall trade
reached its peak and attacks on US vessels by French privateers intensified.
Saint-Domingue had consolidated its status as the Pearl of the United States.

While preexisting trade meant the United States was well-positioned to
dominate the market from the outset, the so-called Saint-Domingue refugees

Table 8.1 **Entries into Port-de-Paix and Value of Cargoes, 1794–1795**

Rank	Port	Livres coloniales
1	Philadelphia	1,329,449
2	Baltimore	801,620
3	Charleston	714,154
4	Boston	560,996
5	New York	507,907
	All other ports	1,357,432
	Total	5,271,558

Source: CADN, Baltimore, 12, "Réponse de l'Ordonnateur civil."

Table 8.2 **Entries from Saint-Domingue Ports**

Years	Baltimore		New York		Philadelphia	
	Ships	Tons	Ships	Tons	Ships	Tons
1792	74	8,580	52	4,921	155	14,653
1793	153	26,248	84	10,518	169	?
1794	94	9,272	90	6,522	106	?
1795	156	13,523	104	?	228	?
1796	179	17,503	116	?	282	?
1797	199	19,076	117	?	203	?
1798	166	17,466	94	?	119	?

Sources: NARA RG36 1149, vols. 6-7; 903; NYHS, United Insurance Company Records; Dun, "What Avenues of Commerce, Will You, Americans, Not Explore!."

also played a role in this commercial growth. They were estimated to be around 10,000, but as no census was carried out and many refugees were highly mobile— resettling in Saint-Domingue, moving back to another US port, returning to the metropole, or trying their luck in Santiago de Cuba, Kingston, or Caracas—this figure should be taken with a grain of salt. Their influence had less to do their quantity than to the capital these planters and traders poured into the US market, which contributed to redrawing commercial routes and transforming the economic landscape of the greater Caribbean. The destruction of the colony's main trading center, Cap Français, marked a turning point, with many of these major traders flocking to the United States. Between June and November 1793, forty-eight large ships, designed to cross the Atlantic and weighing on average 264 tons (more than three times that of a standard American vessel sailing to the Caribbean), entered the chief port of Maryland. As merchant Bentalou recalled, "The total destruction of Cape Francois had taken place and shipping, people and wealth of that great mart, had poured into Baltimore." There were also thirty-five French ships in Norfolk, ten in New York, and others in Philadelphia, Savannah, and Boston. In addition to masses of coffee, sugar, and cotton, many captains and a considerable number of traders and clerks were on board. Their arrival provided human resources that American traders could easily marshal. In a world where personal face-to-face meetings were essential for building trust and relationships, the influx of so many powerful capitalists changed the scope of US- Caribbean trade.[5]

Some Saint-Domingue planters attempted to recreate their lifestyle in the United States and invested in land. In 1793, a handful moved to French Azilum, a planned settlement in Bradford County, Pennsylvania, which ultimately failed.

Jean Payen De Boisneuf founded a notorious plantation called L'Hermitage in Fredericktown near Baltimore, where ninety enslaved people, many from the French colony, worked in atrocious conditions. But the great majority remained in the port-cities, expecting to return to Saint-Domingue or leave for France. Several planters reinvented themselves as merchants and attempted to regain control of their plantations from the North American continent, signaled by the large number of notarial deeds giving power of attorney to relatives in the French consulates. A sea captain, brother, cousin, husband, or wife, whether passing through the colony or residing in the vicinity, could be legally authorized to manage a plantation, challenge the sequestration of an estate, or proceed with the loading of brigantines destined for the United States. Members of a household, dispersed across the continent and the islands, coordinated attempts to import colonial produce.[6]

Charles-Robert Legrand de Boislandry, who had moved to the French colony from Orléans in 1785 to manage his stepfather's plantations, created a new mercantile house. Charged by Saint-Domingue's Southern Provincial Assembly with requesting US aid, he settled in Baltimore in March 1792. His plantation in the parish of Torbeck had been "reduced by the colonial revolution to a state of absolute devastation" before being sequestered and leased by the republican government. Deprived of his property, Boislandry started a partnership with an American merchant named William McCreery and made use of his vast network within the planters' world. Their brigantine, the *Betsy & Patsy*, carried out four commercial ventures to Les Cayes, two to Môle Saint-Nicolas, and one to Cuba. However, having lost cargoes loaded on other ship owners' vessels and confiscated by French privateers, the company went bankrupt in 1798. Despite his eventual failure, Boislandry exemplified the kind of Saint-Domingue entrepreneur chasing new commercial opportunities in the United States.[7]

The business community was well represented among the refugees. In New York alone, eighty-five ship owners, traders, and supercargoes were registered at the French consulate between 1793 and 1798. While some were only passing through, several settled down, less out of necessity than from an entrepreneurial spirit. Most firms specialized in importing Caribbean goods and reexporting them to Europe, and some reached the top of the US trading elite. In Baltimore, John/Jean Carrère, for example, became one of the city's principal ship owners. In 1798 in New York, five of the twelve main importers from Saint-Domingue were registered as "refugees." The driving force, however, was less this elite than the subordinates: clerks and plantation managers. These less affluent individuals had to secure employment, and many sought to use their specialized skills in accounting and languages at trading houses. Advertisements such as this appeared in local newspapers:

A Frenchman, former captain, naturalized American, speaking and
writing English, would like to find employment either as a captain or as
supercargo, commissioner or commercial agent for claims, or for such
other matters like those, and in any part of the world you would like.

Familiarity with markets, goods, local merchants, and languages was essential
for the success of business transactions. The mass of unemployed clerks would
form the merchants' commercial army.[8]

Connected with the "refugees," the powerful traders of French metropolitan
ports indirectly contributed to this expansion. The ship owners in Bordeaux,
Le Havre, and Nantes required US neutral coverage to maintain some hold on
the flows from the French colonies and looked for local partners to help navigate the specific commercial intricacies of the United States. Moïse Gradis, a
member of one of the most influential merchant families in Bordeaux, settled
in Philadelphia and started a trading business with Saint-Domingue, redirecting
produce to Europe via the United States. Pierre Changeur, a slave trader from
Bordeaux who had formerly backed a commercial branch in Cap-Français, had
his two sons work with the seasoned smuggler Bentalou in Baltimore. They were
to import coffee from Saint-Domingue and reexport the produce to Europe. In
1794, Félix Cossin and Nicolas Schweighauser, whose father had supplied the
American insurgents during the previous war, moved from Nantes to New York.
Granted a permit by the Committee of Public Safety, they were to "neutralize"
property owned by the Nantes' Community and ship the goods to France. These
firms sparked another "triangular" trade, between Saint-Domingue, the United
States, and France.[9]

Francophile Trade or Casino Capitalism?

Did this trade have any political meaning for the main practitioners? Were
politicized merchants driven by ideological motives? These are not just abstract
questions. The French consuls in the United States were charged with securing
contracts with "pro-French" traders committed to supplying the French Antilles.
The official *commission des subsistances,* responsible for provisioning France from
foreign sources, had drawn up an ideal portrayal of the merchants they should
entrust with these operations, stressing skills and political affiliation. They
needed to be good republicans.[10]

All consuls and vice-consuls posted in the United States surrounded themselves with a minority of actively pro-French traders. One such "French party"
in the New York mercantile community was famously at odds with a "British
faction," dominated by the towering figure of Alexander Hamilton. In December

1793, Ebenezer Stevens organized a patriotic celebration bringing together all merchants favorable to France in honor of ambassador Genet. His enthusiasm was not unrelated to a contract he had signed to supply the French fleet stationed in New York. Stevens was also a major player in the burgeoning Bordeaux trade. One of the most powerful families in the city were the Livingstons, who had produced a state chancellor and a member of Congress; they were key part-ners of the French consul and urged steadfastness against Britain. Brookholst Livingston was the consulate's lawyer, and John Livingston's trading house secured a contract with the ambassador to ship food to the French metropole. Their brother Peter then signed a contract with Saint-Domingue's govern-ment in a deal so large it attracted suspicions of corruption and was eventually canceled. In all respects, the Livingston family embodied the "French party" of New York.[11]

Some merchants were politically active on the national stage. No substantial US traders identified more with French republicanism than Samuel Smith and Stephen Girard. A true Francophile, Smith had become a prominent Republican-Democrat during the Jay Treaty debate, when he unsuccessfully supported a bat-tery of retaliatory laws against Britain. At the local level he headed the political machine for Republican-Democrats in Baltimore. As Franco-American tensions escalated, Smith repeatedly intervened in Congress to delay and avoid a dec-laration of war, even attempting to justify French seizures of neutral vessels in Saint-Domingue and Guadeloupe by declaring that the injured traders could not allege any legal basis for their claims. In Philadelphia, Girard, a former Bordelais and a prominent member of the local Jacobin club, distinguished himself during the crisis of 1793–1794 by championing the interests of the French Republic. Whereas the majority of US traders had signed petitions requesting adoption of the Jay Treaty, Girard chaired a committee that authored a counter-petition on April 16, 1796. He unequivocally condemned the accord as "unequal in its stipulations, derogatory to our national character, injurious to our general interests, and as offering insult instead of redress." In private correspondence he railed against the corruption of the mercantile elite and their anti-republicanism. His correspondent, Bentalou, decried businessmen who "would sacrifice the most imprescriptible rights to their selfishness" and hoped that "republican virtue" in the countryside would preserve US independence. They belonged to a small group of highly politicized merchants.[12]

On a commercial level, these traders secured supply contracts with the French administration. Smith was close to the Baltimore consul; Girard regularly visited the Consul General of France to consult him on all matters concerning Saint-Domingue. He was also the main supplier of Raymond Labatut, a republican who ruled Tortuga Island and whose family moved to the United States. Girard was the banker for many refugees stranded in Philadelphia, while Smith helped

Saint-Domingue colonists secure relief funds. Both were invested in the success of the French and Saint-Domingue revolutions, which served their interests reasonably well and could be rationalized as a just cause.[13]

The two merchants shipped cargoes to republican ports but also occasionally partnered with merchants based in the British colonies and occupied ports. Whether slavery was abolished or not played little part in their investment decisions, the only issue being whether the port could provide sugar, coffee, or cotton. Girard shipped goods to republican Gonaïves, Toussaint Louverture's headquarters, where "produce was more abundant than elsewhere." Smith lobbied for a bill providing financial aid to white colonists, but also traded with those he called the "republican negroes." However, the reputation of a merchant as a French or a British sympathizer did matter. As his supercargo had the same name as a prominent Federalist in Baltimore, one of Smith's ships was seized by a privateer from Guadeloupe; the ship was released "as soon as it was known that the vessel belonged to general SMITH."[14]

In trading with the British, these merchants saw no contradiction with their support for the republican cause. Girard had no qualms about sending the *Nancy* to Massac & Cie, a trading house operating in occupied Port-au-Prince. Making profits and exchanging goods under the best possible conditions were their main objectives, but these merchants were also defending the national principle of gaining access to foreign markets. Girard grew more critical of France over time, although he remained convinced the French Revolution was a continuation of the American Revolution. He once refused to hire a Scottish captain because he preferred "Americans especially when they are good republicans, any other principle would not suit me," and described the "pirates of Guadeloupe" as "so-called republicans," who could no longer claim a title to which the merchant attached great value. When the *Kitty* was seized by French privateers, Girard even refused to complain to the federal government so as not to harm France's cause. In sum, political convictions did influence the behavior of the most activist merchants, but only marginally.[15]

The bottom line for most traders was to preserve and expand their business in a context of great confusion. In peacetime, eighteenth-century mercantile decision-making was based on a variety of factors: climatic conditions, harvest expectations, the legal context of transactions, and traders' networks. But war heightened levels of uncertainty and increased price volatility. "Those sudden changes are common with us and are productive of extraordinary variations," a Port-au-Prince trader explained. "We have often observed in less than eight days the two opposite extremes in prices." Constant fluctuations, due to sudden blockades closing markets or the arrival of thousands of soldiers producing high demand, meant merchants were fumbling in the dark, while ship owners could hit the jackpot on one venture or send too many goods to the wrong place at the wrong time and go bankrupt. As historian Cathy Matson emphasized, merchants always had to gamble.[16]

Such casino capitalism was all the more hazardous as the safety of vessels, property, and crew was unpredictable. A sea voyage was never trivial: the captain and sailors risked their lives by subjecting themselves to hurricanes or other life-threatening conditions. The war, with the mass circulation of European troops, also encouraged epidemics. Yellow fever in Saint-Domingue caused the death of nearly 11,000 British soldiers as well as innumerable sailors. Commercial ships were suspected of spreading the disease from the colony to Philadelphia and Baltimore, where tragic outbreaks occurred in 1793, 1797, and 1798. A captain would arrive in a port and find "nothing there, but sickness and death." Given the precariousness of maritime life, ship owners ensured that if a captain died on a voyage he would be replaced by the first mate.[17]

In addition to health risks, merchants dreaded the slaughtering of their crews and the pillaging of cargoes, and therefore they endeavored to get as clear a picture of the battlefield as possible. Samuel Smith wrote a revealing letter to his captain in which he attempted to decipher Saint-Domingue's chaotic military and economic landscape:

> We have certain accounts that F. Dauphin was taken by the Brigands and every white person whether on shore or on board the vessel was put to death so that it will be perfectly unsafe for you to go there.... By Captain Ross we have the following information, that Cape Francois is possessed by the Republican negroes. But that there is no safety there. That at Port au Paix the French are strong and not afraid. That Jacmel is possessed by the Republican negroes. That the English port of St. Domingo was stocked with flour which was selling from 4 to 7 dollars.

Tellingly, this ship owner combined information on prices with military news. Protecting crews and cargoes prevailed over any ideological considerations. His captains were authorized to negotiate with the French or the British, Blacks or whites. The war context, much more than the flag or the race of potential partners, dictated merchants' decisions.[18]

The main hazards were at sea. European law deregulated privateering and paved the way for institutionalized piracy. The British order of November 6, 1793, appeared to legitimize violence against neutrals and, despite being canceled less than two months later, unleashed fury. The Bermuda Admiralty Court was condemning US vessels on the basis of the British order long after its repeal. Many passengers were held in Jamaican prisons while others complained of molestations and robberies. On the French side, all republican leaders distributed letters of commission to privateers. The Directory's decree of Messidor 14,

Year IV (July 2, 1796), which legalized the seizure of US ships, gave considerable leeway to local authorities. Abuses, looting, and brutalities were common. On March 2, 1797, the French government made a *rôle d'équipage*, an official document listing crewmembers, a legal requirement, without which vessels could be legally confiscated. Since American captains did not have such paperwork, as the French well knew, US vessels were especially vulnerable to republican privateers.[19]

Maritime rules varied significantly from one place to another. In the occupied part of Saint-Domingue, the Môle-Saint-Nicolas Vice-Admiralty court "was notorious for its cruelty and extortion towards Americans." In Guadeloupe, civil commissioner Victor Hugues demanded that the Basse-Terre prize court condemn all captured US vessels. In Saint-Domingue, not knowing what the National Assembly's intentions were, republican leaders improvised until 1796, when the civil commissioners gradually rallied to a rigorous interpretation of directorial decrees. Sonthonax initially insisted that forced sales follow "the principles of justice and generosity" and be conducted at market prices, but as fear of a British blockade increased, the commission progressively strengthened the rules. The proclamation of 7 Frimaire year V (November 27, 1796) legalized the capture of neutrals intended for the British colonies, and that of 6 Nivôse year V (December 6, 1796) specifically targeted US trade with the occupied part of Saint-Domingue. The commission considered it was "against all principle to treat a horde of rebels, without country, without government, without flag, with the same respect as politicized nations have towards each other in wartime." In fact, Sonthonax translated the legal rules of 1704 and 1744, which authorized the privateering of neutral ships supplying ports under siege, into revolutionary language. The commissioners confirmed captured vessels as "good prizes" in the large majority of cases, but they also invalidated others for lack of evidence. Treatment of American captains depended on the local court. The US press railed at "a mulatto by the name of Gaston," justice of the peace in Petit-Goâve, claiming the sun had never shone on "a more complete infamous scoundrel." But Rigaud, who controlled the southern part of the colony, and Toussaint Louverture, chief of military forces, vehemently opposed the legal extension of privateering. The general, increasingly popular in the United States, was "furious at the piracy against the Americans" and refused to be "executor of the infamous orders."[20]

Anxious merchants did everything they could to avoid conviction; not conveying "enemy" cargoes was the most obvious move. When trading with Saint-Domingue, Smith barred his captains from loading French cargoes, taking French passengers onboard, or forwarding letters written in French. Everything and everyone had to be American, ideally "by birth." The nationality of commodities was defined by the owner's citizenship and could be evidenced by invoices and manifests. In some cases, fake sales and strawmen were used in attempts to circumvent the rules, but this presented the possibility of merchandise being stolen and vanishing. Some traders took the risk of claiming ownership of goods for a fee, "Americanizing" them to avoid confiscation.[21]

Ship owners and captains could rely on their long experience with smuggling, although some wartime adaptations were necessary. Privateering significantly increased danger on the high seas, and corsairs had no incentive to turn a blind eye, as a prize was invariably more lucrative than any payoff. However, the merchants' many skills acquired in smuggling were highly useful: flags were changed, goods were unloaded in remote ports, and routes were taken via impractical archipelagos. In March 1797, Girard, who had already lost vessels to the British and the French, provided his captain with forged sea letters. The first one read:

> The Brig *Sally* under your command being ready for sea, you are to proceed with all possible dispatch to the port of Gonaives in the Island of Hispaniola. . . . At your arrival at Gonaives, you will deliver yourself the letters which you have for General Toussaint Louverture and for Mr. Carrère père.

On the same day he wrote another letter stating his true orders, asking the captain not to pay any attention to the previous one, which was merely intended to fool potential French privateers:

> The brig *Sally* under your command being ready for sea, you are to embrace the first favorable wind to proceed to Cape Nicolas Mole in the Island of Hispaniola, having attention to keep your vessel 24 of thirty Miles of that Island and the one called *La Tortue* until you have run down far enough to the west ward to render necessary to shape your course for the Mole.

Such letters were common practice, though savvy captains usually destroyed them when under threat, leaving few behind in the archives. Captain Henry William Bool of the *Pattern* did not have the chance—or foresight—to do this when captured by *La Trompeuse*. The discovery of sea letters in English, French, and Dutch, intended to protect the vessel and its cargo under any circumstances, actually led to confiscation of the *Pattern* on 15 Pluviôse year V (February 3, 1797).[22]

Traders took considerable risks without always being able to insure their goods, as the rates levied by marine insurance companies were increasing to unsustainable levels. In Philadelphia, insurance rates on vessels and cargoes destined for the West Indies rose to 5 to 6 percent at the end of 1796 (instead of 2.5–3 percent); they increased to 10–15 percent in 1797, and to 25 percent in 1798. Saint-Domingue was considered the riskiest destination in the world for US vessels. Indeed, reversals of fortunes were commonplace. Merchant Bentalou considered it "imprudent to the highest degree, and particularly for beginners to risk anything to that devoted country." The future proved him right: his partner's ships, the *Margaret* and the *Abigail*, were both captured by privateers. Almost all ship owners suffered such setbacks, losing cargoes and wasting inconceivable funds. It was not uncommon for a vessel to be seized several times on one voyage by different factions. The *Nancy*, for instance, was captured on its way to Cap-Français by the British *Embuscade*. It was then taken by a French privateer from Port-de-Paix. Following release and heading for Tortuga Island, the *Nancy* was seized once more by the British on November 7, 1797, and condemned at the vice-admiralty court of Môle-Saint-Nicolas. The Saint-Domingue civil commission not only condemned 200 vessels but also left tens of vessels "lying there, waiting for payment of their cargoes." The time wasted in these proceedings could be as punitive as a condemnation. Since merchants were interconnected through a complex web of credit, the domino effect of uncollected accounts had devastating consequences. Bankruptcies swept away the most robust merchant houses, such as Garrick & Westphal, the leading New York firm on the Saint-Domingue market. Philadelphia endured 150 bankruptcies in December 1796 causing panic to overwhelm Baltimore the following year.[23]

The New Commercial Circuits

In attempts to mitigate the lack of information, US merchants generally delegated decision-making to their agents, either captains or supercargoes. Therefore, ascribing a political meaning to a shipments' destination makes their behavior unintelligible. Any snippets of news about conditions in the West Indies were almost always out of date by the time they reached the United States. In New York, Philadelphia, and Charleston, merchants were at a loss to know where to ship cargoes, what kind of produce to buy, or what price to pay. As Smith confessed to his supercargo: "Your own knowledge of the trade will be a much better guide than any directions we could possibly give." Captains had to be "governed by circumstances." This delegation of responsibility made all the more sense with the war constantly disrupting commercial networks. Merchants, unaware whether the commissioners they intended to work with would still be in place when their ship arrived, recommended multiple correspondents and consignees to their agents. Many trading houses attempting to navigate this revolutionary turmoil would relocate numerous times.[24]

A new commercial hierarchy of Saint-Domingue's ports was emerging. The British-occupied ports, particularly Port-au-Prince and Jérémie, were benefiting most from US commercial redeployment. Under pressure from Jamaica's lobbyists, British merchants barely attempted to capture the market. Dalton, Leriche & Co., which invested in the leases of five Cul-de-Sac sugar plantations, was the only major British firm in Port-au-Prince. Some government officials, such as the custom officer in Jérémie, were in fact merchants from Kingston and engaged in commercial activities. Established traders and firms relocating from Cap-Français nevertheless dominated business. Massac & Cie became Girard's main Saint-Domingue partner, reexporting high-quality coffee from Philadelphia to Hamburg. Dutilh & Wachsmuth traded almost exclusively with Jean Dutilh and Armand Morin in Port-au-Prince. Meanwhile, the port-city of Jérémie experienced its commercial golden age, taking advantage of a fertile hinterland, relatively spared from revolts, its isolation, and a vibrant trading community. The Grande Anse region, where half of the 200 plantations were devoted to coffee, had been the first to welcome the English. While only a dozen commercial vessels and slightly fewer coasters frequented the port annually before 1789, this figure increased more than tenfold after 1794. The area had become the stronghold of slavery capitalism in Saint-Domingue and the harbor swarmed with vessels under the US flag.[25]

Conversely, most "republican" ports experienced a sharp commercial decline. Le Cap-Français, once feverish with activity, sank into lethargy. Gonaïves, Toussaint Louverture's headquarters, and especially Les Cayes, the southern capital, were major exceptions. Before 1789, Les Cayes, despite its *entrepôt* privilege, had never been as large as the other provincial capitals, the port accounting for only 9 percent of Saint-Domingue's transatlantic trade that year. Late regional development and a less accessible harbor hampered development, but its specific profile was better adjusted to the exceptional context of the 1790s. Autonomous from the rest of the colony, the four surrounding parishes experienced delayed prosperity based on indigo and coffee. Neglected by the French slave trade, the southern part had engaged in smuggling—an essential part of life in this colonial frontier—with Jamaica, Curaçao, and Saint-Eustatius from early on. Local Jewish-Dutch networks, linked to the rising population of free people of color, had enabled Les Cayes to prosper in previous wars. In the five years following Polverel's crushing of the slave insurrection in January 1793, Les Cayes underwent spectacular growth. Heading the powerful Légion de l'Egalité, an army of 5,000 men, Rigaud established a strict socioeconomic organization and a militarized labor system. Merchants traded with the United States, Curaçao, and Saint-Thomas, exporting coffee, raw sugar, and cotton. The US traders were so satisfied with the local government that they unequivocally sided with Rigaud when he rebelled against Sonthonax in 1796. Under his rule, Les Cayes became a bustling trading center attracting an increasing number of ships. Entries of vessels from Saint-Domingue in the port of New York show the predominance of the trade with ports occupied by the British—Jérémie and Port-au-Prince in particular—and indicate the growing significance of Les Cayes between 1794 and 1797.[26]

Navigation patterns also changed. Vessels no longer rotated between two major economic centers (such as Philadelphia and Port-au-Prince) but made stopovers in a succession of smaller locations. The port network had become so decentralized that a simple pier, disconnected from any urban environment, could emerge as a major hub. This circulation blended the logics of vast Atlantic trade, Caribbean commerce, and local shipping. Vessels frequently sailed from port to port, replacing Saint-Domingue's coasters, and often traveled under the protection of British convoys in the occupied region. Transporting cargo belonging to Charleston merchants, the *James* headed for Port-de-Paix, stopped at Jean Rabel to recruit sailors, then docked at Petit-Goâve to load coffee, and eventually ended its journey at Miragoâne, where it was prevented from completing its mission by a British ship on May 27, 1797. Another example was *The Honest Friend* of Baltimore, redirected from its original destination, Jacmel, where the market turned out to be "bad," to Aquin in May 1798, where, had it not been captured, it would have taken 535 bags and 50 barrels of coffee onboard.[27]

The Spanish part of Hispaniola, Dutch Curaçao, and Danish Saint-Thomas were integrated into captains' navigation strategies. In 1795–1796, both Spain

Table 8.3. **Number of Vessels Entering New York from Saint-Domingue**

Port	1794		1795		1796		1797
Jérémie	26	Port-au-Prince	21	Port-au-Prince	32	Les Cayes	23
L'Arcahaye	14	Jérémie	18	Jérémie	15	Port-au-Prince	21
Môle St. Nicolas	12	Les Cayes	15	Môle St. Nicolas	14	Môle St. Nicolas	19
Jacmel	8	Gonaïves	10	Le Cap Français	11	Le Cap-Français	13
Port-au-Prince	6	Jacmel	7	Les Cayes	9	Jacmel	9
Les Cayes	6	Le Cap Français	6	Gonaïves	8	Port-de-Paix	9

Sources: NARA RG36 1149, 903; NYHS, United Insurance Company Records.

and the Netherlands were forced into an alliance with France, and their colonies expected to provide safe layovers. Saint-Thomas enjoyed Danish neutrality, which was more highly respected than US neutrality. Leaving from Saint-Thomas in February 1798, *The Hope* went to Les Cayes and from there attempted to enter Coro (in today's Venezuela), but Spanish coast guards prohibited its admission. After this setback, the *Hope* set sail for Curaçao and Aruba to be loaded with cattle. The little forty-two-ton schooner left for Les Cayes to load sugar and coffee intended for Baltimore, where the cargo would be reexported to Europe. But the *Hannibal*, a British privateer, intercepted *The Hope* and led it to Môle-Saint-Nicolas, where the vice-admiralty court tried the crew and confiscated their coffee and syrup in June 1798. Captain Francis Glavany, born in Constantinople of French parents and designated a "Greek," had lived for some time in Marseilles, Toulon, and various US ports, smuggling sugar, coffee, and flour for a living. In front of the British judges, he claimed to be a Danish bourgeois of Saint-Thomas. The majority of crews were multinational and *The Hope* was no exception. The five mariners who accompanied Glavany hailed from the Netherlands, Germany, the Spanish colonies, and the United States. British investigators found a Swedish flag, which Glavany claimed belonged to the previous owner. Glavany's biography and *The Hope*'s transnational circuit and crew epitomized what US trade had become in the revolutionary Caribbean.[28]

Prey or Predator?

The relationship between trade and privateering was complex. Privateers were privately owned, armed vessels commissioned by a belligerent state to attack enemy ships, usually vessels of commerce. The twisted routes undertaken by commercial vessels crossed and shadowed those of the corsairs attempting to capture them, in a game of hide and seek between players belonging to a shared floating world. Although merchants complained of being defenseless prey, it appears they were not the terrified victims they claimed to be.

The two worlds of privateers and contraband were not hermetic. The war prompted captain/smugglers to become captain/corsairs, such as Jean-Antoine Garriscan who, having previously illegally transported flour into Saint-Domingue, joined the French Navy. Some merchants also converted. The Moline brothers in Cap-Français had illegally imported enslaved people with the help of a New York firm in 1791 before going bankrupt and being imprisoned by the Pennsylvania Supreme Court. On release they returned to Saint-Domingue and launched a privateering business, outfitting several armed vessels. The Les Cayes firm, Nathan frères, was the Rigaud administration's main supplier and had many trade connections in the United States. It was also the foremost patron of corsairs in the South.[29]

The "republican" privateering business blossomed both in the Caribbean and the United States, albeit in disparate ways. At the beginning of the war, Saint-Domingue, like Guadeloupe, was a hotbed of privateers. In the northern part of the colony alone, between 10 Prairial year IV (May 29, 1796) and 14 Pluviôse year V (February 2, 1797), the governor distributed eighty-five letters of marque (a license to fit out an armed vessel). Most of these vessels were small, armed with only four guns and weighing on average eighteen tons. Only three weighed over 100 tons and nine exceeded thirty tons, while the word "barge" would more accurately describe fifty-four of these vessels, weighing ten tons or less. The majority of captains were former coasters embracing privateering after the war had ended the "entrepôt privilege."[30]

Privateering from the United States involved players of a different level. While Saint-Domingue's barges never approached the North American continent, the much larger privateer ships from metropolitan France made New York their base of attack. Unlike the crews arriving from Europe, some local captains and many sailors were Black or mixed-race. Despite these differences, US-based privateering was also intimately connected with the Caribbean. French consuls delivered letters of commission and auctioned prizes. Charleston emerged as the main North American rear base for French West Indian privateering. Charleston and Savannah hosted the adjudications for 142 British, Spanish, and Dutch ships and cargoes. Other ports in the United States, such as Baltimore, also passed judgment on and sold smaller amounts of plunder.[31]

No matter how indignant merchants were about privateering, they did not hesitate to profit from it whenever they could. The process only made sense because some merchants were prepared to buy prizes, and most of these were American traders. In Les Cayes, droves of US captains took part in coldly premeditated transactions. A ship owner from Baltimore wrote to his correspondent at Port-de-Paix: "As it seems that there are a number of American vessels condemned, we have authorized Captain Tupper to buy one if he can . . . cheap and of good quality." The sugars and coffees seized from American vessels by privateer ships were then sold to other American captains who reexported the cargoes to Europe. Privateering produced less an interruption of US trade than a new intermediation on the market: shrewd traders played all commercial roles.[32]

The privateers' networks connected ports of the greater Caribbean where prizes could be sold, ships repaired, sailors hired, and ammunition acquired. As it was too perilous to convey goods over long distances, multiple drop-off points were used to make quick transactions and avoid reprisals. This is clearly demonstrated by papers found on the privateer *La Liberté*, captured by a British frigate on May 11, 1797. This vessel, originally called *Bellone*, was bought in

Wilmington by Baltimore merchant Jean Nadau and entrusted to captain Jean Joseph Icard, who obtained a letter of marque in Cap Français on April 8, 1797. In his instructions, Nadeau indicated a list of contacts with whom Icard should trade any prizes *La Liberté* secured. If war with the United States broke out, he was to sell in Cuba, Santo Domingo, or Puerto Rico. If American neutrality was maintained, he was to deal with trusted traders, preferably of French origin but recently naturalized and established in US ports.[33]

Republican officials matched the privateers' efforts by increasing the number of places where captured ships could be condemned. The Directory's agents wanted to ensure that 15 percent of sales would go to France's coffers and the third of the profit intended for a crew was diligently paid. Prizes were initially assessed within the colony in tiny ports, the commission merely confirming or overturning the judgment as a last resort. Saint-Domingue's twenty-five justices of the peace followed a well-established procedure: they affixed seals, appointed an onboard guard, inventoried papers, and questioned at least three members of the crew. Beyond Saint-Domingue, the commission, with the minister of the navy's approval, appointed prize officers in colonies belonging to allied or neutral powers. This trans-imperial practice had existed previously. The United States, for example, had established a prize agency in Martinique during the War of Independence. Following this tradition, the commission had French agents based in Curaçao, Havana, Santiago de Cuba, the smuggling node of Montechrist on the Spanish border, Santo Domingo, and Puerto Rico.[34]

Prize officers, most of whom were merchants, acted as informal diplomatic agents, taking part in prize litigation while also coordinating the provisioning of Saint-Domingue, observing local political developments, and circulating diplomatic news. There was usually some tension in their relationships with the Spanish and Dutch governors who secretly opposed the French alliance. Local authorities complained that the French agent in Santiago de Cuba was fostering hostility between republicans and royalists. Under the leadership of Guadeloupe's commissioner, Victor Hugues, prize agents also played a decisive role in the defense of Trinidad and Puerto Rico against the British in 1797. The most significant intervention was that of Jean-Baptiste Tierce in the coups that shook the Dutch island of Curaçao, then divided between loyalists (Orangists) and patriots. Tierce had been appointed by Rigaud, who needed strong connections with Curaçao for the Southern Departement's provisioning. Then directorial agents confirmed his appointments. From the Dutch colony, Tierce coordinated maritime expeditions to ensure the continuation of US trade while allying himself with patriots who followed their own plans. Curaçao was the meeting point of the French, the Dutch, and the Saint-Domingue revolutions in the context of US commercial expansion, imperial warfare, and local politics.

Such an entanglement of privateering, trading, and governing shaped French imperial policy on the ground.[35]

Negotiating Citizenship in Revolutionary Times

Although the French were cracking down on neutrals trading with the enemy, they also needed those very same merchants to bypass the British Navy and supply the colony; therefore, French consuls turned to the smugglers that they had hunted down only a few years earlier. Experts in the art of camouflage and knowledge of the Saint-Domingue coast had now become the republic's natural allies. The Baltimore vice-consul approached Cazenave & Walker, a firm that had taken part in many smuggling schemes during the 1780s, and Bentalou, one of the "very small number of democrats, good merchants who deserve esteem." The latter was responsible for supplying French frigates. In Charleston, Abraham Sasportas, a Jewish merchant once vilified for illegal trade, was an active member of the Jacobin Club and outfitted two vessels, the *Sophie* and the *Agnès*, on behalf of the republic to transport cargoes to Saint-Domingue. Yesterday's smugglers, like captains Jacques Latouche and Jean Garriscan, were singled out as the most ardent "patriots" serving the Republic.[36]

Recruiting these men involved embracing and adapting to their smuggling methods. Not only merchants but also French officials were being disingenuous. Consuls offered to "neutralize" vessels by making them fly the US flag, "naturalize" the cargoes, and conceal the real names of recipients. When shipping war ammunition, consuls needed to hide shipments not only from the British but also from the US government, which prohibited such trade to protect its neutrality. The French embassy galvanized private traders by assuring them that ships would not be captured by republican privateers. Merchants who wished to benefit from the French Republic's protection had to follow a tried and tested revolutionary procedure: presenting themselves at the consulate to take an oath to serve the French Revolution. Merchants then legalized the "real" destination of the vessel, as distinct from that declared to US Customs. The statement made by the German merchant Cornelius Westphall, formally a clerk at a major Port-au-Prince firm before moving to New York, is typical of such notarial deeds. On 8 Pluviôse, Year III (January 27, 1795), he declared his desire to "give proof of his attachment to the glorious French Revolution." Having been informed of the "scarcity in which the colony of Saint-Domingue now stands," he shipped the brigantine *Nancy* under captain John May and loaded with "supplies calculated on the needs he believes most urgent of the said colony." As "prudence or, to put it better, the necessity, forces him to dispatch the said brig," the consul agreed to conceal the *Nancy*'s true destination:

Cape John May for the Neutral Isle of St. Thomas, so that in the event of an encounter with an English privateer or some other nation presently at war with the Republic, he may brave their inspection and escape their rapacity of which he could not guarantee his brigantine if his expeditions were openly for the port of Les Cayes.

The New York Consular Archives hold a bulky file of such letters of recommendation, intended to protect vessels destined for an enemy port. This strategy was at times so effective that a colonial agent would not believe the consuls' recommendations. In fact, Westphal's vessels were condemned in Saint-Domingue. As a Federalist journalist noticed: "Many of our merchants know, by sorrowful experience, that the strongest recommendations did not save their property, on their arrival at St. Domingo, from the rapacity of the agent of the French republic."[37]

For the majority of traders, declaring love for the republic was an expedient move. While not masked counterrevolutionaries or necessarily hypocrites, many viewed this formality more as a bureaucratic chore than as a sincere declaration. A good merchant and captain—a one-man band par excellence—had to recite the expected words and follow the rituals of the revolutionary scene. But this masquerade did not go unnoticed. It was becoming increasingly hard for consuls in the United States and republican agents in the Caribbean to regulate migration and the flow of goods. On the one hand, the needs of the colony forced them to turn a blind eye to merchants trading with the enemy if they were also supplying the French Antilles. On the other hand, they were under pressure from the central government not only to crack down on the British but also on their potential allies, whether "French" or "US citizens."

Legislation relating to émigrés complicated the rules of commercial law. A French person who had left voluntarily for counterrevolutionary purposes was regarded as an émigré. The law of March 28, 1793, brought in the death penalty and confiscation of property for this treasonous crime. In the French Caribbean these regulations required the differentiation of refugees and émigrés, conducted according to National Assembly categorizations of whether migration had been voluntary (and thus deemed political) or coerced. Should migrants from the colonies be regarded as enemies of the republic and stripped of their civic rights? Should their belongings be confiscated? Or were they victims, deserving of help or even compensation for their losses? The émigré was the enemy whereas the refugee was the victim. Yet the same individual could alternately and retroactively hold both positions. To confuse matters further, these distinctions were constantly shifting, with fifteen different decrees passed in quick succession, creating a legal quagmire.[38]

The Executive Directory believed many French traders taking refuge in the United States were merely camouflaged émigrés serving British economic interests. The government was determined to confiscate émigrés' property, thereby providing much needed support for the war effort. Those under suspicion were unlikely to confess their crimes:

> [They would] protest their loyalty to the republican government with the minister of the Republic, demonstrate with the marks of equality, then later display the old decoration they held from the tyrant, the white cockade, and appear in that costume before the consul or the minister of England and swear in their hands the pledge of allegiance to Great Britain. Legislators, those are the men whose fate you have to seal; those are the men who must at last be classified between the French or the English.

The French embassy and consuls undertook to classify every single French person who resided in or had passed through the United States. As they needed certificates of residence to avoid confiscation, migrants had an incentive to fulfill these formalities and demonstrate republicanism. Consuls kept a registry of those able to produce the mandatory paperwork and the French were required to publicly perform their patriotism by displaying a tricolor cockade at all times.[39]

However, as the vast variety of migrant cases did not easily fit the binaries of revolutionary rhetoric, this bureaucratic and political classification posed many problems. Consuls distinguished six categories of migrants from Saint-Domingue, whose status depended on the time and cause of their departure. Moreover, this classification was exclusively political and did not recognize migrants who sailed to the United States for business purposes. Local authorities were generally given leeway to resolve such delicate issues as they saw fit, and many traders were subjected to arbitrary rulings. Overzealous consuls would identify many "aristocratic" traders, whereas their colleagues would often prove far more lenient.[40]

To avoid being registered as an émigré, French merchants attempted to claim refugee status. Those without a republican passport who had resided for too long in Port-au-Prince or Jérémie needed to justify themselves, often through a formal "declaration of hatred" delivered at the chancery of the consulate. This ritualized procedure included the merchant's claim of having been forcefully detained by the "despicable English." Merchant Jean-Baptiste Charlestéguy, for instance, having only arrived in the United States on July 15, 1795, had to account for his late departure from Port-au-Prince. Born in Bayonne and residing on Water Street in New York, Charlestéguy declared that, as a proud republican abused by the English, his only motive for not evading the "odious victors" was to provide for "the needs of the Colony." Although "determined to sacrifice all his interests," and "run away from the tyranny of the Enemies of the *patrie*," the British had not only refused to give him a passport but kept him "under constant surveillance and prevented him from escaping." Charlestéguy did his best to translate his commercial activities in the strongly politicized rhetoric of patriotism, yet his alibi appears rather weak. It is unlikely that the French consul believed any of this; it was political theater, a ritualistic game of honor. The French consul needed such documents to justify his own behavior and his helplessness. The basic needs of the colony in food, weapons, and money trumped the ideological commitment he claimed to defend.[41]

Not only did any trader from Saint-Domingue registered on the list of émigrés have strong motivation to request US citizenship, but ship owners were also demanding that their Dominguan supercargoes and captains naturalize. If a ship was seized by the British, US citizenship offered some protection, and in Saint-Domingue's revolutionary context it was far safer to be "American" than "French." A ship owner from Philadelphia explained that US citizens were considered "good whites" due to the abolitionist laws implemented in northern states, and Blacks preferred dealing with them than the British and French slavers. With the resurgence of proslavery speech in France in 1796–1797 and the rise of Black people in the upper ranks of the military, French traders were being treated with increasing suspicion. Henry Corbières, a merchant passing through Norfolk, explained that "the situation of the French inhabitants, there was so desagreable [*sic*] that he had rather left the place for some time." However, he intended "to return there, but only as American . . . having been naturalized in 1793; as . . . Americans were perfectly tranquil." This case illustrates the entanglement of political, legal, and racial identities, a blurry configuration that left substantial room for negotiation.[42]

Colonial officials, however, were becoming less tolerant of these inconsistent practices. The Saint-Domingue governor complained to the minister of the navy that "émigrés embrace US citizenship, and under that pretext, go on the American vessels to do their business, take away whatever they can from this colony, and when they are arrested on American ships, they present their naturalization." The governor questioned whether these naturalized French émigrés should be regarded as French at all: the very meaning of French citizenship was at stake, with suspicion pointed at the "so-called refugees" and "so-called Americans." In August 1795, the Court of Admiralty in Petit-Goâve confirmed seizure of the brigantine *Harmonie* because the vessel belonged to a Philadelphia trading company previously based in Port-au-Prince. Although they had resettled in the United States in 1790, naturalized or not, these ship owners were deemed to be nothing but émigrés. Frustrated colonial officials tended to adopt a rigid conception of nationality.[43]

The legal imbroglio reached its climax in relation to French people of color on the high seas or the soil of the United States. Recently naturalized US citizens from Saint-Domingue would claim the abolition decree did not affect the enslaved people they intended to trade. This distinction between French Blacks and foreign Blacks was crucial: if the former were regarded as citizens, could the latter be treated as marketable property? Did the naturalization of an owner extend to the enslaved? The French consul in New York had no idea how to deal with the arrival of white refugees and their Black servants. Whereas planters referred to "their property," revolutionary law predisposed him to regard the Blacks as migrants and citizens with rights. Moreover, many northern states forbade the introduction of enslaved people from the French Antilles. In Saint-Domingue, suspecting that US captains were conducting a disguised form of slave trade through which "French people" sold other "French people," civil commissioners prohibited the departure of US ships with "black passengers." When the privateer *Hasard* seized the *Lark* in the vicinity of Môle-Saint-Nicolas, Sonthonax ordered the emancipation of five Black citizens. Modeste, Bernard, Jean-Charles, Jean-Pierre, and Marie had all been sold to Daniel and Charles O'Hara, merchants in Charleston. The commission declared it could not tolerate this "violation of human rights" and reasserted its support of the emancipation decree.[44]

Black migrants were well aware of their precarious status on the high seas. Realizing that having their Frenchness acknowledged could improve their legal security, they also made statements at consulate chanceries so that their freedom would be recognized and bureaucratically established. At times, they also complained about former masters who still claimed ownership. Romaine, a Black woman, made a formal statement at the New York consulate to combat the risk of reenslavement. Her former master and current employer was returning to Petit-Goâve in the south of Saint-Domingue but she adamantly refused to embark on a US vessel, declaring she would not risk being captured by a privateer who might "compromise her freedom." So fragile was US neutrality that she could step onboard a free woman, yet be treated as an acquirable property if the ship was seized. Romaine knew the risks of Atlantic migrations and was aware of what historians Rebecca Scott and Jean Hébrard describe as "the pervasive general threat of enslavement and reenslavement." While merchants had interests in "Americanizing" their passports, the newly free held fast to their French citizenship.[45]

French officials were suspicious of slavers whose names sounded far too French for them not to be émigrés. But what about the majority, whose names were often indistinguishable from the British? These Americans might be viewed as Britons in disguise since many British merchants established in the United States would apply for US citizenship in order to import goods from the Caribbean under the flag of neutrality. Moreover, the British did not acknowledge American naturalizations, for every citizen of the United States was still considered a British subject. The principle of perpetual allegiance justified the impressment—kidnapping and forced enrollment on British vessels—of thousands of sailors. Therefore, the French consul in New York recommended that France should pay "no regard for the rules of nationality": US citizens had never ceased being "English subjects."[46]

Attacks on US neutrality produced nationalistic responses and resulted in the criteria for naturalization being strengthened. During the 1780s, the process was adjudicated by local states but included significant local variation and flexibility. The Naturalization Act of 1790 conferred legal power to the federal state, which demanded two years of residence and reserved the possibility of naturalization to whites. However, enforcement of the law remained accommodating. The war context prompted a new and highly restrictive law in 1795, requiring five years of residence. This change was driven by the political desire to clearly distinguish between nationals and foreigners so as to fully enforce the policy of neutrality adopted by Washington.[47]

Since the proclamation of 1793, US courts of justice and the federal government had been bogged down in a series of legal disputes about the national definition of privateers. Citizens of the United States had been banned from serving on ships armed by any nation at war. This principle, simple in theory, was extremely difficult to enforce in practice. In 1793, Gideon Henfield, a native of Salem, violated this prohibition by becoming captain of the privateer, *Citoyen Genet,* and his trial caused immense public controversy. Journalists and democratic societies believed the president was not only trespassing on the prerogatives of executive power but also that patriotism did not exclude a form of cosmopolitism. This episode was only the first in a long series of similar cases, the most striking being that of the *Cassius,* which involved the federal government, the courts of justice in Pennsylvania, and the French ambassador. *Les Jumeaux* had been illegally fitted out in Philadelphia in September 1794 and had managed to leave the port by evading the US coast guards. However, it returned to Philadelphia in September 1795 under the new name of *Cassius* and was provided with a letter of marque from the governor of Saint-Domingue. James Yard, a ship owner whose brigantine had been captured by the aforementioned Henfield, recognized the vessel and accused the captain of having violated neutrality. Afterward, the US chief justice even prohibited the selling of all French prizes. As such changes of "national identity" undermined the authority of executive power, Federalists deemed them unacceptable.[48]

In their eyes, the early US republic was threatened by neo-colonial subjugation to directorial France and they supported their claims by citing how the French exploited "sister republics" in Europe. "Holland and Italy present to our immediate observation examples as decisive as they are deplorable," commented the *Gazette of the United States*. A wave of increasingly racialized Francophobia swept through the press and parts of American society.[49]

One of the consequences of this nationalistic ferment was the toughening of rules governing the right to citizenship. Despite Thomas Jefferson's opposition, the Alien and Sedition Acts in 1798 drastically transformed the law on nationality in the United States and were specifically aimed at the French: fourteen years of residence were required to qualify for American citizenship, and the nationals of enemy countries could be deported by order of the president. Both parties used the press to question the "real" nationality of the opposing camp and cast doubt on the loyalty of merchants involved in the debate through petitions and committees. The pro-French newspaper *Aurora* demanded that "NATIVE AMERICANS" be distinguished "from the FOREIGNERS."[50]

In 1798, two American merchants, Samuel A. Otis and Samuel Smith, clashed in Congress. Otis, a Federalist whose son had conducted business in Saint-Domingue, suggested barring entry to "French passengers," who as foreign nationals and providers of "French Negroes" were deemed subversive and therefore likely to spread slave revolts on the continent. Since most newcomers came from the British-occupied area of Saint-Domingue, the question of their nationality was raised. Some had been naturalized in the United States. Otis warned that, despite naturalization, "A Frenchman is a Frenchman." Although Samuel Smith victoriously opposed this measure by mobilizing the "American-French traders," the debate had brought to light the different ways in which citizenship was considered. The contradictions between the growth of the nation-state, traditional patterns of migration, flows of goods, and the needs of a war economy had become unmistakable.[51]

———

The war consolidated the commercial partnership between Saint-Domingue, which exported coffee in substantial quantities, and the United States, which provisioned the island. While the early American republic became more independent from France through the Jay Treaty, the French West Indies grew more dependent on the US trading networks. Out of republicanism, Anglophobia, or opportunism, a minority of US-based merchants remained loyal to France and the French Revolution across borders. Their commitment, however, did not conflict with their willingness to trade with the enemy either in the Caribbean or Europe and profit made in republican Saint-Domingue also went "into British coffers." Merchants continued to employ formulas that had enabled them to slip through the net of empires throughout the early modern period. Fully aware that US neutrality was a frail bulwark against the naval supremacy of European powers, ship owners were prepared to equivocate, utilizing the usual subterfuges, forged documents, and layovers in Scandinavian colonies. The increasing ambitions of states to control the flow of goods and people did not translate into systematically repressive practices; public officials still depended on cooperation with merchants to obtain food, credit, and ammunition.[52]

Yet trading with the enemy in a context of radicalization and foreign occupation did complicate the situation. Foreign merchants had been temporarily tolerated or brutally excluded for "national," "social," and/or "religious" reasons in the name of the colonial monopoly since the beginning of European colonization. However, the specific nature of the revolutionary wars implied that traders should classify their activities in political terms. Depending on the circumstances, they defined themselves as French, American, British, or Danish, refugee or deportee, royalist or republican, privateer or smuggler by negotiating their political, legal, and administrative categorization with local authorities. The chaotic construction of imperial nation-states and their bureaucratic infrastructures made such transactions increasingly difficult and explosive. An undeclared naval war between France and the United States started in 1798.

9

Trade and War: A Fiscal-Military State Within the French Empire, 1797–1801

Saint-Domingue had been a major export market for US merchants for years, but once the newly free had gained more purchasing power, would these "new people" remain the same kind of consumers as when they had been enslaved? Was the political revolution a consumer revolution? And if so, what should traders ship to Hispaniola? The Philadelphia newspaper, *Aurora*, published one merchant's speculations on the new consumption politics playing out in revolutionary Saint-Domingue. Well acquainted with the latest developments, he explained that the whites "consumed immensities, when in affluence, of all the articles which were imported." But he went on to warn that traders should "not infer from the liberty of the new citizens, that they will spend more in fineries or delicacies than before," as the newly free had an "extremely frugal way of living," eating "bananas, cassava, and ground provisions, with a herring, a piece of cod-fish, or mackerel, or any other salt meat," but "no bread. They use no butter, no lard, no candles." Their sobriety, he appeared to suggest, made the newly free republicans in a classical sense, immune to the lure of luxury and the depravations of commercial society, a major concern in US political debate. Shippers should therefore calibrate their cargoes accordingly since the time of flour fever was over; Saint-Domingue's formidable army merely needed "salt provisions" and "coarse articles."[1]

However, a "small proportion of fine goods, plain, striped, and cross-bar muslin, East-India handkerchiefs, a few muslin shawls, ginghams" would suit an emerging revolutionary elite whose consumption choices remained associated with Frenchness and whiteness. Indeed, Susanne Toussaint Louverture, wife of the new leader and a capable manager of her husband's estates, would order red wine, fine oil, sausages, ham, and "good cheese" from Dupuch &

Entrepôt of Revolutions. Manuel Covo, Oxford University Press. © Oxford University Press 2022.
DOI: 10.1093/oso/9780197626382.003.0010

Ducasse, a Philadelphia-based firm that had originated in Bordeaux. Personal tastes undoubtedly influenced her selection, but public office and social distinction required the consumption of refined French products. Household meals performed a diplomatic role as Toussaint Louverture declared both autonomy and a place in the French Empire for Saint-Domingue while negotiating with British and US emissaries. For this purpose, the official table required bread, cheese, and beef, not plantains and yams.[2]

In fact, the food and commercial politics of Toussaint Louverture were integral to the final chapter in Saint-Domingue prior to Haitian independence. Toussaint, who had successively been enslaved, a free person of color, a slaveholder, an insurrectionist, a Spanish auxiliary, and a French republican general, became the uncontested ruler of the colony. Having dismissed Sonthonax in 1796, he was free to pursue four distinct, yet related, state-building goals. Toussaint intended to unite Saint-Domingue's territory by expelling the British, crushing Rigaud's southern government in a bloody war, and annexing the Spanish part of the island. He was committed to upholding the abolition of slavery and recognizing laborers as wage earners, but he was also determined to rebuild and energize the plantation complex by encouraging white colonists to return and creating a new class of indentured servants under military control. As soon-to-be governor for life, Toussaint concentrated power around himself and a privileged military class. Ultimately, he wished to redefine the contractual relationship between the metropole and the colony, within a new French-Dominguan confederation based on equal co-sovereignty, appropriating and subverting the agenda of the white colonists. This would entail reshaping links between Saint-Domingue and the United States, Britain, and the greater Caribbean, as food dependence and reliance on exports remained insurmountable obstacles to Saint-Domingue's quasi-sovereignty. In other words, Toussaint Louverture would consume French cheese as long as he could buy it from the United States.[3]

The French Directory responded with ambivalence to Toussaint's commercial ambitions and political maneuvering. The regime, challenged from the right and left in the metropole, confirmed the abolition of slavery, but also reopened the *exclusif* pandora's box in light of new geopolitical circumstances: the creation of subordinate sister-republics in Italy, Switzerland, and the Batavian [Dutch] Republic; a new Spanish alliance; the fleeting conquest of Egyp; and a British-US rapprochement. New questions arose: was an inclusive republican empire sustainable and desirable? Was the "Great Nation" compatible with colonialism and, if so, in what form? Should France engage with a "new colonization" without slavery, departmentalize the existing colonies, or facilitate colonial independence? The French Revolution and the Saint-Domingue Revolution followed divergent paths as metropolitan designs were increasingly out of touch with the Caribbean realities. Toussaint Louverture was building a new political entity,

Figure 9.1 Toussaint Louverture, Général en Chef à St. Domingue by Nicolas de Bonneville. Paris musées/musée Carnavalet, G.39307, etching, 21.5 x 17.8 cm.

the contours of which remained blurry, in a process that not only involved state actors but also rival trading networks vying for control of the Saint-Domingue market.[4]

Theoretical Exclusif and de Facto Exclusif

The abolition of slavery, the Jay Treaty, the privateers' war in the Caribbean, and the shrinking fiscal revenues of a bankrupt state pushed Directory republicans to revisit the exclusif. The constitution of year III declared the "colonies integral parts of the Republic" (article 6), constitutionalized "general liberty," and promised to "departmentalize" the colonies (article 7), that is, to fully incorporate them into the French political community. Whether restoration of the plantation complex should be carried out within the framework of commercial republicanism was still an issue. If overseas departments were still subject to the national monopoly, did they remain colonies in spite of a different designation?[5]

The National Convention that put an end to the Terror has often been presented as liberal and business oriented, but it was concerned mainly with saving the republic against all odds. The Assembly gradually repealed the Maximum law on the domestic market, while maintaining customs on the French borders. The Convention recalibrated the tariff of 1791 several times, modulating custom duties to encourage or restrict imports on specific goods. Deputy François-Antoine Boissy d'Anglas, one of the new regime's founders, placed importance on the exclusif from the outset. In a report on the colonies delivered on 17 Thermidor Year III (August 4, 1795), he strongly rejected the "system of independence" demanded by followers of the "economists." Breaking with the Girondins' optimism, he warned that in the event of secession, France could compete "neither with England in Europe, nor with the United States in America" and "would be forced to abdicate in their favor all the advantages it can derive from a better-established order." Without the legal protection of the exclusif, Boissy d'Anglas argued, French traders were not in a position to contain combined Anglo-American power. The French flour trade would collapse and coffee would transit via New York, not Bordeaux. US vessels glutting the Saint-Domingue market provided a taste of the looming commercial invasion already threatening other parts of the empire, especially Ile-de-France (Mauritius).[6]

Some of Boissy d'Anglas' colleagues would not relinquish the republican ambitions encapsulated by the Navigation Act, which they associated with a regulated version of free trade. Deputy Joseph Eschassériau, a member of the Committee of Public Safety on several occasions, was anxious to restore the "true bases of political economy." Trade would strengthen the navy of the republic, he believed, while also improving relations between peoples on the basis of a fair economic reciprocity. Diplomat Charles-Guillaume Thérémin, whose report was translated into English and praised by Republican-Democrats in the United States, lambasted the "monopolistic and warmongering commerce" of the British, which was corroding the republic's very foundations. In a pamphlet published in 1797, *The Liberty of the Seas*, Bertrand Barère, distant from power and free to articulate his own vision of political economy, reverted to a cosmopolitan, anticolonialist, and Anglophobic approach. The colonial system, the vices of which were identified with England, needed to be replaced by a republican, European system. Barère advocated the foundation of an authentic "commercial democracy" based on emancipation of the seas, which would grant all nations the political and natural rights of equal citizens. The 1793 Act of Navigation was no longer thought of as heir to the exclusif but would become the basis of a regulated international order. This economic policy would engender an internationally negotiated legal model that incorporated European colonies.[7]

A minority opinion interpreted recent events through a physiocratic lens and favored colonial independence. In a pamphlet that did not find much favor,

Charles Gilloton de Beaulieu, translator of the Italian economist Giuseppe Gorani and a friend of the deceased Girondin Clavière, insisted the colonies were the main cause of European wars and therefore a false economy. The exclusif provoked incessant armed conflicts that depleted the states' financial resources. Gilloton de Beaulieu recommended that Europeans completely and definitively open colonial ports to foreign trade. The islands would bind "all of them and with the United States of America, defensively and commercially, for their common and reciprocal interests." Such a Caribbean confederation would prepare the region for a negotiated freedom and independence. Similarly, Guillaume Le disputeur—a pseudonym most likely concealing a former member of the first Saint-Domingue Colonial Assembly—declared the exclusif to be the cause of most evils harming France. The prohibitive regime had benefited only a small class of "merchants" and weakened France's global status. The government should prioritize the consumer, the real engine of the economy, whose tastes could overcome all customs borders. Declaring colonies independent from French sovereignty and creating a West Indian Confederation could generate a new form of global cooperation. A forerunner of the United Nations' mandate over a century later, this program would involve the creation of an international protectorate to ensure the Confederation's security.[8]

In contrast with the lack of interest in these utopian projects, Charles-Maurice de Talleyrand Périgord popularized the theory that the French economy had everything to gain from colonial secession. Having played a leading role at the start of the French Revolution by calling for the confiscation of church property, Talleyrand had gone into exile in the United States during the Terror. Based in Philadelphia, he engaged in various land speculations and fraternized with businessmen, influential members of Congress, and wealthy Saint-Domingue refugees, experiences that convinced Talleyrand that the old colonial system could not survive and European nations must design a new imperial model. A member of the "political economy" section of the National Institute, he delivered two resounding speeches on his return to Paris. The first, dated 15 Germinal year V (April 4, 1797), dealt with "trade relations of the United States with England," and the second, on 15 Messidor year V (July 3, 1797), questioned the "advantages to be gained from new colonies in the present circumstances." This latter speech incited the government to redirect its colonial policy toward Africa and embrace wage labor on a global scale.[9]

Talleyrand's first address, taking stock of fifteen years of the Franco-American alliance, suggested ways of revitalizing the French colonial agenda. Thriving trade between Great Britain and the United States challenged the deeply held belief that the exclusif was an effective tool of imperial governance. The independent republic, which consumed twice as many English goods in 1797 as in 1783, was economically more profitable for Britain for cultural reasons:

Anyone who has observed America well can no longer doubt that in most of its habits it has remained English; that its old trade with England had even gained activity, instead of losing it, since the time of the independence of the United States, and that consequently independence, far from being disastrous to England, was in several respects advantageous.

Cultural community, linguistic identity, credit facilities, and commercial habits on the part of the United States had generated a voluntary monopoly. Talleyrand implied that France could and should replicate the same pattern. A de facto monopoly was preferable to an abstract monopoly. These speeches won him great praise in the moderate press. The newspaper *Décade Philosophique*, which dedicated considerable space to colonial matters, underlined its innovative character, and the liberal thinker Jean-Baptiste Say would later absorb and disseminate many of Talleyrand's insights in his 1803 *Treaty of Political Economy*.[10]

Blossoming British trade in North America inflamed the rage of French republicans against the United States. France had helped the early republic secure a "false independence"—

what contemporary scholars would probably term a postcolonial deference toward the former homeland. Sonthonax was also disillusioned by the Americans, who were "thirsty for enormous profits" and "would go to hell to seek gold there if they knew that there were some to win." American traders "gave preference to English ports" in Saint-Domingue because of "the resemblance of manners, habit, and language." Jean Antoine Joseph Fauchet, Genet's successor as ambassador to Philadelphia, dejectedly concluded that "if one judged by the current state of trade between the United States and Great Britain," "one could believe that the former is still a colony of the latter." This trade was not benign, and British wealth was corrupting the polity and betraying the ideals of the American Revolution. This analysis gained traction as the French republican press unleashed fury against a "treacherous" republic that increasingly resembled a monarchy. Less idealistically, Moreau de Saint-Méry invited France to replicate the British strategy of commercial invasion through "agents" and "loans," without maintaining a costly administration.[11]

France forced Spain to enter into its alliance in 1796. One of the reasons for this diplomatic move was the desire to expand trade with the Spanish colonies and find new sources of provisioning for Saint-Domingue. But this perspective proved disappointing because the British were much more successful at controlling the markets and the Caribbean seas. The hawkish Ministry of Foreign Affairs, headed by Charles-François Delacroix, was less concerned with the exclusif per se than with containing Britain's hegemonic ambitions and taking action against the Federalist government. Former ambassadors, consuls, and influential refugees from Saint-Domingue dispelled the myth that free trade in the West Indies benefited the French economy and helped Delacroix design a new policy toward America. France had to find a way to break the "co-exclusive" system the United States and Great Britain were establishing in the Caribbean. The Franco-American and republican binational empire was on the verge of being replaced by a new binational, despotic, and monarchizing commercial empire. Delacroix's advisors feared the Federalist government was laying the groundwork for an effective territorial conquest that would oust continental Europe from the Americas. One former consul predicted a rising power "that would swallow up the world," while another decried the emergence of "another England, growing under the allegiance of the old, ruling with and for her over the American seas." A 1796 report warned that the real purpose of the British-US alliance was "to take joint possession of all the French islands and to share the trade." This apprehension was not entirely unfounded.[12]

Delacroix, who assimilated international relations with commercial relations, was fixated on expanding the republic's trade through diplomacy. Although the Jay Treaty had made the Anglo-American empire a formidable entity based on "exclusive privileges," he believed France had become even more powerful thanks to the abolition of slavery. The vast new army of citizen-soldiers from Saint-Domingue provided France with prodigious strength. This transformation, Delacroix predicted, will support "the commercial independence in which, in the course of time, we must place this revolution, from which it will result for us, the ability to open or close our ports to the Americans, at all times." He thought the government should reactivate the exclusif as soon as it had the capacity to do so. The ministry determinedly retained a traditional understanding of the colonial monopoly, setting boundaries on the legal integration of overseas departments.[13]

Lawmakers did not remain idle in this debate, but the crypto-royalist Clichyiens, who won the elections of February 1797, were divided on the subject. The colonists' lobbyists, aware of Saint-Domingue's food dependence, advocated a policy of appeasement toward the United States. Vincent-Marie Viénot-Vaublanc, a former planter and leader of the right in the Council of Five Hundred, called for "a careful distinction between the effects of the trade in the Colonies, and the effects of the monopoly of this trade," which "are always and necessarily harmful." A Republican deputy derided this speech, claiming that Vaublanc was merely repeating the "commonplaces" of Adam Smith and Jacques Necker that "everyone knows by heart." The final intendant of Saint-Domingue, François Barbé-Marbois, who had secured a deputy seat, also disagreed with his colleague Vaublanc. Backing the policy he followed in the West Indies, Barbé-Marbois stated that "these distant establishments" could not be assimilated to any department of European France. "The real goal" of the colonial system, he stated, "is the absolute independence of a great nation that has to rely on itself for its defense. It needs wealth to maintain its power, and conversely its power ensures and retains its wealth."[14]

The issue of US neutrality was far more contentious. Despite divisions on the right, the Councils were embroiled in bitter debate over the Directory's American policy. In the Council of Five Hundred, the Clichyien Emmanuel Pastoret launched an offensive against the directorial decree of 12 ventôse Year V (March 2, 1797), which required *rôles d'équipage* from US captains. Pastoret did not overly care about the Americans' fate, but this strategic attack was intended to weaken the republicans; Pastoret was playing a long game to challenge the abolition decree and damage the republic. The Clichyiens criticized the Directory for giving free rein to the "piracies" of the civil commissioners. Sonthonax, by claiming to "retaliate" against the United States, was accused of appropriating the law of war and peace and suspected of inciting "independence" to ensure his own "dictatorship." However, the leftist press and lobbyists for privateer ship owners endorsed directorial US policy. The newspaper *Le Républicain des colonies* regularly published lists of vessels condemned in Saint-Domingue and supported the commissioners' stance. Its editor, François Marie Bottu, eagerly awaited a time when Americans no longer benefited from "the exclusive privilege of trade in our colonies."[15]

The Clichyiens' American strategy did not gain unanimous support from the business community. Metropolitan merchants had conflicting interests. On one hand, they needed neutrals to import colonial goods from the Antilles and Mascarene islands; on the other, those who backed privateers also wanted prizes to be legal. Félix Cossin, the wealthiest merchant in Nantes in 1799, embodied this contradiction. In a memorandum to the Directory he requested "vigorous, clear and positive measures towards the Neutral Powers, who abuse their neutrality to serve our Enemies." At the same time, his New York firm was outfitting vessels for the colonies under the US flag.[16]

The coup of 18 Fructidor year V (September 4, 1797), which purged the Councils of Clichyiens by exiling many deputies to the "dry guillotine" of tropical disease-ridden Cayenne, held the royalists in check. Directory policy became clearer: the abolition of slavery was confirmed, the exclusif was to be implemented, and the privateers' war on neutrals was to continue. The law of *départementalisation*, voted on soon after, marked the constitutional integration of Saint-Domingue: the absolute legal equality of citizens within the republic, whatever their color. The two councils hosted a two-month debate, in which two committees and twenty-two representatives participated, including several deputies from the colonies. The commissions responsible for presenting the bill made conservative comments on the exclusif. Joseph Eschassériaux, abandoning his earlier support for free trade, rejected "any change . . . that would deliver the trade of your colonies to foreign powers." Pierre Chassiron made a theoretical distinction between the old form of "monopoly," enforced by "necessity and the right of the strongest," and the colonial pact, a "free agreement between free men for their advantage" enhanced by a "contract of voluntary restriction of trade." However, this restriction should be accompanied by tax relief. Other deputies, rejecting such republican packaging, bluntly insisted that the exclusif was "the basis of the modern colonial system" and could not be considered a tax. As one deputy sarcastically commented, "We have to decide whether our colonies should belong to foreign nations, or to the French Republic." This false alternative meant everything.[17]

The organic law of 12 Nivôse year VI (January 1, 1798) surreptitiously reestablished the exclusif as a valid principle. Article 41 of Title XII enabled agents of the Directory to authorize foreign goods on neutral vessels in specific circumstances. Article 45 stipulated that "all laws on the commerce of the colonies will have their full execution." The Councils circled back to Old Regime regulations and the decrees of March 8 and 28, 1790, ending ambiguity and voiding the decree of February 19, 1793, of its anticolonial ambitions. Paradoxically, it was Talleyrand who would deliver the fatal blow to the French-American alliance of 1778. Having succeeded Delacroix at the Ministry of Foreign Affairs, Talleyrand abandoned the innovative ideas he had expressed only a few months earlier. He humiliated US envoys in the notorious XYZ affair by demanding a bribe and endorsed plans to recover Louisiana, envisioned as a check on Anglo-American power and the possible anchor of the French West Indies. However, Talleyrand was anxious to avoid all-out war with the United States. Victor Dupont de Nemours, consul in Charleston and son of the famous physiocrat, had warned him about the "excesses" of privateers. Eager to restore proper procedures and, for that purpose, the authority of metropolitan France, Talleyrand began to espouse a very traditional form of colonialism. Commercial republicanism was dying out.[18]

A Break from Colonial Autonomism?

The contrast between the French debate on the exclusif and Caribbean realities, where metropolitan authority was deemed irrelevant, was striking. The Directory's agent, General Gabriel de Hédouville, a minor hero of the Vendée war, was dispatched to enforce the new colonial law in March 1798 escorted by a small fleet and a few hundred soldiers. He was immediately confronted by the strong man of Saint-Domingue, Toussaint Louverture. The general was pursuing an autonomous policy at this point and did not aspire to independence, although governments in the United States, Britain, Spain, and France believed he was preparing for secession. In fact, many of the measures that Hédouville would take were in line with Toussaint's policies. Constraints imposed by the international environment and food dependence convinced the directorial agent to pursue rather different colonial legislation than that decreed in Paris.

On an international level, Toussaint Louverture successfully juggled pressures exerted by foreign powers and competing merchant networks. The complicated game in which Toussaint, the US government, and British agents took part became a well-known chapter in Haitian revolutionary history. There was something truly exceptional about the partnership on quasi-equal terms between President John Adams and Toussaint. However, it is also important not to exaggerate the break between Toussaint's foreign policy and the autonomism of earlier French colonial agents. Inheriting quasi-diplomatic practices, Toussaint solidified autonomy beyond cyclical adjustments and gave it a theoretical base, helping to shape a self-governing Louverturian state, which, for a brief moment, was imagined as part of the French imperial project.[19]

Hédouville and Toussaint Louverture shared a similar perspective with regard to the United States. On his arrival in the colony, the French agent noted the enormous progress achieved by Cap-Français, resurrected from the ashes and reemerging as the colony's primary port. Soaring production of coffee had even provided the Saint-Domingue market with a positive trade balance in Floréal year VI (April–May 1798), for the first time since August 1793. Confronted with Saint-Domingue's colossal food dependence, Hédouville took steps to encourage production of local food crops, such as yams, cassava, and bananas, but like his predecessors, he was well aware these measures alone would not feed the colony. Arguing that he could not afford to undermine "the confidence of traders," Hédouville exempted US vessels from the law of 29 Nivôse year VI (January 18, 1798) authorizing corsairs to capture ships carrying English goods. Although President Adams had embargoed France, and the Directory retaliated by banning the US flag, Hédouville still granted admission to US vessels "loaded with edibles or dry goods" on 30 Messidor year VI (July 18, 1798). Under the pretext of article 41 of the new colonial law, which authorized temporary relaxations on the exclusif, Hédouville even invited French consuls in the United States to conceal shipments by using the Danish flag. This strategy was intended to "pit the particular interest of American trading houses with the malice of the federal government." Following Directory orders, Hédouville restored the rule of law in regard to privateering, repressing the "overly glaring abuses," murders, looting, and disguised slave trade practiced by certain "pirates" in the name of the Republic.[20]

When eventually driven from the colony by Toussaint, Hédouville accused the general of "being sold to the Americans," but Toussaint was only consolidating an existing policy driven by structural issues. Indeed, the impact of the British blockade and US Intercourse bill had been formidable: in the first half of 1799, only sixteen US ships docked in the harbor of Cap-Français, about three times fewer than in the first half of 1797. In March and April of 1799, only one vessel had entered the port. Smugglers were unable to counter the combined maritime power of Britain and the United States. As Toussaint's appeals for help in the winter of 1799 indicate, the colony was in dire straits; he needed both ammunition and food. One merchant had previously noted there was "in the stores a little coffee and a little sugar which is not sold for lack of ships. This non-sale of the commodity somewhat slows the ardor of blacks to work because they are not paid." The resistance of unpaid cultivators demonstrates their ability to exert pressure on Toussaint Louverture, who was implored to open the market as scarcity threatened to destabilize the regime. An American merchant observed that some cultivators were refusing to eat yams, potatoes, and plantains as a "luxurious indulgence has taken hold of the negroes" and if "the country should be reduced to roots and vegetables, I think both the whites and mulattoes would fall a sacrifice to the fury of the Black." Beyond the racist cliché of Black savagery and indolence, this suggests that Toussaint's foreign policy was in part driven by internal consumer politics.[21]

In spite of official directorial policy towards royalists and émigrés, Toussaint amnestied colonists who had remained in British occupied areas on 18 Floréal (May 7, 1798) and encouraged white refugees in the United States to return on 25 Fructidor year VI (September 11, 1798). Although Hédouville had received instructions to "fight émigrés," he applauded these proclamations. Both men were intent on revitalizing the plantation economy, reasserting owners' property rights, and restoring the colony to its "old splendor." As Toussaint Louverture declared in front of inhabitants who had been under British occupation: "without culture, no commerce, and without commerce, no colony." At the same time, Sonthonax was voicing support for a similar policy at the Ministry of the Navy in Paris.[22]

Agent Philippe-Rose Roume, who replaced Hédouville and would be the final Directory representative, also supported most of Toussaint Louverture's bold initiatives. The general's diplomatic maneuvers with Britain and the United States reopened trade despite the embargo on France decreed by Adams in June–July 1798. The decrees of 6 Floréal (April 25, 1799) and 14 Thermidor Year VII (August 1), admitted US ships to Cap-Français and Port-Républicain (the new name for Port-au-Prince), a strategy that proved instantly successful. As shown in more detail in table 9.1, more US vessels entered Saint-Domingue's major ports in year VIII (1799–1800) than in 1788.[23]

Saint-Domingue was producing almost no refined sugar or indigo. The large sugar factories of the northern plain were far from being restored in 1799, but table 9.2 shows that exports of coffee and cotton reached one-third of the amount

Table 9.1 **Saint-Domingue Trade in Year VIII (September 23, 1799–September 22, 1800)**

	Imports		Exports	
	Vessels	Value (livres coloniales)	Vessels	Value (livres coloniales)
Le Cap	492	28,221,034	388	25,432,355
Total colonie	598	44,720,261	1,173	48,565,380

Source: ANOM, CC9a 28, "Commerce de la Colonie pendant l'an VIII."

Table 9.2 **Volume of Goods Exported from Saint-Domingue in Year VIII (September 23, 1799–September 22, 1800)**

	Volumes (quintals)	In comparison with 178–1789
Raw Sugar	167,850	10 %
Refined Sugar	289	
Coffee	277,441	35 %
Indigo	19	
Cotton	23,419	33 %
Cocoa	945	6.5 %
Tobacco	10	
Leather	1,891	
Syrup	120,504	
Taffia	259	
Timber	62,195	

Source: ANOM, CC9a 28, "Commerce de la Colonie pendant l'an VIII."

annually shipped from the French Antilles to mainland France. Considering that, before the Revolution, Saint-Domingue had produced almost half the world's coffee, and that the following data did not include production from the southern *département*, this was a considerable figure.

The Directory was deeply ambivalent toward Toussaint's strategy vis-à-vis Britain and the United States but could not ignore the colony's economic revival. Etienne Laveaux, an influential member among the "new Jacobins" at the Council of the Ancients, tirelessly lobbied on the general's behalf. Toussaint also

had spokesmen in Paris to combat accusations that he was pursuing independence, most notably made by Sonthonax, as a member of the Council of Five
Hundred. The Colonial Office in Paris approved of opening the Saint-Domingue
market and the minister of the navy, Marc-Antoine Bourdon de Vatry, argued
that Toussaint was merely pursuing the autonomist policy that had been in
place for years. In Philadelphia, during the House of Representatives' debate
on the advisability of reestablishing trade relations with Saint-Domingue,
Samuel Smith made the case that Toussaint's policy was very much in line
with that of his predecessors. Autonomism had become the norm among all
administrators: "Santhonax [*sic*] made no scruple to set aside the decrees of
France; and in this manner has Rigaud ever done, repealing and preventing
the execution of the decrees of France, whenever he disliked them. . . . Here,
then, we see Hédouville setting aside the decrees of France." Smith, unlike his
Republican-Democratic colleague, Albert Gallatin, favored legalization of US
trade with Saint-Domingue to discourage colonial secession. Rather than fear
of political independence, racial anxieties were the foremost cause of representatives' misgivings about Toussaint Louverture.[24]

There is no denying that Toussaint crossed a line and decisively broke with
the French Republican government when dealing with Britain and its representative, Thomas Maitland. Roume, scandalized by the access granted to
British ships, rebuked the general-in-chief, by—unsuccessfully—reasserting
prohibition of British trade in the colony. Toussaint believed the agreement
with the Americans only made sense if British privateers did not prevent
neutrals from supplying Saint-Domingue. He knew that "the English government is the most dangerous for me and the most treacherous for France, it
did everything to have the exclusive trade of the island, but it had only what
was impossible that it wouldn't have." The British government, which had exhausted financial and demographic resources in an unsuccessful occupation,
believed it would profit more from Toussaint Louverture's heavy-handed command. In the United States, Republican-Democrats weaponized the general's
strategy to attack the Federalists, and began to depict Toussaint Louverture as
a British royalist puppet with authoritarian intents, in contrast to the French
Republican Rigaud.[25]

The general was willing to sabotage the Directory's Caribbean plans to safe-
guard his agreement with Maitland and avoid immediate retaliation. In fact,
British dominance of the Atlantic protected him from potential French reprisals.
Toussaint Louverture revealed to the British the existence of a republican con-
spiracy to spread slave revolt across the Caribbean and spark an uprising among
Jamaica's maroons. On the basis of his denunciation, one of the plotters, Isaac
Sasportas, was publicly hanged in Kingston. Sasportas was a Jewish merchant
trading in the Caribbean from Curaçao and a committed republican whose

uncle had been a key ally to French delegates in Charleston. In a way, the general was attempting to "stop" the revolution by solidifying Saint-Domingue's autonomism. In addition to Toussaint Louverture's obvious realpolitik, the capacity of the general to regulate and control a fluid, subversive trade was at stake, that is, his ability to hold commercial republicanism in check.[26]

Toussaint Louverture's Political Economy

Although he challenged the exclusif, Toussaint did not intend to pursue a deregulated free-trade agenda and never considered opening all the colony's ports to foreign merchants or eliminating custom duties. His primary objective was to strengthen the military. Unlike well-armed Rigaud, Toussaint needed ammunition and weapons, but the US embargo had been remarkably effective at dissuading merchants to take risks. Through General Christophe, who was fluent in English, Toussaint Louverture petitioned Philadelphia merchant John Hollingsworth to send his vessels to Cap-Français rather than to the ports of his rival.

Toussaint Louverture expected the Anglo-American navy to embargo the southern ports under Rigaud's rule. The "triple alliance" between Saint-Domingue, the United States, and Great Britain served the interests of the latter two powers, who wished to permanently oust "French" trade from the colony. However, it also provided the means of eliminating competition from Rigaud, and Toussaint, who understood how to wage colonial wars in the Caribbean, intended to starve his enemy. On August 1, 1799, President Adams, betting on Toussaint rather than Rigaud—who embodied the metropole's interests—legalized American trade with Cap-Français and Port-Républicain. At a time when British privateers had brought trade with the southern ports to a virtual standstill, the ship on which the US consul sailed to Saint-Domingue, the Kingston, was well-stocked with food.[27]

This strategy proved extremely effective. Toussaint outfitted a handful of privateers to fight Rigaud's barges, but his maritime weakness forced him to rely on foreign powers to carry out a siege. Indeed, patrolling US Navy warships soon inflicted devastating blows on the southern département. Rigaud's troops were hungry and "to have a few bananas they are forced to go 3 or 4 leagues by running the greatest risks," as one colonist observed. Correspondence from Edward Hall, an American merchant based in Les Cayes, highlighted the success of the Anglo-American blockade. "All communication with neutral nations is nearly cut off," he lamented, "No Americans, no Danes, much misery and absolutely dead business." At first, Hall was hopeful the US consul's talks with Toussaint would benefit all the ports of Saint-Domingue, including Les Cayes, as there was much

talk of "free trade to this Island in neutral bottoms, of an exclusive trade in favor
of the English, and even of Independence." However, Hall realized too late that
Les Cayes was the target of a blockade and his business was annihilated. Soon
after, the US warship *General Green* bombarded the port of Jacmel, hastening
Rigaud's downfall. As Toussaint's army destroyed southern plantations, the civil
war also disrupted local production of sugar and coffee. The war of attrition had
achieved its objective.[28]

Following victory over Rigaud, Toussaint adjusted his fiscal policy. Not
only did he see that trade with Les Cayes was legalized, but he also employed
custom duties to boost Saint-Domingue's economic development. Taxation
was intended to shape incoming merchandise according to what Toussaint
Louverture believed his soldiers coveted. Neutral ships with cargoes that did
not include flour were to pay 12.5 percent in taxes. Gradually uniting the island
territory under his authority, Toussaint also wanted to boost the economy of
underexploited and underpopulated areas of Hispaniola. To this end he authorized foreign trade in only nine ports, sparking protests from the US consul general. Conversely, ports located in the formerly Spanish area benefited from tax
relief. Having found culture and trade in a "state of nullity," Toussaint fixed import duties at 6 percent, unlike the 20 percent levied on the rest of the island.
The general hoped to bring the region "out of thin air" by stimulating "the emulation of the old inhabitants by incentives which should at the same time, attract
new settlers." Customs regulations were intended to energize expansion of the
plantation economy.[29]

The stakes rapidly became essentially financial. Toussaint could no longer
count on credit from the French legation in the United States, which, year on
year, had enabled the colony to survive. The balance of the debt, transferred to
James Swan in 1795, had been exhausted by the end of 1796, prompting the
French ambassador to find new financial intermediaries able to deliver bills of
exchange on Hamburg. The consul general had also called on Saint-Dominguan
money handlers and concluded secret transactions with Baltimore merchant-
bankers. Yet all these solutions proved temporary or illusory as the number of
unpaid US creditors increased. France's 1798 financial collapse in America had
a dismal outcome: the arrest for debts of the consul general, Philippe Joseph
André Létombe, who was serving as an informal ambassador. By treating the
French representative as an ordinary trader, the United States was plainly hu-
miliating the Republic. All drafts on Paris provided by the consul general had
been disputed. John Coffin Jones, a merchant close to the Federalist Party,
sued Létombe, whose title did not confer diplomatic immunity, prompting
a marshal to appear at his door and order his imprisonment. The consul general could secure release only by paying a deposit of 90,000 dollars with
money advanced by two "pro-French" merchants. The charge collapsed when

judges concluded that Létombe had spent only public money, not his personal capital. But the financial rout of the French republic had one major consequence: Toussaint Louverture was isolated and had to find local resources to feed an army of nearly 50,000 men, import timber for reconstruction, and compensate civil servants.[30]

Since the general rejected Guadeloupe's strategy of frantic privateering, he had no choice but to establish a sustainable tax system. The Councils in the metropole had discussed the topic at length, entirely redesigning colonial taxation. The organic law of 12 Nivôse year VI (January 1, 1798) included thirty articles relating to the provision of colonial expenses. The Directory agreed to allocate limited credit to the National Treasury, arguing that, like metropolitan départements, the colonies had to financially contribute to the commonwealth. For local expenses, the law recommended implementing indirect taxes and drawing income from the national domain: property confiscated from émigrés. Without challenging the entire law, Toussaint selected the provisions most suited to the Saint-Domingue economy. For example, he verified *patentes* (trading licenses) but rejected registration fees and abandoned land contributions in order to restore crops and encourage private owners. A battery of fiscal incentives was designed to motivate colonists to revive plantations: exemption from the right of subsidy, deadlines granted on the repayment of debts, and action against the "squandering" of absentee owners' incomes. Toussaint intently prioritized custom duties and the taxing of foreign trade to provide a fiscally advantageous environment for returning white colonists.[31]

These decisions were part of a coherent and substantial program, buttressed by Toussaint Louverture's sophisticated political economy. Justifying this fiscal strategy to the US consul general, he explained that his inspiration came from the American model:

> Reasoning in cold blood, there can be no government without tax, and it is impossible to establish one that does not weigh on anyone. . . . It is the consumer to which this contribution relates . . . and the United States can all the less complain that their contribution system is mainly based on customs duties and that by establishing it in the colony, I have only imitated the example on which your country found it just to establish its resources, which nevertheless did not slow down its prosperity, and the first truth is in the final analysis that the consumer pays and not the merchant.

This letter demonstrates that Toussaint was well acquainted with the customs system designed by Alexander Hamilton and was familiar with the language of European political economy. The general benefited from multiple sources of information and could rely on commercial brokers who had spent considerable time on the North American continent. A number of his advisors, who composed what an observer coined his "White Committee," had been French diplomatic staff in the United States. His personal secretary, Pascal, had worked for ambassador Edmond-Charles Genet in 1793 and been part of the third civil commission in 1796. Joseph-Antoine Idlinger, his *ordonnateur*, and his treasurer, Bizouard, had both engaged in business when in the United States and could provide valuable insights. Taking advantage of these multiple channels of firsthand information, Toussaint was not a mere replicator: he borrowed the regulations that suited him and adapted them to the local context. When the US consul suggested implementing a drawback system (the refund of custom duties on imported and reexported goods), the general deemed the proposal unsuitable given Saint-Domingue's administrative inadequacies.[32]

Building a financially autonomous state was no easy matter. Toussaint hesitated between fixing a stable tariff to bolster commercial confidence and constantly adjusting it to respond to market prices. Initially favorable to a ten-year system with periodic renovation, he realized the logistical means to implement such a complex organization were lacking and decided on a fixed tariff. He was soon faced with the recurring problems of any customs administration: fraud and corruption. As before, captains sought to evade taxes and take specie out of the Saint-Domingue market. Citing Louis XIV's ordinance of 1669 and revolutionary laws, Toussaint attempted to curb the silver flight by jailing anyone who "exported cash" and granting any informant a quarter of the confiscated money. Americans were alarmed that duties were to be paid in "HARD CASH, which excludes the Americans from a speculation on their *assignats*, and consequently renders the duties higher than before." A merchant in Port-Républicain worried that under such a strenuous policy, "it will be merely impossible to stay or do business in any of these ports." Traders responded by exerting pressure on Toussaint's government, at times effectively, and notably through the US consul. Twice, the general was forced to back down: he lowered import duties from 12.5 percent to 10 percent and, having attempted to double this rate in 1801, once more yielded to traders' demands.[33]

Toussaint Louverture's experiments were intended to create a coherent administrative, economic, and fiscal framework. Fighting carelessness, corruption, and rogue employees, he made public accountants responsible for their administration under his own authority. This administrative structure was not built along republican lines but around the person of Toussaint, his generals—who had also become major proprietors—and his army. In contrast to republican principles, the customs directors were accountable to military officers, not a representative assembly. This was significant. Under Toussaint Louverture's leadership, customs had become the regime's financial foundation. In 1791–1792, public debt on the National Treasury accounted for two-thirds of Saint-Domingue's budget. Ten years later, custom duties accounted for over 40 percent of revenue and taxes on national domains contributed 32 percent. Food provisioning and army supplies absorbed more than 60 percent of the budget (10 million *livres coloniales*), which were paid for mainly in colonial goods. Military, fiscal, and foreign policy went hand with hand.[34]

Due to the lack of a powerful navy, Toussaint could not count only on Saint-Domingue's resources to build the new state. He needed to collaborate with the United States and Britain, whose objectives and interests only partially overlapped. The control of circulation was part of a three-way effort to establish Toussaint Louverture as sole authority on the island and oust French metropolitan traders. Universal access was granted to Cap-Français and Port-Républicain, but special authorizations were required whenever a captain wished to dock at another harbor. Passengers applied to the "commander of the place" for a passport, while those who embarked for the United States or a neutral port needed their papers checked by the general himself or an agent of the Directory. In addition, sea captains required formal approvals from the representative of Britain and the US consul general.[35]

This triple passport system immediately became the source of mass confusion. Saint-Domingue's admiralty courts had previously struggled to identify the nationality of vessels, goods, and individuals, and the procedure reached a new level of complexity as different parts of the colony were subjected to different rules. How could they distinguish the French vessels of Guadeloupe, the barges of Rigaud, the corsairs of Toussaint as well as those of Roume, whose status was uncertain? In November 1799, the captain of a schooner captured by USS *Boston* produced documents signed by the US consul general. However, his commission letter was issued by Roume rather than Toussaint, the cargo belonged to Bertrand from Jérémie, and the crew was Spanish. British agent Edward Corbet also complained that US captains exploited the tripartite convention to trade freely between Saint-Domingue and Jamaica.[36]

The unintended consequence of the new system was an increase in the number of vessels flying the Danish flag, which many "Americans" had adopted. This posed a serious diplomatic problem for the young republic: having made the defense of neutrality the center of its diplomacy since 1793, was it legitimate and possible to convict the Danes, some of whom were former US citizens or recently naturalized French? The US fleet shunted responsibility onto the British to arrest the supposed Scandinavians. The Cayes-based trader Hall decried that "the English have taken over the poor neutrals" and "make great Havock among the Danes," who were sentenced ruthlessly in Jamaica. The entanglement of conflicts and players exacerbated confusion to the point that even seasoned captains became lost in the mess of disparate rules. Chaos boosted the circulation of forged passports, creating a whole new market for counterfeiters. One supercargo berated the proliferating experts in forgery as "figureheads" who were merely "profit eaters." In fact, these fake documents did little to protect captains due to the arbitrary behavior of British warships. As the US consul general pointedly stated, US vessels were seized for the sole reason of having "valuable cargoes," sparking outrage against Britain in the United States. It was clear the British would comply with the tripartite agreement only to the extent that they benefited.[37]

US Partisan Politics, Commercial Cartels, and the Fiscal-Military State

Despite Toussaint Louverture's efforts to be in control, were public officials really the main players or did businessmen have the upper hand? During his speech to Congress on November 22, 1797, President Adams had made it clear that the federal state should be placed at the service of its merchants as "commerce has made this country what it is, and it cannot be destroyed or neglected without involving the people in poverty and distress." The government was ready to protect US commercial interests against foreign aggressors, that is, France, and policy was designed by a small number of merchants with the ear of prominent Federalists. Ignoring Congress, Timothy Pickering, secretary of state, sought advice from the Philadelphia Chamber of Commerce and obtained vital information from merchants in Saint-Domingue acting as spies. Pickering appointed Dr. Edward Stevens, a merchant in Philadelphia from the West Indies and a personal friend of Hamilton, as US consul general in Saint-Domingue. Pickering's letters to Stevens, in which he articulated his policy in the vocabulary of markets, goods, and capital, resemble business correspondence.[38]

Another key department of the United States government, the secretary of the navy, a position created in April 1798 to organize the country's maritime defense, also mobilized traders. That same year, the government issued 365 letters of marque, 54 percent of which were supplied by Philadelphia, New York, and Baltimore. Many of these ship owners were supposedly Francophile "patriots" calling themselves "friends of France." One foot inside, one out, and constantly hoping to eliminate competition, these merchants benefited from the reopening of the Dominguan market. They also invested financially in the construction of frigates to fight French corsairs, with the chambers of commerce of the four main ports—Philadelphia, New York, Boston, and Baltimore—funding four warships. Adams authorized merchants to outfit armed commercial vessels and capture enemy privateers. The Republican-Democrats protested in vain against the establishment of a public navy and the proliferation of private armed forces in the service of "speculators." In the eyes of Jeffersonians, commerce was corrupting and militarizing the state and the nation.[39]

At the same time, alongside the returning white owners, a new class of military planters was developing mutually beneficial connections with US merchants, required by Saint-Domingue's new elite to sell their coffee and cotton. Generals Hyacinthe Moyse, Henri Christophe, and Jean-Jacques Dessalines, among others, had become large plantation owners in need of outlets. Pierre Granier, a merchant from Cap-Français, was the broker for Christophe and Pascal. Toussaint's envoy to Philadelphia, Joseph Bunel, was the colony's treasurer and a formerly bankrupt trader. His wife, Fanchette/ Marie, who was a powerful Black merchant probably far more effective at business than her husband, became a key player in the US-Saint-Domingue relationship. The overlap between trade, diplomacy, and corruption was illustrated by a certain citizen Dambugeac's trip to New York. Dambugeac had been Laveaux's secretary, but later claimed he sailed to New York at Toussaint Louverture's request and had important dispatches for Napoléon Bonaparte. Formerly a "prize officer" in Danish Saint Thomas and a "seasoned plotter" according to the French consul, Dambugeac met with prominent republican politicians/businessmen such as Aaron Burr, Samuel Smith, and members of the Livingston family, who welcomed him "at great cost." The number of merchant/diplomats with dubious letters of credence was immeasurable. It was not a new phenomenon either. Since 1791, colonial authorities had consistently commissioned "supply agents" (agents pour l'approvisionnement) to US ports, where they repeatedly attempted to meet with US officials. The difference in 1798 was that John Adams's republic of merchants agreed to negotiate.[40]

Shrewd traders capitalized on the ongoing international rivalries and domestic political upheaval. The personal conflict between the consul general of the United States, Stevens, and the consul of Cap-Français, Jacob Mayer, whose business rivalry devolved into a full-blown national crisis, epitomizes the entanglement of trade and politics. The men's careers were highly similar. Originally from Philadelphia, Mayer had long been a well-known merchant in Saint-Domingue. Appointed consul general in 1797, he had accompanied Bunel to negotiate the reopening of trade between the United States and Saint-Domingue. However, when Mayer returned to the colony in April 1798, he was demoted to the post of ordinary consul in Cap-Français, under the command of his replacement, Dr. Stevens. Stevens was also a merchant, based in Philadelphia, but had better connections with the federalist establishment and was a personal friend with Hamilton.[41]

The scandal was prompted by a letter from Mayer to his partners in Philadelphia. This memo accused Stevens of exploiting his position as informal ambassador to speculate on the Saint-Domingue market before official enactment of the trade deal. Mayer was aware that commercial correspondence at that time was often printed as news in the press and was therefore quasi-public speech. He hoped his claim would be discussed at the stock market and in coffee houses, and it was; the left-leaning *Aurora* newspaper repeated his accusations. Mayer criticized Stevens for making American captains pay for British passports, lamenting that the "American character has fallen in consequence of his abominable speculation, preying on the very vitals of the people." But Stevens was guilty of a far more offensive activity. According to Mayer, he had committed what would now be called insider trading, exploiting non-public information and his official position for personal gain. In coalition with merchants William Crammond, who owned the *Kingston,* and his brother-in-law, James Yard, Stevens had dispatched agents to various parts of the colony to purchase all available goods, including almost 300,000 pounds of sugar, before the end of the blockade. The *Aurora* made it clear that the arch-Federalist secretary of state had granted "the exclusive privilege of making millions to MR. Cramon, Mr Yard, and Dr. Stevens, who must be bad merchants if they have not succeeded in monopolizing the produce of St. Domingo to the exclusion of our native citizens." Drawing on Mayer's denunciation, the *Aurora* journalist claimed that "some have lost their whole fortune, by the secret management of certain persons in public stations in the St. Domingo treaty—while others have made an immense sum, by holding the secret from the public." The charges were probably true, as evidenced by the *Oceania,* which entered the New York harbor with a considerable quantity of produce, dispatched by Stevens from Gonaïves, Toussaint Louverture's stronghold. In volume and value, the cargo far exceeded average shipments from Saint-Domingue. Stevens, the only person to know the outcome of negotiations, did capitalize on knowledge gained through his civil duties.[42]

The conflict was viewed through the lens of US race politics. While Mayer prided himself on having the confidence of white officials, he vilified Stevens for having sold himself to the Black generals, Toussaint, Moyse, and Christophe. Stevens countered that Mayer was malignantly spreading vicious rumors not just to ruin his reputation but, through him, that of the United States. He also accused Mayer of embracing the "democratic party," and of colluding with captains who were the "enemies of the Government." By questioning the moral qualities of his subordinate, Stevens directly targeted Mayer's reputation as a merchant and his honor as a US representative. The consul general mocked Mayer's drinking habits and labeled him a "Jacobin," a toxic designation after the Terror, encompassing moral defects, demagoguery, and an appetite for violence. Both men appropriated the vitriolic rhetoric of the time, as the confrontation between Federalists and Republican-Democrats threatened the very existence of the Union.[43]

When the scandal came to the secretary of state's attention, both men were forced to justify themselves. Both mobilized their networks in attempts to safeguard their reputations, vital to a merchant's identity and success; a disreputable, dishonorable trader would soon be out of business in the eighteenth century. In Philadelphia, the Petit & Bayard firm took Mayer's side, while the merchant James Yard relayed Stevens's grievances. In a letter to the secretary of state signed by twenty-five "inhabitants, traders and commissioners of Gonaïves," the consul general maintained that he had not monopolized colonial produce for his personal interest. Mayer forwarded a petition in his support signed by forty French or American merchants from Cap-Français, who all enjoyed "public esteem." Despite such politicking, both merchants lost their standing. Mayer was dismissed in May 1800, James Yard became insolvent, and Stevens had to negotiate with his creditors to avoid bankruptcy. The consul general lost all his properties, which, according to Girard, amounted to "not half of what he owed."[44]

In the meantime, the feud had significant diplomatic and commercial consequences. In response to the scandal, resident "French" commissioners lobbied Toussaint Louverture to secure the monopoly on consignments of foreign goods. Mayer even convinced "American" traders who had resided in the country for several years to sign the petition. This shift in policy would exclude American newcomers from Saint-Domingue. By becoming indispensable middlemen, residents could form cartels and establish themselves as gatekeepers, providing access to the market in return for a commission.[45]

Toussaint, reputedly hostile to the colonial exclusif, nonetheless approved the policy and decided to grant the monopoly of consignments to "French" traders and long-time residents. Objections by the American consul general temporarily suspended the measure, but it was definitively implemented by Toussaint on 18 Floréal, year IX (May 8, 1801). Article IX stated:

> No one will be admitted to be a Consignee, if he is not 1 a French citizen; 2 if in any circumstance he has breached his commitments; 3 ° if he does not have a sufficient fortune to establish a liability, except for the exceptions to be made in favor of foreign merchants, to whom the Government reserves to grant the same right, after having examined their good faith, their credit and their morality. As a result, Lists of Negotiators in the Colony's Commercial Cities will have the qualifications required to be admitted as Consignees. These Lists, approved by the Chief General, will remain posted in Chambers of Commerce.

This law suggests Toussaint Louverture still envisioned Saint-Domingue within a French imperial entity but, even more important, viewed the privilege granted to French citizenship as a tool that could help him counter foreign ambitions. The policy would ensure tax revenues, aid the fight against fraud, and position merchants among his clientele and under his protection. It is also likely the deeply Catholic Toussaint Louverture insisted on the morality clause. Some "Americans," hoping to monopolize the market and eliminate competition, supported the legal alliance with the Louverturian state. "Americanity" and "Frenchness" were instruments in the competition for state power, especially the regulatory power to block market access to newcomers.[46]

This alliance was sealed in blood at the end of Toussaint's regime. On November 11, 1801, "American" merchants based in Saint-Domingue thanked the governor for maintaining order and tranquility in the department. Calling themselves "friends of Liberty" while emphasizing that freedom could only be preserved by "the establishment of good order and perfect security," these merchants were delighted with Toussaint Louverture's crackdown on the mutinous workers in the Plaisance and Marmelade neighborhoods, close to Cap-Français. The governor, with the help of Dessalines and Christophe, had violently repressed the revolt against his harsh regulations, killing many plantation managers. The governor accused General Moyse, his own nephew, of having incited the revolt and endangering the economic recovery. He sentenced him to death. In the aftermath of the failed revolt, Toussaint addressed US merchants, pledging to guarantee "a lasting tranquility, which will allow you to engage in security and confidence in the Speculations of your Commerce." Officer-planters, supporting a militarized production system, collaborated with cartels intent on monopolizing the market against newcomers. The construction of a fiscal-military state dictated an alliance that redefined the boundary between the exclusif and free trade on local terms.[47]

On 18 Messidor, "the ninth year of the one and indivisible French Republic" (July 7, 1801), one of the "most brilliant" ceremonies "Saint-Domingue has seen in a great number of years" was held on the Place-d'Armes at Cap-Français. The national guard and the army formed a square battalion, into which entered Governor Toussaint Louverture, preceded by the civil authorities and accompanied by all his generals. Jérôme-Maximilien Borgella, president of the central assembly of Saint-Domingue, went up into the gallery to proclaim the "local constitution" the colony had awaited for "so long." The general-in-chief, Borgella declared to the crowd, had succeeded in "ensuring respect for the French name," been able to "supply Ports, invigorate Cultures, call back trade, restore Cities" and "discipline the Troops." Toussaint Louverture then took the floor and addressed the "people of Saint-Domingue." The ensuing banquet concluded with a series of toasts: to the governor, the French Republic, the central assembly, the colonial constitution, the generals and, finally, the United States:

> *By the new Consul of the United States*: May the links between the Government of the United States and that of Saint-Domingue be cemented by Justice and protected by Liberty!
>
> *By the Governor of Saint-Domingue*: May the feelings of Friendship that inspire us towards the Government of the United States be reciprocal!

This ceremony, intended to demonstrate the unity of the colony, resembled the starched festivals that punctuated the revolutionary decade in metropolitan France, although on the island republican symbolism had been replaced with militaristic bravado. The ritual signified that the colony belonged to the French Empire, while the constitution proclaimed a double identity, French and colonial. The military and commercial orientations of the new regime were displayed, revolving around the representative of the United States, who shared the "friendship" of Saint-Domingue with metropolitan France.[48]

The ceremony was also the climax of an unstable and explosive sequence of events in which Toussaint Louverture had refashioned both the French-American alliance and the French Empire on his own terms, creating a de facto confederation with the metropole, in spite of republican "assimilation." This fleeting moment rested on multiple compromises and precarious conditions. The general, subject to extreme pressure from within and without, had scrambled to make a new political entity viable. Biographies that idolize or demonize Toussaint Louverture do not underscore the sophistication of his political economy and his contributions to the Atlantic debate over the exclusif, free trade, and statecraft. Saint-Domingue's quasi-sovereignty buttressed the emergence of a new fiscal-military state within the French confederation. This quasi-state remained caught between the ambitions of rival empires, the overreach of powerful merchants, growing internal popular resistance, and a looming metropolitan backlash.

Epilogue

The Collapse of Commercial Republicanism and the Enduring Power of Imperial Trade

The war of Haitian independence, spanning 1802 to 1804, offers an enlightening counterpoint to the distinctive sequence of events between 1776 and 1801. At the very beginning of the nineteenth century, commercial republicanism ceased to underpin the triangular relationship between Saint-Domingue, France, and the United States. The alliance between Toussaint Louverture and John Adams and the creation of the Haitian quasi-state rested on fragile compromises, antagonizing French metropolitan power. The British Navy retained dominance in the Caribbean despite the military retreat from Saint-Domingue. Both republicanism and the "liberty of commerce" significantly receded as unifying transatlantic principles for political legitimacy.

Although the new consular regime in France formally remained a republic, its democratic features were rapidly unraveling as power became concentrated in the hands of First Consul Napoléon Bonaparte. While Bonaparte's governance has been considered a mix of revolutionary fervor, old regime legacy, and military charisma, his colonial policy was far more straightforward and unambiguous: Bonaparte embraced a wholly counterrevolutionary project in the Americas. Intending to topple governor Toussaint Louverture and secretly reestablish slavery—though he was undecided on a timeframe—Bonaparte demanded implementation of the exclusif, experimenting with a policy he would carry out in Europe a few years later with the Continental Blockade. The Treaty of Amiens signed by Britain and France in early 1802 provided the opportunity for his imperial aims. France was able to gather its military forces and direct the navy to Saint-Domingue without fear of British aggression. A 20,000-strong expedition force—later expanded to 30,000—was launched to impose the first consul's uncontested authority.[1]

Entrepôt of Revolutions. Manuel Covo, Oxford University Press. © Oxford University Press 2022.
DOI: 10.1093/oso/9780197626382.003.0011

Bonaparte definitively abandoned the policy imagined by Etienne-François de Choiseul, contracted by Charles Gravier de Vergennes, and attempted by Edmond-Charles Genet. Giving instructions to his brother-in-law and expedition commander, Charles-Victoire-Emmanuel Leclerc, Bonaparte clarified his demands: "Commerce must during the first, second and third epochs be accessible to Americans, but after the third epoch only French people will be admitted, and the old regulations before the revolution will be reinstated." The question was no longer whether to prohibit foreign trade but when and how to implement the ban. Bonaparte regarded the provisioning of Saint-Domingue from the United States as a temporary measure and blamed the rise of Toussaint Louverture on US complicity and ill-conceived economic designs. François Barbé-Marbois, chased out of Saint-Domingue in October 1789 for his restrictive policy on foreign trade and banished to Guyane in 1797 under suspicion of royalist sympathies, had his chance for revenge. As one of the first consul's prominent colonial advisors he could pursue his centralizing agenda and drive US merchants out of Saint-Domingue. Dismissing the planters' more imaginative projects, he wanted to put the early American republic back in its place, that of a secondary power in the Concert of Nations.[2]

Bonaparte had the power to implement his plan, but this unraveling had been years in the making. The election of John Adams, maritime skirmishes, and the Jay Treaty between the United States and Great Britain in November 1794 had already gravely damaged the principle of a republican free-trade zone. In January 1798, the Directorial Republic had relegalized the exclusif, prompting metropolitan merchants to lobby for effective implementation. At the same time, Foreign Minister Charles-Maurice de Talleyrand, having forsaken the greater colonial reinvention he had advocated just a few years earlier, was endeavoring to recover Louisiana from Spain, hoping to intimidate the United States, stop British progress on the continent, and feed Saint-Domingue from a French colony, thereby bypassing US intervention. In 1802, Napoleon's assertion of authority had nothing to do with commercial republicanism.[3]

On the other side of the Atlantic, Toussaint Louverture, although dependent on the US alliance, had progressively divorced the nascent country from republicanism. Saint-Domingue's constitution of 1801 had named him governor-for-life, solidifying his dictatorship. Adamant that abolition be preserved, Toussaint Louverture actively militarized the economy and did not flinch from suppressing popular resistance, although a democratic life persisted at the local level. Deeply Catholic, he believed in a strong association between church and state. Fostering privileged relationships with an elite of "merchants" under his protection, Toussaint Louverture was intent on defending the quasi-sovereignty he had consolidated and legitimized. The fiscal-military state he commanded was fundamentally commercial but only nominally republican.[4]

Meanwhile, despite the alliance with Toussaint Louverture, the US government grew more detached from Saint-Domingue. Abolitionism was inspiring enslaved people to revolt and making white planters uneasy; Haiti, not the French Revolution, was to be the enduring source of hope for the enslaved in antebellum America. Moreover, the US balance of trade had become less dependent on Saint-Domingue's market. The Adams administration advocated the "free admission of our vessels" in the French colonies but also conceded that "if France will not allow a trade with her colonies, on the terms which may be agreed in respect to the parent state, we should be silent on the subject." The US government wanted to normalize its relationship with France and eliminate Article 11 of the 1778 Treaty of Alliance, under which the United States was obliged to honor French sovereignty over its colonies. The Treaty of Mortefontaine signed on September 30, 1800, fulfilled this desire, concluding the quasi-war with France, as well as the alliance.[5]

A Commercial Counterrevolution

To Napoleon and French metropolitan merchants, 1802 was a time for retribution. Rejoicing at the full-blown recreation of the "colonial system," former *commissionnaires* returned to Saint-Domingue en masse, expecting to make the fortunes they felt entitled to and deprived from by the revolution. Anticipating a return to slavery and expulsion of the "Americans" once and for all, many traders followed the Expedition in the hope of rebuilding Saint-Domingue as it had been, or perhaps as they imagined it had been. One former commissionaire, confident that Bonaparte would eventually reestablish slavery, left Philadelphia, where he had been a refugee, to found a firm in Cap-Français and export coffee and cotton: he believed resources would "soon become substantial again, when people and things are put back in their place." Companies in Bordeaux and Nantes were also eager to take advantage of the "peace in Europe" and "reestablishment of order in [these] regions."[6]

The Haitian War of Independence has been the subject of many books, which have largely focused on the terrible violence that took place but have paid little attention to the bustling trade occurring at the time of invasion. The arrival of such a substantial military force from Europe prompted immense provisioning contracts, and merchants, blind to the devastation, were preoccupied with resuming business as usual for pre-revolutionary times. Although Cap-Français was reduced to "ruin and dung" and "abound[ed] in dead and dying," the idea that France could lose Saint-Domingue forever remained unthinkable to the majority of merchants, who faithfully believed trade would flourish once again. Yves Bizouard, previously a senior official in the Louverturian state, adjusted to the new circumstances by abandoning Toussaint Louverture and quitting his position as a public accountant to establish a new company. The wording of the flyer sent to his potential customers could not convey the morbid mercantile euphoria displayed in Cap-Français more clearly: although "most of the colony" was "only destruction and ashes," the "vigorous" policies of the French government would produce "a happy future" and had persuaded him to create a new merchant house. Thirty-one years of experience in "trade, administration and colonial business" were the credentials that would help Bizouard stand out from his competitors.[7]

Newcomers and returning entrepreneurs jostled to make a profit. Bewildered by this new rush to Saint-Domingue, one established merchant derided the incoming "herd," "the multitude of people, administrators, small, large inspectors, suppliers of such and such items." The divide between public service and private interest was irrelevant. "Employees" wanted "to make their fortune in six months. These gentlemen didn't come to have a change of heart"; they had crossed the Atlantic to "pick up gold bars." The highest civil official, the colonial prefect Pierre Benezech, was himself a "businessman." However, the glutted market was not big enough for all these vindictive entrepreneurs. Merchants pressured the government to reinstate the French colonial monopoly and drive out those who had parasitized French wealth: the "American" intruders.[8]

The French merchants' agenda aligned with the new regime's open hostility to "Americans" for ideological and geopolitical reasons. Reestablishment of the exclusif, the first consul believed, was part of a larger project that went beyond French national interests. He argued that the expedition was a crusade of European civilization against the threats posed by Americans. Like Montesquieu, he also believed European public law was based on a "colonial system" the US-Saint-Domingue commercial alliance was eroding. Pierre-Auguste Adet, former head of the Colonial Office and former ambassador to the United States, used such an argument to justify the preservation of slavery in the colonies that Britain had returned to France: "Europe is a large family, each part of which is bound by laws adopted for the preservation of all." As William Eden had warned in 1786, Britain was France's true natural ally. The American mirage had dissipated: Europe and America had diametrically opposed interests. From this perspective, the idea of European civilization was inseparable from a colonial conception of the world.[9]

This explains why the Leclerc Expedition was also a punitive enterprise against the United States, whose commercial ambition threatened European colonization and had facilitated the rise of Toussaint Louverture. Considering the assistance US merchants and privateers gave to independence movements in Latin America two decades later, this was a prescient analysis. Some officials believed the real enemy of France was neither Saint-Domingue's general-in-chief

Figure E.1 Prise du Cap Français par l'Armée Française, sous le Commandement du Général Leclerc; le 15 et 20 Pluviôse an 10, 1802, by Pierre-Adrien Lebeau and Naudet. Collection de Vinck, 6049. Bibliothèque nationale de France, etching, 33.2 x 48.6 cm.

nor Britain, but the young American republic. Bonaparte's spies in the colonies wrongly suspected the federal administration was plotting to separate Saint-Domingue from France and even seize the French colonies. According to Leclerc, it was "here and at this moment that the question was judged whether Europe would retain colonies in the West Indies." The French minister of the navy added: "The only power to which you have to show hostility is the United States." Leclerc, struggling to establish his authority and quell insurrection, accused the United States of providing "rifles, cannons, gunpowder and all the munitions of war." As the Americans planned to enable "the independence of all the Antilles" to secure "their exclusive trade," England and France should "come together to intimidate them." It was in the common interest of the two imperial powers to crush this stateless nation of merchants, no matter if their names were "French," "English," or anything else. As French consuls had in the 1780s, Leclerc viewed the United States with anti-semitic bigotry: "The Americans [were] of all Jews the most Jewish."[10]

When the general and his formidable fleet entered Saint-Domingue, they discovered harbors packed with American vessels: sixty brigantines and schooners were docked in Cap-Français alone. Leclerc immediately took retaliatory measures against the "American traders" equated with representatives of the American state, arresting diplomat-businessmen, such as Joseph Bunel and Pierre Granier,

deemed too closely allied with the Black generals. Leclerc took a series of vigorous steps: he embargoed the island; requisitioned American goods and ships;
fixed prices for foodstuffs, without leaving the slightest margin for negotiation
by captains and supercargoes; and imposed payments on bills in the National
Treasury. As the Treaty of Mortefontaine denied the United States the right
to consuls in the French colonies, Leclerc revoked the exequatur of the consul
general, Tobias Lear, who, at Jefferson's instigation, had replaced Dr. Edward
Stevens in 1801. Lear, having lost his public position, could only continue his
duties in a private capacity.[11]

Leclerc was convinced that "American" traders were supplying the
"insurgents" with arms, ammunition, and food, reprising an anxiety that had
troubled colonists since 1791. He condoned French soldiers retaliating against
US captains, regarded as Toussaint's accomplices. It was unclear whether US
citizens were "friends and allies of the French Republic" or the enemy. Leclerc
mobilized roughly fifty Americans in Cap-Français for the war effort, drafting
them into the national guard. Subjected to bureaucratic harassment and arbitrary
requisitions, captains petitioned Lear to protest against their mistreatment: as
one captain complained, each day produced "new instances of oppression and
vexation."[12]

Albeit wounded, US trade did not disappear from Saint-Domingue. In year
X (from September 1801 to September 1802), 224 "foreign" vessels entered Les
Cayes, where only fourteen French ships were docked. In Thermidor (August
1802), the vast number of Americans in Port-Republicain brought prices down,
infuriating French metropolitan merchants. Under pressure from the latter, the
minister of the navy demanded that Leclerc fully enact the exclusif: foreign
imports should be only goods the French were unable to supply since "this was
the first basis of the colonial system." Although Leclerc agreed with this restrictive policy, he had no choice but to perpetuate the customs system developed by
his predecessors, from Sonthonax to Toussaint Louverture. Facing a calamitous
financial shortage and with the colony's only local resource being custom duties,
he raised the rate to 15 percent, despite an outcry from Americans and French
alike. Scarcity of coinage was endemic. Based in New York, Victor Dupont de
Nemours, a former French consul in Charleston, volunteered to deliver Spanish
pesos via Vera Cruz and Havana. The plan proved to be fruitless as well as disastrous for the Dupont de Nemours company.[13]

Leclerc had to deal with these contradictory pressures in a context of civil
war. To promote trade with metropolitan France he established a discriminatory tariff for "foreigners" "so excessive" that Les Cayes trader Edward Hall
could not imagine "how the Americans [could] continue to use [the] ports."
In Vendémiaire year XI (September 1802), Leclerc banned certain foreign
foodstuffs that could be supplied by the French, making sure to announce the

measure as late as possible to prevent the colony "being infested with English goods." He also planned to reestablish an entrepôt at Môle Saint-Nicolas in the hope of restoring the *exclusif mitigé* of 1767 rather than that of 1784. This tentative policy infuriated many French merchants, who demanded the "colonial system sine qua non," with French trade exempted from tariff, foreign goods prohibited, and the salaries of Black people suppressed. All these plans came to naught.[14]

Despite early victories, the arrest of Toussaint-Louverture on June 7, 1802, under false pretenses, his deportation to France (where he was to perish), and the rallying of most of its generals, the Leclerc Expedition proved to be a military disaster. Once Haitians learned that General Antoine Richepanse had reestablished slavery in Guadeloupe, they understood their freedom was at stake regardless of Leclerc's reassuring rhetoric, and the civil war resumed, a war that included episodes of extreme, even genocidal violence toward the Black population. Several factors led to these horrific events: escalating racial hatred; a culture of brutality; a yellow fever epidemic that decimated Europeans—including Leclerc—in unprecedented numbers; and the renewed declaration of war by Britain on May 18, 1803, which isolated Saint-Domingue/Haiti from the outside world. Under the new leadership of Donatien de Rochambeau, son of the general who, alongside Washington, had successfully laid siege to Yorktown, warfare methods reached a ferocious intensity.[15]

The new situation had significant impacts on business. The government was the primary customer of most merchants but, one after another, administrators were dying and contractors were not being paid for provisioning the army. Dupont de Nemours, for instance, lost almost everything. His agents in Saint-Domingue, Pierre and Alexandre Bauduy, having attempted to "knock on all doors," eventually secured the good graces of the colonial prefect Benezech, but to no avail, since the prefect died shortly after. Leclerc, who had agreed to their request for payment, also died that November. Soldiers were behaving like an occupying army, vandalizing property and molesting French traders, and it was becoming blatantly obvious the military were not striving to rebuild or pacify but to loot as much as possible. The rout created an apocalyptic atmosphere. With defeat in sight, plunder was the "order of the day," and merchants had become targets, leading Edward Hall to predict "the Colony is *at its lasts gasps*": "We have everything to fear. The English, the Brigands and the famine, of these three evils, it is difficult to guess which will seize us." As in 1791, however, merchants were not helpless victims: they fought back, killing their enemy whenever possible.[16]

The range of potential partners for merchants had significantly expanded. Commercial transactions not only involved white and elite Black and mixed-race traders: the war revealed the extent of Haitians' direct participation in global exchanges. "Cultivators" occupied the Atlantic scene through the markets,

constantly in business with whites, who nevertheless claimed outrage at abolition. In practice, French colonists did not hesitate to buy and sell from "negroes
in the towns," who spent their days "selling their produce and buying returns."
As one planter lamented, "A multitude of white people buy this coffee and encourage this mess." Enslaved people had sold goods at the markets in colonial
times—but officially on behalf of their masters. Although they had conducted
informal business before, selling and buying openly for their own profit was
part of their newly acquired freedom. Recorded comments reflect the radicalization of racial language and the planters' outrage at Haitians' economic independence. Merchant Edward Hall exclaimed, "Flour is abundant at 12 $ and a
very good market, supplied by our allies the Congos. Great God. What Has the
Great nation come to?" A group of "Congo" soldiers, led by Gagnet and Letellier,
had been contracted by the French to fight the Creoles. They were also actively
participating at the market, bartering coffee beans in exchange for arms.[17]

   To Hall, the Expedition, rather than returning people to "their place," had
upended all hierarchies. The "rascals of French generals," he judged, were "a hundred times more brigand than those they qualified as such." In the name of security and national interest, the French Army confiscated property from merchants
and planters alike. Given this context, Hall believed there was nothing immoral
about doing business with the "new government" of Haiti, declared independent
on January 1, 1804. Indeed, US merchants were considered essential to the
new regime. When Jean-Jacques Dessalines ordered the massacre of remaining
French white people, he spared US traders along with Polish soldiers who had
been drafted into the Napoleonic army. This event epitomized the "beginning of
the fraught project of postcolonial, antislavery statehood."[18]

The French Revolution was not only a significant event in the history of political sovereignty but also engaged with a broader debate over commercial
sovereignty in a world of empires and nascent nation-states. Commercial republicanism emerged as a potential solution to reconcile global capitalism with
the assertion of popular sovereignty and a reorganization of the international
order. A consensus existed among the French revolutionary elite that, if France
wanted to be a sovereign nation, it could not and should not turn its back on
global trade. This concern traversed the entire sequence of events, independent
from the chronological milestones associated with traditional narratives of the
French Revolution. But how to conciliate global trade with a national community of citizens was a far more controversial matter. Divisions along and across
political factions, politicking by economic lobbies, and pressure from the streets
went beyond simple dogmatic debates on political economy. Disputes and

revolts erupted over whether a colonial economy should be predicated on racial slavery. The "liberty of commerce" could not easily be defined, the compatibility of departmentalized colonies with equality was debatable, and republicanism had unleashed apprehension. The status of merchants and their role in the polity as commercial experts also remained uncertain. Neither free trade nor protectionism won. What the French state should become was not only up for debate but in fact would trigger a bloody fight.

This history, from above and below, cannot be approached within a narrow framework. The variation of scales and the multi-centered approach of this study expose the tensions between national power and trade, the breach between ideological intents and pragmatic implementations, disruptions caused by Atlantic communication, and the incongruity between delineated boundaries and the flow of goods and money. For more than two decades, the French-Saint-Domingue-US alliance ceaselessly remade the relationship between the metropole and the colonies, with the British and Spanish empires persistently in the backdrop or foreground. Despite an undeniable exchange of ideas, there was no single revolution spreading homogenous concepts of freedom, equality, and democracy. Revolutionary connections were at times mutually reinforcing but more often explosive. The clash of the American, French, and Haitian revolutions produced unexpected outcomes. Mercantile transactions, public contracts, and financial debts traded revolutions and triggered commercial wars.

Taking trade as the object of study reveals a hidden cartography of the Atlantic world, in which Saint-Domingue/Haiti was recognized as the "first province" of the French Empire and operated as a magnet for the new early American republic. In the nineteenth century, Haiti lost its economic prominence but became central to the history of human rights and decolonization, although Haitian leaders and Haitian society struggled to secure formal acknowledgment of the new, independent state. General Jean-Louis Ferrand, commanding the last French troops in the formerly Spanish part of the island, fought Haitians until 1808 when he committed suicide after a military defeat. Yet, despite diplomatic isolation, the great powers were unable, and secretly unwilling, to prevent what they deemed to be a Haitian intrusion on the global scene.[19]

Official recognition from France was only granted in 1825—twenty-one years after independence had been declared—and was contingent on Haiti's reimbursing planters for the so-called "property" they had lost. France's brutal demand of payment was to profoundly hurt Haitian economy for decades to come, as emphasized by a 2022 *New York Times* investigation which drew from numerous studies written by historians in Haiti, Europe, and the United states. Over the course of 64 years, Haiti made payments amounting to 112 million francs – around 560 million dollars. Due to this immense transfer of funds, Haiti's economy might have lost about 21 billion dollars in the past two centuries.

At the beginning of the nineteenth century, trading networks connecting US ports with the Caribbean adapted. As markets in the Spanish Empire opened up to US trade and the early American republic had other commercial wars to fight with the British, Haiti lost a degree of its economic significance. Despite Jefferson's retaliatory blockades in 1807 and 1808, neutrality provided US merchants with a twenty-year period of expansion. Vessels were redirected from Haiti to the flourishing slave economy of Cuba, which emerged as the new "Pearl of the Caribbean." On the North American continent, Louisiana's plantation economy was beginning to thrive, inciting businessmen to relocate to New Orleans. The early American government and ship owners were bracing for a new chapter of commercial expansion. However, the United States kept preying on Haiti for a long period of time. Recognition was not forthcoming from the United States until its own civil war brought an end to slavery, but in the twentieth century, through occupation and financial plundering, the United States kept exploiting Haitian resources. [20]

These developments were also the consequences of Saint-Domingue's historical significance in the US economy. Several prominent nineteenth-century merchants, already searching for new paths to wealth, owed much of their fortune to the colony. Stephen Girard, who had launched his career in the smuggling trade, became one of the wealthiest individuals in the country, purchasing the majority of shares in the first Bank of the United States in 1812. The Perkins family, among other "Brahmins" in Boston, controlled a commercial empire extending to China. Francophile merchant Samuel Smith entered the Jeffersonian administration as secretary of the navy. Through them and others, Saint-Domingue trade had substantial impacts on the US economy and politics, the magnitude of which is only just beginning to be understood.

At the Atlantic level, the triangular association between Haiti, France, and the United States brutally declined, both in the materiality of trafficked commodities and in its fantasized form as a politically regenerative trade. The failure of that relationship was a decisive factor in the collapse of the French Empire and its reformulation in the nineteenth century. The communal aspirations encapsulated in the notion of "empire of liberty" had not prevented commercial republicanism from capitulating to a multitude of contradictions. But the collapse under way was part of a larger picture and a feature of the longer-term destruction of early modern empires in the Americas. Soon Spanish colonies on the continent were to follow suit. In the cauldron of revolution, emancipation, and war, Great Britain was to embrace the trade regime forged by the United States on the remnants of a French imperial vision. A new rivalry of free-trade imperialism would erupt on the shores of South America. Despite slave insurrections and the existence of Haiti, these free-trade practices did not naturally lead to the abolition of slavery in the Americas; in fact, a second form of slavery expanded in the United States, Cuba, and Brazil. Merchants kept playing a leading role: they withstood and created crises; promoted "free trade," and maneuvered to monopolize markets; lobbied and undermined nascent governments. Trade remained a driving force in its own right, reshaping the geopolitics of the Atlantic world.

NOTES

Abbreviations

ADLA	Archives départementales de Loire-Atlantique, Nantes
AMV	Archives du ministère de la Défense, Vincennes
AN	Archives nationales de France, Paris and Pierrefitte-sur-Seine
ANOM	Archives nationales d'Outre-Mer, Aix-en-Provence
APS	American Philosophical Society, Philadelphia, PA
BL	British Library, London, United Kingdom
BNF	Bibliothèque nationale de France, Paris
BVP	Bibliothèque de la ville de Paris, Paris
CADN	Centre des archives diplomatiques de Nantes
CUL	Columbia University Library, New York, NY
DPL	Detroit Public Library, Detroit, MI
HM	Hagley Museum and Library, Wilmington, DE
HL	Huntington Library, San Marino, CA
HSP	Historical Society of Pennsylvania, Philadelphia, PA
JCB	John Carter Brown Library, Providence, RI
LC	Library of Congress, Washington, DC
MAE	Archives du ministère des Affaires étrangères, La Courneuve
MHS	Maryland Historical Society, Baltimore, MD
MassHS	Massachusetts Historical Society, Boston, MA
NARA	National Archives and Records Administration, Washington, DC, College Park, MD, New York, NY, and Philadelphia, PA
NYHS	New York Historical Society, New York, NY
NYPL	New York Public Library, New York, NY
NYPL-SC	New York Public Library Schomburg Center, New York, NY
NYSA	New York State Archives, Albany, NY
PRO	Public Record Office (National Archives), Kew, United Kingdom
TUL	Temple University Library, Philadelphia, PA

Introduction

1. MHS, *Barney Papers*, "Extrait du procès-verbal de la Convention nationale du 25 Fructidor an IIe de la République"; *Gazette nationale ou le Moniteur universel*, September 14. 1794, 2; Mary Barney, *A Biographical Memoir of the Late Commodore Joshua Barney* (Boston: Gray & Bowen, 1832), 185–87.

2. On Barney's mission to Saint-Domingue: HSP, *Barney Papers*, "Instructions pour le citoyen Barney, capitaine de vaisseau, commandant la Frégate l'Harmonie," May 19, 1796. On his life

as a slaveholder in Kentucky, see: MHS, *Barney Papers*, Joshua Barney's will and correspondence. Accounts of Barney's life are hagiographies. See, for instance, Louis A. Norton, *Joshua Barney|: Hero of the Revolution and 1812* (Annapolis, MD: Naval Institute Press, 2000).

3. For syntheses on the longer history of the French Empire, see Gilles Havard and Cécile Vidal, *Histoire de l'Amérique française* (Paris: Flammarion, 2003); Bernard Gainot, *L'Empire colonial français: De Richelieu à Napoléon* (Paris: Armand Colin, 2015); Brett Rushforth and Christopher Hodson, *Discovering Empire: France and the Atlantic World from the Age of the Crusades to the Rise of Napoleon* (Oxford University Press, forthcoming). For a historiographical discussion on the idea of the colonial empire in the French context, see François-Joseph Ruggiu, "Des nouvelles France aux colonies—Une approche comparée de l'histoire impériale de la France de l'époque moderne," *Nuevo Mundo Mundos Nuevos* (2018), doi: 10.4000/nuevomundo.72123. On the political economy of early modern empires and charter companies: James D. Tracy, ed., *The Political Economy of Merchant Empires* (Cambridge: Cambridge University Press, 1991); Eric Roulet, *La Compagnie des îles de l'Amérique 1635–1651: Une entreprise coloniale au XVIIe siècle* (Rennes: Presses universitaires de Renne, 2017). On rogue colonialism and its mutations in the age of revolutions: Shannon Lee Dawdy. *Building the Devil's Empire: French Colonial New Orleans* (Chicago: University of Chicago Press, 2008); Vanessa Mongey, *Rogue Revolutionaries: The Fight for Legitimacy in the Greater Caribbean* (Philadelphia: University of Pennsylvania Press, 2020).For the French trade with South Asia: Philippe Haudrère, *Les Compagnies françaises des Indes au XVIII siècle: 1719–1795* (Paris: Librairie de l'Inde, 1989); Felicia Gottman, *Global Trade, Smuggling, and the Making of Economic Liberalism* (Basingstoke, UK: Palgrave Macmillan, 2016).

4. Historians have debated the extent to which the slave trade and colonial economies benefited French capitalism beyond metropolitan ports: Paul Butel, *Les négociants bordelais, l'Europe et les Îles au XVIIIe siècle* (Paris: Aubier, 1974); Olivier Pétré-Grenouilleau, *L'argent de la traite: Milieu négrier, capitalisme et développement: un modèle* (Paris: Aubier, 1996); Guillaume Daudin, *Commerce et prospérité: la France au XVIIIe siècle* (Paris: Presses de l'Université Paris-Sorbonne, 2011). For the big picture of the French colonial trade in that period, see Robert Louis Stein, *The French Sugar Business in the Eighteenth Century* (Baton Rouge: Louisiana State University Press, 1988); Butel, "Succès et déclin du commerce colonial français, de la Révolution à la Restauration," *Revue économique* 40, no. 6 (1989): 1079–96; David Geggus, "The French Slave Trade: An Overview," *William and Mary Quarterly* 58, no. 1 (2001): 119–38. On the Saint-Domingue economic boom, see Trevor Burnard and John Garrigus, *The Plantation Machine: Atlantic Capitalism in French Saint-Domingue and British Jamaica* (Philadelphia: University of Pennsylvania Press, 2016). On the impact in metropolitan France, see Michael Kwass, *Contraband: Louis Mandrin and the Global Underground* (Cambridge, MA: Harvard University Press, 2015), 9. On the violence of the French slave trade and the resistance to it by enslaved men and women, see Jessica Marie Johnson, *Wicked Flesh: Black Women, Intimacy, and Freedom in the Atlantic World* (Philadelphia: University of Pennsylvania Press, 2020).

5. On the vulnerability of Saint-Domingue's colonial capitalism, see Paul Cheney, *Cul de Sac: Patrimony, Capitalism, and Slavery in French Saint-Domingue* (Chicago: University of Chicago Press, 2017). On the role of maritime expansion and slavery in the making of early modern French sovereignty: Helen Dewar, "Souveraineté dans les colonies, souveraineté en métropole: le rôle de la Nouvelle-France dans la consolidation de l'autorité maritime en France, 1620–1628," *Revue d'histoire de l'Amérique française* 64, no. 3–4 (2011): 63–92; Malick W. Ghachem, *The Old Regime and the Haitian Revolution* (Cambridge: Cambridge University Press, 2012). On the role of colonies in French diplomacy: Eric Schnakenbourg and François Ternat, eds., *Une diplomatie des lointains: La France face à la mondialisation des rivalités internationales, XVIIe-XVIIIe siècles* (Rennes: Presses universitaires de Rennes, 2020). On the debates regarding the notion of the fiscal-military state:John Brewer, *The Sinews of Power: War, Money, and the English State, 1688–1783* (London: Unwin Hyman, 1989); Steve Pincus and James Robinson, "Wars and State-Making Reconsidered—The Rise of the Developmental State," *Annales. Histoire, Sciences Sociales: English Edition* 71, no. 1 (2016): 9–34. On the Hundred Years' War in the long eighteenth century: Jean Meyer and John S. Bromley, "La seconde guerre de Cent Ans (1689–1815)," in *Dix siècles d'histoire franco-britannique: de Guillaume*

le Conquérant au Marché Commun (Paris: Albin Michel, 1979), 153–90. On French-British cooperation, see Renaud Morieux, *The Channel: England, France and the Construction of a Maritime Border in the Eighteenth Century* (Cambridge: Cambridge University Press, 2016). On entanglements and imperial sovereignty in the early modern world: Eliga H. Gould, "Entangled Histories, Entangled Worlds: The English-Speaking Atlantic as a Spanish Periphery," *American Historical Review* 112, no. 3 (2007): 764–86; Lauren Benton, *A Search for Sovereignty: Law and Geography in European Empires, 1400–1900* (Cambridge: Cambridge University Press, 2009).

6. On Colbert's commercial policy in the colonies and Colbert's legacy in the eighteenth century: Stewart Lea Mims, *Colbert's West India Policy* (New Haven, CT: Yale University Press, 1912); Philippe Minard, *La Fortune du colbertisme: État et industrie dans la France des Lumières* (Paris: Fayard, 1998). On the monopoly economy and the merchants' dual language: Jean-Pierre Hirsch, *Les deux rêves du commerce: entreprise et institution dans la région lilloise, 1780–1860* (Paris: Éditions de l'École des hautes études en sciences sociales, 1991); Jeff Horn, *Economic Development in Early Modern France: The Privilege of Liberty, 1650–1820* (Cambridge: Cambridge University Press, 2015). On the new charter companies and their role in French politics construed more broadly: Elizabeth Cross, "India and the Compagnie des Indes in the Age of the French Revolution," *French Historical Studies* 44, no. 3 (2021): 455–76.

7. Richard Pares, *Yankees and Creoles: The Trade Between North America and the West Indies Before the American Revolution* (Cambridge, MA: Harvard University Press, 1956); Dorothy Burne Goebel, "The 'New England Trade' and the French West Indies, 1763–1774: A Study in Trade Policies," *William and Mary Quarterly* 20, no. 3 (1963): 332–72; John J. McCusker, *Rum and the American Revolution: The Rum Trade and the Balance of Payments of the Thirteen Continental Colonies* (New York: Garland, 1989); Willem Gerrit Klooster, *Illicit Riches: Dutch Trade in the Caribbean, 1648–1795* (Leiden: KITLV Press, 1998); Christian J. Koot, *Empire at the Periphery: British Colonists, Anglo-Dutch Trade, and the Development of the British Atlantic, 1621–1713* (New York: New York University Press, 2011); Gregory E. O'Malley, *Final Passages: The Intercolonial Slave Trade of British America, 1619–1807* (Chapel Hill: University of North California Press, 2014); Karwan Fatah-Black, *White Lies and Black Markets: Evading Metropolitan Authority in Colonial Surinam, 1650–1800* (Leidon: Brill, 2015); Ernesto Bassi, *An Aqueous Territory: Sailor Geographies and New Granada's Transimperial Greater Caribbean World* (Durham, NC: Duke University Press, 2017); Jesse Cromwell, *The Smugglers' World: Illicit Trade and Atlantic Communities in Eighteenth-century Venezuela* (Chapel Hill: University of North Carolina Press, 2018).

8. Catherine Larrère, *L'invention de l'économie au XVIIIe siècle: du droit naturel à la physiocratie* (Paris: Presses universitaires de France, 1992); Jean-Claude Perrot, *Une histoire intellectuelle de l'économie politique: XVIIe–XVIIIe siècle* (Paris: Éditions de l'École des hautes études en sciences sociales, 1992); Marc Belissa, *Fraternité universelle et intérêt national (1713–1795): les cosmopolitiques du droit des gens* (Paris: Kimé, 1998); John Shovlin, *The Political Economy of Virtue: Luxury, Patriotism and the Origins of the French Revolution* (Ithaca, NY: Cornell University Press, 2006); Cheney, *Revolutionary Commerce: Globalization and the French Monarchy* (Cambridge, MA: Harvard University Press, 2010); Anoush Fraser Terjanian, *Commerce and Its Discontents in Eighteenth-Century French Political Thought* (New York: Cambridge University Press, 2013); Arnault Skornicki, *L'Economiste, la cour et la patrie. L'Economie politique dans la France des Lumières* (Paris: CNRS, 2015); Caroline Oudin-Bastide and Philippe Steiner, *Calculation and Morality: The Costs of Slavery and the Value of Emancipation in the French Antilles* (Oxford: Oxford University Press, 2019).

9. On the reorientation of French colonial policy: Jean Tarrade, *Le commerce colonial de la France à la fin de l'Ancien Régime: l'évolution du régime de l'exclusif de 1763 à 1789* (Paris: Presses universitaires de France, 1972); Charles Frostin, "Histoire de l'autonomisme colon de la partie française de St-Domingue aux XVIIe et XVIIIe siècles, contribution à l'étude du sentiment américain d'indépendance" (PhD diss., Université de Lille III, 1973); Edmond Dziembowski, *Un nouveau patriotisme français, 1750–1770: la France face à la puissance anglaise à l'époque de la guerre de Sept ans* (Oxford: Voltaire Foundation, 1998); François-Joseph Ruggiu, "India and the Reshaping of the French Colonial Policy (1759–1789)," *Itinerario* 25,

no. 2 (2011): 25–43; Pernille Røge, *Economistes and the Reinvention of Empire: France in the Americas and Africa, c. 1750—c. 1815* (Cambridge: Cambridge University Press, 2019). On British global expansion and reorientation: Vincent Todd Harlow, *The Founding of the Second British Empire, 1763–1793* (London: Longmans, Green, 1952); Christopher Alan Bayly, *Imperial Meridian: The British Empire and the World, 1780–1830* (London: Longman, 1989). On *entrepôts* in the Caribbean: Frances Armytage, *The Free Port System in the British West Indies, a Study in Commercial Policy, 1766–1822* (London: Longmans, Green, 1953); Linda M. Rupert, *Creolization and Contraband: Curaçao in the Early Modern Atlantic World* (Athens: University of Georgia Press, 2012); Jeppe Mulich, *In a Sea of Empires: Networks and Crossings in the Revolutionary Caribbean* (Cambridge: Cambridge University Press, 2020).

10. Eric Hobsbawm, by contrasting the political revolution in France and the industrial revolution in Britain, contributed to this interpretation. Immanuel Wallerstein also adopted this approach, stating that the French Revolution "occurred in the wake of, and as a consequence of, France's sense of impending defeat in this struggle." On the geopolitical analysis of French weakness in Europe, see Bailey Stone, *Reinterpreting the French Revolution: A Global-Historical Perspective* (Cambridge: Cambridge University Press, 2002). On the history of the "dying" French Empire and British superiority in the late eighteenth century, see François Crouzet, *De la supériorité de l'Angleterre sur la France: l'économique et l'imaginaire, XVIIe–XXe siècles* (Paris: Perrin, 1985); Immanuel Wallerstein, *The Modern World-System*, vol. 3, *The Second Era of Great Expansion of the Capitalist World-Economy, 1730–1840s* (New York: Academic Press, 1989), 94; Jean Meyer, "De l'apogée économique à l'effondrement du domaine colonial (1763–1803)," in *Histoire de la France coloniale, 1: Des origines à 1914*, Jean Meyer et al. (Paris: Armand Colin, 1991), 197–314; Alan Forrest, *The Death of the French Atlantic: Trade, War, and Slavery in the Age of Revolution* (Oxford: Oxford University Press, 2020). On the "new history of capitalism," which particularly focuses on the connections between slavery and capitalism, building on Eric Williams's foundational work but centered on a global United States, see Eric Eustace Williams, *Capitalism and Slavery* (Chapel Hill: University of North Carolina Press, 1944); Sven Beckert and Seth Rockman, eds., *Slavery's Capitalism: A New History of American Economic Development* (Philadelphia: University of Pennsylvania Press, 2016). For critics of the new history of capitalism, see Eric Hilt, "Economic History, Historical Analysis, and the "New History of Capitalism," *Journal of Economic History* 77, no. 2 (2017): 511–36; Trevor Burnard and Giorgio Riello, "Slavery and the New History of Capitalism," *Journal of Global History* 15, no. 2 (2020): 225–44.

11. Guillaume Daudin, "Profitability of Slave and Long-Distance Trading in Context: The Case of Eighteenth Century France," *Journal of Economic History* 64, no. 1 (2004): 144–71. I also share Jeff Horn's skepticism toward the anglocentrism of the literature. See Jeff Horn, *The Path Not Taken: French Industrialization in the Age of Revolutions (1750–1830)* (Boston: MIT Press, 2006), 4. On the notion of "imperial revolution" and political economy in the Spanish imperial context, see Jeremy Adelman, "An Age of Imperial Revolutions," *American Historical Review* 113, no. 2 (2008): 319–340; Federica Morelli, Clément Thibaud, and Geneviève Verdo, eds., *Les empires atlantiques des Lumières au libéralisme, 1763–1865* (Rennes: Presses universitaires de Rennes, Réseau des universités de l'Ouest Atlantique, 2009). On the transition between the first and the second colonial empire, through free trade, see Røge, *Economistes*; Marcel Dorigny and Bernard Gainot, eds., *La colonisation nouvelle (fin XVIIIe siècle—début XIXe siècle)* (Paris: L'Harmattan, 2018); David Todd, "A French Imperial Meridian, 1814–1870?," *Past and Present* 210, no. 1 (2011): 155–86.

12. This approach is indebted to scholarship produced by Jean Jaurès, Anna J. Cooper, and C. R. L. James. Published in the first half of the twentieth century, their research connected the French revolution with the history of colonialism and slavery and placed it within a larger narrative of global capitalism from a Marxian perspective. However, for a long time these interpretations were sidelined from the grand narratives of the French Revolution. A major reason for this disregard was the "silencing" of the Haitian Revolution, diagnosed by Michel-Rolph Trouillot. A less acknowledged explanation is the attack on the "rise of the bourgeoisie" framework of analysis. While Jaurès and James both emphasized the power of a capitalist bourgeoisie deriving its wealth from colonial trade, most historians belonging to "the Jacobin school," such as Georges Lefebvre and Albert Soboul, were more interested in

writing a "history from below"—of peasants and *sans-culottes*. Conversely, in the footsteps of François Furet, the "revisionists" argued that noble and bourgeois elites were one and the same, going as far as presenting the bourgeoisie as a "myth." See Jean Jaurès, *Histoire socialiste de la Révolution française* (Paris: Éditions sociales, 1968–1972); Anna Julia Cooper, *L'attitude de la France à l'égard de l'esclavage pendant la Révolution* (Paris: Imprimerie de la Cour d'Appel, 1925); C. L. R. James, *The Black Jacobins: Toussaint L'ouverture and the San Domingo Revolution* (New York: Vintage Books, 1963); Michel-Rolph Trouillot, *Silencing the Past: Power and the Production of History* (Boston: Beacon Press, 1995). For an extensive list of publications on the history of Atlantic Revolutions and the more recent scholarship on the impact of the Haitian Revolution, see Allan Potofsky, "The One and the Many: The Two Revolutions Question and the 'Consumer-Commercial' Atlantic, 1789 to the Present," in *Rethinking the Atlantic World: Europe and America in the Age of Democratic Revolutions*, ed. Manuela Albertone and Antonino De Francesco (Basingstoke, UK: Palgrave Macmillan, 2009), 17–45; Alyssa Goldstein-Sepinwall, ed. *Haitian History: New Perspectives* (New York: Routledge, 2012); Manuel Covo and Megan Maruschke, "The French Revolution as an Imperial Revolution," *French Historical Studies* 44, no. 3 (2021): 371–97.

13. "Letter to John Livingston," June 3, 1783, in Robert Joseph Taylor and Gregg L. Lint, eds., *Papers of John Adams, June 1783–January 1784* (Cambridge, MA: Harvard University Press, 2010), 49. On the political economy of the Revolution and in the early years of the Republic: Drew R. McCoy, *The Elusive Republic: Political Economy in Jeffersonian America* (Chapel Hill: University of North Carolina Press, 1996); T. H. Breen, *The Marketplace of Revolution: How Consumer Politics Shaped American Independence* (Oxford: Oxford University Press, 2005).

14. On the political economy of the US state formation, see Cathy Matson and Peter Onuf, *A Union of Interests: Political and Economic Thought in Revolutionary America* (Lawrence: University Press of Kansas, 1990); Max M. Edling, *A Revolution in Favor of Government: Origins of the US Constitution and the Making of the American State* (Oxford: Oxford University Press, 2008); Steve Pincus, *The Heart of the Declaration: The Founders' Case for an Activist Government* (New Haven, CT: Yale University Press, 2016). On the entanglement of US formation with Borderland and Atlantic dynamics: Richard White, *The Middle Ground: Indians, Empires, and Republics in the Great Lakes Region, 1650–1815*, 20th anniversary ed. (Cambridge: Cambridge University Press, 2011); Eliga H. Gould, *Among the Powers of the Earth: The American Revolution and the Making of a New World Empire* (Cambridge, MA: Harvard University Press, 2012); Kathleen DuVal, *Independence Lost: Lives on the Edge of the American Revolution* (New York: Random House, 2015); Nathan Perl-Rosenthal, *Citizen Sailors: Becoming American in the Age of Revolution* (Cambridge, MA: Belknap Press of Harvard University Press, 2015). On the early American republic as an empire in the making, see Peter Kastor, *The Nation's Crucible: The Louisiana Purchase and the Creation of America* (New Haven, CT: Yale University Press, 2004); Ned Blackhawk, *Violence over the Land: Indians and Empires in the Early American West* (Cambridge, MA: Harvard University Press, 2006); Bethel Saler, *The Settlers' Empire: Colonialism and State Formation in America's Old Northwest* (Philadelphia: University of Pennsylvania Press, 2015).

15. This work draws inspiration from Alain Turnier, *Les Etats-Unis et le marché haïtien* (Washington DC, 1955); Vertus Saint-Louis, *Aux origines du drame d'Haïti: droit et commerce maritime (1794–1806)* (Port-au-Prince: Bibliothèque nationale d'Haïti, 2006); Peter Linebaugh and Marcus Rediker, *The Many-Headed Hydra: Sailors, Slaves, Commoners, and the Hidden History of the Revolutionary Atlantic* (Boston: Beacon Press, 2013); Julius Scott, *The Common Wind: African-American Currents in the Age of the Haitian Revolution* (London: Verso, 2018). For the notion of Haitian "layered sovereignty," see Julia Gaffield, *Haitian Connections in the Atlantic World: Recognition after Revolution* (Chapel Hill: University of North Carolina Press, 2015).

16. This question should be replaced within the broader debate over the transformation of the French nation-state cum colonial empire. See Cécile Vidal, ed., *Français?: La nation en débat entre colonies et métropole, XVIe–XIXe siècle* (Paris: Éditions de l'école des Hautes études en Sciences Sociales, 2014); Josep M. Fradera, *The Imperial Nation: Citizens and Subjects in the British, French, Spanish, and American Empires*, trans. Ruth MacKay (Princeton, NJ: Princeton University Press 2018).

17. On merchants in the American Revolution, see for instance, Thomas M. Doerflinger, *A Vigorous Spirit of Enterprise: Merchants and Economic Development in Revolutionary Philadelphia* (Chapel Hill: University of North Carolina Press, 1986); Tyson Reeder, *Smugglers, Pirates and Patriots: Free Trade in the Age of Revolution* (Philadelphia: University of Pennsylvania Press, 2019). The two only and dated studies on merchants in colonial Saint Domingue are focused on transatlantic connections. See Pierre Léon, *Marchands et spéculateurs dauphinois dans le monde antillais du XVIIIe siècle: les Dolle et les Raby* (Paris: Les Belles lettres, 1963); Françoise Thésée, *Négociants bordelais et colons de Saint-Domingue, liaisons d'habitations, la maison Henry Rombert, Bapst et Cie, 1783–1793* (Abbeville: Imprimerie F. Paillart, 1972). On Guadeloupe's privateers, see Anne Pérotin-Dumon, "Cabotage, Contraband and Corsairs: The Port Cities of Guadeloupe and Their Inhabitants (1650–1800)," in *Atlantic Port Cities: Economy, Culture, and Society in the Atlantic World, 1650–1850,* ed. Franklin | Knight and Peggy Liss (Knoxville: University of Tennessee Press, 1991), 58–86. On free people of color and female merchants in Saint-Domingue: Dominique Rogers, "Les libres de couleur dans les capitales de Saint-Domingue: fortune, mentalités et intégration à la fin de l'Ancien Régime (1776–1789)" (PhD diss., Université de Bordeaux III, 1999).

18. On self-organizing merchant networks, see, for instance, David Hancock, "The Triumphs of Mercury. Connection and Control in the Emerging Atlantic Economy," in *Soundings in Atlantic History: Latent Structures and Intellectual Currents, 1500–1830,* ed. Bernard Bailyn and Patricia L. Denault (Cambridge, MA: Harvard University Press, 2009), 112–40. On merchants, profit, and institutions within and beyond imperial borders: Cathy Matson, *Merchants and Empire: Trading in Colonial New York* (Baltimore: Johns Hopkins University Press, 1998); Dominique Margairaz, Yannick Lemarchand, and Pierre Gervais, eds., *Merchants and Profit in the Age of Commerce, 1680–1830* (New York: Routledge, 2015); Silvia Marzagalli, *Bordeaux et les États-Unis: 1776–1815: politique et stratégies négociantes dans la genèse d'un réseau commercial* (Geneva: Droz, 2015); Cátia Antunes and Amelia Polónia, eds., *Beyond Empires: Global, Self-organizing, Cross-imperial Networks, 1500–1800* (Leiden: Brill, 2016).

19. On *jeux d'échelles*: Jacques Revel, ed., *Jeux d'échelles: la micro-analyse à l'expérience* (Paris: Gallimard, Seuil, 1996); Rebecca J. Scott, "Small-Scale Dynamics of Large-Scale Processes," *American Historical Review* 105, no. 2 (2000): 472–79; Lara Putnam, "To Study the Fragments/Whole: Microhistory and the Atlantic World," *Journal of Social History* 39, no. 3 (2006): 615–30. On connected histories and *histoire croisée*: Sanjay Subrahmanyam, "Connected Histories: Notes toward a Reconfiguration of Early Modern Eurasia," *Modern Asian Studies* 31, no. 3 (1997): 735–62; Michael Werner and Bénédicte Zimmermann, "Penser l'histoire croisée: entre empirie et réflexivité," *Annales. Histoire, Sciences Sociales* 58, no. 1 (2003): 7–36. On brilliant examples of variations of scale to analyze port-cities in the Atlantic world: Elena A. Schneider, *The Occupation of Havana: War, Trade, and Slavery in the Atlantic World* (Chapel Hill: University of North Carolina Press, 2018); Cécile Vidal, *Caribbean New Orleans: Empire, Race, and the Making of a Slave Society* (Chapel Hill: University of North Carolina Press, 2019).

Chapter 1

1. Thomas Paine, *Lettre adressée à l'abbé Raynal sur les affaires de l'Amérique septentrionale. . . . Traduite de l'anglois de M. Thomas Payne* (Paris: s.n., 1783), 65; Guillaume-Thomas Raynal, *Considérations sur la paix de 1783, envoyées par l'abbé Raynal au prince Frédéric Henri de Prusse qui lui avait demandé ce qu'il pensait de cette paix* (Berlin: H. La Garde, 1783).

2. Traditional scholarship based on a nation-state framework includes Samuel Flagg Bemis, *The Foundations of American Diplomacy, 1775–1823,* vol. 1, *The Diplomacy of the American Revolution* (New York: D. Appleton-Century, 1935); William C. Stinchcombe, *The American Revolution and the French Alliance* (Syracuse, NY: Syracuse University Press, 1969); Ronald Hoffman and Peter J. Albert, eds., *Diplomacy and Revolution: The Franco-American Alliance of 1778* (Charlottesville: University Press of Virginia, 1981); Jonathan Dull, *A Diplomatic History of the American Revolution* (New Haven, CT: Yale University Press, 1985); Alexander DeConde, "Historians, the War of American Independence, and the Persistence of the Exceptionalist Ideal," *International History Review* 5, no. 3 (August 1983): 399–430. The

subject has been touched on in Roopnarine John Singh, *French Diplomacy in the Caribbean and the American Revolution* (Hicksville, NY: Exposition Press, 1977).

3. Edward Corwin's interpretation that the defense of the colonies was only a pretext has remained largely unchallenged: Edward Samuel Corwin, *French Policy and the American Alliance of 1778* (Princeton, NJ: Princeton University Press, 1916).

4. Paul Cheney, "A False Dawn for Enlightenment Cosmopolitanism? Franco-American Trade During the American War of Independence," *William and Mary Quarterly* 63, no. 3 (July 2006): 463–88; Henri Doniol, *Histoire de la participation de la France à l'établissement des États-Unis d'Amérique*, vol. 1 (Paris: Impr. nationale, 1886), 244, 278; Isaac Nakhimovsky, "Vattel's Theory of the International Order: Commerce and the Balance of Power in the Law of Nations," *History of European Ideas* 33, no. 2 (June 2007): 157–73.

5. On Gournay's circle, see Simone Meyssonnier, *La balance et l'horloge: la genèse de la pensée libérale en France au XVIIIe siècle* (Montreuil: Édition de la Passion, 1989), 203; Jacob Viner, "Power Versus Plenty as Objectives of Foreign Policy in the Seventeenth and Eighteenth Centuries," in *Theories of Empire, 1450–1800*, ed. David Armitage (Aldershot, UK: Ashgate, 1998), 277–305; Fréderic Lefebvre, Loïc Charles, and Christine Théré, eds., *Le cercle de Vincent de Gournay—Savoirs économiques et pratiques administratives en France au milieu du XVIIIe siècle* (Paris: INED, 2011). On the rebuilding of the French Navy, see Jonathan Dull, *The French Navy and American Independence: A Study of Arms and Diplomacy, 1774–1787* (Princeton, NJ: Princeton University Press, 1975).

6. Manuscripts are transcribed in Cornélis Henri de Witt, *Thomas Jefferson, étude historique sur la démocratie américaine* (Paris: Didier, 1861), 452–54; Eugène Théodore Daubigny, *Choiseul et la France d'outre-mer après le traité de Paris: étude sur la politique coloniale au XVIIIe siècle* (Paris: Hachette, 1892), 176; Doniol, *Histoire de la participation*, 1: 244–45, 279, 571–72, 576, 586, 588, 2: 466. On Franklin's intervention and the policy of Congress, see Vernon G. Setser, *The Commercial Reciprocity Policy of the United States, 1774–1829* (Philadelphia: University of Pennsylvania Press, 1937), 15–16; Gerald Stourzh, *Benjamin Franklin and American Foreign Policy* (Chicago: University of Chicago Press, 1954); Manuela Albertone, *National Identity and the Agrarian Republic: The Transatlantic Commerce of Ideas Between America and France (1750–1830)* (Farnham, UK: Ashgate, 2014), 101–38.

7. Doniol, *Histoire de la participation*, 1: 245, 2: 466; John Shovlin, "Selling American Empire on the Eve of the Seven Years War: The French Propaganda Campaign of 1755–1756," *Past and Present* 206, no. 1 (2010): 121–49.

8. Georges Weulersse, *Les Physiocrates sous le ministère de Turgot* (Poitiers: Impr. du Poitou, 1925), 11; André Labrouquère, *Les Idées coloniales des physiocrates* (Paris: Presses universitaires de France, 1927), 28; Alain Clément, "Du bon et du mauvais usage des colonies: politique coloniale et pensée économique française au XVIIIe siècle," *Cahiers d'économie politique/Papers in Political Economy* 56, no. 1 (2009): 101–27; Pernille Røge, *Economistes and the Reinvention of Empire: France in the Americas and Africa, c.1750–1802* (Cambridge: Cambridge University Press, 2019).

9. Anne Robert Jacques Turgot, *Mémoire sur les colonies américaines, sur leurs relations politiques avec leurs métropoles et sur la manière dont la France et l'Espagne ont dû envisager les suites de l'indépendance des États-Unis de l'Amérique, par feu M. Turgot* (Paris: Impr. de Du Pont, député de Nemours, 1791), 17.

10. Turgot, *Mémoire sur les colonies américaines*, 18–19.

11. Turgot, *Mémoire sur les colonies américaines*, 21, 22, 25, 31. On the usage of the slavery metaphor, see Peter Dorsey, "To "Corroborate Our Own Claims": Public Positioning and the Slavery Metaphor in Revolutionary America," *American Quarterly* 55, no. 3 (2003): 353–86.

12. Turgot, *Mémoire sur les colonies américaines*, 35; Marc Belissa, *Fraternité universelle et intérêt national (1713–1795): les cosmopolitiques du droit des gens* (Paris: Kimé, 1998), 28.

13. Adam Smith, *Fragment sur les colonies en général et sur celles des Anglois en particulier. Traduit de l'anglois* (Lausanne: chez la Société typographique, 1778); Siegmund Feilbogen, *Smith und Turgot: ein Beitrag zur Geschichte und Theorie der Nationalökonomie* (Genève: Slatkine Reprints, 1970); Emma Rothschild, "Commerce and the State: Turgot, Condorcet and Smith," *Economic Journal* 102, no. 414 (1992): 1197–210; Kathleen Wilson, *The Sense of the People: Politics, Culture and Imperialism in England, 1715–1785* (Cambridge: Cambridge

University Press, 1995); Kenneth E. Carpenter, *The Dissemination of The Wealth of Nations in French and in France: 1776–1843* (New York: Oak Knoll Press, 2002).

14. Jean Tarrade, *Le commerce colonial de la France à la fin de l'Ancien Régime: L'évolution du régime de "l'Exclusif" de 1763 à 1789*, vol. 1 (Paris: Press Universitaires de France, 1972), 431, 443; Singh, *French Diplomacy in the Caribbean*, 161–76.

15. *Traité d'amitié et de commerce, conclu entre le Roi et les États-Unis de l'Amérique septentrionale, le 6 février 1778* (Paris: Impr. royale, 1778), 5, 20.

16. Charles Frostin, *Histoire de l'autonomisme colon de la partie française de St-Domingue aux XVIIe et XVIIIe siècles: contribution à l'étude du sentiment américain d'indépendance*, vol. 2 (Lille: Service de reproduction des thèses, 1973), 808; Tarrade, *Le commerce colonial*, 1: 455–59; Patrick Villiers, "Les moyens navals de la France aux Antilles au XVIIIe siècle," in *L'espace Caraïbe: théâtre et enjeu des luttes impériales, XVIe–XIXe siècle*, ed. Paul Butel and Bernard Lavallé (Bordeaux: Maison des Pays ibériques, 1996), 11–38.

17. Pierrette Girault de Coursac and Paul Girault de Coursac, *Guerre d'Amérique et liberté des mers: 1783–1983*, (Paris: La Ville, 1983), 71.

18. Edmond Dziembowski, *Un nouveau patriotisme français, 1750–1770: la France face à la puissance anglaise à l'époque de la guerre de Sept ans* (Oxford: Voltaire Foundation, 1998), 59–62; Franz Bosbach, "The European Debate on Universal Monarchy," in *Theories of Empire*, ed. Armitage, 81–98; Steven Pincus, "The Making of a Great Power? Universal Monarchy, Political Economy, and the Transformation of English Political Culture," *European Legacy* 5, no. 4 (2000): 531–45; Renaud Morieux, *Une mer pour deux royaumes: la Manche, frontière franco-anglaise, XVIIe–XVIIIe siècles* (Rennes: Presses universitaires de Rennes, 2008) 150–53; Joseph Mathias Gérard de Rayneval, *Observations sur le Mémoire justificatif de la Cour de Londres* (Paris: Impr. royale, 1780), 36.

19. Martin Hubner, *Doutes et questions proposées par Montanus à Batavus sur les Droits de la Neutralité*, (London: s.n., 1781); Ferdinando Galiani, *De' Doveri de' principi neutrali verso i principi guerregianti e di questi verso i neutrali libri due* (Milan: s.n., 1782); Richard Pares, *Colonial Blockade and Neutral Rights, 1739–1763* (Philadelphia: Porcupine Press, 1975); Ole Feldbæk, "Privateers, Piracy and Prosperity: Danish Shipping in War and Peace, 1750–1807," in *Pirates and Privateers: New Perspectives on the War on Trade in the Eighteenth and Nineteenth Centuries*, ed. David John Starkey (Exeter, UK: University of Exeter Press, 1997), 227–44; Andrew Jackson O'Shaughnessy, *An Empire Divided: The American Revolution and the British Caribbean* (Philadelphia: University of Pennsylvania Press, 2000), 217–20; Koen Stapelbroek, "Neutrality and Trade in the Dutch Republic (1775–1783): Preludes to a Piecemeal Revolution," in *Rethinking the Atlantic World: Europe and America in the Age of Democratic Revolutions*, ed. Manuela Albertone and Antonino De Francesco (Basingstoke, UK: Palgrave Macmillan, 2009), 100–19; Victor Enthoven, ""That Abominable Nest of Pirates": St. Eustatius and the North Americans, 1680–1780," *Early American Studies: An Interdisciplinary Journal* 10, no. 2 (2012): 239–301.

20. Jean Baptiste Coeuilhe, *La liberté des mers: poème qui a remporté le prix de l'Académie des Marseille, en 1781* (Paris: P. F. Gueffier, 1782), 3–4.

21. *Les Affiches américaines*, September 28, 1779; February 18, 1784; Dorothy Burne Goebel, "The "New England Trade" and the French West Indies, 1763–1774: A Study in Trade Policies," *William and Mary Quarterly* 20, no. 3 (1963): 332–72; Frostin, "Saint-Domingue et la Révolution américaine," *Bulletin de la Société d'histoire de la Guadeloupe* 22 (1974): 1–44; John Garrigus, *Before Haiti: Race and Citizenship in French Saint-Domingue* (New York: Palgrave Macmillan, 2006), 207–10; Robert Taber, ""Le Sens Commun": Atlantic Pathways and Imagination in Saint-Domingue's *Affiches Américaines*," *Latin Americanist* 61, no. 4 (2017): 569–83.

22. François Bellec, "L'iconographie de la guerre d'Amérique," in *Les marines française et britannique face aux États-Unis de la guerre d'indépendance à la guerre de sécession (1776–1865)*, ed. Jean-Charles Lefebvre (Vincennes: Service historique de la Marine, 1999), 139–53; Hervé-Thomas Campangne, "La réception du traité de Paris (1783) et l'imaginaire des relations franco-américaines," *Transatlantica*, no. 2 (2020). On the role of the Spanish alliance in French maritime successes, see Larrie D. Ferreiro, *Brothers at Arms: American Independence and the Men of France and Spain Who Saved It* (New York: Vintage, 2017).

23. Rayneval, *Observations*, 68; Lauren Benton, *A Search of Sovereignty: Law and Geography in European Empires, 1400–1900* (Cambridge: Cambridge University Press, 2010), 104–61.

24. Martin Hübner, *De la saisie des bâtimens neutres, ou Du droit qu'ont les nations belligérantes d'arrêter les navires des peuples amis* (The Hague: s.n., 1759); François Véron Duverger de Forbonnais, *Essai sur l'admission des navires neutres dans nos colonies* (s.l., 1756); Antonella Alimento, "Competition, True Patriotism and Colonial Interests: Forbonnais Vision of Neutrality and Trade," in *COLLeGIUM: Studies Across Disciplines in the Humanities and Social Sciences*, ed. Koen Stapelbroek, vol. 10, *Trade and War:The Neutrality of Commerce in the Inter-State System* (Helsinki: University of Helsinki, Helsinki Collegium for Advanced Studies, 2011).

25. Cheney, *Revolutionary Commerce.*

26. The histories of the American Revolution from a French colonial perspective include Pierre-Ulric Dubuisson, *Abrégé de la Révolution de l'Amérique angloise, depuis le commencement de l'année 1774 jusqu'au premier janvier 1778* (Paris: Cellot et Jombert fils jeune, 1778); Michel-RenéHilliard d'Auberteuil, *Essais historiques et politiques sur la révolution de l'Amerique septentrionale* (Bruxelles, 1781); Guillaume-Thomas Raynal, *Révolution de l'Amérique, par M. l'abbé Raynal, auteur de l'Histoire philosophique et politique des établissemens et du commerce des Européens dans les deux Indes* (London: L. Davis, 1781). On French colonial enlightenment see Robert Darnton, *The Forbidden Best-Sellers of Pre-Revolutionary France* (New York: W. W. Norton, 1995), 65–66; Sankar Muthu, *Enlightenment Against Empire* (Princeton, NJ: Princeton University Press, 2003); Gene E., "The Eternal Power of Reason and the Superiority of Whites: Hilliard d'Auberteuil's Colonial Enlightenment," *French Colonial History* 3, no. 1 (2003): 35–50; Gene E. Ogle, "The Trans-Atlantic King and Imperial Public Spheres: Everyday Politics in Pre-Revolutionary Saint-Domingue," in *The World of the Haitian Revolution*, ed. David Patrick Geggus and Norman Fiering (Bloomington: Indiana University Press, 2009), 79–96; Anja Bandau, Marcel Dorigny, and Rebecca von Mallinckrodt, eds., *Les mondes coloniaux à Paris au XVIIIe siècle: circulation et enchevêtrement des savoirs* (Paris: Éd. Karthala, 2010); James E. McClellan and François Regourd, *The Colonial Machine: French Science and Overseas Expansion in the Old Regime* (Turnhout: Brepols, 2011).

27. Michel-René Hilliard d'Auberteuil, *Considérations sur l'état présent de la colonie française de Saint-Domingue:ouvrage politique et législatif*, vol. 1 (Paris: Grangé, 1776), 4, 10, 26–27.

28. Hilliard d'Auberteuil, *Considérations*, 1: 267, 276, 281. Hilliard d'Auberteuil's interpretation took many liberties with historical facts. See Frostin, *Les révoltes blanches à Saint-Domingue aux XVIIe et XVIIIe siècles* (Rennes: Presses Universitaires de Rennes, 2007), 48–65.

29. Hilliard d'Auberteuil, *Considérations*, 1: 11, 156, 231, 297, 299; Dubuisson, *Nouvelles considérations sur Saint-Domingue, en réponse à celles de M. H. D.* (Paris: Cellot et Jombert, 1780), 5.

30. Raynal, *Histoire philosophique et politique des établissemens et du commerce des Européens dans les deux Indes*, vol. 10 (Geneva: J.-L. Pellet, 1781), 388. See also Edoardo Tortarolo, "La Révolution américaine dans l'Histoire des deux Indes: la narration comme dialogue?," in *Lectures de Raynal: l'Histoire des deux Indes en Europe et en Amérique au XVIIIe siècle*, ed. Hans-Jürgen Lüsebrink and Anthony Strugnell (Oxford: Voltaire Foundation, 1995), 205–21.

31. ANOM, C9a 153, extraits des registres du Conseil supérieur du Cap; *Affiches américaines*, February 25, 1784, no. 8, 134; Richard Brandon Morris, *The Peacemakers: The Great Powers and American Independence* (Boston: Northeastern University Press, 1983); Andrew Stockley, *Britain and France at the Birth of America: the European Powers and the Peace Negotiations of 1782–1783* (Exeter, UK: University of Exeter Press, 2001).

32. AN, 306 AP 17, "Journal du Maréchal de Castries," 135, 142, 147,150; Marie Donaghay, "Calonne and the Anglo-French Commercial Treaty of 1786," *Journal of Modern History* 50, no. 3 (1978): 1157–84; Donaghay, "The Maréchal De Castries and the Anglo-French Commercial Negotiations of 1786, 1787," *The Historical Journal* 22, no. 2 (1979): 295–312.

33. ANOM, F2b 9, Bruny to Castries, July 6,1783, 472; Frederick Louis Nussbaum, "The French Colonial *arrêt* of 1784," *South Atlantic Quarterly*, no. 27 (1928): 62–78; Louis Reichenthal Gottschalk, *Lafayette and the Close of the American Revolution* (Chicago: University of Chicago Press, 1942), 176–77, 357; Gottschalk, "Lafayette as Commercial Expert," *American*

Historical Review 36, no. 3 (1931): 561–70; François Furstenberg, "Atlantic Slavery, Atlantic Freedom: George Washington, Slavery, and Transatlantic Abolitionist Networks," *William and Mary Quarterly* 68, no. 2 (2011): 247–86.

34. ANOM, F2b 9, "Lettre de Jean Dutasta," December 5, 1783, 365–6; MAE, MD EU 9, "Observations sur le commerce de l'Amérique par un négociant de Marseille," fo. 5. These Voltairian ideas were not really new; see Cheney, *Revolutionary Commerce*, 37. Chambre d'agriculture du Cap-Français, *Mémoire sur le commerce étranger avec les colonies françaises de l'Amérique, présenté à la chambre d'agriculture du Cap le 17 février 1784* (Paris: Cuchet, 1785), 1.

35. MAE, MD EU 9, "Observations d'un négociant marseillais sur le commerce d'Amérique," 7.

36. Josiah Child's treaties were translated by Vincent de Gournay in 1754. Josiah Child, Jacques Marie Claude Vincent de Gournay, and Simone Meyssonnier, *Traités sur le commerce* (Paris: L'Harmattan, 2008); Josephine Grieder, *Anglomania in France, 1740–1789: Fact, Fiction and Political Discourse* (Geneva: Droz, 1985); Richard Whatmore, *Republicanism and the French Revolution: An Intellectual History of Jean-Baptiste Say's Political Economy* (Oxford: Oxford University Press, 2001), 37–60; Whatmore, "Dupont de Nemours et la politique révolutionnaire," *Revue Française d'Histoire des Idées Politiques* 20, no. 2 (2004): 111–27; Arnault Skornicki, "England, England. La référence britannique dans le patriotisme français au 18e siècle," *Revue française de science politique* 59, no. 4 (2009): 681–700; Cheney, *Revolutionary Commerce*, 21–51.

37. Philippe Minard, ""France colbertiste" versus Angleterre "libérale"? Un mythe du XVIIIe siècle," in *Les idées passent-elles la Manche?: savoirs, représentations, pratiques*, ed. François-Joseph Ruggiu and Jean-Philippe Genet (Paris: Presses universitaires de Paris-Sorbonne, 2007), 197–210; Vincent Todd Harlow, *The Founding of the Second British Empire, 1763–1793* (London: Longmans, Green, 1952); Charles R. Ritcheson, "The Earl of Shelbourne and Peace with America, 1782–1783: Vision and Reality," *International History Review* 5, no. 3 (1983): 322–45; Andrew Hamilton, *Trade and Empire in the Eighteenth-Century Atlantic World* (Newcastle, UK: Cambridge Scholars, 2008), 25–41; Hannah Barker and Simon Burrows, eds., *Press, Politics and the Public Sphere in Europe and North America, 1760–1820* (Cambridge: Cambridge University Press, 2002); William Slauter, "News and Diplomacy in the Age of the American Revolution" (PhD diss., Princeton University, 2007); Albertone, *National Identity*, 199.

38. Setser, *The Commercial Reciprocity Policy*, 38–39; Gregg L. Lint, "Preparing for Peace," in *Peace and the Peacemakers:Tthe Treaty of 1783*, ed. Peter J Albert and Ronald Hoffman (Charlottesville: University Press of Virginia, 1986), 30–51; P. J. Marshall, "Empire and Authority in the Later Eighteenth Century," *Journal of Imperial and Commonwealth History* 15, no. 2 (1987): 105–22; O'Shaughnessy, "The Formation of a Commercial Lobby: The West India Interest, British Colonial Policy and the American Revolution," *Historical Journal* 40, no. 1 (1997): 71–95; Daeryoon Kim, "Political Convention and the Merchant in the Later Eighteenth Century," in *Regulating the British Economy, 1660–1850*, ed. Perry Gauci (Farnham, UK: Ashgate, 2011), 123–37.

39. ANOM, F2b 8, "Commerce maritime—États-Unis," 43; MAE, CP EU 25, Pierre Texier to Vergennes, July 29, 1783, 107.

40. ANOM, F2b 8, "Mémoire sur le commerce entre les isles françoises et les États-Unis de l'Amérique," fo. 226. MAE, MD EU, 8, "Mémoire sur le commerce des États-Unis," 190; ANOM, F2b 9, "Lettre de Gouverneur à M. le Mis de Chatelux, traduit de l'anglois," June 17, 1784, 523.

41. ANOM, F2b 9, fo. 473.

42. ANOM, F2b 9, 47; John Baker Holroyd, *Observations on the Commerce of the American States with Europe and the West Indies, Including the Several Articles of Import and Export, and on the Tendency of a Bill now Depending in Parliament [by Lord Sheffield]* (London: J. Debrett, 1783); Jeremy Black, *British Foreign Policy in an Age of Revolutions, 1783–1793* (Cambridge: Cambridge University Press: 1994), 29. On Vergennes's East Indian and British policy, see John Shovlin, *Trading with the Enemy: Britain, France, and the 18th-Century Question for a Peaceful World Order* (New Haven, CT: Yale University Press, 2021), 260–72.

43. ANOM, F2b 9, "Les négociants du Havre, 17 mars 1783", 461; ANOM, F2b 8, "Mémoire sur le commerce entre les isles françoises et les États-Unis de l'Amérique," 212.

44. Peter Hill, "La suite imprévue de l'alliance: l'ingratitude américaine, 1783-1789," in *La Révolution américaine et l'Europe*, ed. Claude Fohlen and Jacques Godechot (Paris: Éditions du C.N.R.S, 1979), 385–89; Silvia Marzagalli, "The Failure of a Transatlantic Alliance? Franco-American Trade, 1783–1815," *History of European Ideas* 34, no. 4 (2008): 456–64; Marzagalli, *Bordeaux et les Etats-Unis* (Geneva: Droz, 2015); ANOM, F2b 9, "Lettre de Marbois à Castries, 3 juin 1783," fo. 180; ANOM, F2b 9, "Lettre du chevalier d'Annemours," 476; ANOM, F2b 9, "Mémoire sur le commerce de France avec les États-Unis," fo. 24.

45. On the role of boycott at the beginning of the American Revolution, see T. H. Breen, *The Marketplace of Revolution: How Consumer Politics Shaped American Independence* (Oxford: Oxford University Press, 2005); MAE, MD EU 8, "Mémoire sur le commerce des États-Unis," 174; ANOM, F2b 9, La Luzerne to Castries, May 22, 1782, 450; Gottschalk, "Lafayette as Commercial Expert," 570.

46. ANOM, F2b 9, "Question sur le commerce de France avec les colonies et les Amériquains," 178; F2b 9, December 5, 1783, 358; F2b 9, "Sur le commerce des États-Unis avec nos colonies," 224; "Réflexions sur les liaisons de commerce qu'il convient de former entre la France et l'Amérique unie," 495; F2b 9, "Rapport de Sabatier de Cabres," July 20, 1783, 442; Thomas Pownall, *Mémoire adressé aux souverains de l'Europe, sur l'état présent des affaires de l'ancien et du nouveau monde* (Needham, UK: E. Flon, 1781).

47. ANOM, F2b 9, "Commerce entre les Colonies françoises et les États-Unis," 216–17; F2b 8, "Avis des députés du commerce sur l'observation rigoureuse ou la modification des loix prohibitives du commerce étranger dans nos colonies," 401; MAE, MD EU 9, "Observations sur le commerce de l'Amérique par un négociant de Marseille."

48. ANOM, F2b 9, "Question sur le commerce de France, les colonies et les Américains," fo. 178; "Rapport de Sabatier de Cabres," July 20,1783, 448. On the significance of sexual metaphors in justifications of colonialism, see Kathleen Wilson, *The Island Race: Englishness, Empire and Gender in the Eighteenth Century* (London: Routledge, 2003).

49. ANOM, F2b 9, "Mémoire sur les motifs qui nécessittent les permissions aux Anglo-amériquains d'introduire plusieurs sortes d'objets dans nos colonies," 298.

50. Chambre d'agriculture du Cap-Français, *Mémoire sur le commerce*, 23.

51. ANOM, F2b 8, fo. 188. On Castries's reforms of colonial regulations, see Malick W. Ghachem, *The Old Regime and the Haitian Revolution* (Cambridge: Cambridge University Press, 2012), 229.

52. *Observations des négocians de Bordeaux sur l'arrest du Conseil du 30 août 1784* (Paris, 1784); ANOM, F2b 8, fo. 120; Chambre de Commerce de Nantes, *Requête présentée par les députés du Commerce de Nantes, aux États & au Parlement de Bretagne* (Paris, 1785); Dubuisson, *Lettres critiques et politiques sur les colonies et le commerce des villes maritimes de France: adressées à G.-T. Raynal* (Genève, 1785), 10, 20.

53. Dubuisson, *Lettres critiques et politiques*, 241–42.

Chapter 2

1. In addition to the *South Carolina Weekly Gazette*, the same article was also published in the *United States Chronicle*, September 16, 1784. Figures were compiled from the slavevoyages. org database.

2. On the trade of cattle with the Spanish part of the islands, see Louis-Médéric Moreau de Saint-Méry, *Description topographique et politique de la partie espagnole Isle St.-Domingue*, vol. 2 (Philadelphia, 1796): 111–40.

3. The debate about whether historians should rely on these sources has been controversial for a long time. See Pierre Léon, "Structure du commerce extérieur et évolution industrielle de la France à la fin du XVIIIe siècle," in *Conjoncture économique, structures sociales: Hommages à Ernest Labrousse*, ed. Fernand Braudel (Paris: Mouton, 1974), 407–32; Michel Morineau, *Pour une histoire économique vraie* (Lille: Presses Universitaires de Lille, 1985); François Crouzet, *La guerre économique franco-anglaise au XVIIIe siècle* (Paris: Fayard, 2008), 24–34. On Arnould

and the Bureau, see Guillaume Daudin and Loïc Charles, "La collecte du chiffre au XVIIIe siècle: le Bureau de la balance du commerce et la production des données sur le commerce extérieur de la France," *Revue d'histoire moderne et contemporaine* 58, no. 1 (2011): 128–55; Ambroise-Marie Arnould, *De la Balance du commerce et des relations commerciales extérieures de la France dans toutes les parties du globe*, vol. 1 (Paris: Buisson, 1791), 124–25, 234, 333–35; Tarrade, *Le commerce colonial*, 2: 752.

4. ANOM, C4a 82, fo. 180; on the emergence of a "statistical state" in the eighteenth century, see Minard, "Volonté de savoir et emprise d'État," *Actes de la recherche en sciences sociales* 133, no. 1 (2000): 62–71; *The Political Intelligencer and New-Jersey Advertiser*, July 27, 1785, 2.

5. Nussbaum, "American Tobacco and French Politics 1783–1789," *Political Science Quarterly* 40, no. 4 (1925): 497–516; Jacob M. Price, *France and the Chesapeake, A History of the French Tobacco Monopoly, 1674–1791*, vol. 2 (Ann Arbor: University of Michigan Press, 1973), 761–69; MAE, CP EU 31, fo. 76, 378–84; MAE, CP EU 32, fo. 107–10, Calonne to Jefferson, October 22, 1786; MAE, CP, EU 32, fo. 416–17.

6. Jean Philippe Garran de Coulon, *Rapport sur les troubles de Saint-Domingue, fait au nom de la Commission des colonies, des Comités de salut public, de législation et de marine, réunis*, vol. 3 (Paris: Imprimerie Nationale, 1799), 400–404; ANOM, CC9a 11, "Commission déléguée aux Iles sous le vent: correspondance avec le ministre de la marine," 18 Brumaire year V (November 8, 1796); AN, D XXV 76, reg. 750, fo. 34; reg. 75, fo 15; reg. 753, fo. 22–25; Peter Hill, "La suite imprévue de l'alliance: l'ingratitude américaine, 1783–1789," in *La Révolution américaine et l'Europe*, ed. Claude Fohlen and Jacques Godechot (Paris: CNRS, 1979); Claude-Corentin Tanguy de La Boissière, *Mémoire sur la situation commerciale de la France avec les États-Unis de l'Amérique, depuis l'année 1775, jusques et y compris 1795, suivi d'un sommayre d'observations sur les États-Unis de l'Amérique* (s.l., 1795), 10, table C.

7. Tanguy de La Boissière, *Mémoire sur la situation commerciale de la France*, 38.

8. On consuls, see Anne Mézin, *Les consuls de France au siècle des Lumières: 1715–1792* (Paris: Ministère des affaires étrangères, Direction des archives et de la documentation, 1997); Jörg Ulbert, "La fonction consulaire à l'époque moderne: définition, état des connaissances et perspectives de recherches," in *La fonction consulaire à l'époque moderne: l'affirmation d'une institution économique et politique, 1500–1800*, ed. Jörg Ulbert and Gérard Le Bouëdec (Rennes: Presses universitaires de Rennes, 2006), 9–20; Stéphane Bégaud, Marc Belissa, and Joseph Visser, *Aux origines d'une alliance improbable: Le réseau consulaire français aux États-Unis (1776–1815)* (Bruxelles: Peter Lang, 2005), 130–47; Allan Potofsky, "Le corps consulaire français et le débat autour de la 'perte' des Amériques. Les intérêts mercantiles franco-américains et le commerce atlantique, 1763–1795," *Annales historiques de la Révolution française* 363, no. 1 (2011): 33–57; AN, AE, B I 372, Chateaufort to the Ministry, May 12, 1785.

9. AN, AE, B I 372, Chateaufort to the Ministry, September 12, 1785; AN, AE, B I 210, copy translated from the customs officer, March 24, 1787; AN, AE, B I 909, Laforest to the Ministry, January 6, 1786; AN, AE, B I 909, Laforest to the Ministry, August 1, 1786; AN, AE, B I 946, Barbé-Marbois to the Ministry, November 30, 1784; AN, AE, B III 445, Oster to the Ministry, January 5, 1787. The quote is from CADN, Philadelphie, consulat général, 119, "Laforest-De Marbois"; AN, AE, B I 210, Létombe to the Ministry, June 26, 1788. On Customs Houses in the United States, Gordon C., *Stagnation and Growth in the American Economy, 1784–1792* (New York: Garland, 1985), 52; Gautham Rao, *National Duties: Custom Houses and the Making of the American State* (Chicago: University of Chicago Press, 2016): 53–74.

10. P. C. Emmer, "Jesus Christ Was Good, but Trade Was Better; An Overview of the Transit Trade of the Dutch Antilles, 1634–1795," in *The Lesser Antilles in the Age of European Expansion*, ed. Robert L. Paquette and Stanley L. Engerman (Gainesville: University Press of Florida, 1996), 206–22; Victor Enthoven, "'That Abominable Nest of Pirates': St. Eustatius and the North Americans, 1680–1780," *Early American Studies* 10, no. 2 (2012): 239–301; DPL, Dutilh Papers, box 11, Pizany and Dubuc to Dutilh, August 2, 1789; APS, GP, *lett.* 2, S. Girard to J. Girard, April 22, 1789; MHS, MS 1152, vol. 2, Smith to John Stran, January 29, 1789.

11. AN, AE, B III 445; AN, AE, B I 372 Chateaufort to the Ministry, August 28, 1786; AN, AE, B I 372, letter no. 55, July 13, 1788; AN, AE, B I 910, Laforest to the Ministry, May 9, 1788; AN, AE, B I 372, Pétry to the Ministry, February 20, 1787; AN, AE, B I 946, November 15,

1784; AN, AE, B I 372; CADN, Philadelphia, consulat général, 119, Laforest to the Ministry, November 28, 1786. The quote is from ANOM, C9a 158, common letter no. 417.

12. AN, AE, B III 944 "Imports and Consumption of Sugar in Massachusetts," by Létombe|, March 26, 1785.

13. Richard Pares, *Yankees and Creoles: The Trade Between North America and the West Indies Before the American Revolution* (Cambridge, MA: Harvard University Press, 1956); Goebel, "The "New England Trade" and the French West Indies"; John J. McCusker, *Rum and the American Revolution: The Rum Trade and the Balance of Payments of the Thirteen Continental Colonies* (New York: Garland, 1989); Russell R. Menard and John J. McCusker, *The Economy of British America, 1607–1789* (Chapel Hill: University of North Carolina Press, 1985); Ronald Hoffman, ed., *The Economy of Early America: The Revolutionary Period, 1763–1790* (Charlottesville: University Press of Virginia, 1988); Bjork, *Stagnation and Growth*, 67, 77, 83, 97; Brooke Hunter, "Wheat, War, and the American Economy During the Age of Revolution," *William and Mary Quarterly* 62, no. 3 (2005): 505–26.

14. On the connection between New York and the Dutch Islands, see Cathy Matson, *Merchants and Empire: Trading in Colonial New York* (Baltimore: Johns Hopkins University Press, 1998), 191; AN, AE, B I, 444–45.

15. APS, GP, roll 2, J. Girard to S. Girard, October 3, 1784; CADN, New York 63, "passeports délivrés aux capitaines destinés aux ports des Antilles."

16. ANOM, C9a 158, common letter no. 466, March 25, 1787.

17. AN, AE, B I 909–10; AN, AE, B III 444–45.

18. For more economic data on port-cities: David Patrick Geggus, "Urban Development in 18th Century Saint-Domingue," *Bulletin du Centre d'histoire des espaces atlantiques* 5 (1990): 197–228; Geggus, "The Major Port Towns of Saint-Domingue in the Later Eighteenth Century," in *Atlantic Port Cities: Economy, Culture, and Society in the Atlantic World, 1650–1850,* ed. Franklin W. Knight and Peggy K. Liss (Knoxville: University of Tennessee Press, 1991), 87–116; Tarrade, *Le commerce colonial,* 2: 659–60.

19. The first quote is from AN, AE, B I 372, Chateaufort to the Ministry, July 19, 1785; the second quote: APS, GP, roll 2, J. Girard to S. Girard, October 3, 1784; the third quote: ANOM, C9a 158, common letter no. 466, March 25, 1787; CADN, New York 72, fo. 27, act of December 5, 1785; ANOM, C9a 159, intendant to the Ministry, November 20, 1787; MHS, MS 1152, vol. 2, S. Smith to William B. Smith, July 21, 1787.

20. APS, GP, bobine 2, fo. 113, December 3, 1784. Figures established from AN, AE, B I 209–10; CADN, New York 100, fo. 20–21; AN, AE, B I 372, Delaforest to the Ministry, October 7, 1784; AN, AE, B I 372, Delaforest to the Ministry, October 7, 1784; ANOM, C9a 159, letter du Commissaire de la Marine, March 1, 1787.

21. MHS, JSS, vol. 2, Smith to Captain William Denney, July 17, 1787; CADN, Philadelphie, Consulat général, 119, November 9, 1786; AN, AE, B I 210, Boston Consul to the Ministry, October 24, 1786. An almost identical denunciation took place at the Baltimore consulate on April 17, 1786. Three sailors accused Captain Nabre of the vessel Saint-Domingue of Bordeaux, of having deceived them by changing their destination from Le Havre to Baltimore. The captain fired the French crew to Americanize the vessel, prompting the retaliation of the sailors. See CADN, Baltimore, 81, no. 106; AN, AE, B III 449, Beudé to the Ministry of the Navy, November 13, 1787.

22. The rules regarding the nationality of vessels were defined in the navy ordinance, the Strasbourg decree of 1681, the ordinance of October 20, 1723, and the king's declaration of December 24, 1726. See René-Josué Valin, *Nouveau commentaire sur l'ordonnance de Marine du mois d'août 1681,* vol. 1 (La Rochelle: Chez Jérôme Légier et Pierre Mesnier, 1760), 279, 528, 533. See, for instance, the sale of five brigantines and schooners by American traders in 1784: ANOM, DPPC, NOTREP 131; ANOM, C9a 158, common letter no. 509, April 29, 1787. On what these constant changes meant for sailors, see Nathan Perl-Rosenthal, *Citizen Sailors: Becoming American in the Age of Revolution* (Cambridge, MA: Belknap Press of Harvard University Press, 2015), 88–93.

23. On the role of family ties in imperial governance, see Zacharias Moutoukias and Annie Vignal-Ramos, "Réseaux personnels et autorité coloniale: les négociants de Buenos Aires au XVIIIe siècle," *Annales. Histoire, Sciences Sociales* 47, no. 4–5 (1992): 889–915. On French colonial

careers in the eighteenth century, see Michel Vergé-Franceschi, "Fortune et plantations des administrateurs coloniaux aux îles d'Amérique aux XVIIe et XVIIIe siècles," in *Commerce et plantation dans la Caraïbe, XVIIIe et XIXe siècles*, ed. Paul Butel (Bordeaux: Maison des Pays ibériques, 1992), 115–43; Céline Ronsseray, "Administrer Cayenne: sociabilités, fidélités et pouvoir des fonctionnaires coloniaux en Guyane française au XVIIIe siècle" (PhD diss., Université de La Rochelle, 2007); Zélie Navarro-Andraud, "Les élites urbaines de Saint-Domingue dans la seconde moitié du XVIIIe siècle: la place des administrateurs coloniaux (1763–1792)" (PhD diss., Université de Toulouse II-Le Mirail, 2007).

24. AN, AE, B III 439, Ministry of the Navy to consuls and vice-consuls, January 23, 1785; AN, AE, B I 946, the Consul general to consuls et vice-consuls, June 15, 1785; AN, AE, B I 909, Consul general to the Ministry of Navy, January 6, 1786; ANOM, B I 192, fo. 59; AN, AE, B I 312, no. 65, consul at Charleston to the Ministry of Navy, March 9, 1789; ANOM, C9a 158, common letter to the Ministry, May 30, 1787.

25. On the identification revolution, see John Torpey, *The Invention of the Passport: Surveillance, Citizenship and the State* (Cambridge: Cambridge University Press, 2000). The policy of "registration" is a defining feature of the French monarchical state in the 1750s–1770s. See Vincent Denis and Vincent Milliot, "Police et identification dans la France des Lumières," *Genèses*, no. 54 (2004): 4–27; ANOM, B 192, fo. 59–61; ANOM, C9a 157, intendant to the Ministry, August 30, 1787.

26. Cathy Matson, "The Revolution, Constitution and the New Nation," in *The Cambridge Economic History of the United States*, ed. Stanley Engerman and Robert E. Gallman (Cambridge: Cambridge University Press, 2001), 1:363–401; Marie-Jeanne Rossignol, *The Nationalist Ferment: The Origins of U.S. Foreign Policy, 1789–1812* (Columbus: Ohio State University Press, 2004); *Cumberland Gazette*, August 24, 1786, 2; AN, AE, B I 906, Laforest to the Ministry, March 2, 1786; AN, AE, B I 372, Pétry to the Ministry, March 27, 1789.

27. On prejudices toward creoles and the fractiousness of creole identities, see Cécile Vidal, "Francité et situation coloniale. Nation, empire et race en Louisiane française (1699–1769)," *Annales. Histoire, Sciences sociales* 64, no. 5 (2009): 1019–50. The quotes are from MAE, CCC Portsmouth, Ducher to the Ministry, July 6, 1786; AN, AE, B I 209, fol. 310; ANOM, F2b 8, "Mémoire sur la contrebande, 1787," fo. 283; AN, AE, B I 209, fo. 364; Raynal, *Essai sur l'administration de Saint-Domingue* (Paris, 1785): 26–27.

28. AN, AE, B I 372, Chateaufort to the Ministry, September 12, 1785. This prejudice was linked to the common bias toward the "Usurer Jew" in eighteenth-century France. See Francesca Trivellato, "Credit, Honor, and the Early Modern French Legend of the Jewish Invention of Bills of Exchange," *Journal of Modern History* 84, no. 2 (2012): 289–334; MAE, MD, EU 9, "mémoire de Létombe pour l'année 1785," fo. 65.

29. CADN, Philadelphie, consulat général, 19, administrateurs de Saint-Domingue au consul général, September 27, 1787; APS, GP, bobine 2, J. to S. Girard, October 24, 1784, fo. 88; AN, AE, B I 210, consul de Boston to the Ministry, no. 42, January 19, 1787; AN, AE, B I 946, consul général to the Ministry de la Marine, no. 100, June 16, 1785; ANOM, F2b 8, "Mémoire sur la contrebande, 1787," fo. 264.

30. MAE CP EU 31, "tableau des navires et matelots employés pour le commerce de la Grande-Bretagne avec les États-Unis de l'Amérique septentrionale" February 20, 1786, fo. 133–136, fo. 199; MAE, CCC suppl. 4, fo. 312; Frances Armytage, *The Free Port System in the British West Indies, a Study in Commercial Policy, 1766–1822* (London: Longmans, 1953), 56. On the luxury debate, see Henry C. Clark, *Compass of Society. Commerce and Absolutism in Old-Regime France* (Plymouth, MA: Lexington Books, 2007), 257–82; Shovlin, "The Cultural Politics of Luxury in Eighteenth Century France," *French Historical Studies* 23, no. 4 (2000): 578–84; ANOM, F2b 8, "Mémoire sur la contrebande, 1787," fo. 224. On the debate between Dupont and Beccaria, see Cesare Beccaria, *Des délits et des peines* (Paris: Flammarion, 1991), 151–53; Bernard E. Harcourt, *The Illusion of Free Markets: Punishment and the Myth of Natural Order* (Cambridge, MA: Harvard University Press, 2011), 60–62; Michael Kwass, "The Global Underground," in *The French Revolution in Global Perspective*, ed. Suzanne Desan, Lynn Hunt, and William Max Nelson (Ithaca, NY: Cornell University Press, 2013), 15–31, 26–27.

31. In 1784, French merchants officially bought ten brigantines or schooners from American sellers in New York, and twenty-nine in Boston. See AN, AE, B I 372, Pétry to the Ministry de

la Marine, January 12, 1786; AN, AE, B I 946, Laforest to Castries, March 14, 1785; AN, AE, B I 372, Pétry to La Luzerne, January 6, 1789; AN, AE, B I 910, Laforest to La Luzerne, May 9, 1788.

32. On the role of credit and trust in global trade, see Pierre Gervais, "Neither Imperial, Nor Atlantic: A Merchant Perspective on International Trade in the Eighteenth Century," *History of European Ideas* 34, no. 4 (2008): 465–73; Marzagalli, "Establishing Transatlantic Trade Networks in Time of War: Bordeaux and the United States, 1793-1815," *Business History Review* 79, no. 4 (2005): 811–44; Xabier Lamikiz, *Trade and Trust in the Eighteenth-Century Atlantic World: Spanish Merchants and Their Overseas Networks* (Woodbridge, UK: Boydell & Brewer, 2010); Tijl Vanneste, *Global Trade and Commercial Networks: Eighteenth-Century Diamond Merchants* (London: Routledge, 2011): 84–88.

33. On the role of sea captains in the French colonial trade, see M. Weuves, le jeune, *Réflexions historiques et politiques sur le commerce de France avec ses colonies de l'Amérique* (Geneva: Chez L. Cellot, 1780), 29–34. On the risks involved, see Marzagalli, *Bordeaux et les États-Unis*, 262–66. On merchants' skills: Pierre Jeannin, "Distinction des compétences et niveaux de qualification: les savoirs négociants dans l'Europe moderne," in *Marchands d'Europe: pratiques et savoirs à l'époque moderne* (Paris: Presses de l'Ecole Normale Supérieure, 2002), 309–40. Another example is the planter Roberjot Lartigue who entrusted the management to the Port-au-Prince firm Daubagna Trigant & Cie which imported foodstuffs from the United States. See CADN, Philadelphie, consulat général, 119, Roberjot Lartigue to Laforêt, February 3, 1786. On Packer Dering: NYPL, *Henry Packer Dering Papers (HPDP)*, diary, February 3, 1786; April 4, 1787; July 31, 1787; August 6, 1787.

34. On merchants in revolutionary Philadelphia, see Cathy Matson, "A Port in the Storm: Philadelphia's Commerce During the Atlantic Revolutionary Era," in *Revolution! The Atlantic World Reborn*, ed. Bender Thomas, Dubois Laurent, and Rabinowitz Richard (New York: New York Historical Society, 2011), 65–90; John Bach McMaster, *The Life and Times of Stephen Girard: Mariner and Merchant* (London: J. B. Lippincott, 1918), 122–65; Albert J. Gares, "Stephen Girard's West Indian Trade 1789-1812," *Pennsylvania Magazine of History and Biography* 72, no. 4 (1948): 312; MHS, MS 1152; NYHS, *Lynch & Stoughton papers*, *Gelston & Saltonstall papers*; NYPL *Gouverneur & Kemble letterbook*.

35. Richard Smith Chew, "The Measure of Independence: From the American Revolution to the Market Revolution in the Mid-Atlantic" (PhD diss., College of William and Mary, 2002), 138; Stuart Weems Bruchey, *Robert Oliver, Merchant of Baltimore, 1783-1819* (Baltimore: Johns Hopkins University Press, 1956), 33; NARA, Mid-Atlantic Regional Branch, Philadelphia, RG 36 1149, vol. 2; CADN, Charleston, 143, Gadelins to Hamelin, July 2, 1785.

36. Thomas M. Doerflinger, *A Vigorous Spirit of Enterprise: Merchants and Economic Development in Revolutionary Philadelphia* (Chapel Hill: University of North Carolina Press, 1986), 246–50; NYSA, *Mumford papers*, 7, Mumford to Daniel Rodman, December 7, 1790; Carl Seaburg and Stanley Paterson, *Merchant Prince of Boston: Colonel T. H. Perkins, 1764-1854* (Cambridge, MA: Harvard University Press, 1971); MHS, MS 1152, vol. 2, Smith to Donnell, December 17, 1790.

37. JCB, Brown & Benson Papers, box 351, Wall & Tardy to Nicholas Brown, January 3, 1783; GHC, 97, October 1997, 20; Élisabeth Escalle and Mariel Gouyon Guillaume, *Francs-maçons des loges françaises "aux Amériques" 1770-1850. Contribution à l'étude de la société créole* (Paris: E. Escalle et M. Gouyon-Guillaume, 1993), 212, 825; Butel, *La croissance commerciale bordelaise dans la seconde moitié du XVIIIe siècle*, vol. 2 (Lille: Service de reproduction des thèses, Université de Lille III, 1973), 903, 973–78; Philippe Gardey, *Négociants et marchands de Bordeaux: de la guerre d'Amérique à la Restauration (1780-1830)* (Paris: Presses de l'Université Paris-Sorbonne, 2009), 146; Jacques de Cauna, *L'Eldorado des Aquitains: Gascons, Basques et Béarnais aux îles d'Amérique (XVIIe–XVIIIe siècles)* (Biarritz: Atlantica, 1998), 365; "American War of Independence—At Sea, Officers," http://www.awiatsea.com/Officers/Officers%20A.html; Manuel Covo, "I, François B.: Merchant, Protestant and Refugee—a Tale of Failure in the Atlantic World," *French History* 25, no. 1 (2011): 69–88.

38. On the strategy of commercial integration, see Albane Forestier, "A 'Considerable Credit' in the Late Eighteenth-Century French West Indian Trade: The Chaurands of Nantes," *French History* 25, no. 1 (2011): 48–68. On Seguineau, see Roger Massio, "Un dossier de

plantation de Saint-Domingue (1745–1829)," *Revue d'histoire de l'Amérique française* 5, no. 4 (1952): 542–77; Cheney, *Cul de Sac*, 114–15. On Cottineau: CADN, Baltimore 80, bilan de la société Monbos, Latil & Cie, May 15, 1785; Gabriel Debien, *Plantations et esclaves à Saint-Domingue: sucrerie Cottineau* (Dakar: Université de Dakar, Publications de la section d'histoire, 1962).

39. ANOM, DPPC, NOTSDOM 1681, inventaire après décès, April 1790. For comparison with some of the richest free people of color's wealth, see Dominique Rogers, "De l'origine du préjugé de couleur en Haïti," in *Haïti, première république noire*, ed. Marcel Dorigny (Paris: Société française d'histoire d'outre-mer, 2003), 83–101, 90–91.

40. CADN, New York, 72, no. 13; ANOM, C9a 157, common letter no 76, April 29, 1786.

41. *Independent Chronicle*, August 30, 1781, 2; ANOM, DPPC, NOTSDOM 411, acte July 11, 1786; ANOM, DPPC, NOTSDOM 1362; ANOM, DPPC, NOTSDOM 411, acte August 26, 1786; *Almanach royal de Saint-Domingue*, 71; *État détaillé des indemnités* (Paris: Imprimerie Royale, 1831), 214–15; ANOM, DPPC, NOTSDOM 870, actes de procuration June 6, 1788. For instance, Jacques Gramon, a sea captain officially based in Providence, Rhode Island, was constantly traveling between the United States and Cap-Français. Abel Hamelin, a merchant from Rennes, who moved to Philadelphia in March 1782 and filed for bankruptcy in July 1784, tried his luck again in Charleston by multiplying ventures to Cap-Français. See *Supplément à la feuille du Cap-François*, April 12, 1788, 789; LC, D&W, *lett.*, fo. 171; CADN, Charleston, 143, "letters from Abel Hamelin."

42. ANOM, DPPC, NOTSDOM 1681, inventaire après décès, April 1790; AN, AE, B I 209, fo. 364; AN, 208 Mi 1, "Compromise and reparation, Jacob Mayer and John Girard de Mombrun."

43. McMaster, *The Life and Times of Stephen Girard*, 72; LC, D&W, *lett.*, Dutilh to Dursse, February 21, 1785; ANOM, C9a 157, common letter to the Ministry, May 29, 1786; HSP, Claude Unger Collection, Box 9; MHS, MS 1152, vol. 2, Smith to Perkins Burling & Perkins, June 7, 1789; DPL, Dutilh Papers, box 3, Mesniers frères to Dutilh, May 3 1785.

44. On the role of the law in market rules of the eighteenth century, see Amalia D. Kessler, *A Revolution in Commerce: The Parisian Merchant Court and the Rise of Commercial Society in Eighteenth-Century France* (New Haven, CT: Yale University Press, 2007), 141–87; McMaster, *The Life and Times of Stephen Girard*, 115–20.

45. MHS, MS 125, 1–4; CADN, Baltimore, 81, "papiers concernant les Srs. Casenave, Dumeste et Bentalou."

46. ANOM, E 218, "Hasket-Derbie, négociant de Salem, Comté d'Essex, dans l'Amérique septentrionale contre Barrère (Jean-Marc), LeMayre (Alexandre), négociants à Port-au-Prince, 1785–1787."

Chapter 3

1. *Réflexions sur le commerce* (Paris, 1789), 4; *The Papers of Thomas Jefferson (JP)* (Princeton : Princeton University Press, 1955-), vol. 16, 104.

2. Léon Deschamps, *Les colonies pendant la Révolution: la Constituante et la réforme coloniale* (Paris: Perrin, 1898); Jules François Saintoyant, *La colonisation française pendant la Révolution (1789–1799)*, vol. 1, *Les assemblées révolutionnaires et les colonies* (Paris: La Renaissance du livre, 1930); Valerie Quinney, "Decisions on Slavery, the Slave-Trade and Civil Rights for Negroes in the Early French Revolution," *Journal of Negro History* 55, no. 2 (1970): 117–30; Tarrade, "Les colonies et les principes de 1789: les Assemblées révolutionnaires face au problème de l'esclavage," *Revue française d'histoire d'outre-mer* 76, no. 282–83 (1989): 9–34; Geggus, "Racial Equality, Slavery, and Colonial Secession During the Constituent Assembly," *American Historical Review* 94, no. 5 (1989): 1290–308; Tarrade, "La Révolution et le commerce colonial: le régime de l'Exclusif de 1789 à 1800," in *État, finances et économie pendant la Révolution française*, ed. Comité pour l'histoire économique et financière de la France (Paris: CHEFF, 1991): 553–64; Florence Gauthier, *L'aristocratie de l'épiderme: le combat de la Société des citoyens de couleur, 1789–1791* (Paris: CNRS, 2007); Josep M. Fradera, "L'esclavage et la logique constitutionnelle des empires," *Annales. Histoire, Sciences Sociales* 63, no. 3 (2008): 533–60.

3. Shovlin, *Political Economy of Virtue: Luxury, Patriotism, and the Origins of the French Revolution* (Ithaca, NY: Cornell University Press, 2006), 5. For a broader discussion on the notion of regeneration as a leitmotif of the French Revolution, see Mona Ozouf, "La Révolution française et la formation de l'homme nouveau," in *L'Homme régénéré: essais sur la Révolution française* (Paris: Gallimard, 1989), 116–57; Alyssa Goldstein Sepinwall, "Les paradoxes de la régénération révolutionnaire," *Annales historiques de la Révolution française*, no. 321 (2000): 69–90; Jeremy J. Whiteman, *Reform, Revolution, and French Global Policy, 1787–1791* (Aldershot, UK: Ashgate, 2003), 139–68; William Max Nelson, "Colonizing France. Revolutionary Regeneration and the First French Empire," in *The French Revolution in Global Perspective*, ed. Suzanne Desan, Lynn Hunt and Nelson, 73–85.

4. Henri Sée, "The Normandy Chamber of Commerce and the Commercial Treaty of 1786," *Economic History Review* 2, no. 2 (January 1930): 308–13; Jean-Pierre Hirsch, "Les milieux du commerce, l'esprit de système et le pouvoir à la veille de la Révolution," *Annales. Économies, Sociétés, Civilisations* 30, no. 6 (1975): 1337–70; Morieux, "Les nations et les intérêts. Les manufacturiers, les institutions représentatives et le langage des intérêts dans le traité de commerce franco-anglais de 1786–1787," in *La concurrence des savoirs. France-Grande-Bretagne, XVIIIe-XIXe siècles*, ed. Christophe Charle and Julien Vincent (Rennes: Presses universitaires de Rennes, 2011), 39–74; Charles Walton, "The Fall from Eden. The Free-Trade Origins of the French Revolution," in Desan, Hunt and Nelson, *The French Revolution in Global Perspective*, 44–56; Tarrade, *Le commerce colonial*, 2: 706–11; Charles Frostin, *Histoire de l'autonomisme colon*, 2: 812.

5. Steven L. Kaplan, *Bread, Politics and Political Economy in the Reign of Louis XV* (The Hague: Martinus Nijhoff, 1976); Cynthia A. Bouton, *The Flour War: Gender, Class, and Community in Late Ancien Régime French Society* (University Park: Pennsylvania State University Press, 1993); Debien, "La nourriture des esclaves sur les plantations des Antilles françaises aux XVIIe et XVIIIe siècles," *Caribbean Studies* 4, no. 2 (1964): 3–27; Bernard Foubert, *Les habitations Laborde à Saint-Domingue dans la seconde moitié du dix-huitième siècle: contribution à l'histoire d'Haïti* (Lille: ANRT, 1991), 283–91; Bertie Mandelblatt, "How Feeding Slaves Shaped the French Atlantic: Mercantilism and Food Provisioning in the Franco-Caribbean during the 17th and 18th centuries," in *The Political Economy of Empire in the Early Modern World*, ed. Pernille Røge and Sophius Reinert (New York: Palgrave Macmillan, 2013), 192–220.

6. Elijah Wilson Lyon, *The Man Who Sold Louisiana: The Career of Francois Barbe-Marbois* (Norman: University of Oklahoma Press, 1942), 3–71; Ronsseray, "Administrer Cayenne"; Loïc Charles and Paul Cheney, "The Colonial Machine Dismantled: Knowledge and Empire in the French Atlantic," *Past & Present* 219, no. 1 (2013): 127–63, 140–46; Alexandre-Stanislas de Wimpffen and Pierre Pluchon, *Haïti au XVIIIe siècle: richesse et esclavage dans une colonie française* (Paris: Karthala, 1993), 176; Vergé-Franceschi, "Fortune et plantations," 115–43; Navarro-Andraud, "Les élites urbaines de Saint-Domingue"; LC, "Journal de la commission de Saint-Domingue," fo. 148; François Regourd, "Hommes de pouvoir et d'influence dans une capitale coloniale: Intendants et gouverneurs à Port-au-Prince dans la seconde moitié du XVIIIe siècle," in *Des hommes et des pouvoirs dans la ville, XIVe-XXe siècles: France, Allemagne, Angleterre, Italie*, ed. Josette Pontet (Talence: CESURB Histoire, Université Michel de Montaigne-Bordeaux 3, 1999), 208; Prosper Boissonnade, *Saint-Domingue à la veille de la révolution et la question de la représentation coloniale aux États généraux (Janvier 1788–7 juillet 1789)* (Paris: J. Geuthner, 1906), 46.

7. ANOM, C9a 162, Barbé-Marbois to the Minister of the Navy: "Ordonnance portant permission d'introduire jusqu'au premier Juillet de cette année dans les ports d'entrepôt de la partie française de St. Domingue des farines et du biscuit de farine étrangère"; ANOM, C9a 163, Du Chilleau to the Minister, March 28, 1789.

8. ANOM, C9a 163, "Ordonnance de M. le gouverneur général concernant la liberté du commerce pour la Partie du Sud de St. Domingue"; Marie Charles du Chilleau, *Ordonnance (de M. le Gouverneur général) concernant l'introduction des farines étrangères dans les ports d'entrepôt de la partie française de l'isle de Saint-Domingue* (Port-au-Prince: Imprimerie de Bourdon, 1789); ANOM, C9a 163, "Discours de Barbé de Marbois prononcé dans la cour, délibérant

sur le nouveau régime proposé par M. le Gouverneur Général pour l'admission des étrangers dans la partie du Sud de la Colonie," May 27, 1789.

9. Maurice Begouën Demeaux, *Mémorial d'une famille du Havre, Stanislas Foäche, Négociant de Saint-Domingue, 1737–1806*, vol. 1 (Paris: Larose, 1951), 132, 134; ANOM, C9a 163, "lettre de l'intendant n° 525," May 29, 1789; ANOM, C9a 163, Barbé-Marbois to the Minister, May 24, 1789; May 29, 1789; M. Portelance, *Cahier d'un philosophe, commissaire de la noblesse dans deux bailliages ou Doléances d'un Américain persécuté* (Paris, 1789), 25–26; Forestier, "A 'Considerable Credit,'" 48–68.

10. *Affiches américaines*, July 15, 1789, 387; Demeaux, *Mémorial*, 1: 133.

11. *Arrêt de l'assemblée provinciale de la partie du nord de Saint-Domingue, séant au Cap, contre Barbé-Marbois, ses conseils, complices et adhérents, en date du 21 septembre 1789* (s.l., 1789); Blanche Maurel, *Saint-Domingue et la Révolution française, les représentants des colons en France de 1789 à 1795* (Paris: Presses universitaires de France, 1943), 10; François Barbé de Marbois, *Mémoire et observations du sieur Barbé de Marbois, sur une dénonciation signée par treize de MM. les députés de Saint-Domingue, et faite à l'Assemblée nationale au nom d'un des trois comités de la colonie. (18 juin 1790.)* (Paris: Knapen et fils, 1790), 48; Jean-Michel Deveau, *Le Commerce rochelais face à la Révolution* (La Rochelle: Rumeur des âges, 1989), 193; *Lettre de l'assemblée générale de la partie française de Saint-Domingue aux chambres du commerce et manufactures du royaume* (Paris, 1790), 5.

12. *New York Daily Gazette*, October 27, 1789; *New York Daily Gazette*, November 25, 1789, 2.

13. Oliver Gliech, *Saint-Domingue und die Französische Revolution: Das Ende der weissen Herrschaft in einer karibischen Plantagenwirtschaft* (Cologne: Böhlau Verlag, 2011), 225, 232; Jeremy D. Popkin, "Saint-Domingue, Slavery, and the Origins of the French Revolution," in *From Deficit to Deluge: The Origins of the French Revolution*, ed. Dale Kenneth Van Kley and Thomas E Kaiser (Stanford, CA: Stanford University Press, 2011), 220–48; Maurel, *Cahiers de doléances de la colonie de Saint-Domingue pour les États généraux de 1789* (Paris: E. Leroux, 1933), 71; *Réclamations pour les colonies des Antilles adressées au Roi et à la nation* (Paris, 1789), 39; *Lettre des Commissaires de la Colonie de Saint-Domingue au Roi* (Paris, 1788), 7.

14. Karine Audran, "Les négoces portuaires bretons sous la Révolution et l'Empire: bilan et stratégies" (PhD diss., Université de Bretagne-Sud, 2007), 1: 446; Jacques Godechot, "Les relations économiques entre la France et les États-Unis de 1778 à 1789," *French Historical Studies* 1, no. 1 (1958): 26–39; Hill, "La suite imprévue de l'alliance" 385–98; Marzagalli, "The Failure of a Transatlantic Alliance?," 456–464; Joseph Letaconnoux, *Le Comité des députés extraordinaires des manufactures et du commerce de France et l'œuvre économique de l'Assemblée constituante, 1789–1791* (Paris: E. Leroux, 1913), 7.

15. Gliech, *Saint-Domingue und die Französische Revolution*, 246; Ronsseray, "De l'aventurier au fonctionnaire ou la transformation de l'administrateur colonial au XVIIIe siècle en Guyane française," in *GIS Réseau Amérique latine. Actes du 1er Congrès du GIS Amérique latine: Discours et pratiques de pouvoir en Amérique latine, de la période précolombienne à nos jours, 3–4 novembre 2005, Université de La Rochelle* (November 2005), https://halshs.archives-ouvertes.fr/hal shs-00005635/document.

16. LC, "Lettre de M. Malouet| à M. le Mis de Gouy d'Arsy, le 4 novembre 1788" in *Journal de la commission de Saint-Domingue*; Jérémy Richard, "Droits de l'Homme, droits de l'Humanité et droits naturels: la question de l'esclavage des Noirs dans l'argumentaire de la Société des Amis des Noirs et du Club Massiac" in *Droits de l'homme et colonies: de la mission de civilisation au droit à l'autodétermination*, ed. Alexandre Deroche, Éric Gasparini and Martial Mathieu (Aix-en-Provence: Presses universitaires d'Aix-Marseille, 2017), 83–99.

17. Garrigus, "'Des François qui gémissent sous le joug de l'oppression': Les libres de couleur et la question de l'identité au début de la Révolution française," in *Français? La nation en débat entre colonies et métropole*, ed. Cécile Vidal (Paris: Éditions de l'École des hautes études en sciences sociales, 2013), 149–68, 154–56.

18. Maurel, *Saint-Domingue et la Révolution française*, 9; Gliech, *Saint-Domingue und die Französische Revolution*, 242–49; Letaconnoux, *Le Comité des députés extraordinaires*, 8; George Chalmers, *Analyse de la force de la Grande-Bretagne sous le règne de Georges III et sous les quatre règnes précédens* (London, 1789); Jacques-François Bégouën, *Précis sur l'importance des colonies et sur la servitude des Noirs* (Paris, 1789).

19. Étienne Clavière and Jacques-Pierre Brissot de Warville, *De la France et des États-Unis* (Paris: Éditions du CTHS, 1996); Jean-Antoine-Nicolas de Caritat marquis de Condorcet, *De l'influence de la Révolution d'Amérique sur l'Europe* (1786; repr., Houille: Éditions Manucius, 2009); Max M. Mintz, "Condorcet's Reconsideration of America as a Model for Europe," *Journal of the Early Republic* 11, no. 4 (1991): 493–506; Jean Barré de Saint-Venant, *Mémoire sur le commerce étranger avec les colonies françaises de l'Amérique, présenté à la chambre d'agriculture du Cap, le 17 février 1784* (Paris: Cuchet, 1785); Brissot de Warville, *Réflexions sur l'admission aux états généraux des députés de Saint-Domingue* (Paris, 1789), 7–8. More specifically on the debate over the profitability of enslaved labor and wage labor, see Caroline Oudin-Bastide and Philippe Steiner, *Calcul et morale. Coûts de l'esclavage et valeur de l'émancipation (XVIIIe–XIXe siècles)* (Paris: Albin Michel, 2015), 52–57.

20. Louis-Marthe de Gouy d'Arsy, *Précis remis par M. le marquis De Gouy D'Arsy, aux commissaires auxquels l'Assemblée nationale a renvoyé l'examen de la demande faite par les représentans de la colonie, pour obtenir provisoirement la liberté de se procurer des farines, dont elle manque absolument* (Versailles: Baudoin, 1789); Nicolas-Robert de Cocherel, *Réplique de M. de Cocherel, député de St.-Domingue, aux inculpations du commerce contre M. le marquis Du Chilleau* (Versailles: Baudoin, 1789); Cocherel, *Motion de M. de Cocherel, député de Saint-Domingue, à la séance du 29 août 1789* (Versailles: Baudoin, 1789); Jean-François Reynaud de Villevert, *Motion de M. le Comte de Reynaud, député de Saint-Domingue à la séance du 31 août* (Versailles: Baudouin, 1789); Philippe-Denis Pierres, *Réponse des députés des manufactures et du commerce de France, aux motions de MM. de Cocherel & de Raynaud, députés de l'isle de St. Domingue à l'Assemblée nationale.—Signé par 21 députés des ports de mer français et daté du 24 septembre 1789* (Versailles: Imprimerie de Ph.-D. Pierres, 1789); *Réponse succincte des députés de S.-Domingue au Mémoire des commerçants des ports de mer, distribué dans les bureaux de l'Assemblée nationale, le 9 octobre 1789* (Versailles: Baudouin, 1789); Cocherel, *Dernière Réponse de M. de Cocherel, député de S. Domingue, à MM. les députés du commerce* (Versailles: Baudoin, 1789).

21. Jean-Yves Grenier, "Faut-il rétablir l'esclavage en France?," *Revue d'histoire moderne et contemporaine* 57, no. 2 (2010): 7–49, 37–49; Reynaud de Villevert, *Motion de M. le Comte de Reynaud*; Cocherel, *Motion de M. de Cocherel*; Marcel Gauchet, *La Révolution des droits de l'homme* (Paris: Gallimard, 1989), 36–59; Antoine de Baecque, Wolfgang Schmale, and Michel Vovelle, *L'an 1 des droits de l'homme* (Paris: Presses du CNRS, 1988), 13.

22. Saint-Venant, *Mémoire*.

23. Laure Pineau-Defois, "Une élite d'ancien régime: les grands négociants nantais dans la tourmente révolutionnaire (1780–1793)," *Annales historiques de la Révolution française*, no. 358 (2010): 97–118; BNF, Arsenal, *Le système des colonies*, H 14339 (7), 3; Debien, "Les débuts de la Révolution à Saint-Domingue vus des plantations Bréda," *Notes d'histoire coloniale*, no. 45 (1956): 143–73, 165.

24. Moreau de Saint-Méry, however, thought that this donation was a pure invention. See ANOM, 87 MIOM 95, fo. 214, April 30, 1791; *Lettre des colons résidens à St. Domingue, au Roi. le 31 mai 1788. Signé, les propriétaires planteurs de la colonie de Saint-Domingue* (Paris, 1788), 11; BNF, Arsenal, 8 H 14342 (1), *Requête présentée aux États-Généraux du royaume, le 8 juin 1789, par les députés de la colonie de Saint-Domingue*; Jacques-Louis de Thébaudières, *Vues générales sur les moyens de concilier l'intérêt du commerce national avec la prospérité des Colonies* (Paris, 1789), 11.

25. Frostin, *Les révoltes blanches*, 241; Gauthier, *L'aristocratie de l'épiderme*, 50–52; *Archives parlementaires (AP)*, vol. X, 266–67.

26. *L'Ami des Patriotes ou le Défenseur de la Révolution*, vol. 3, no. 44 (Paris: Demonville, 1791), 404; *Adresse à l'Assemblée nationale par les représentants de la Commune de Rouen* (Paris, 1789), 9. .

27. *AP*, t. X, 351; *AP*, t. XII, 322–23; Emmanuel-Joseph Sieyès, *Observations sur le rapport du comité de constitution concernant la nouvelle constitution de la France* (Versailles, 1789), 4.

28. Éric Gojosso, *Le concept de République en France (XVIe–XVIIIe siècle)* (Aix-en-Provence: Presses universitaires d'Aix-Marseille, 1998), 392–98; Pierre Serna, "Toute révolution est guerre d'indépendance," in *Pour quoi faire la Révolution*, ed. Jean-Luc Chappey et al. (Marseille: Agone, 2012), 19–49; Marie-Vic Ozouf-Marignier, *La formation des départements: la représentation du*

territoire français à la fin du 18e siècle, 2nd ed. (Paris: Édtitions de l'École des hautes études en sciences sociales, 1992); Roland Debbasch, *Le Principe révolutionnaire d'unité et d'indivisibilité de la République: essai d'histoire politique* (Paris: Economica, 1988), 79, 90–94.

29. *AP,* t. VIII, 553–54; Letaconnoux, *Le Comité des députés extraordinaires,* 22 Louis-Charles Gillet-Lajaqueminière, *Rapport fait au nom de la section du comité d'agriculture et de commerce, chargée par l'Assemblée nationale de l'examen de la réclamation des députés de Saint-Domingue, relative à l'approvisionnement de l'isle* (Paris: Baudouin, 1789), 41–42; AN, D XXV 89, vol. 1, fo 4, 86th session, January 20, 1790.

30. ADLA, C 592, "Délibérations de la Chambre de commerce de Nantes," session of September 2, 1789, fo. 14; Deveau, *Le Commerce rochelais,* 135–36; *JP,* vol. 16, 87; Bégouën, *Précis,* 24–25.

31. On the free trade crisis in the Lesser Antilles and the tensions between white planters and free people of color, see William S. Cormack, *Patriots, Royalists, and Terrorists in the West Indies: The French Revolution in Martinique and Guadeloupe, 1789–1802* (Toronto: University of Toronto Press, 2019), 63, 67–84. On Barnave: *Patriote français,* March 2, 1790, 1; *AP,* t. XII, 6, 78–92; Souad Degachi, *Barnave, rapporteur du comité des colonies* (Révolution Française.net., 2007). https://revolution-francaise.net/editions/barnave_colonies_degac hi2.pdf.

32. *AP,* t. XII, 71–72.

33. Deveau, *Le Commerce rochelais,* 203; Jean-Baptiste Duvergier, *Collection complète des lois, décrets, ordonnances, règlemens et avis du Conseil d'État,* vol. 1 (Paris: Imprimerie A. Guyot, 1834), 165. On the debates over the liberalizing of the East Indian Trade, see Whiteman, *Reform, Revolution and French Global Policy,* 191–99; Elizabeth Cross, "India and the Compagnie des Indes in the Age of the French Revolution," *French Historical Studies* 44, no. 3 (2021): 455–76.

34. Demeaux, *Mémorial,* 135, 139; AN, D XXV 59, dos. 583, "Discours de Bacon de la Chevalerie"; Debien, "Nouvelles de Saint-Domingue: 1re Assemblée coloniale, avril-août 1790, soulèvement des gens de couleur, août-octobre 1791," *Annales historiques de la Révolution française* 31, no. 158 (1959) and 32, no. 160 (1960): 7.

35. *Débats entre les accusateurs et les accusés, dans l'affaire des colonies,* vol. 1 (Paris: Imprimerie nationale, 1794), 65; *Ouverture de tous les ports de la colonie aux étrangers* (Port-au-Prince: Imprimerie de Mozard, 1790); Martine Kahane, "La première assemblée coloniale révolutionnaire à Saint-Domingue: l'assemblée de Saint-Marc" (PhD diss., École des Chartes, 1970); Debien, *Nouvelles de Saint-Domingue,* 23; AN, D XXV 59, dos. 586; Garrigus, *Before Haiti,* 171–94; Gliech, *Saint-Domingue und die Französische Revolution,* 265.

36. J.-Félix Carteau, *Soirées Bermudiennes, ou Entretiens sur les évènemens qui ont opéré la ruine de la partie française de l'île Saint-Domingue, ouvrage où l'on expose les causes de ces évènemens, les moyens employés pour renverser cette colonie* (Bordeaux: Pellier-Lawalle, 1802), 45; Debien, *Les colons de Saint-Domingue et la Révolution: Essai sur le Club Massiac (Août 1789-Août 1792)* (Paris: Armand Colin, 1953), 227–34; ANOM, CC9a 4, "Copie de la requête des caboteurs du Port-au-Prince en date du 3 Août 1790"; Garran de Coulon, *Rapport sur les troubles de Saint-Domingue,* 1: 247–51, 267–72; AN, D XXV 65, dos. 658 "registres de la paroisse de l'Acul, 22 août 1790," dos. 659, "registres de Fort-Dauphin, 20 septembre 1790."

37. *Discours prononcé à l'Assemblée nationale le 2 octobre 1790* (Paris, 1790), 17; *AP,* t. XIX, 569; François-Raymond-Joseph de Pons, *Observations sur la situation politique de Saint-Domingue, par M. de Pons, habitant du quartier d'Ouanaminthe, isle & côte de St-Domingue* (Paris: Imprimerie de Quillau, 1790), 10. Among other pamphlets targeting Barnave's colonial policy: Thomas Millet, *Examen du rapport fait par M. Barnave à l'Assemblée nationale sur l'affaire de Saint-Domingue* (Paris: Chez Lejay fils, 1790), 84; Moreau de Saint-Méry|, *Opinion de M. Moreau de Saint-Méry, député de la Martinique à l'Assemblée nationale. Sur les dangers de la division du Ministère de la marine et des colonies, du 28 octobre 1790* (Paris: Imprimerie nationale, 1790), 13.

38. *Journal général de Saint-Domingue,* no. 33, 153; ANOM, F3, 195, "lettre du 12 août 1790"; AN, D XXV 57, dos. 558, August 12, 1790; AN, D XXV 89, registre de la commission générale, session of January 30, 1791; AN, D XXV 57, dos. 558; AMD, BB⁴ 6, "mémoire du roi pour servir d'instruction particulière au Sieur de Villages, commandant les forces navales de l'État stationnées aux Isles Sous-le-Vent," fo. 7–16.

Chapter 4

1. Rogers, "Vincent Ogé," in *Dictionnaire des gens de couleur dans la France moderne. Paris et son bassin*, ed. Erick Noël (Geneva: Droz, 2011), 108–10.

2. Debien, *Les colons de Saint-Domingue et la Révolution*, 287.

3. Gouy d'Arsy, *Louis Marthe Degouy à ses commettants* (Paris, 1791), 4–5; *Extraits des Registres de Délibération de la Chambre de Commerce de la ville de Bordeaux* (Paris: Imprimerie nationale, 1791); Garran de Coulon, *Rapport sur les troubles de Saint-Domingue*, 2: 110, 115; *AP*, t. XXVI, 357–60; AN, D XXV, 65, dos. 655.

4. *Gazette de Saint-Domingue*, July 16, 1791, 717; *Gazette de Saint-Domingue*, August 10, 1791, 777–80; *Moniteur général de Saint-Domingue*, vol. 1, no. 45, December 29, 1791, 182; AN, D XXV 64, Port-au-Prince to Bordeaux, January 4, 1792, 653; *Débats entre accusateurs et accusés*, 1: 133–39. For a broader context on Bordeaux, see Forrest, *The Death of the French Atlantic*, 134–36.

5. Gouy D'Arsy, *Louis Marthe Degouy*, 37; Clavière, *Adresse de la Société des amis des noirs, à l'Assemblée nationale, à toutes les villes de commerce, à toutes les manufactures, aux colonies, à toutes les sociétés des amis de la constitution* (Paris: Desenne, 1791).

6. François de Chabanon, *Plan de constitution pour la colonie de Saint-Domingue* (Paris, 1791), 99; Clavière, *Adresse de la Société des amis des noirs*, 87–103; *La Chronique de Paris*, May 19, 1791. Robert DuPlessis has examined the sartorial practices of free people of color and has shown that this prejudiced assumption was unfounded. See Robert DuPlessis, *The Material Atlantic: Clothing, Commerce, and Colonialism in the Atlantic World, 1650–1800* (Cambridge: Cambridge University Press, 2015), 191–94.

7. Julien Raimond, *Observations sur l'origine et les progrès du préjugé des colons blancs contre les hommes de couleur* (Paris: Desenne, 1791), 10.

8. Gouy D'Arsy, *Louis Marthe Degouy*, 44; Yvonne Eileen Fabella, "Inventing the Creole Citizen: Race, Sexuality and the Colonial Order in Pre-Revolutionary Saint-Domingue" (PhD diss., Stony Brook University, 2008), 208–63; Dominique Margairaz, "L'économie d'Ancien Régime comme économie de la circulation," in *La circulation des marchandises dans la France de l'Ancien régime*, ed. Denis Woronoff (Paris: Comité pour l'histoire économique et financière de la France, 1998), 1–5; *Mercure national et étranger, ou journal politique de l'Europe*, May 13, 1791, 417–18.

9. *AP*, t. XXVI, 55. On intellectual debates regarding race in the eighteenth century, see Nelson, "Making Men: Enlightenment Ideas of Racial Engineering," *American Historical Review* 115, no. 5 (2010): 1364–94; Andrew S. Curran, *The Anatomy of Blackness: Science and Slavery in an Age of Enlightenment* (Baltimore: Johns Hopkins University Press, 2011); Claude-Olivier Doron, *L'Homme altéré. Races et dégénérescence (XVIIe—XIXe siècles)* (Paris: Champs Vallon, 2016).

10. On the wide circulation of Maury's speech in Saint-Domingue, see Garran de Coulon, *Rapport sur les troubles de Saint-Domingue*, 2: 221; *Gazette de Saint-Domingue*, July 20, 1791, vol. 2, no. 58, 727–30; Pierre Léon, *Marchands et spéculateurs dauphinois dans le monde antillais du XVIIIe siècle: les Dolles et les Raby* (Paris: Les belles lettres, 1963), 142. On race, sex, and representations of miscegenation see Doris Lorraine Garraway, *The Libertine Colony: Creolization in the Early French Caribbean* (Durham: Duke University Press, 2005); Marlene Daut, *Tropics of Haiti: Race and the Literary History of the Haitian Revolution in the Atlantic World, 1789–1865* (Liverpool: Liverpool University Press, 2015).

11. *AP*, t. XXI, 211–12; *AP*, t. XXXI, 280; *AP*, t. XXXI, 203–35.

12. *JP*, vol. 20, Jefferson to Short, July 28, 1791, 688.

13. Frostin, "L'Intervention britannique à Saint-Domingue en 1793," *Revue française d'histoire d'outre-mer* 49, no. 176–77 (1962): 306; Debien, *Esprit colon et esprit d'autonomie à Saint-Domingue au XVIIIe siècle* (Paris: La Rose, 1954), 7; Geggus, *Slavery, War, and Revolution: The British Occupation of Saint-Domingue 1793–1798* (New York: Oxford University Press, 1982), 46; Christian de Parrel and Gabriel Debien, *Les Colons des Antilles et la contre-Révolution, 1791-1793* (Paris: Congrès des Sociétés Savantes, 1966): 292–340.

14. Tim Matthewson, *A Proslavery Foreign Policy: Haitian-American Relations during the Early Republic* (Westport: Praeger, 2003), 22–23; Alexander Dun, *Dangerous Neighbors: Making*

the Haitian Revolution in Early America (Philadelphia: University of Pennsylvania Press, 2016), 70–71.

15. Frederick J. Turner, *Annual Report of the American Historical Association for the Year 1903: Correspondence of the French Ministers to the United States, 1791–1797* (Washington, DC: Government Printing Office, 1904), 47.

16. MAE, CP EU suppl. 36, Ternant to Blanchelande, September 24, 1791; Blanchelande| to Ternant|, April 13, 1792. AN, 416 Mi 4, no. 57, M. Otto to the Ministry of Foreign Affairs, March 12, 1791; ANOM, CC9a 5, "consulat général près des États-Unis," no 347, December 3, 1791; MAE, CP EU suppl. 36, fo. 33, "Lettre de l'assemblée générale au Congrès des États-Unis," October 13, 1791; ANOM, F3 197, Roume to the President of the Colonial Assembly.

17. *JP*, vol. 22, Jefferson to Short, November 24, 1791, 330; Rainford Logan, *The Diplomatic Relations of the United States with Haiti, 1776-1891* (Chapel Hill: University of North Carolina Press, 1941), 35.

18. *AP*, t. XXXV, 467.

19. Dorigny, "Le mouvement abolitionniste français face à l'insurrection de Saint-Domingue ou la fin du mythe de l'abolition graduelle," in *L'insurrection des esclaves de Saint-Domingue: 22-23 août 1791*, ed. Laënnec Hurbon (Paris: Karthala, 2000), 97–113; *AP*, t. XXXV, 473–90.

20. Richard Whatmore and James Livesey, "Étienne Clavière, Jacques-Pierre Brissot et les fondations intellectuelles de la politique des girondins," *Annales historiques de la Révolution française*, no. 321 (2000): 1–26, 13–14.

21. Dorigny, "Recherches sur les idées économiques des Girondins," in *Actes du Colloque Girondins et Montagnards*, ed. Albert Soboul (Paris: Société des études robespierristes, 1980), 79–102; Dorigny, "La Société des Amis des Noirs, les Girondins et la question coloniale," in *Esclavage, colonisations, libérations nationales de 1789 à nos jours: colloque* (Paris: L'Harmattan, 1990), 69–78.

22. *Moniteur général de Saint-Domingue*, December 10, 1791, 103; Garran de Coulon, *Rapport sur les troubles de Saint-Domingue*, 2: 187–89; MassHS, Cutting Diary, November 29, 1791; MassHS, Cutting Diary, December 13, 1791.

23. AN, D XXV, 61, dos. 612, "lettre de M. de Grimouard à l'assemblée provinciale de l'Ouest"; CADN, Philadelphie, consulat général, 106, Stewart & Plunket to Genet, Baltimore, May 30, 1793; *Moniteur général de Saint-Domingue*, December 28, 1791, 179; MassHS, Cutting Diary, January 26, 1792.

24. AN, D XXV 1, dos. 1, no. 9, "copie d'une lettre à M. de Grimouard par le bureau de police de Léogane," January 1792.

25. MassHS, "Nathan Cutting Diary," December 21, 1791, fo. 263.

26. AN, D XVI 5, fo. 4, sessions of November 10 and 11, 1791; Armand Guy Kersaint, *Moyens proposés à l'Assemblée nationale pour rétablir la paix et l'ordre dans les colonies*, vol. 2 (Paris: Imprimerie du cercle social, 1792), 2–3, 14, 23.

27. Kersaint, *Moyens proposés à l'Assemblée nationale*, 1: 10.

28. *AP*, t. XXXIX, 209-20.

29. *AP*, t. XL, 374.

30. Clavière, "De l'alliance avec l'Angleterre," in *La chronique du mois ou les cahiers patriotiques de E. Clavière, C. Condorcet, L. Mercier, A. Auger, J. Oszqld, N. Bonneville, J. Bidermann, A. Broussonet, A. Guy-Kersaint, J. P. Brissot, J. Ph. Garran de Coulon, J. Dussaulx, F. Lanthenas et Collot-d'Herboit (Février)* (Paris: Imprimerie du cercle social, 1792), 67–74, 67.

31. Nussbaum, *Commercial Policy in the French Revolution: A Study of the Career of G. J. A. Ducher* (Washington, DC: American Historical Association, 1923); Potofsky, "The Political Economy of the French-American Debt Debate," *William and Mary Quarterly* 63, no. 3 (July 2006): 489–516.

32. Gaspard Joseph Amand Ducher, *Suppression des barrières entre la France et les colonies* (Paris, s.n., 1792), 3, 5, 10. On the project of a "French Customs Union," see John Francis Bosher, *Single Duty Project: A Study of the Movement for a French Customs Union in the Eighteenth Century* (London: University of London, Athlone Press, 1964).

33. AN, 416 Mi 4, "Projet d'un pacte commercial et économique avec les États-Unis de l'Amérique"; Dorigny, "Brissot et Miranda en 1792, ou comment révolutionner l'Amérique espagnole," in *La France et les Amériques au temps de Jefferson et de Miranda*, ed. Dorigny and Rossignol (Paris: Société des études robespierristes, 2001), 93–105; *AP*, t. XL, 353.

34. *AP*, t. LIX, 16.
35. MAE, CP, Espagne 635, fo. 375.
36. Charles Schmidt and Fernand Gerbaux, eds., *Procès-verbaux des comités d'agriculture et de commerce de la Constituante, de la Législative et de la Convention*, vol. 3 (Paris: Imprimerie nationale, 1908), 20–26; *AP*, t. LX, 692–93.
37. AN, 416 Mi 4, the Ministry of Foreign Affairs to Citizen Genet, no. 7, April 11, 1793.

Chapter 5

1. MassHS, *Cutting Diary*, November 3, 1791. Biographical information on Cutting can be found in Simon P. Newman, "American Political Culture and the French and Haitian Revolutions: Nathaniel Cutting and the Jeffersonian Republicans," in *The Impact of the Haitian Revolution in the Atlantic World*, ed. Geggus (Columbia: University of South Carolina Press, 2001), 72–89. Simon Newman, however, did not examine Cutting's business activities.
2. On the luddism of the enslaved, see Johnhenry Gonzalez, *Maroon Nation: A History of Revolutionary Haiti* (New Haven, CT: Yale University, 2019).
3. Albert J. Gares, "Stephen Girard|'s West Indian Trade 1789–1812," *Pennsylvania Magazine of History and Biography* 72, no. 4 (1942): 311–42, 314; John H. Coatsworth, "American Trade with European Colonies in the Caribbean and South America, 1790–1812," *William and Mary Quarterly* 24, no. 2 (April 1967): 243–66; Michelle Craig McDonald, "The Chance of the Moment: Coffee and the New West Indies Commodities Trade," *William and Mary Quarterly* 62, no. 3 (July 2005): 441–72.
4. DPL, *Dutilh Papers*, 10, Dominique François to Etienne Dutilh, February 7, 1789; 10, J. Dutilh to E. Dutilh, March 12, 1789; 10, J. Dutilh to E. Dutilh, April 3, 1789; 11, James Morphy to John Wachsmuth, July 24, 1789; 12, E. Dutilh to Dutilh & Wachsmuth, March 20, 1790; NYSA, *Mumford Papers*, 7, Mumford to Daniel Rodman, December 11, 1790.
5. AN, AE, B I 910, De La Forest to the Ministry of the Navy, February 25, 1790. For the role of wheat in the US economy, see Brooke Hunter, "Wheat, War, and the American Economy During the Age of Revolution," *William and Mary Quarterly* 62, no. 3 (July 2005): 505–26.
6. JCB, *Brown Family Papers*, 527, Brown to James Munro, August 24, 1790; Munro to Brown & Benson, September 10, 1790; Munro to Brown & Benson, October 1, 1790; AN, Fonds Archives étrangères, B I 210, Létombe to the Ministry of the Navy, May 19, 1790.
7. On the understanding of profits in the early modern period, see Pierre Gervais, "Why Profit and Loss Didn't Matter: The Historicized Rationality of Early Modern Merchant Accounting," in *Merchants and Profit in the Age of Commerce, 1680–1830*, ed. Pierre Gervais, Yannick Lemarchand, and Dominique Margairaz, 33–52. Quotes from DPL, *Dutilh Papers*, 11, J. Dutilh to E. Dutilh, July 12, 1789; APS, Girard Papers, *Letterbook* 2, E. Girard to J. Girard, June 21, 1789; MHS, JSS, vol. 2, Smith to Buchanan, June 27, 1789.
8. DPL, Dutilh Papers, 12, E. Dutilh to J. Wachsmuth, May 7, 1790; E. Dutilh to J Wachsmuth, June 26, 1790; AN, AE, La Forest to the Ministry of the Navy, December 1, 1789; DPL, Dutilh Papers, Sol de Water to Wachsmuth, May 29, 1790.
9. APS, GP, Aubert to Girard, October 24, 1792; Aubert to Girard, December 7, 1792; DPL, *Dutilh Papers*, Box 20, August 22, 1793.
10. On family matters, intimacy, and commercial correspondence, see Sarah M. S. Pearsall, *Atlantic Families: Lives and Letters in the Later Eighteenth Century* (Oxford: Oxford University Press, 2008), 179–209; Toby Ditz, "Formative Ventures: Eighteenth-Century Commercial Letters and the Articulation of Experience," in *Epistolary Selves: Letters and Letter-writers, 1600–1945*, ed. Rebecca Earle (Aldershot, UK: Ashgate, 1999), 59–78. On the planters' racial thinking see Popkin, *Facing Racial Revolution: Eyewitness Accounts of the Haitian Insurrection* (Chicago: University of Chicago Press, 2007). APS, GP, Jean to Stephen Girard, December 24, 1792, fo. 377; February 14, 1793, fo. 52.
11. Covo, "I, François B.,"; MassHS, NC diary, November 3, 1791; DPL, *Dutilh Papers*, 15, Etienne Dutilh to Dutilh and Wachsmuth, September 18, 1791; Dun, ""What Avenues of Commerce, Will You, Americans, Not Explore!": Commercial Philadelphia's Vantage onto the Early Haitian Revolution," *William and Mary Quarterly* 62, no. 3 (July 2005): 473–504, 479.

12. MassHS, NC diary, November 14, 1791, November 8, 1791.
13. DPL, Dutilh Papers, 15, Collette to Dutilh & Wachsmuth, October 15, 1791; De Water & Lapeyre to Dutilh & Wachsmuth, October 3, 1791; MassHS, NC diary, January 23, 1792. For a discussion on emotions during the Haitian Revolution, see Alejandro E. Gómez, *Le spectre de la Révolution noire. L'impact de la révolution haïtienne dans le monde atlantique, 1790–1886* (Rennes: Presses universitaires de Rennes, 2013).
14. DPL, *Dutilh Papers*, 15, De Water & Lapeyre to Dutilh & Wachsmuth, October 3, 1791; MassHS, NC diary, November 3, 1791; March 31, 1792.
15. Dun, *Dangerous Neighbors*, 59; APS, GP, *lett.* 3, Girard to Samatan, October 10, 1791, fo. 248; NYHS, G&S, Gelston to W. Joseph et R. Hart, September 19, 1791; DPL, Dutilh Papers,15, Etienne Dutilh to Dutilh and Wachsmuth, September 11, 1791; MassHS, NC diary, November 18, 1791; NYSA, *Mumford Papers*, 7, Mumford to Gelston & Saltonstall, September 14, 1791.
16. DPL, Dutilh Papers, 15, Etienne Dutilh to Dutilh & Wachsmuth, September 11, 1791; TUL, SCA, "French Businessman's Autobiography, 19th century," 1820, fo. 102; MHS, MS 1300, "memorandum book at aux Cayes," Girault frères to Hall & Sanderson, October 9, 1791; APS, GP, roll 9, Aubert, Chauveau & Bacon to Girard, April 14, 1793, fo. 146; DPL, Dutilh Papers, 15, Pillé & E. Dutilh to Dutilh & Wachsmuth, September 13, 1791; NYHS, *Gelston & Saltonstall papers, letterbook* 1, Gelston to Joseph Pellerin, January 23, 1793; AN, AE B I 910, Marbois to the Ministry of Navy, date unknown but received on June 20, 1792.
17. MassHS, NC diary, December 21, 1791, February 16, 1792, April 11, 1792. Rousseau Bonaventure indicated that he "rallied" around ten enslaved people who agreed to work on his plantation near Cap-Français in February 1793. See CADN, New York, 72, "Declaration de Rousseau Bonaventure." For a comparison with the varied attitude of the enslaved in time of revolts, see Marjoleine Kars, "Dodging Rebellion: Politics and Gender in the Berbice Slave Uprising of 1763," *American Historical Review* 121, no. 1 (2016): 39–69.
18. AN D XXV 24, "Entrepôt du Port-au-Prince, mois de May 1793"; "Entrepôt du Port-au-Prince, année 1793"; CADN Boston 79 "Récapitulation des Résultats comparés"; "Entrées et sorties des quarante un ports de l'état de Massachusetts pendant l'année 1791."
19. The figures are derived from the slave-trade database. MassHS, Cutting Diary, June 2, 1792; DPL, *Dutilh Papers*, 14, Reinhold to Dutilh, July 12, 1791. On the British debates regarding abolition, see Srividhya Swaminathan, *Debating the Slave Trade: Rhetoric of British National Identity, 1759–1815* (Burlington, UK: Ashgate, 2009), 191–202.
20. MassHS, Cutting Diary, February 11, 1792.
21. MassHS, Cutting Diary, January 1, 1792, February 10, 1792. On Woodville and the British slave traders who settled in Le Havre, see Edmond Delobette, "Ces Messieurs du Havre. Négociants, commissionnaires et armateurs de 1680 à 1830" (PhD diss., Université de Caen, 2005), 689. On the sales of slaves in Saint-Marc: Debien, "Les esclaves des plantations Mauger à Saint-Domingue (1763–1802)," *Bulletin de la société d'histoire de la Guadeloupe*, no. 43-44 (1980): 31–164, 64. On the lives of enslaved women in the Caribbean, see Marisa J. Fuentes, *Dispossessed Lives: Enslaved Women, Violence and the Archive* (Philadelphia: University of Pennsylvania Press, 2016).
22. For the global context of the intercolonial slave trade, see Gregory E. O'Malley and Alex Borucki, "Patterns in the Intercolonial Slave Trade Across the Americas Before the Nineteenth Century," *Tempo* 23, no. 2 (2017): 314–38. On the French legislation on the foreign slave trade, see Tarrade, *Le commerce colonial* 2: 622–33. On the illegal slave trade with Jamaica, see Geggus, "La traite des esclaves aux Antilles françaises à la fin du XVIIIe siècle: quelques aspects du marché local," in *Négoce, Ports et Océans: XVIe–XXe siècles*, ed. Silvia Marzagalli and Hubert Bonin (Bordeaux: Presses universitaires de Bordeaux, 2000), 235–45. On the marginal role of US slavers, see Leonardo Marques, *The United States and the Transatlantic Slave Trade to the Americas, 1776–1867* (New Haven, CT: Yale University Press, 2016), 39. The quote is from François Chabanon, *Plan de constitution pour la colonie de St. Domingue* (Paris, 1791), 82.
23. The anxiety around "French negroes" in the United States and the illegal import of slaves have been expertly analyzed in Ashli White, *Encountering Revolution: Haiti and the Making of Early Republic* (Baltimore: Johns Hopkins University Press, 2010), 151–52. On Dutilh's rejection of

the slave trade, see DPL, *Dutilh Papers*, 10, Dominique François to Etienne Dutilh, February 7, 1789.

24. Elena Schneider, "African Slavery and Spanish Empire: Imperial Imaginings and Bourbon Reform in Eighteenth-Century Cuba and Beyond," *Journal of Early American History* 5, no. 1 (2015): 3–29; Ada Ferrer, *Freedom's Mirror: Cuba and Haiti in the Age of Revolution* (Cambridge: Cambridge University, 2014), 17–43; MassHS, *Cutting Diary*, December 28, 1791, January 27, 1792.

25. MassHS, *Cutting Diary*, December 28, 1791.

26. As Gregory O'Malley has demonstrated, this was a common feature of the intercolonial slave trade. Gregory O'Malley, *Final Passages: The Intercolonial Slave Trade of British America, 1619–1807* (Chapel Hill: University of North Carolina Press, 2014); MassHS, Cutting Diary, March 15, 1792. On the commercial changes in Cuba, see Dale Tomich, "La richesse de l'Empire: esclavage et production sucrière à Cuba après la Révolution de Saint-Domingue," in *Rétablissement de l'esclavage dans les colonies françaises, 1802. Ruptures et continuités de la politique coloniale française (1800–1830). Aux origines d'Haïti*, ed. Yves Bénot and Marcel Dorigny (Paris: Maisonneuve & Larose, 2003), 329–62; Linda K. Salvucci, "Atlantic Intersections: Early American Commerce and the Rise of the Spanish West Indies (Cuba)," *Business History Review* 79, no. 4 (2005): 781–809; Alain Yacou, *Essor des plantations et subversion antiesclavagiste à Cuba, 1791–1845* (Paris: Karthala, 2010), 55–61.

27. MassHS, Cutting Diary, March 29, 1792. The figures on Havana's imports are drawn from Ernesto Bassi, "Mobility, Circulation, Spatial Configurations and Respatialization in the Wake of the Haitian Revolution: A View from New Granada's Shores," in *The French Revolution as a Moment of Respatialization*, ed. Megan Maruschke and Matthias Middell (Berlin: De Gruyter Oldenbourg, 2019), 107–28, 124. The table of Port-au-Prince's exports can be found in AN, D XXV 24, "Entrepôt du Port-au-Prince, année 1793."

28. DPL, *Dutilh Papers*, 15, Etienne Dutilh to Wachsmuth, November 29, 1791.

29. *Moniteur général de la partie française de Saint-Domingue*, November 17, 1791, 10; CADN, Philadelphie, consulat général, 119, Laforest| to Pouget, March 27, 1792; consular minutes, November 19, 1792 and January 17, 1793; MAE, CCC, Baltimore, vol. 1; NARA, RG 36, 1214, 22, vol. 1, no. 52. MHS, *John Smith & Sons letterbook*, vol. 2, Smith to Perkins|, June 8, 1792; to George Stiles, November 7, 1792; to captain Anthony Daniels, November 20, 1792.

30. CADN, Philadelphie, consulat général, 119, Proisy to the Colonial Assembly, April 30, 1792; Proisy to Laforest, April 13, May 13, 1792; Blanchelande| to Laforest, May 9, 1792; MAE, CP EU suppl. 37, Wante| to Genet|, September 8, 1793; APS, GP, roll 9, Delonguemarre|, Paouilhac & Cie to Girard, October 7, 1792, fo. 282; Aubert|, Chauveau| & Cie to Girard, October 8, 1792, fo. 288; AN, D XXV 17, dos. 161, Boislandry| to Wante|, September 12, 1793; CADN, Baltimore 91, acte de mariage du 9 thermidor an IV (July 27, 1796); MAE, CC, Baltimore, vol. 1, Bizouard| to Genet|, September 12, 1793; MAE, CC, Baltimore, vol. 1, Moissonnier to Fauchet, 10 Prairial Year 2 (May 29, 1794).

31. Howard C. Rice, "James Swan|: Agent of the French Republic 1794–1796," *New England Quarterly* 10, no. 3 (1937): 464–86; Eleanor Pearson DeLorme, "The Swan Commissions: Four Portraits by Gilbert Stuart," *Winterthur Portfolio* 14, no. 4 (1979): 361–95; Mark Peterson, "Boston à l'heure française: religion, culture et commerce à l'époque des révolutions atlantiques," *Annales historiques de la Révolution française*, no. 363 (2011): 7–31, 13; James Swan, *Causes qui se sont opposées aux progrès du commerce entre la France et les États-Unis de l'Amérique, avec les moyens de l'accélérer & la comparaison de la dette nationale de l'Angleterre, de la France, & des Etats-Unis; en six lettres adressées à M. le marquis de La Fayette. Traduit sur le manuscrit anglais du colonel Swan* (Paris: Imprimerie de L. Potier de Lille, 1790).

32. AN, D XXV 63, dos. 632, "Au comité colonial de l'Assemblée," February 1792; CADN, Boston 76, "Soumission," November 2, 1792; "Procès-verbal constatant la qualité bonne, loyale et Marchande de 750 barils de Bœufs salés et de 750 barils de Porcs salés destinés par tiers de 500 barils pour le Cap, le Port au Prince et les Cayes Isle St. Domingue," January 15–27, 1793.

33. CADN, New York 63, "marché conclu entre les régisseurs des vivres et James Swan." |

34. Marzagalli, *Bordeaux et les États-Unis*, 153–59; Pierre Caron, *La commission des subsistances de l'an II. Procès-verbaux et actes*, vol. 1 (Paris: E. Leroux, 1925), 168, 174, 228; Rice, "James Swan," 472; Albert Hall Bowman, *The Struggle for Neutrality: Franco-American Diplomacy*

During the Federalist Era (Knoxville: University of Tennessee Press, 1974), 228–29; James Monroe, *The Writings of James Monroe, Including a Collection of His Public and Private Papers and Correspondence, Now for the First Time Printed*, vol. 2, *1794–1796* (New York: G. P. Putnam's Sons, 1899), 313; Alphonse Aulard, "La dette américaine envers la France," part 2, *Revue de Paris* 32, no. 11 (June 1925): 546; Annie Jourdan, "A Tale of Three Patriots in a Revolutionary World: Théophile Cazenove|, Jacques-Pierre Brissot|, and Joel Barlow|," *Early American Studies: An Interdisciplinary Journal* 10, no. 2 (2012): 360–81; Georges Lefebvre, *La France sous le Directoire: 1795–1799* (Paris: Éditions sociales, 1978), 137–41. There were a lot of twists and turns in Swan's career. He eventually went bankrupt and was imprisoned for debts in Paris in 1808. He died just after his liberation from prison where he had spent 22 years. See: Erika Vause, "'The Great Air of Liberty Choked Him': Finance, Freedom, and the Legendary Death of Colonel James Swan," *Age of Revolutions*, online (June 2021).

35. François Barbé de Marbois, *État des finances de Saint Domingue contenant le résumé des Recettes et Dépenses de toutes les caisses publiques, depuis le 1er janvier 1788 jusqu'au 31 décembre de la même année* (Paris: Imprimerie royale, 1790); Chevalier de Proisy|, *État des finances de Saint Domingue contenant le résumé des Recettes et Dépenses de toutes les caisses publiques, depuis le 1er janvier 1789 jusqu'au 31 décembre de la même année* (Paris: Imprimerie royale, 1790): AN, D XXV 56, dos. 545, Minister of the Navy to the President of the National Assembly, August 8, 1792; dos. 546, "mémoire sur les lettres de change"; MassHS, *Cutting Diary*, June 11, 1792.

36. AN, D XXV 56, dos. 545, Pouget to the President of the National Assembly, June 2, 1792; D XXV 59, dos. 576, Pouget to the Ministry of the Navy, August 18, 1792: APS, GP, roll 9, Aubert to Girard, April 19, 1793, fo. 156; Robert Lacombe, *Histoire monétaire de Saint Domingue et de la République d'Haïti des origines à 1874* (Paris: Larose, 1958), 17; Gérard Gabriel Marion, *L'administration des finances en Martinique, 1679–1790* (Paris: Harmattan, 2000), 122–200; Dominique Margairaz, *François de Neufchâteau. Biographie intellectuelle* (Paris: Publications de la Sorbonne, 2005), 135–40; Louis Dermigny, "Circuits de l'argent et milieux d'affaires au XVIIIe siècle," *Revue historique* 212 (1954): 239–78; Morineau, *Incroyables gazettes et fabuleux métaux: les retours des trésors américains d'après les gazettes hollandaises: XVIe–XVIIIe siècles* (Paris: Éditions de la Maison des sciences de l'homme, 1984), 425–60; Matthieu de Oliveira, *Les routes de l'argent. Réseaux et flux financiers de Paris à Hambourg (1789–1815)* (Paris: CHEFF, 2011), 175–89.

37. Rebecca Spang, *Stuff and Money in the Time of the French Revolution* (Cambridge, MA: Harvard University Press, 2015), 112–23; *Moniteur général de la partie française de Saint-Domingue*, December 30, 1791, 187; December 31, 1791, 192; MassHS, Cutting Diary, January 5, 1792.

38. Courts were opened on January 17, 1792, closed on January 23, opened on June 3 to be closed again on June 22, before the decree of July 11, 1792. See *Moniteur général de la partie française de Saint Domingue*, January 19, 1792, 267–68; June 18, 1792, 139; June 22, 1792, 155; MassHS, Cutting Diary, February 8, 1792.

39. AN, D XXV 59, dos. 576, Pouget to the Ministry of the Navy, August 18, 1792; *AP*, t. XL, 533–35; *AP*, t. XLV, 593–95; t. LIII, 117–20; t. LXIV, 354–57, t. LXXXV, 110–18.

40. Potofsky, "The Political Economy"; *AP*, t. XL, 533–35; Aulard, "La dette américaine envers la France," part 1, *Revue de Paris* 32, no. 3 (May 1925): 319–38; part 2, *Revue de Paris* 32, no. 11 (June 1925): 524–50; *AP*, t. XLV, 593–95; Matthewson, *A Proslavery Foreign Policy*, 37–44.

41. CADN, Philadelphie consulat général 120, "Sommaire des tirages effectués par le Trésorier principal de la colonie de St. Domingue sur le consul général de la République française près des États-Unis," April 2, 1793; AN, D XXV 59, dos. 583, Wante| to Genet|, September 8, 1793; CADN, Philadelphie, consulat général 106, dos. "Utilisation des fonds de 3 millions de livres tournois [*sic*]"; "Statement of the payments at the Treasury on Account of the Debt due to France"; "Réclamations des négociants américains."

42. *Moniteur général de la partie française de Saint-Domingue*, May 25, 1793, 41.

43. *Moniteur général de la partie française de Saint-Domingue*, May 25, 1793, 41.

44. DPL, *Dutilh Papers*, 19, Soulier to Dutilh, May 23, 1793; 20, Soulier to Dutilh, June 5, 1793: Soulier to Dutilh, June 11, 1793; APS, GP, roll 9, Aubert to Girard, May 26, 1793, fo. 218.

45. DPL, *Dutilh Papers*, 20, Soulier to Dutilh, June 11, 1793; *Moniteur général de la partie française de Saint-Domingue*, June 17, 133–35; June 18, 138–39.

& Cie, March 6, 1796; APS, GP, Dutilh|, Morin & Cie to Girard, November 13, 1792, fo. 330; Louis-Élie Moreau de Saint-Méry|, Marcel Dorigny, and Étienne Taillemite, *La descrip-tion topographique, physique, civile, politique et historique de la partie française de l'isle Saint-Domingue*, vol. 3 (Saint-Denis: Publications de la Société française d'histoire d'outre-mer, 2004) 1380–83.

26. Geggus, "Urban Development in Eighteenth Century Saint-Domingue," *Bulletin du Centre d'Histoire des Espaces Atlantiques*, no. 5 (1990): 197–228, 222, 224; Garrigus, *Before Haiti*, 21–50; Giovanni Venegoni, "La contrebande caraïbe et la première "américanisation" de l'empire (1723-1763)," *Cahiers d'Histoire* 32, no. 2 (2013): 41–59; Israel, "The Jews of Curaçao, New Amsterdam and the Guyanas," 511–32; Garrigus, "Blue and Brown: Contraband Indigo and the Rise of a Free Colored Planter Class in French Saint-Domingue," *The Americas* 50, no. 2 (1993): 233–63; Fick, *The Making of Haiti*, 143–56; ANOM, DPPC, NOTSDOM 456, Act of April 17, 1796; CADN, Philadelphia, Consulat général 122, Rigaud| to Duval, Prairial 25, year III (June 13, 1795); ANOM, F3 200, "Petition of American merchants, supercargoes and captains." On the conflict between Rigaud and the third civil commission, see Covo, "Le massacre de Fructidor An II à Saint-Domingue," 143–69.

27. Geggus, *Slavery, War, and Revolution*, 258; PRO, HCA 49 53, *James*; PRO, HCA 49 47, *Honest Friend*.

28. Glavany had been hired by the firm Pellicot and Co. as the captain of *Jolie Nanette*, destined for Baltimore on April 29, 1791. Then he started smuggling flour to Saint-Domingue. See CADN Baltimore 83, dos. "Concernant la *Jolie Nanette*"; PRO, HCA 49 47, "The Hope." On the multi-national character of the crews, see Perl-Rosenthal, *Citizen-Sailors*.

29. Pérotin-Dumon, *La ville aux îles, la ville dans l'île*, 232–33; Melvin H. Jackson, *Privateers in Charleston, 1793–1796: An Account of a French Palatinate in South Carolina* (Washington, DC: Smithsonian Institution Press, 1969), 115–25; NYHS, *Lynch & Stoughton letterbooks*, Lynch to Randolph, November 1792; Lynch to Moylan, May 7, 1793; ANOM, SUPSDOM 13, Act of April 16, 1793; BNF, Fr. 8986, commission to Moline, Thermidor 4, year IV (July 22, 1796), fo. 75.

30. Pérotin-Dumon, "Économie corsaire et droit de neutralité: les ports de la Guadeloupe pendant les guerres révolutionnaires," in *L'Espace Caraïbe*, ed. Butel and Lavallé, 232. Figures calculated from ANOM, CC9a 14, "Privateers outfitted by the third civil commission."

31. W. Jeffrey Bolster, *Black Jacks: African American Seamen in the Age of Sail* (Cambridge, MA: Harvard University Press, 2009); Bégaud, Belissa, and Visser, *Aux origins d'une alliance improbable*, 212–19; CADN, Philadelphia, Consulat général, 41, "État des prises."

32. PRO, HCA 49 49, *Peggy*, Valck to Louis Lacoste, October 26, 1797; ANOM, DPPC, NOT Delestang 455–65.

33. PRO, HCA 49 48, "La *Liberté*."

34. Françoise Bléchet, "La seconde mission de Sonthonax| à Saint-Domingue d'après sa correspondance (mai 1796–août 1797)," in *Léger-Félicité Sonthonax: la première abolition de l'esclavage la Révolution française et la Révolution de Saint-Domingue*, ed. Dorigny (Saint-Denis: Société française d'histoire d'outre-mer, 2005), 79–93, 81, 86; AN, D XXV 45, dos. 423, "Instructions pour les citoyens Sonthonax|, Leblanc|, Giraud, Raymond et Roume"|; ANOM, CC9a 16, Brumaire 3, year V (October 24, 1796); Pluviôse 6, year V (January 25, 1797).

35. ANOM, CC9a 18, Beauvais| to Tierce|, Nivôse 7, year VI (December 27, 1797) and Pluviôse 28, year VI (February 16, 1798); BNF, Fr. 8987, Sonthonax| to Paris, Germinal 6, year V (March 26, 1797); Sonhonax to Rondineau, Germinal 10, year V (March 30, 1797); Maria Elena Orozco-Melgar, "Cuba et les îles sous-le-vent: la course comme facteur identitaire," in *Le monde caraïbe: défis et dynamiques. Géopolitique, intégration régionale, enjeux économiques*, ed. Christian Lerat (Bordeaux: Maison des sciences de l'homme d'Aquitaine, 2005), 97–116; Agnès Renault, *D'une île rebelle à une île fidèle: les Français de Santiago de Cuba (1791-1825)* (Mont-Saint-Aignan: Publications des universités de Rouen et du Havre, 2012), 238–56; Karwan Fatah-Black, "The Patriot Coup d'État in Curaçao, 1796," in *Curaçao in the Age of Revolutions, 1795-1800*, ed. Wim Klooster and Gert Oostindie (Leiden: KITLV Press, 2011), 123–40; Han Jordaan, "Patriots, Privateers and International Politics: The Myth of the Conspiracy of Jean Baptiste Tierce| Cadet," in *Curaçao in the Age of Revolutions, 1795-1800*, ed. Klooster and Oostindie, 141–70.

36. MHS, MS 125, July 1793; CADN, Baltimore 7, Moissonnier to Genet, June 15, 1793; APS, GP, lett. 6, Girard to Bentalou, May 11, 1796, fo. 2; Kennedy, "Le club jacobin de Charleston," 438.

37. DPL, Dutilh Papers, 19, Chabaud to Dutilh and Wachsmuth, April 3, 1793; CADN, New York, 72, fo. 348–49; New York, 63, dos. "Protection accordée par le consulat"; ANOM, CC9a 16, Séances des 13 et 15 frimaire an V; *Gazette of the United States*, April 15, 1797.

38. On the distinction between *émigré* and *réfugié*, see Potofsky, "The "Non-Aligned Status" of French Emigrés and Refugees in Philadelphia, 1793–1798," *Transatlantica*, no. 2 (2006).

39. Message from the Directory: Pluviôse 15, year IV (February 4, 1796); *Recueil des lois relatives à la marine et aux colonies*, vol. 6 (Paris: Imprimerie de la République, 1797–1800), 251; MAE, CP EU 46, fo. 302; John McNelis O'Keefe, "From Legal Rights to Citizens' Rights and Alien Penalties: Migrant Influence, Naturalization, and the Growth of National Power over Foreign Migrants in the Early American Republic" (PhD diss., George Washington University, 2012), 27–28.

40. CADN, Philadelphia, Consulat général 64, New York Vice-Consul to the General Consul in Philadelphia, Frimaire 18, year V (December 8, 1796); CADN, Baltimore 6, Moissonnier to Genet, September 3, 1793.

41. CADN, New York 74, Acte du 11 nivôse an V, December 31, 1796. Afterward, he came to support Toussaint Louverture; see De Cauna, "Charlesteguy, un Basque fondateur de la franc-maçonnerie haïtienne," *Bulletin du Centre Généalogique du Pays-Basque et du Bas-Adour*, no. 12 (1992): 2–5.

42. AN, 208 Mi 1, Richard Yates to Timothy Pickering, April 30, 1798; MassHS, *Perkins Papers*, Corbières to James and Thomas Perkins, December 30, 1799.

43. On the broader debate regarding citizenship, see Peter Sahlins, *Unnaturally French: Foreign Citizens in the Old Regime and After* (Ithaca, NY: Cornell University Press, 2004); ANOM, CC9a 10, Laveaux to the Ministry of the Navy, Vendémiaire 19, year III (October 8, 1794); CADN, Philadelphia, Consulat général 115, file *Le Résolu Républicain*.

44. BNF, fr. 8987, Sonthonax to the Society of the Friends of the Blacks in Philadelphia, Germinal 20, year V (April 9, 1797); ANOM, CC9a 16, dos. *Lark*, Nivôse 8, year V (December 28, 1796); MAE, CCC, New York, vol. 3, fo. 74.

45. CADN, New York 76, Declaration of June 15, 1798, fo. 89; Rebecca J. Scott and Jean Hébrard, *Freedom Papers: An Atlantic Odyssey in the Age of Emancipation* (Cambridge, MA: Harvard University Press, 2012), 57. The legal strategy demonstrated by Romaine is reminiscent of notarial practices in old regime Saint-Domingue; see Ghachem, *The Old Regime*, 105–11. For the larger context regarding the circulation of enslaved people to the United States, see Martha S. Jones, "Time, Space, and Jurisdiction in Atlantic World Slavery: The Volunbrun Household in Gradual Emancipation New York," *Law and History Review* 29, no. 4 (2011): 1031–60.

46. MAE, CCC New York, vol. 3, Rozier to the Ministry of Foreign Affairs, Frimaire 3, year V (December 23, 1796); Denver Brunsman, "Subjects vs. Citizens: Impressment and Identity in the Anglo-American Atlantic," *Journal of the Early Republic* 30, no. 4 (2010): 557–86, 561; MAE, CCC, New York, vol. 3, Rozier to the Ministry of Foreign Affairs, Thermidor 24, year V (August 11, 1797); MAE, CP, EU 47, fo. 247.

47. Douglas Bradburn, *The Citizenship Revolution: Politics and the Creation of the American Union, 1774–1804* (Charlottesville: University of Virginia Press, 2009), 104–7.

48. Marilyn C. Baseler, *"Asylum for Mankind": America, 1607–1800* (Ithaca, NY: Cornell University Press, 1998), 251–52; O'Keefe, "From Legal Rights to Citizens' Rights and Alien Penalties," 8–10; Bradburn, *The Citizenship Revolution*, 101–3, 108–27; Young, "Connecting the President and the People," 435–66; Gordon S. Brown, *Toussaint's Clause: The Founding Fathers and the Haitian Revolution* (Jackson: University Press of Mississippi, 2005), 106–9.

49. *Gazette of the United States*, February 16, 1797; February 21, 1797; Hale, "'Many Who Wandered in Darkness': The Contest over American National Identity, 1795–1798," *Early American Studies: An Interdisciplinary Journal* 1, no. 1 (2003): 127–75; Cotlar, "The Federalists' Transatlantic Cultural Offensive of 1798 and the Moderation of American Democratic Discourse," in *Beyond the Founders: New Approaches to the Political History of the Early American Republic*, ed. Jeffrey L. Pasley, David Waldstreicher, and Andrew W. Robertson (Chapel Hill: University of North Carolina Press, 2004), 274–99.

de fonctionnaires publics, Prairial 21, year VIII (June 10, 1800); ANOM, CC9a 28, "Dette publique sur le Trésor de St. Domingue, constatée le 25 frimaire an IX"; Pamphile de Lacroix, *La Révolution de Haïti* (Paris: Karthala, 1995), 268–74.

35. ANOM, CC9b 18, Arrêté contenant des mesures pour la suppression des pirateries exercées par les rebelles du département du Sud, Thermidor 14, year VII (August 1, 1799); Arrêté sur la délivrance des passeports du 16 thermidor an VII, August 3, 1799; AN, 208 Mi 1, Roume to Stevens, Frimaire 3, year VIII (November 24, 1799); Dumaine to Stevens, Frimaire 12, year VIII (December 3, 1799); Frimaire 18, year VIII (December 9, 1799); AN, 208 Mi 3, Lear to Madison, July 25, 1801.

36. AN, 208 Mi 1, "Copy of communication from capt. Bainbridge"; AN, 208 Mi 2, Chevret to Henri Christophe, no date; Stevens to Pickering, December 9, 1799; AN, 208 Mi 3, Corbet to Lear, September 23, 1801.

37. AN, 208 Mi 2, Stevens to Pickering, February 13, 1800; MHS, MS 1300, Hall to Bonnefils, Ferrete & Santon, Ventôse 5, year VII (February 23, 1799); Hall to McIntosh, March 31, 1799; NYHS, Jumel papers, 4, Allain to Dupan, March 24, 1799; AN, 208 Mi 3, Dandrige to Madison, July 23, 1801; PRO, FO 5 33, Barclay to Grenville, March 12, 1801; Julia Gaffield, "Haiti and Jamaica in the Remaking of the Early Nineteenth-Century Atlantic World," *William and Mary Quarterly* 69, no. 3 (2012): 583–614.

38. http://www.presidency.ucsb.edu/ws/index.php?pid=29439; Perl-Rosenthal, "Private Letters and Public Diplomacy: The Adams Network and the Quasi-War, 1797–1798," *Journal of the Early Republic* 31, no. 2 (2011): 283–311; AN, 208 Mi 1, Pickering to Lee, February 20, 1799; Richard Yates to Pickering, April 30, 1798; Pickering to Stevens, July 3, 1799.

39. United States. Office of Naval Records and Library, *Naval Documents Related to the Quasi-War with France* (Washington DC: US gov. print. off., 1935-1938), vol. 1, 135–37, 143–47; McCoy, *The Elusive Republic*, 174–76.

40. Debien, "A propos du trésor de Toussaint-Louverture," *Revue de la société d'histoire et géographie d'Haïti* 17, no. 62 (1946): 30–40: Pierre Pluchon, *Toussaint Louverture: Un Révolutionaire noir d'ancien régime* (Paris: Fayard, 1989), 413–15; Girard, "Trading Races: Joseph and Marie Bunel, a Diplomat and a Merchant in Revolutionary Saint-Domingue and Philadelphia," *Journal of the Early Republic* 30, no. 3 (2010): 351–76; Girard, "Jean-Jacques Dessalines and the Atlantic System: A Reappraisal," *William and Mary Quarterly* 69, no. 3 (2012): 549–82, 556; ANOM, CC9a 18, Raimond to Tierce, Floréal 2, year VI (April 21, 1798); BL, Péries, "Révolution de Saint-Domingue," fo. 45; Charles Victor Emmanuel Leclerc, *Lettres du général Leclerc, commandant en chef de l'armée de Saint Domingue en 1802* (Paris: Société de l'histoire des colonies françaises), 92; CADN, Philadelphia, Consulat général 65, Arcambal to Pichon, Ventôse 15, year IX (March 6, 1801) and Germinal 17, year IX (April 7, 1801).

41. On US consuls, see Marzagalli, "Les débuts des services consulaires des États-Unis. L'exemple de Bordeaux de la guerre d'Indépendance américaine à la fin du Premier Empire," in *La fonction consulaire*, eds. Ulbert and Le Bouëdec, 279–296, 282–284.

42. On eighteenth-century letter writing, see Ditz, "Formative Ventures," 70; *Aurora*, July 27, 1799. The captain of *Oceania* paid 16,204 dollars in duties, an extraordinary amount for a ship coming from Saint-Domingue. Stevens shipped coffee, sugar, cotton, and timber. This document does not tell whether Stevens was the full owner of the cargo or just the commissioner. See NARA, RG 36, 956 28, *Inward foreign manifest*, December 16, 1799.

43. AN, 208 Mi 1, Mayer to Petit & Bayard, October 22, 1799; *Aurora*, January 8, 1800. On verbal violence and anti-jacobinism, Hale, "'Many Who Wandered in Darkness,'" 127–75; Cotlar, "The Federalists' Transatlantic Cultural Offensive of 1798," in *Beyond the Founders*, ed. Pasley, Waldstreicher, and Robertson, 274–99; Bradburn, "A Clamor in the Public Mind: Opposition to the Alien and Sedition Acts," *William and Mary Quarterly* 65, no. 3 (2008): 565–600; Cleves, "'Jacobins in this Country,'" 410–45. On credit and honor, see Ditz, "Shipwrecked; or, Masculinity Imperiled: Mercantile Representations of Failure and the Gendered Self in Eighteenth-Century Philadelphia," *Journal of American History* 81, no. 1 (1994): 51–80; John Smail, "Credit, Risk, and Honor in Eighteenth-Century Commerce," *Journal of British Studies* 44, no. 3 (2005): 439–56; Pearsall, *Atlantic Families*, 113–18; Xabier Lamikiz, *Trade and Trust*, 142. See Nuala Zahedieh, "Credit, Risk and Reputation in Late Seventeenth-Century Colonial Trade," *Research in Maritime History*, no. 15 (1998): 53–74;

Cathy Matson, ed., "Forum: Reputation and Uncertainty in America," *Business History Review* 78, no. 4 (2004): 595–702.

44. AN, 208 Mi 2, Pétition du 12 vendémiaire an VIII, October 4, 1799; Pétition du 26 pluviôse an VIII, February 15, 1800. The suspicious dismissal was discussed in the press. See, for instance, *Alexandria Times*, May 28, 1800; *Philadelphia Gazette*, May 23, 1800; APS, GP, lett. 8, Girard to Domergue, May 24, 1802.

45. AN, 208 Mi 2, Stevens to Pickering, November 3, 1799; Lalandelle to Stevens, November 3, 1799.

46. ANOM, CC9b 18, Règlement du 18 floréal an IX, May 8, 1801.

47. This new configuration gave way to what Carlo Celius calls a new social contract: Carlo Avierl Célius, "Le contrat social haïtien," *Pouvoirs dans la Caraïbe. Revue du CRPLC*, no. 10 (1998): 25–67. ANOM, CC9b 18, "Adresse des citoyens des États-Unis d'Amérique résidant au Cap-Français au citoyen Toussaint Louverture, gouverneur de St. Domingue," November 11, 1801; "Le Gouverneur de St. Domingue aux Citoyens des États-Unis d'Amérique, résidant au Cap-Français," Brumaire 21, year X (November 12, 1801). On Moyse's revolt, see Dubois, *Les vengeurs du Nouveau monde. Histoire de la révolution haïtienne* (Rennes: Les Perséides, 2005), 233–34; Girard, *The Slaves Who Defeated Napoleon: Toussaint Louverture and the Haitian War of Independence, 1801–1804* (Tuscaloosa: University of Alabama Press, 2011), 76–79.

48. ANOM, CC9b 18, "Extrait des Registres . . ." 2–3. Mona Ozouf has shown that such solemnities were intended to institute and perpetuate a new, fragile order. See Ozouf, *La Fête révolutionnaire: 1789–1799* (Paris: Gallimard, 1988). On Toussaint Louverture's colonial constitution, see Claude Moïse, *Le projet national de Toussaint Louverture: la Constitution de 1801* (Port-au-Prince: Mémoire, 2001).

Epilogue

1. Napoleon Bonaparte's views on the colonies have been described in Bénot, *La démence coloniale sous Napoléon*; Thierry Lentz and Pierre Branda, *Napoléon, l'esclavage et les colonies* (Paris: Fayard, 2006); Christophe Belaubre, Jordana Dym, and John Savage, eds., *Napoleon's Atlantic: The Impact of Napoleonic Empire in the Atlantic World* (Leiden: Brill, 2010); Girard, *The Slaves Who Defeated Napoleon*. For primary sources, see: "Notes pour servir aux instructions à donner au capitaine général Leclerc|", Brumaire 9, year X (October 31, 1801) in Leclerc, *Lettres du général Leclerc*, 44–45, 269; ANOM, CC9a 28, "Projet d'une nouvelle organisation de la colonie de St. Domingue," Germinal 1, year IX (March 22, 1801). On Dominguan colonists' projects, see Røge, "The Directory and the Future of France's Colonial Possessions in Africa, 1795–1802," *French Historical Studies* 44, no. 3 (2021): 477–97. On the European Colonial Blockade, see Marzagalli, *Les boulevards de la fraude. Le négoce maritime et le Blocus continental (1806–1813)* (Lille: Septentrion, 1999).

2. Elijah Wilson Lyon, *The Man Who Sold Louisiana: The Career of Francois Barbé-Marbois* (Norman: University of Oklahoma Press, 1942).

3. I detailed the Louisiana politics of the French Revolution in Covo, "Why did France Want Louisiana Back? Imperial Ventures, Political Economy, and Revolutionary Schemes in a Caribbean Borderland," in *The French Revolution as a Moment of Respatialization*, 23–46.

4. For an up-to-date summary on Toussaint Louverture's government, see Sudhir Hazareesingh, *Black Spartacus: The Epic Life of Toussaint Louverture* (New York: Farrar, Straus and Giroux, 2020).

5. ASP, FR II, 303; On the negotiations of the Mortefontaine Convention: Ulane Bonnel, *La France, les États-Unis et la guerre de course (1797–1815)* (Paris: Nouvelles Éditions latines, 1961), 119-40, 159.

6. HM, VDP, A. Philibert Travi to Dupont, May 26, 1802; ADLA, 3 J 36, Gerbier to Trottier, May 15, 1802; HSP, Borie Family Papers, 7, folder 9, Circulaire d'Armand Diuhoulec et Jean Fagouet, Bordeaux, Messidor 5, year X (June 24, 1802); 5, folder 6, Paul Nairac to Jean-Claude Sulauze, Frimaire 1, year X (November 22, 1801).

7. For the military campaign, see Girard, *The Slaves Who Defeated Napoleon*, 86–100, 113–38. An important exception is Marcel Bonaparte Auguste and Claude Bonaparte Auguste, *La Participation étrangère à l'expédition française de Saint-Dominigue* (Montreal: Claude et Marcel

Bonaparte Auguste, 1980). See NYPL-SC, *Haiti Miscellaneous Collection*, SCM 82–16, Memo by Yves Bizouard, April 4, 1802.

8. HM, VDP, A, Bauduy to Dupont, April 3, 1802; AN, 505 Mi 81, Treuil to Foäche|, December 18, 1802; Leclerc|, *Lettres du général Leclerc*, 115.

9. On the relationship between Napoleon and Europe, see Jean-Clément Martin, ed., *Napoléon et l'Europe: colloque de La Roche-sur-Yon* (Rennes: Presses universitaires de Rennes, 2002); Thierry Lentz, ed., *Napoléon et l'Europe: regards sur une politique* (Paris: Fayard, 2005). Pierre-Auguste Adet, *Tribunat. Rapport fait par P.-A. Adet sur le projet de loi relatif aux colonies restituées par le traité d'Amiens, et aux autres colonies françaises. Séance du 29 floréal an X* (Paris: Imprimerie nationale, 1802), 3. On the notion of European civilization at that particular moment, see Antoine Lilti, ""Et la civilisation deviendra générale": L'Europe de Volney ou l'orientalisme à l'épreuve de la Révolution," *La Révolution française. Cahiers de l'Institut d'histoire de la Révolution française*, no. 4 (2011), https://journals.openedition.org/lrf/290.

10. Christian Schneider, "Le colonel Vincent|," 120; ANOM, CC9a 27, Ventôse 4, year VIII (February 23, 1800); Leclerc|, *Lettres du général Leclerc*, 90–91, 97, 290.

11. AN, 135 AP 1, "Liste des bâtiments américains qui sont dans la rade du Cap à l'époque du 20 ventôse an X"; AN, 208 Mi 4, Madison to Lear, January 8, 1802; Thomas Lawrason to Lear, January 10, 1802; Leclerc| to Lear, Germinal 27, year X (April 17, 1802); Leclerc|, *Lettres du général Leclerc*, 92, 125; Matthewson, *A Proslavery Foreign Policy*, 109.

12. AN, 208 Mi 4, Lear to Boyer, March 15, 1802; Boyer to Lear, Pluviôse 30, year X (February 19, 1802); Petition, March 23, 1802; HM, VDP, A 10, A. Bauduy to Dupont, May 6, 1802; AN, 505 Mi 81, Treuil to Foäche|, May 18, 1802; MSH, MS 1300, Hall to Ritchie, July 15, 1803.

13. Decrès to Leclerc|, June 26, 1802 in Leclerc, *Lettres du général Leclerc*, 286; AN, 135 AP 1, Benezech to Boyer, Ventôse 19, year X (March 10, 1802); HM, VDP C 23, memo starting with "Deux opérations très profitables se présentent en ce moment aux négociants des États-Unis"; AN, 135 AP 3, "Tableau des droits de douanes payés par les bateaux dans le port des Cayes pendant l'an X"; HM, VDP, A 9, A. Bauduy to V. Dupont, August 24, 1802. Dupont de Nemours's provisioning contracts have been studied in Bouton, "Flour for Pesos: Precarious Atlantic Financial Interdependency and the Provisioning of the Leclerc Expedition, 1802–1803," *Atlantic Studies* 15, no. 4 (2018): 504–22. On the larger picture of Dupont de Nemours's numerous entrepreneurial pictures, Martin Giraudeau, "Performing Physiocracy: Pierre Samuel Du Pont de Nemours and the Limits of Political Engineering," *Journal of Cultural Economy* 3, no. 2 (2010): 225–42.

14. MHS, MS 1300, Hall to Antoine Alezard, September 7, 1802; Leclerc|, *Lettres du général Leclerc*, 135, 215.

15. Gainot, ""Sur fond de cruelle inhumanité'; les politiques du massacre dans la Révolution de Haïti," *La Révolution française. Cahiers de l'Institut d'Histoire de la Révolution Française*, no. 3 (2011), https://journals.openedition.org/lrf/239; Girard, *The Slaves Who Defeated Napoleon*, 159-81.

16. Leclerc|, *Lettres du général Leclerc*, 139, 164, 189; HM, VDP A 9, P. Bauduy to Dupont, Germinal 16, year X (May 13, 1802); A. Bauduy to Dupont, June 15, 1802; A. Bauduy to Dupont, December 26, 1802; VDP A 10, Bauduy to Dupont, November 1, 1802; MHS, MS 1300, Hall to Dallest, August 26, 1803.

17. Quotes from AN, 505 Mi 81, Treuil to Foäche|, May 8, 1802; MHS, MS 1300, Hall to Hopfengartner, August 15, 1803; BL, Péries "Révolution de St. Domingue," fo. 163. On the intervention of enslaved people on markets in other Caribbean societies, see Beckles, "An Economic Life of Their Own: Slaves as Commodity Producers and Distributors in Barbados," *Slavery and Abolition* 12, no. 1 (1991): 31–47; Berlin and Morgan, eds., *Cultivation and Culture: Labor and the Shaping of Slave Life in the Americas*; Shauna J. Sweeney, "Market Marronage: Fugitive Women and the Internal Marketing System in Jamaica, 1781–1834." *William and Mary Quarterly* 76, no. 2 (2019): 197–222.

18. MHS, MS 1300, Hall to Malter and Delmas, December 16, 1803; Chelsea Stieber, *Haiti's Paper War: Post-Independence Writing Civil War, and the Making of the Republic, 1804-1954* (New York: New York University Press, 2020): 1.

19. Benoît Joachim, "La reconnaissance d'Haïti par la France (1825): naissance d'un nouveau type de rapports internationaux," *Revue d'histoire moderne et contemporaine* 22, no. 3 (1975): 369-396; Jean-François Brière, *Haïti et la France, 1804-1848: le rêve brisé* (Paris: Karthala, 2008);

Frédérique Beauvois, "L'indemnité de Saint-Domingue: "Dette d'indépendance" ou "rançon de l'esclavage"?," *French Colonial History* 10, no. 1 (2009): 109–24; Gaffield, *Haitian Connections in the Atlantic World* (Chapel Hill: University of North Carolina Press, 2015); Nathalie Pierre, "Liberal Trade in the Postcolonial Americas: Haitian Leaders and British Agents, 1806–1813," *Journal of Haitian Studies* 21, no. 1 (2015): 68–99; Daut, *Baron de Vastey and the Origins of Black Atlantic Humanism* (New York: Palgrave Macmillan, 2017); Gusti-Klara Gaillard-Pourchet, "Haïti-France. Permanences, évolutions et incidences d'une pratique de relations inégales au XIXe siècle," *La Révolution française* 16 (2019), online ; Lazaro Gamio, Constance Méheut, Catherine Porter, Selam Gebrekidan, Allison McCann and Matt Apuzzo, "The Ransom: Haiti's Lost Billions," *New York Times*, May 20, 2022. .

20. Ferrer, *Freedom's Mirror*, 146–88; Douglas R. Egerton, *Gabriel's Rebellion: the Virginia Slave Conspiracies of 1800 and 1802* (Chapel Hill: University of North Carolina Press, 1993); White, *Encountering Revolution*, 166–202; Dun, *Dangerous Neighbors*, 179–208.

INDEX

Printed in the USA/Agawam, MA
October 17, 2022

799893.009